JUDGMENT IN MANAGERIAL DECISION MAKING

JUDGMENT IN MANAGERIAL DECISION MAKING

EIGHTH EDITION

Max H. Bazerman
Harvard Business School

Don A. Moore
The University of California, Berkeley

Wiley Custom

ISBN 9781119427384

This book was set in 10/12 New Caledonia by Thomson Digital

Printed in the United Kingdom by CPI Antony Rowe, Ltd.

Contents

Chapter 1 Introduction to Managerial Decision Making 1

The Anatomy of Decisions 1
System 1 and System 2 Thinking 3
The Bounds of Human Attention and
Rationality 5
Introduction to Judgmental Heuristics 7
An Outline of Things to Come 10

Chapter 2 Overconfidence 14

The Mother of All Biases 14
Overprecision 16
Overestimation 22
Overplacement 26
Let's Hear it for Well-Calibrated Decision Making 28

Chapter 3 Common Biases 31

Biases Emanating from the Availability Heuristic 34
Biases Emanating from the Representativeness
Heuristic 38
Biases Emanating from the Confirmation
Heuristic 46
Integration and Commentary 57

Chapter 4 Bounded Awareness 60

Inattentional Blindness 65
Change Blindness 66
Focalism and the Focusing Illusion 67
Bounded Awareness in Groups 69
Bounded Awareness in Strategic Settings 71
Discussion 81

Chapter 5 Framing and the Reversal of Preferences 82

Framing and the Irrationality of the Sum of Our Choices 85
We Like Certainty, Even Pseudocertainty 87
Framing and The Overselling of Insurance 90

What's It Worth to You? 91
The Value We Place on What We Own 93
Mental Accounting 94
Rebate/Bonus Framing 96
Joint-versus-Separate Preference Reversals 98
Conclusion and Integration 100

Chapter 6 Motivational and Emotional
Influences on Decision Making 103

When Emotion and Cognition Collide 105
Self-Serving Reasoning 112
Emotional Influences on Decision Making 114
Summary 117

Chapter 7 The Escalation of Commitment 119

The Unilateral Escalation Paradigm 121
The Competitive Escalation Paradigm 123
Why Does Escalation Occur? 127
Integration 131

Chapter 8 Fairness and Ethics in Decision Making 132

Perceptions of Fairness 133
When We Resist "Unfair" Ultimatums 135
When We are Concerned about the Outcomes
of Others 139
Why do Fairness Judgments Matter? 142
Bounded Ethicality 143
Overclaiming Credit 145
In-Group Favoritism 146
Implicit Attitudes 147
Indirectly Unethical Behavior 151
When Values Seem Sacred 152
The Psychology of Conflicts of Interest 154
Conclusion 158

Chapter 9 Common Investment Mistakes 160

The Psychology of Poor Investment Decisions 162
Active Trading 170
Action Steps 171

Chapter 10 Making Rational Decisions in Negotiations 175

A Decision-Analytic Approach to Negotiations 176
Claiming Value in Negotiation 179
Creating Value in Negotiation 180

	The Tools of Value Creation	185
	Summary and Critique	191

Chapter 11 Negotiator Cognition   193

The Mythical Fixed Pie of Negotiation   193
The Framing of Negotiator Judgment   195
Escalation of Conflict   196
Overestimating Your Value in Negotiation   198
Self-Serving Biases in Negotiation   200
Anchoring in Negotiation   203
Conclusions   205

Chapter 12 Improving Decision Making   206

Strategy 1: Use Decision-Analysis Tools   208
Strategy 2: Acquire Expertise   213
Strategy 3: Debias Your Judgment   216
Strategy 4: Reason Analogically   219
Strategy 5: Take an Outsider's View   222
Strategy 6: Understand Biases in Others   223
Strategy 7: Nudge Wiser and More Ethical Decisions   226
Conclusion   228

References   **231**

Index   **261**

CHAPTER ONE

Introduction to Managerial Decision Making

The human mind packs spectacular power into its modest three-pound mass. With little effort, we can accomplish sophisticated tasks, such as recognizing faces or catching balls, that remain beyond the abilities of even the most powerful computers and sophisticated robots.

Yet most people remain largely unaware of how their minds accomplish complex tasks, and introspection and experience offer poor guidance. The fact that we lack an "operating manual" for our minds might not seem important. In fact, however, our lack of knowledge about how our minds work has profound consequences. Without an understanding of our thoughts and behavior, we cannot anticipate when the cognitive processes that usually serve us so well are likely to lead us astray.

Fortunately, psychological research has uncovered many of the clever and sophisticated shortcuts on which our brains rely to help get us through the day—as well as common errors that these shortcuts lead us to make on a regular basis. These errors can lead to relatively minor problems, such as buying the wrong product, hiring the wrong employee, or selecting the wrong investment. They also can contribute to big problems, such as bankruptcy, government inefficiency, and social injustice.

Even the brightest of people are susceptible to many of these errors. In fact, intelligent people who receive high scores on college entrance exams are just as vulnerable to many of these errors as are people with lower scores (Stanovich & West, 2008). This book will introduce you to a number of cognitive biases that are likely to affect the judgment of all types of professionals, from auditors to managers to politicians to salespeople. You are likely to recognize your own tendencies in the research results that we'll cover. The strategies that we suggest for overcoming these biases will give you the skills you need to become a better decision maker and to protect yourself, your family, and your organization from avoidable mistakes.

THE ANATOMY OF DECISIONS

The term *judgment* refers to the cognitive aspects of our decision-making process. To fully understand judgment, we must first identify the components of the decision-making process that require it. To get started, consider the following decision situations:

- You are finishing your MBA at a well-known school. Your credentials are quite good, and you expect to obtain job offers from a number of consulting firms. How will you select the right job?
- You are the director of the marketing division of a rapidly expanding consumer company. You need to hire a product manager for a new "secret" product that the company plans to introduce to the market in fifteen months. How will you go about hiring the appropriate individual?
- As the owner of a venture capital firm, you have a number of proposals that meet your preliminary considerations but only a limited budget with which to fund new projects. Which projects will you fund?
- You are on the corporate acquisition staff of a large conglomerate that is interested in acquiring a small-to-moderate-sized firm in the oil industry. What firm, if any, will you advise the company to acquire?

What do these scenarios have in common? Each one proposes a problem, and each problem has a number of alternative solutions. If you don't have alternatives to choose from, you don't have a decision to make. But as long as you have alternatives—and we often have far more interesting alternatives than we assume—you have a decision to make. Let's look at six steps you should take, either implicitly or explicitly, when applying a "rational" decision-making process to each scenario:

1. Define the problem. The problem has been fairly well specified in each of the four scenarios. However, managers often act without a thorough understanding of the problem to be solved, leading them to solve the wrong problem. Accurate judgment is required to identify and define the problem. Managers often err by (a) defining the problem in terms of a proposed solution, (b) missing a bigger problem, or (c) diagnosing the problem in terms of its symptoms. Your goal should be to solve the problem, not just eliminate its temporary symptoms.

2. Identify the criteria. Most decisions require you to accomplish more than one objective. When buying a car, you may want to maximize fuel economy and comfort while minimizing cost. The rational decision maker will identify all relevant criteria in the decision-making process.

3. Weigh the criteria. Different criteria will vary in importance to a decision maker. Rational decision makers will know the relative value they place on each of the criteria identified (for example, the relative importance of fuel economy versus cost versus comfort). The value may be specified in dollars, points, or whatever scoring system makes sense.

4. Generate alternatives. The fourth step in the decision-making process requires identification of possible courses of action. Decision makers often spend an inappropriate amount of time seeking alternatives. An optimal search continues only until the cost of the search outweighs the value of the added information.

5. Rate each alternative on each criterion. How well will each of the alternative solutions achieve each of the defined criteria? This is often the most difficult stage of the decision-making process, as it typically requires us to forecast future events. The rational decision maker carefully assesses the potential consequences of selecting each of the alternative solutions on each of the identified criteria.

6. Compute the optimal decision. Ideally, after all of the first five steps have been completed, the process of computing the optimal decision consists of (1) multiplying the ratings in step five by the weight of each criterion, (2) adding up the weighted ratings across all of the criteria for each alternative, and (3) choosing the solution with the highest sum of the weighted ratings.

The rational model of decision making assumes that people follow these six steps optimally. That is, it assumes that decision makers (1) perfectly define the problem, (2) identify all criteria, (3) accurately weigh all of the criteria according to their preferences, (4) know all relevant alternatives, (5) accurately assess each alternative based on each criterion, and (6) accurately calculate and choose the alternative with the highest perceived value.

Depending on how scholars conceptualize these steps and their components, not everyone identifies exactly six steps. Some separate them into more steps; some collapse them into fewer (Hammond, Keeney, & Raiffa, 1999). However, scholars generally agree on the essential components of rational decision making, as well as the fact that we as individuals very rarely employ them optimally.

SYSTEM 1 AND SYSTEM 2 THINKING

Do people actually reason in the logical manner described above? Sometimes they do, but not most of the time. Stanovich and West (2000) make a useful distinction between System 1 and System 2 cognitive functioning. System 1 thinking refers to our intuitive system, which is typically fast, automatic, effortless, implicit, and emotional. We make most decisions in life using System 1 thinking. For instance, we usually decide how to interpret verbal language or visual information automatically and unconsciously. By contrast, System 2 refers to reasoning that is slower, conscious, effortful, explicit, and logical (Kahneman, 2003). The logical steps above provide a prototype of System 2 thinking.

In most situations, our System 1 thinking is quite sufficient; it would be impractical, for example, to logically reason through every choice we make while shopping for groceries. But System 2 logic should preferably influence our most important decisions.

People are more likely to rely on System 1 thinking when they are busier, more rushed, and when they have more on their minds. In fact, the frantic pace of managerial life suggests that executives often rely on System 1 thinking (Chugh, 2004). Although a complete System 2 process is not required for every managerial decision, a key goal for managers should be to identify situations in which they should move from the intuitively compelling System 1 thinking to the more logical System 2.

Many people have a great deal of trust in their intuitions—their System 1 thinking. To prepare for the rest of the book, which is designed to challenge this confidence, consider the following diagram from Shepard (1990):

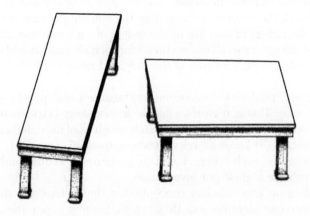

Like most people, you probably saw the table on the right as more of a square than the one on the left, which appears to be longer and skinnier. Well, your System 1 processing is failing you, as it fails most people in this instance. Don't believe it? Try this System 2 strategy: put a sheet of tracing paper over the drawing and trace the top of either table. Now line up your tracing over the other table, and see how your intuition has failed you!

Throughout this book, we will provide you with plenty of other reasons to question your intuition. Even the brightest people make judgmental errors on a regular basis. These errors, or biases, are much more likely to occur in System 1 thinking than in System 2 thinking. At the same time, any methodical System 2 process will use some intuitive System 1 shortcuts. In fact, the two systems frequently work in tandem, with modification of the quick, initial response of System 1 thinking after more in-depth consideration by the System 2 mind.

Sometimes, however, System 2 thinking does not fully adjust. For example, most people have a sensible aversion to eating from a container labeled as containing the poison cyanide. However, they have trouble overcoming this impulse even when they themselves were the ones to write "cyanide" on an otherwise clean container (Rozin, Markwith, & Ross, 1990). System 1 leads people to feel an aversion to eating from the container. Even after their System 2 thinking tells them that this aversion is utterly illogical, people still cannot bring themselves to eat.

THE BOUNDS OF HUMAN ATTENTION AND RATIONALITY

In this book, the term *rationality* refers to the decision-making process that is logically expected to lead to the optimal result, given an accurate assessment of the decision maker's values and risk preferences.

The rational model is based on a set of assumptions that prescribe how a decision *should* be made rather than describing how a decision *is* made. In his Nobel Prize–winning work, Herbert Simon (March & Simon, 1958; Simon, 1957) suggested that individual judgment is bounded in its rationality and that we can better understand decision making by describing and explaining actual decisions rather than by focusing solely on prescriptive ("what would rationally be done") decision analysis.

Two schools of thought. As Simon's work implies, the field of decision making can be roughly divided into two parts: the study of prescriptive models and the study of descriptive models. Prescriptive decision analysts develop methods for making optimal decisions. For example, they might suggest a mathematical model to help a decision maker act more rationally. By contrast, descriptive decision researchers consider how decisions are actually made.

This book takes a descriptive approach. Why, when a prescriptive approach should lead to an optimal decision? First, understanding our own decision-making processes helps clarify where we are likely to make mistakes and therefore when better decision strategies are needed. Second, the optimal decision in a given situation often depends on the behavior of others. Understanding how others will act or react to your behavior is critical to making the right choice. Third, plenty of good advice about making decisions is available, but most people do not follow it. Why not? Because they do not understand how they actually make decisions, they do not appreciate the need to improve. Indeed, some of the intuitions that lead us astray also undermine our willingness to implement good advice, as we will explore in Chapter 2. An understanding of this fact is needed to motivate people to adopt better decision-making strategies.

Why we "satisfice." While Simon's bounded-rationality framework views individuals as attempting to make rational decisions, it acknowledges that they often lack important information that would help define the problem, the relevant criteria, and so on. Time and cost constraints limit the quantity and quality of available information. Decision makers retain only a relatively small amount of information in their usable memory. Moreover, intelligence limitations and perceptual errors constrain the ability of decision makers to accurately "calculate" the optimal choice from the universe of available alternatives.

Together, these limitations prevent us from making the optimal decisions assumed by the rational model. The decisions that result typically overlook the full range of possible consequences. We forgo the best solution in favor of one that is acceptable or reasonable. That is, we *satisfice*: rather than examining all possible alternatives, we simply search until we find a *satisfactory* solution that will *suffice* because it is good enough.

A broader look at bias. The concepts of bounded rationality and satisficing show us that human judgment deviates from rationality. Specifically, these concepts help us identify situations in which we may be acting on the basis of limited information. However, these concepts do not tell us *how* our judgment will be biased—they do not help diagnose the specific systematic, directional biases that affect our judgment.

Fifteen years after the publication of Simon's work, Amos Tversky and Daniel Kahneman (Tversky and Kahneman, 1974) continued what he had begun. They filled in critical details about specific systematic biases that influence judgment. Their work laid the foundation for our modern understanding of judgment.

Specifically, researchers have found that people rely on a number of simplifying strategies, or rules of thumb, when making decisions. These simplifying strategies are called *heuristics*. As the standard rules that implicitly direct our judgment, heuristics serve as a mechanism for coping with the complex environment surrounding our decisions.

In general, heuristics are helpful, but their use sometimes leads to severe errors. A central goal of this book is to identify and illustrate these heuristics and the biases that can result from their use by managers. We will use examples of a variety of heuristics and biases to explain how people deviate from a fully rational decision-making process in individual and competitive situations.

New findings. Since Simon, bounded rationality has served as the integrating concept of the field of behavioral decision research. With time, we have refined and clarified our understanding of exactly how human judgment is bounded. Richard Thaler (2000) suggested that decision making is bounded in two ways not precisely captured by the concept of bounded rationality. First, our willpower is bounded, such that we tend to give greater weight to present concerns than to future concerns. As a result, our temporary motivations are often inconsistent with our long-term interests in a variety of ways, such as the common failure to save adequately for retirement (we discuss this issue in Chapters 6 and 9). Second, Thaler suggests that our self-interest is bounded; unlike the stereotypic economic actor, we care about the outcomes of others (Chapter 8 explores this topic).

Furthermore, we will explore two other bounds on human judgment. First, Chapter 4 explores the concept of *bounded awareness*, including the broad category of focusing biases, or the common tendency to overlook obvious, important, and readily available information that lies beyond our immediate attention. Second, Chapter 8 discusses *bounded ethicality*, a term that refers to the notion that our ethics are limited in ways of which we are unaware.

Overall, this book develops a systematic structure for understanding the bounds to our decision making, including bounded rationality, bounded willpower, bounded self-interest, bounded awareness, and bounded ethicality.

INTRODUCTION TO JUDGMENTAL HEURISTICS

Consider the following example:

> While finishing an advanced degree in computer science, Marla Bannon put together a Web-based retailing concept that many of her colleagues consider to be one of the best ever developed. While the product is great, Marla has far less skill in marketing her ideas. She decides to hire a marketing MBA with experience in Web-based environments to formalize the business plan she will use to approach venture capitalists. Marla follows the heuristic of limiting her search to new MBAs from the top six management schools. How would you evaluate her strategy?

If we evaluate this strategy in terms of the degree to which it follows the rational model outlined earlier, Marla's heuristic of limiting her search to six schools will be deficient, because her search will not be complete. Her heuristic may eliminate the best possible candidates from consideration if they do not attend one of the top schools. However, the heuristic also has some benefits. While it could eliminate the best choice, the expected time savings of focusing on only six schools may outweigh any potential loss resulting from Marla's limited search strategy. For this reason, this job search heuristic could produce more good decisions than bad ones. In fact, economists would argue that individuals use heuristics such as this because the benefit of time saved often outweighs the costs of any potential reduction in the quality of the decision.

Heuristics provide time-pressured managers and other professionals with a simple way of dealing with a complex world. But reliance on heuristics creates problems, primarily because people are typically unaware that they rely on them. One consequence is that we are prone to misapplying heuristics to inappropriate situations, a tendency that leads us astray. When managers become aware of the potential adverse impact of using heuristics, they become capable of deciding when and where to use them, thus minimizing their reliance on problematic heuristics.

People use a variety of types of heuristics. The poker player follows the heuristic "never play for an inside straight." The mortgage banker follows the heuristic "spend only 35 percent of your income on housing." Although an understanding of these specific heuristics is important to these professionals, our concern in this book is with more general cognitive heuristics that virtually everyone uses. The heuristics described next are not specific to particular individuals; rather, research has shown that they can be applied across the population. The four general heuristics on which we focus here are (1) the availability heuristic, (2) the representativeness heuristic, (3) the confirmation heuristic, and (4) the affect heuristic.

The Availability Heuristic

People assess the frequency, probability, or likely causes of an event by the degree to which instances or occurrences of that event are readily "available" in memory (Tversky & Kahneman, 1973). An event that evokes emotions and is vivid, easily imagined, and specific will be more available than an event that is unemotional in nature, bland, difficult to imagine, or vague.

For example, a subordinate who works in close proximity to the manager's office is likely to receive a more critical performance evaluation at year-end than a worker who sits down the hall because the manager will be more aware of the nearby subordinate's errors. Similarly, a product manager will base her assessment of the probability of a new product's success on her recollection of the successes and failures of similar products in the recent past.

The availability heuristic can be a very useful managerial decision-making strategy, since our minds generally recall instances of events of greater frequency more easily than rare events. Consequently, this heuristic will often lead to accurate judgments. This heuristic is fallible, however, because the availability of information is also affected by factors unrelated to the objective frequency of the judged event. These irrelevant factors (such as vividness) can inappropriately influence an event's immediate perceptual salience, the vividness with which it is revealed, or the ease with which it is imagined. Peter Lynch, the former director of Fidelity's Magellan Fund (one of the largest mutual funds), argues in favor of buying stock in firms that are unavailable in the minds of most investors (for example, due to their blandness); the more available the stock is, he notes, the more overvalued it will be.

The Representativeness Heuristic

When making a judgment about an individual (or object or event), people tend to look for traits the individual may have that correspond with previously formed stereotypes. "A botanist assigns a plant to one species rather than another by using this judgment strategy," wrote Nisbett and Ross (1980, p. 7). "The plant is categorized as belonging to the species that its principal features most nearly resemble."

Managers also use the representativeness heuristic. They may predict a person's performance based on an established category of people that the individual represents for them. If a manager thinks that the best salespeople are likely to be extroverts, ex-athletes, or white men, for instance, then the manager will favor those sorts of people for their sales jobs. Similarly, bankers and venture capitalists will predict the success of a new business based on the similarity of that venture to past successful and unsuccessful ventures. If an entrepreneur pitching an idea reminds a venture capitalist of Amazon.com founder Jeff Bezos, the entrepreneur may be more likely to obtain funding than an entrepreneur who reminds the venture capitalist of the founder of a less successful company.

In some cases, use of the representativeness heuristic offers a good first-cut approximation, drawing our attention to the best options. At other times, this heuristic can lead to serious errors. For instance, the germ theory of disease took a long time to catch on, because people had a hard time accepting the notion that something as miniscule as viruses and bacteria could produce such powerful consequences as tuberculosis and the plague. Instead, relying on the representativeness heuristic, people believed for centuries that disease was caused by malevolent agents, such as evil spirits or magic spells. In the meantime, innumerable people died unnecessary deaths from easily preventable diseases because physicians carried infections from one patient to another, or even from cadavers to surgery patients, without washing their hands.

The representativeness heuristic can also work on an unconscious level, causing a person to engage in race discrimination or other behavior that he or she would consider reprehensible if he or she were consciously aware of it. Unfortunately, people tend to rely on representative information even when that information is insufficient to make an accurate judgment or when better, less obviously representative information is available.

The Confirmation Heuristic

Consider your response to the following questions:

1. Is marijuana use related to delinquency?
2. Are couples who marry under the age of 25 more likely to have bigger families than couples who marry at an older age?

In assessing the marijuana question, most people typically try to remember several marijuana users and recall whether these individuals were delinquents. However, a proper analysis would require you to recall four groups of people: marijuana users who are delinquents, marijuana users who are not delinquents, delinquents who do not use marijuana, and non-delinquents who do not use marijuana.

The same analysis applies to the marriage question. A rational assessment of whether those who marry young are more likely to have large families than those who marry later would include four groups: couples who married young and have large families, couples who married young and have small families, couples who married older and have large families, and couples who married older and have small families.

Indeed, there are always at least four separate situations to consider when assessing the association between two events, assuming each one just has two possible outcomes. However, our everyday decision making commonly neglects this fact. Instead, we intuitively use selective data when testing hypotheses, such as instances in which the variable of interest (e.g., marijuana use or early marriage) is present (Klayman & Ha, 1987). Our focus on selective data or a single possible cause of an effect such as delinquency or a large family may lead us to neglect alternative causes of the effect and conclude that the association between the single cause and effect that we are considering is stronger than it is in reality (Fernbach, Darlow, & Sloman, 2011). Thus, we may conclude that marijuana use has a stronger association with delinquency than it does in reality and that early marriage has a stronger association with large families than it does in reality.

This simple search heuristic turns out to have profound consequences. For instance, in the absence of evidence to the contrary, people tend to behave as if they assume that a given statement or hypothesis is true (Gilbert, 1991; Trabasso, Rollins, & Shaughnessy, 1971). This tendency in turn can lead to the *confirmation bias*, in which we search for and interpret evidence in a way that supports the conclusions we favored at the outset (Nickerson, 1998). It can also explain the power of *anchoring*, in which some irrelevant initial hypothesis or starting point holds undue sway over our judgments. Finally, positive hypothesis testing can trigger the *hindsight bias*, in which we too quickly dismiss, in retrospect, the possibility that things could have turned out differently than they did. We explore these issues, as well as other biases resulting from the confirmation heuristic, in Chapter 2.

The Affect Heuristic

Most of our judgments follow an affective, or emotional, evaluation that occurs even before any higher-level reasoning takes place (Kahneman, 2003). While these affective evaluations are often unconscious, Slovic, Finucane, Peters, and MacGregor (2002) provide evidence that people nonetheless use them as the basis of their decisions rather than engaging in a more complete analysis and reasoning process.

A manifestation of System 1 thinking, the *affect heuristic* is all the more likely to be used when people are busy or under time constraints (Gilbert, 2002). For example, appraisals of potential employees can be affected by a wide variety of variables that influence a manager's affect, independent of applicant quality. These variables could include the mood of the manager or the degree to which the applicant reminds the manager of his or her former spouse. Environmental conditions that change peoples' feelings can also influence decision making. Stock prices go up on sunny days, presumably due to the good mood and optimism induced by the weather. And feelings can override more reasoned decisions in the court of law. Evidence suggests that juries decide penalties and awards in large part based on their feelings of outrage rather than on a logical assessment of harm created by the defendant (Kahneman, Schkade, & Sunstein, 1998). Chapters 4, 5, and 7 will develop the affect heuristic in more detail.

AN OUTLINE OF THINGS TO COME

The main objective of this book is to improve your judgment. As a preview of what you will learn, let's consider how we might improve the judgment of Marla Bannon, the entrepreneur who is looking to hire a marketing MBA to help formalize her business plan. First, we must identify the errors in her intuitive judgment and make her aware of biases that are likely to affect her decision. This awareness will improve her current decision-making process and lead to a more beneficial outcome.

Yet Lewin (1947) suggests that for change to occur and last over time, an individual must do more than simply be aware of imperfections. For change to be successful, Lewin argues, it is necessary to (1) get the individual to "unfreeze" existing decision-making processes, (2) provide the information necessary to promote change, and (3) create the conditions that "refreeze" new processes, thus making the change part of the individual's standard repertoire.

This book will attempt to unfreeze your present decision-making processes by demonstrating how your judgment systematically deviates from rationality. You will also be given tools to allow you to change your decision-making processes. Finally, the book will discuss methods that you can use to refreeze your thinking to ensure that the changes will last.

Nisbett and Ross (1980, p. xi–xii) write:

> One of philosophy's oldest paradoxes is the apparent contradiction between the greatest triumphs and the dramatic failures of the human mind. The same organism that routinely solves inferential problems too subtle and complex for the mightiest computers often makes errors in the simplest of judgments about everyday events. The errors, moreover, often seem traceable to violations of the same inferential rules that underlie people's most impressive successes. . . . How can any creature skilled enough to build and maintain complex organizations, or sophisticated enough to appreciate the nuances of social intercourse, be foolish enough to mouth racist clichés or spill its lifeblood in pointless wars?

While Nisbett and Ross refer to the general population, the essence of their question defines a fascinating issue concerning managerial effectiveness. In this book, we approach managers as intelligent people who have been generally successful but whose decisions are biased in ways that seriously compromise their potential. We will show how habit leads people to rely on heuristics that limit the quality of their decisions.

Chapters 2 through 9 focus on individual decision making. In these chapters, we give little attention to the fact that many managerial decisions are made in conjunction with other individuals. Instead, these chapters focus on how individuals approach decisions. Chapters 10 and 11 reexamine judgment in the interpersonal context of negotiation. Chapter 12 summarizes the book's arguments and focuses on how to incorporate the changes suggested throughout into your own decision-making processes.

Specifically, the remaining chapters will focus on the following:

Chapter 2: Overconfidence. We lead with an exploration of this bias for two reasons. First, it is one of the most potent and pervasive biases to which human judgment is vulnerable. Second, it facilitates many of the other biases discussed in this book. Without it, we would be better able to acknowledge our own shortcomings and correct our other biases.

Chapter 3: Common biases. This chapter identifies and illustrates a series of specific biases that affect the judgment of virtually all managers.

These biases are caused by the four heuristics described in this chapter. Quiz items and short scenarios demonstrate these biases and emphasize their prevalence.

Chapter 4: Bounded awareness. This chapter examines how the essential ability of the human mind to focus can prevent us from seeing information that is readily available and important. We will review new research on bounded awareness that shows systematic ways in which sharp focus degrades the quality of decisions.

Chapter 5: Framing and the reversal of preferences. Some of the most striking biases in the decision literature are those that lead managers to reverse their preferences based on information that they would agree should not affect their behavior. This chapter will examine how the framing of information affects decisions.

Chapter 6: Motivation and emotion. Some biases are created by emotions and by the self-serving motivations of individuals rather than by purely cognitive mistakes. This chapter complements the presentation of cognitive biases in Chapters 2, 3, 4, 5, and 7 with an overview of *motivated biases*.

Chapter 7: Escalation of commitment. Managerial decision makers who commit themselves to a particular course of action may make subsequent suboptimal decisions in order to justify their previous commitment. This chapter examines the research evidence and psychological explanations for this behavior. *Escalation of commitment* has a significant effect in a variety of managerial domains, including new product development, bank loans, and performance appraisal.

Chapter 8: Fairness and ethics in decision making. When do people care about fairness? When will individuals accept suboptimal outcomes in order to maintain fairness? This chapter examines how we think about fairness and explores inconsistencies in our assessments of fairness.

Chapter 9: Common investment mistakes. Perhaps the domain that has been most influenced by decision research has been behavioral finance. In the last decade, we have learned a great deal about the mistakes that investors commonly make. This chapter will explore these mistakes and apply the messages of the book to help readers become wiser investors.

Chapter 10: Making rational decisions in negotiation. This chapter outlines a framework to help readers think about joint decision-making between individuals. We focus on how you can make decisions that maximize the joint gain available to both sides while simultaneously thinking about how to obtain as much of that joint gain as possible for yourself.

Chapter 11: Negotiator cognition. This chapter looks at the judgmental mistakes we make in negotiations. The resulting framework shows how consumers, managers, salespeople, and society as a whole can benefit simultaneously from less biased negotiations.

Chapter 12: Seven strategies for improved decision making. The final chapter evaluates seven explicit strategies for improving judgment: (1) use prescriptive decision-making procedures, (2) acquire expertise, (3) debias your judgment, (4) reason analogically, (5) take an outsider's view, (6) identify biases in others, and (7) nudge people toward wiser and more ethical decisions. This chapter will teach you how to use the information in the book to permanently improve your decisions.

CHAPTER TWO

Overconfidence

To begin this chapter, we are going to test your knowledge. Ten quantities appear below. Do not look up any information about these items. For each, write down your best estimate. Next, put a lower and upper bound around your estimate, so that you are 98 percent confident that your range surrounds the actual quantity. Make your range wide enough that there is a 98 percent chance the truth lies inside it.

Estimate	Lower	Upper	
_____	_____	_____	a. Wal-Mart's 2010 revenue
_____	_____	_____	b. Google's 2010 revenue
_____	_____	_____	c. World population, as of January 2012
_____	_____	_____	d. 2010 U.S. Gross Domestic Product
_____	_____	_____	e. Population of China, as of December 2011
_____	_____	_____	f. Rank of McDonald's in the 2010 Fortune 500
_____	_____	_____	g. Rank of General Electric in the 2010 Fortune 500
_____	_____	_____	h. Number of deaths due to motor vehicle accidents in 2008, worldwide
_____	_____	_____	i. The national debt of the U.S. federal government, as of December 2011 (in U.S. dollars)
_____	_____	_____	j. The national debt of Greece, as of December 2011 (in euros)

The answers will appear later in the chapter. First we need to explain why we asked you these questions and what this test demonstrates. For now, let's just say that it illustrates overprecision in judgment and that overprecision is one form of overconfidence.

THE MOTHER OF ALL BIASES

Overconfidence may be the mother of all biases. We mean this in two ways. First, overconfidence effects are some of the most potent, pervasive, and pernicious of any of the biases we document in this book. Griffin and Varey (1996) write that "overconfidence is not only marked but nearly universal." The bias is "the most robust finding in the psychology of judgment," according to DeBondt and Thaler (1995). Overconfidence has been blamed for wars, stock market bubbles, strikes, unnecessary lawsuits, high rates of entrepreneurial bankruptcy, and the failure of corporate mergers and acquisitions. It could also explain the excessively high rate of trading in the stock market, despite the costs, argues Odean (1998). According to Camerer and Lovallo (1999), overconfidence may be the culprit behind high rates of entrepreneurial entry, which occur even though most new businesses go bankrupt within a few short years, having burned through the money provided by backers, investors, and founders. Overconfidence could explain the high rates of corporate mergers and acquisitions, despite the fact that such ventures so often fail, write Malmendier and Tate (2005). Plous (1993) suggests that overconfidence contributed to the nuclear accident at Chernobyl and to the explosion of the Space Shuttle Challenger. We could easily add the U.S. invasion of Iraq and the subprime financial crisis to that list (Gladwell, 2009). "No problem in judgment and decision making is more prevalent and more potentially catastrophic than overconfidence," writes Plous (p. 217).

In addition, overconfidence facilitates many of the other biases discussed in this book. If we were all appropriately humble about the quality of our judgments, we could more easily double-check our opinions and correct our flaws. Instead, we continue to believe that our views and judgments are correct, despite the copious evidence of our own fallibility (Pronin, Gilovich, & Ross, 2004; Schulz, 2010).

Let's take a closer look at that confidence. Overconfidence has been studied in three basic ways: in terms of overprecision, overestimation, and overplacement.

- Overprecision describes the tendency to be too sure our judgments and decisions are accurate, uninterested in testing our assumptions, and dismissive of evidence suggesting we might be wrong. It leads us to draw overly narrow confidence intervals and to be too certain that we know the truth.

- Overestimation is the common tendency to think we're better, smarter, faster, more capable, more attractive, or more popular (and so on) than we actually are. As a consequence, we overestimate how much we will accomplish in a limited amount of time or believe we have more control than we actually do.

- Overplacement is the tendency to falsely think we rank higher than others on certain dimensions, particularly in competitive contexts. Overplacement can lead people to be too interested in competing with others in negotiations, in markets, in the courts, or on the battlefield. There are too many impasses in negotiation, too many lawsuits, and too many wars, and overplacement may partially explain why.

We will describe these three forms of overconfidence in turn, then broaden out to explore the prevalence and limits of overconfidence. When can confidence be beneficial, and when does overconfidence get us into trouble?

OVERPRECISION

The test you took at the outset of this chapter can reveal overprecision. If you have not completed it yet, please go back and do so.

How many of your ten ranges will actually surround the true quantities? If you set your ranges so that you were 98 percent confident, you should expect to correctly bound between nine and ten of the quantities. Let's look at the correct answers:

a. Wal-Mart's 2010 revenue $421,849,000,000 ($421 billion)
b. Google's 2010 revenue $29,321,000,000 ($29 billion)
c. World population, as of January 2012   7,010,895,280 people (7 billion)
d. U.S. Gross Domestic Product in 2010 $14,582,400,000,000 ($15 trillion)
e. Population of China, as of December 2011   1,338,299,500 (1.3 billion)
f. Rank of McDonald's in the 2010 Fortune 500   108
g. Rank of General Electric in the 2010 Fortune 500   4
h. Number of deaths due to motor vehicle accidents in 2008, worldwide   1,209,000 (1.2 million)
i. The national debt of the United States federal government, as of December 2011 (in U.S. dollars) $15,104,054,667,691 ($15 trillion)
j. The national debt of Greece, as of December 2011 (in euros)   €341,371,244,124 (€341 billion)

Most people bound only between three (30 percent) and seven (70 percent) of these quantities, despite being 98 percent confident that each of their ranges will surround the true value. In Alpert and Raiffa's (1969/1982) initial demonstration of overconfidence based on 1,000 observations (100 participants estimating 10 items like those above), 42.6 percent of quantities fell outside of participants' 90 percent confidence ranges. Why? We are more confident than we deserve to be regarding the accuracy of our knowledge. Most of us are overconfident in the precision of our beliefs.

If your answers make you look overconfident, you may wonder whether your unfamiliarity with the 10 topics we asked you about may have contributed to your poor results. It seems logical to predict that we would perform better in domains where we are experts. McKenzie, Liersch, and Yaniv (2008) examined this hypothesis by asking students at the University of California at San Diego and computer-programming professionals working in information technology to answer trivia questions about UCSD and IT, respectively. Indeed, in domains where they were experts, participants' knowledge was more precise; they specified narrower confidence intervals. However, their overconfidence continued. Their confidence intervals narrowed to such a degree that they often failed to capture the correct answer, and their hit rates did not increase. The participants appeared just as overconfident (as measured by accuracy) in domains where they were expert as in domains where they were not expert. You can think about their confidence intervals as the bull's-eye that people draw on the target. The smaller they draw the bull's-eye, the more confident they must be that their aim will be true. But if the bull's-eye shrinks at the same rate as their accuracy increases, they won't wind up hitting the target any more often.

It is rare that people sometimes are asked to specify a bull's-eye, confidence interval around their best estimate of something. Instead, it is more common for us to choose some action that ought to depend on uncertainty about our own accuracy, as well as the consequences of exceeding or falling short of the mark. For instance, you might need to decide how quickly to drive to the airport, given uncertainty about how long it might take to get there. It is obviously worse to arrive too late than to arrive too early for your flight. Or you might have to decide how much money you can spend this weekend, given bills coming due and uncertainty about when the next paycheck will arrive. It is worse for checks to start bouncing than to have a little extra money in the bank.

If we could specify how uncertain people should be and could systematically vary the consequences of over- or underestimation, then we could test whether people shift their behavior as much as they should. Mannes and Moore (2012) did exactly that. The evidence corroborated what many others had already learned about confidence intervals: people act as if they are sure they know the truth. They draw their bull's-eyes too small, make their confidence intervals too narrow, and don't shift their actions as much as they should in the face of uncertainty. The consequence is that, too often, we tumble off a cliff we were too sure we were clear of. We miss our flights and we bounce checks, in part because we underestimate the uncertainties involved.

One social, political, and environmental issue with big consequences and uncertainties is global climate change. There is a strong consensus in the scientific community that the earth is warming and that increased human emissions of greenhouse gasses are to blame (Solomon et al., 2007). But even those who believe that we should take action to alleviate climate change acknowledge that there remains uncertainty regarding the key issue of how much the earth is likely to heat up and how quickly. Zickfeld and his colleagues (2010) consulted experts on the subject to elicit confidence intervals around their estimates. The experts acknowledged uncertainty, but here again, many of their confidence intervals did not overlap with one another, suggesting that many scientists had drawn their confidence intervals too narrowly.

These differences are not purely academic in nature. The evidence for human-caused climate change is overwhelming, and swift action is needed to address the problem. But climate change deniers, including politicians, oil companies, and the coal industry, have exploited disagreements among climate-change experts regarding their predictions of the amount of future warming to question their expertise. The deniers use these disagreements to illogically question the existence of climate change, confuse the public, and forestall regulation.

Is scientists' overprecision on the subject of climate change driven by the highly charged nature of the subject? Could strong opinions about the issue have clouded scientists' expert judgment? It seems less likely that political motives impinged on scientists' estimation of physical constants, such as the speed of light, Planck's constant, Avogadro's number, or the mass or charge of an electron. Early attempts at estimating these quantities were acknowledged as imperfect, and the scientific publications that present these imperfect estimates include confidence intervals intended to reflect the scientists' degree of uncertainty. An analysis by Henrion and Fischhoff (1986) reveals that the confidence intervals were too narrow: The majority failed to include the true value being measured.

Throughout human history, experts' overly precise judgments often have proven disastrous. There are many examples. On August 6, 1997, the pilot of Korean Air flight 801 from Seoul to Guam, sure that he knew what he was doing, did not listen to the concerns of his flight engineer and crashed his Boeing 747 into the side of a hill a few miles from the airport in Guam. On January 3, 2004, the pilot of Flash Airlines Flight 604 from Sharm el-Sheikh, Egypt, to Paris, experienced spatial disorientation and ignored the data from his copilot and the airplane's navigation instruments and crashed his plane into the Red Sea. And on January 13, 2012, the captain of the cruise ship Costa Concordia departed from the officially designated route near the western coast of Italy to plot his own course and ran the half-billion-dollar cruise ship, with 4,200 passengers on board, aground. Add to these brief, limited tragedies the prolonged damage caused by the errors of generals, presidents, and CEOs who have charged confidently forward into the jaws of disaster. By contrast, good managers realistically appraise risks, dangers, and errors, especially their own. In the words of Ray Dalio, the founder of Bridgewater Capital Management, one of the world's most successful hedge funds, "Our greatest power is that we know that we don't know and we are open to being wrong and learning" (Cassidy, 2011). Or in the words of Mahatma Gandhi, "It is unwise to be too sure of one's own wisdom. It is healthy to be reminded that the strongest might weaken and the wisest might err."

To plan effectively, every organization must make forecasts of uncertain events. The number of people to hire, the number of manufacturing plants to build, and the number of units to produce all depend on what sales will look like in the future. Are organizations good at making well-calibrated forecasts of the future? Research by Ben-David, Graham, and Harvey (2010) suggests not. They analyzed over 10,000 forecasts made by financial officers of thousands of firms over many years. The results show that actual market returns fall inside these executives' 80% confidence intervals only 33% of the time. This does not mean that executives are inveterate optimists, always believing that sales would be better than they were. Sometimes they overestimated, and sometimes they underestimated, but they were systematically overprecise.

Confidence can be beneficial in some situations, so how concerned should you be about the risk of reaching overly precise judgments? Consider how the overprecision caused by excess confidence can have these potential adverse effects:

- You are a surgeon who is trying to persuade a patient's family to agree to a difficult operation. When the family asks you to estimate the likelihood that the patient will survive the operation, you respond, "95 percent." If the patient dies on the operating table, was he one of the unlucky five percent, or are you guilty of making an overconfident projection?

- You are the chief legal counsel for a firm that has been threatened with a multimillion dollar lawsuit. You believe you will win in court and are 98 percent confident. Is this degree of certainty sufficient for you to recommend rejecting an out-of-court settlement? Suppose you learn that, if you lose the case, your firm will go bankrupt. Based on what you know now, are you still comfortable with your 98 percent estimate?

- You have developed a marketing plan for a new product based on your forecast of future sales. You are so confident in your plan that you have not developed any contingencies. When sales turn out differently from your forecast, will you be able to change in time, or will your overconfidence blind you to the need to change course?

Causes of overprecision. There are a variety of theories regarding the underlying causes of overprecision in judgment. According to one theory, overprecision springs from the desire to relieve internal dissonance, or a state of tension regarding the right decision or course of action. People in a stressful state of tension feel motivated to relieve this dissonance, even if this requires them to change what they believe. Herzog and Hertwig (2009) employed an innovative approach to resolving internal dissonance. They asked participants in their study to come up with more than one estimate of the exact same quantity. An average of these two estimates produced more accurate final judgments, much in the way the "wisdom of crowds" does simply by averaging across individuals. In essence, asking people to think of a second estimate produced a "crowd" in the individual's mind, and the average of this small crowd's opinion was more accurate than the individual's first estimate. The fact that this technique was effective at correcting for overprecision serves as a reminder that internal dissonance is not a natural state of mind. As evidence, when we are getting advice from others, we prefer to hear perspectives that are similar to our own, despite the fact that hearing different perspectives is more helpful and informative.

In addition to helping us feel sure of ourselves, our outward expressions of confidence help others feel sure about us. Those who express confidence earn trust, credibility, and, ultimately, status. Many Americans took comfort in the confidence and resolve of George W. Bush's leadership. Bush accused his opponent, John Kerry, of being a "flip-flopper"—that is, of changing his mind on important matters, such as military appropriations. During their first presidential debate, in 2004, Bush admonished Kerry for sending "mixed messages" and said, "I just know how this world works, and in the councils of government there must be certainty from the U.S. President." We find confident people to be more persuasive than those who seem less so (Sniezek & Van Swol, 2001). Consequently, we see them as more capable and therefore tend to elevate them to positions of status and influence. When confidence and ability are positively correlated, this makes sense. But contenders for leadership positions quickly learn that, to gain others' support, they must express more confidence than their rivals (Radzevick & Moore, 2011). As a result, rivals end up competing to express more confidence than each other.

But as many learn the hard way, there are costs to being confident and wrong, as Kerry noted in his debate response to Bush's criticism: "It's one thing to be certain, but you can be certain and be wrong." When people who claim certainty later are discovered to have been in error, their credibility is undermined and their reputation suffers (Tenney, MacCoun, Spellman, & Hastie, 2007). Indeed, Bush's steadfast denial that he made any mistakes as president may have contributed to his falling approval ratings in his second term. When reckonings with our mistakes come at all, they often come slowly; moreover, we often fail to seek out the evidence we need to assess whether those around us are overconfident. Confident people tend to get promoted, and by the time their overconfidence is exposed, they often have moved on to another assignment.

Finally, overprecision may be a byproduct of other cognitive processes. Because the human mind is better at searching memory for evidence that confirms rather than disconfirms our beliefs, when we assess our confidence in a belief, it is easier for us to generate supportive rather than contradictory evidence (Klayman & Ha, 1987). Bolstered by supportive evidence that is easily available, we overestimate the accuracy of our knowledge and the truth of our tentative hypotheses. As with the other biases described in this book, this process tends to occur automatically, without conscious awareness.

Interventions that force people to think about alternative perspectives, interpretations, or hypotheses are often effective at shaking their overconfidence and inducing greater realism (Koriat, Lichtenstein, & Fischhoff, 1980). In other words, thinking about why you might be wrong can help correct for the influence of the confirmation bias on your confidence judgments. In fact, Don Moore (one of the authors) and his colleagues have found in their research that simply asking people to explicitly consider the likelihood of alternative outcomes to the one they've proposed increases the accuracy of their judgments (Haran, Moore, & Morewedge, 2010).

As we have shown, there are psychological and social forces that push us toward unwarranted self-assurance. But can we be blamed for wanting to believe that we know what is true and false? If we find out that we were mistaken about something, we move in that instant from the old belief to a new belief. As a consequence, we almost never have the experience of believing something we know to be false. Instead, believing that we are right about everything all of the time becomes the usual state of affairs (Schulz, 2010). No wonder, then, that overprecision is so common.

Consequences of overprecision. Overprecision makes us too sure of our judgments, such that we are often in error yet rarely in doubt. Our assurance makes us too reluctant to take advice from others, suspicious of those whose views differ from our own, too quick to act on our opinions, and too slow to update our erroneous beliefs.

Research on advice giving and advice taking helps us to understand how people learn from others and when they are open to receiving others' wisdom. The single most important and robust finding from this substantial literature is that, reluctant to revise our opinions, we tend to ignore feedback from others on the problems we face (Yaniv & Kleinberger, 2000). Research has often demonstrated this phenomenon by asking people for an estimate of some quantity, such as the number of jelly beans in a jar, the number of flat-screen TVs in China, or the sales of one's company's product the coming quarter. After making an initial estimate, all the participants learn what one other person estimated. Then the participants have the opportunity to individually revise their estimates. On average, if people's faith in their own knowledge were well calibrated, then they should weigh others' knowledge equally with their own—that is, they should simply average the two estimates. Sure, some people may happen to know that they are particularly talented at estimating the number of jelly beans in a jar. But for every such person, there ought to be someone else who knows they perform worse than others on this task, and that, consequently, they should overweight others' advice. In fact, however, there are too few of the latter type of person and too many of the former. We give substantially less weight to others' advice—including very useful advice—than to our own opinions, and our accuracy suffers as a result (Minson, Liberman, & Ross, 2009).

Ross and Ward (1996) use the term naive realism to describe the widespread belief that the way we see the world is the only sensible view. For most of us, the naïve view that our perspective is the only legitimate one is the default. Considering others' perspectives takes energy and attention because it requires us to move from the comfortable familiarity of how we are used to seeing things (Epley, Keysar, Van Boven, & Gilovich, 2004) to the unfamiliar vantage point of an outside view. As we discuss in Chapter 11, an egocentric viewpoint can be a significant impediment to mutual understanding and agreement in negotiation. If we assume that those who see things differently are either stupid (for not seeing the facts right before their eyes) or evil (for seeing the truth but misrepresenting it for their own nefarious ends), we will be unwilling to consider other perspectives and find common ground. The result can be dysfunctional conflict and unnecessary divorces, lawsuits, strikes, and wars (Johnson, 2004).

Another interesting economic implication of overprecision offers a potential explanation for the high amount of trading that occurs in the stock market. Every day, many millions of shares trade on stock markets around the world. Yet strong evidence exists that the more investors trade, the worse their market outcomes become (Barber & Odean, 2000). In case you have ever considered working as a day trader, you should know that this is not a particularly profitable endeavor. Sometimes, of course, trading does make sense, as when you know something the person on the other side of the trade does not, and this knowledge suggests that you're getting a good deal from them. But research in behavioral finance shows that overprecision can make investors too interested in trading. Overprecision deludes people into thinking that their beliefs are more accurate than those of others, and thereby increases their willingness to trade (Odean, 1998). We explore this phenomenon in more depth when we discuss investment decisions in Chapter 9.

Managers' faith in their own judgment also leads them astray in the context of hiring decisions. Hiring and promotion decisions are probably among the most important decisions any organization makes. Recognizing this importance, managers generally give them a great deal of time, attention, and care—which usually means spending a lot of time interviewing candidates. The more important the position, the more interviews a candidate has. Unfortunately, many decades of study and hundreds of published research findings attest to the difficulty of accurately predicting work performance (Schmidt & Hunter, 1998). Moreover, the traditional face-to-face job interview is low on the list of useful tools we have for helping us predict how someone will perform on the job. Other tools, including the simple IQ test, are cheaper to administer, less biased, and better predictors of job performance. Nevertheless, managers stubbornly cling to the notion that even if *others* cannot predict how someone will perform based on interviews, they themselves are solid judges of character (Highhouse, 2008). Reluctant to acknowledge the true uncertainties associated with personnel selection, managers make overly precise forecasts of candidates' potential. In the process, they waste time and effort conducting interviews that aren't predictive of job performance.

If only we were better at acknowledging the imperfections in our knowledge and insights, we could better calibrate our choices to account for our uncertainty. An empowering implication of this realization is that we are capable of outsmarting the many biases and imperfections in human judgment we will catalog in this book. If we could only accept our personal vulnerability to bias, we could better anticipate our biases, correct them, and avoid the errors they cause. Unfortunately, people tend to be resistant to the idea that their views are biased (Pronin, Lin, & Ross, 2002). While we are often ready to acknowledge general imperfections in human judgment, and especially those of others, we are remarkably reluctant to acknowledge that any particular judgment of ours has been tarnished by bias. As we discuss in Chapter 7, our blindness to our own biases can be particularly problematic in ethical domains, making us unwilling to accept correction, guidance, or regulation.

So far, we have explored the pervasiveness, causes, and consequences of overprecision in judgment. We next turn our attention to overestimation, our second type of overconfidence.

OVERESTIMATION

Overestimation describes the common tendency to think you're better across a number of domains than you actually are. Researchers have identified various manifestations of overestimation, including self-enhancement, the illusion of control, the planning fallacy, and optimistic biases.

Self-enhancement. People are motivated to view themselves positively, as opposed to accurately (Dunning, 2005). We tend to believe that the groups to which we belong are superior to other groups (Gramzow & Gaertner, 2005). We even like the letters in our names more than we like other letters (Nuttin, 1985, 1987). In fact, liking our own characteristics may help to explain the endowment effect, which we will discuss in Chapter 4, in which simply owning an object produces a special appreciation that increases its subjective value to us (Morewedge, Shu, Gilbert, & Wilson, 2009; Van Boven, Dunning, & Loewenstein, 2000). Evidence suggests, however, that these effects operate at an unconscious level and are strongest when people are responding quickly and automatically (Koole, Dijksterhuis, & van Knippenberg, 2001). When they think about a question more systematically (engaging System 2 thinking), for instance, people no longer prefer the letters in their names over other letters (Koole et al., 2001).

We also tend to overestimate our own performance, abilities, or talents, a bias sometimes referred to as self-enhancement (Sedikides & Gregg, 2008). There is also evidence that we evaluate ourselves more positively on more desirable traits (Alicke, 1985) than on less desirable traits. This may be, of course, because we convince ourselves that we are better than we actually are on those traits. But it is also possible that this effect arises simply because we strive, quite intentionally, to enact desirable traits such as loyalty, kindness, and cleanliness more often than undesirable traits like being spiteful, snobbish, and meddlesome.

The illusion of control. Sometimes people think they have more control over circumstances than they actually do, a phenomenon know as the illusion of control (S. C. Thompson, 1999). In particular, when people have very little control, they tend to overestimate how much control they do have. Superficial signs of control, such as the chance to pick their own lottery ticket numbers, are enough to lead people to believe that they can exert control over uncontrollable events (Langer, 1975). We also cling to superstitious beliefs about performance and competitive success. There are a long list of baseball superstitions, including the prohibition on commenting on the likelihood of a no-hitter, not washing one's clothes during a series, and, most recently, the popularity of expensive "phiten" necklaces, alleged to "improve bioelectric current" and improve performance. By contrast, when people have a great deal of control, they tend to underestimate it. For instance, people often display fatalistic attitudes toward their health, not getting screened for cancer and otherwise acting as if they lack control over something that they do indeed (at least partially) control.

The planning fallacy. The planning fallacy describes the common tendency to overestimate the speed at which we will complete projects and tasks (Buehler, Griffin, & Ross, 1994). Using data from many major infrastructure projects in various different countries, Flyvbjerg (2003) highlights the dramatic tendency to underestimate the cost and duration of construction projects, including roads, bridges, tunnels, and buildings. Notably, the advocates of such projects, including the firms bidding for contracts to build them, have incentives to make optimistic projections, as their optimism may increase the likelihood that the project will move forward and they will get the business. But we are prone to the planning fallacy even without the help of contractors or others who benefit from encouraging our delusional optimism.

The planning fallacy tends to occur most often in the context of large, complex projects that, by their very nature, are prone to complications. Major construction, home remodeling, and software development projects are all notorious for time and budget overruns. We often fail to anticipate a project's many component parts or the likelihood that complications will arise.

Consider the following real-life scenarios:

- After three years of study, doctoral students typically dramatically overestimate the likelihood of completing their dissertations within a year. This occurs even when they plan how long each component of the project will take. Why do they not finish in one year?
- The manager of a consulting firm led a project in which five internal teams each analyzed a different strategy for a client. The alternatives could not be compared until all of the teams completed their analysis. As the client's deadline approached, three of the five teams were behind schedule but the manager assured the client that all five would be ready on time. In the end, the manager presented only three of the five alternatives to the client, as two were still missing. Unimpressed, the client dropped the consulting firm. Whose fault was it that the project failed?
- In 1991, the City of Boston broke ground on a massive construction project, known as the "Big Dig," to move Interstate Highway 93 below ground as it passes through the city. Based on the estimates of the subcontractors involved, city officials had developed a $2.5 billion budget and calculated that the project would be completed by 1998. As it turned out, the project was not completed until 2007—about nine years late—and went about $12 billion over budget. What went wrong?

Virtually all of us have personally experienced the costly consequences that such optimism produces, if not in the undoing of well-planned budgets, then in the allocation of our own time. It is too easy to make future commitments, believing somehow that we will have more time available at a later date. When the future arrives, it is inevitably as busy as the present, thanks in part to all those commitments we made. Interestingly, however, people actually tend to overestimate completion times for simple tasks (Boltz, Kupperman, & Dunne, 1998; Burt & Kemp, 1994). When there are few potential complications, then our excessive optimism about completion times is not a problem.

Optimistic biases. The tendency to overestimate the rosiness of our future is known as unrealistic optimism (Sharot, Riccardi, Raio, & Phelps, 2007). This type of optimism may be motivated by the simple fact that savoring the prospect of a rosy future feels good. Yet this type of optimism is not universal (Chambers,

Windschitl, & Suls, 2003; Kruger & Burrus, 2004). People believe that they are more likely than others to cut themselves shaving and less likely than others to live past 100. Why don't we observe more consistent evidence of overestimation? After all, it is hard to deny that it feels good to believe in ourselves. Fortunes have been made selling self-help products that offer little more than affirmations of self-worth, ability, and esteem. It would seem that, for this reason alone, we should expect people to consistently exaggerate their abilities, their control, their performance, and their luck. It just feels good to believe in yourself.

But consider that, as we all have experienced, the sweet taste of optimism can turn to bitter disappointment when reality falls short of our grand expectations (McGraw, Mellers, & Ritov, 2004). No wonder, then, that we regularly display what Norem (2002) calls defensive pessimism: we brace ourselves for disappointment by making pessimistic assessments about our own abilities, status, and future performance (Norem & Cantor, 1986; K. M. Taylor & Shepperd, 1998). That may explain why so many Academy Award winners seem caught off guard when called up to the podium: they didn't allow themselves to imagine they would win, lest they be crushed if they lost.

It doesn't feel good when our inflated beliefs collide with reality. As we will discuss in Chapter 4, gains and losses affect our feelings differently, such that a loss of a given size is more painful than a gain of a similar size is pleasurable. That is, if you expect your raise will be 5% and it turns out to be 2%, your disappointment will exceed the pleasure you would have gotten from an 8% raise (Loewenstein & Prelec, 1993). To take one remarkable example, after Greg Lippman's team helped Deutsche Bank produce over $2 billion in profits in 2007, the bank paid Lippmann a stunning $50 million bonus. But Lippmann had expected more. "This is not fair," Lippmann angrily told his superiors, "It's too low!" (as quoted in Zuckerman, 2010, p. 249). McGraw, Mellers, and Ritov (2004) show that individuals who are most optimistic about their abilities end up being most disappointed by their outcomes because reality is likely to fall short of their expectations. The easiest way to surpass expectations is to lower them.

Research on the "moment of truth" effect suggests that we attempt to manage our expectations strategically (Gilovich, Kerr, & Medvec, 1993). We start off full of hope regarding an unknown future outcome. As the moment of receiving actual performance feedback draws near, we tend to reduce our performance expectations, becoming more pessimistic than optimistic. This mindset enables us to experience the pleasure of a positive surprise, or at least avoid the disappointment of falling short—and it probably helps explain why the evidence for overestimation is so inconsistent.

Any theory that attributes optimism to the pleasure of savoring a flattering self-image or positive future must confront the many risks to which such self-delusion exposes us. Consumers who are sure they will be richer in the future too willingly sign up for mortgages whose payments balloon over time or for credit cards with steep interest rates whose balances they (erroneously) expect to pay off each month. Indeed, thriving industries—from payday lenders and pawn shops to banks and credit card companies—have grown to exploit people who make such errors.

If we sometimes believe that we are better than we actually are, do we also believe that we are better than others? This question lies at the heart of research on the third variety of overconfidence: what Larrick, Burson, and Soll (2007) have called overplacement.

OVERPLACEMENT

The term overplacement describes the tendency to believe we are better than others in specific ways when we're actually not. Much of the overplacement research specifically documents the "better-than-average" effect. In one study, for example, 93 percent of American drivers reported themselves to be more skillful than the median American driver (Svenson, 1981). Another highly-cited example comes from the self-evaluations of students preparing to take the Scholastic Aptitude Test. When asked to assess their ability to get along with others, 60 percent of these students rated themselves in the top 10 percent and fully 25 percent rated themselves in the top 1 percent (College Board, 1976–1977). John Cannell (1989) referred to this as the "Lake Wobegon effect"—a reference to the mythical Minnesota town where, according to radio host Garrison Keillor, "all the women are strong, all the men are good-looking, and all the children are above average"—when decrying the common practice of school districts and U.S. states to claim that their children were above average on various dimensions when they were not.

Overplacement can have undesirable consequences. Believing we are more deserving than others can cause us to have inflated expectations that we will be victorious in lawsuits and court battles (Neale & Bazerman, 1985). As a result, we fight too hard and hold out too long, paying our lawyers too much to fight for us (Thompson & Loewenstein, 1992). Entrepreneurs who believe they are more capable than their potential competitors will choose to enter new markets and compete even when their objective chances of success are not particularly good (Åstebro, Jeffrey, & Adomdza, 2007; Koellinger, Minniti, & Schade, 2007). Many people wind up throwing away their life savings on business ideas that fail. Believing that they are better than other managers, many pursue mergers and acquisitions that wind up costing their shareholders handsomely (Malmendier & Tate, 2008). Indeed, evidence suggests, the majority of mergers fail (Ravenscraft & Scherer, 1989).

Some psychologists believe that the accumulated evidence is strong enough to conclude that "for nearly any subjective and socially desirable dimension . . . most people see themselves as better than average" (Myers, 1998, p. 440). More recently, however, research has uncovered evidence of underplacement, or the tendency for people to believe they are worse than others on various dimensions (Moore, 2007). Underplacement occurs most often on difficult tasks. For example, on average, people report themselves to be worse at juggling and unicycle-riding than are others (Kruger, 1999). In a survey, a group of college students estimated that there was a 96% chance they would lose a quiz contest with another randomly selected student on the subject of Baroque music (Windschitl, Kruger, & Simms, 2003).

Just as we believe we would perform worse than others on hard tasks and better than others on easy tasks, we believe we are more likely than others to experience common events but less likely than others to experience rare events (Chambers et al., 2003). For instance, while people believe they are more likely than others to live past 70 (a common event), they also believe that they are less likely than others to live past 100 (a rare event). College students believe they are more likely than their classmates to own their own homes someday, but less likely than their classmates to own their own islands (Kruger & Burrus, 2004).

So if sometimes people believe that they are better than others, and sometimes they think they are worse than others, maybe we should expect that, on average, people are not biased one way or the other? Not quite. Even if the two balanced each other, it would not mean that you need not worry about your own potential for bias—that would be like the person with one hand in fire and the other hand in liquid nitrogen being just right, on average. Both extremes are problematic. The mistake of overplacement has led eager and ambitious entrepreneurs to throw their life savings into ventures that fail. When it turns out that they are no better at managing a restaurant than are the other new entrants and incumbents, they end up broke. The mistake of underplacement, on the other hand, regularly leads to terrible missed opportunities by those who would have succeeded had they only the courage to try. Every parent has seen their child refuse to attempt things that they probably would have enjoyed, simply because they were afraid of being worse than others.

But there are more reasons to be concerned about errors of overplacement than of underplacement. We select career paths, job assignments, and hobbies based in part on our belief in our own "unique" talents (Moore & Cain, 2007; Tesser, 1988). We generally choose to get in and compete where we think we are distinctively good. The aspiring businesswoman chooses to go into marketing for consumer packaged goods because she believes that she has a passion for it that sets her apart from other applicants for the job. If this is how people choose their vocations and avocations, then we should expect that people generally believe themselves to be better than others at those tasks and endeavors that they choose. Most of those who choose to major in physics believe that they are above-average in the subject. And maybe they are, compared to the entire world. But the problem is that we regularly neglect the reference group and fail to appreciate that we will be among a select group of others who, like us, thought they were better than others (Klar, Karelitz, Roziner, & Levi, 2012; Klar, Ravid, & Hallak, 2012; Windschitl, Rose, Stalkfleet, & Smith, 2008).

Indeed, this failure to understand the relevant reference group may help explain a number of biases of both over- and underplacement. When comparing themselves to others, people often fall back on evaluating themselves in some absolute sense, or relative to the population at large, rather than comparing themselves to the special group to which they belong (Zell & Alicke, 2009). By focusing on themselves, people exaggerate their own abilities and limitations, failing to consider the fact that, quite often, others face similar opportunities and challenges (Moore & Kim, 2003). For instance, the fact that most people believe they are happier than others probably has more to do with the fact that they feel good, rather than due to a sophisticated comparison of their own happiness levels with those of others (Klar & Giladi, 1999). This may be an entirely forgivable error if others' true levels of happiness are invisible to us. However, businesses that fail to invest in understanding their markets, competitors, and potential entrants can pay a high price for such omissions (Moore, Oesch, & Zietsma, 2007). It is not enough to know, for instance, that your own organization has a strong team if that team runs headlong into an even stronger team. Even the best entrepreneurial startup, for example, would have trouble creating a portable music player that could successfully compete against Apple's iPod.

LET'S HEAR IT FOR WELL-CALIBRATED DECISION MAKING

Some scholars have argued that, beyond its symbolic value, overconfidence, and positive illusions in particular, can be good for you, especially if optimism enhances psychological resilience and improves well-being. Taylor and Brown (1988) suggest that our positive illusions about ourselves enhance and protect our self-esteem, increase personal contentment and commitment, help us persist at difficult tasks, and facilitate coping with aversive and uncontrollable events. Taylor (1989) even argues that positive illusions are beneficial to physical and mental health. Positive illusions allow us to maintain cognitive consistency, perceived control, and our belief in a just world (Greenwald, 1980). Seligman (1991) advocates the selection of salespeople based on the magnitude of their positive illusions, which he refers to as "learned optimism," on the grounds that unrealistically high levels of optimism help salespeople persist in the face of rejection.

There are clearly some advantages of positive illusions, including a greater capacity to cope with adversity and an improved ability to convince others of your perspective. Yet we know of no study that has shown that positive illusions or, more broadly, overconfidence leads to better decisions. In contrast, much evidence is in the other direction.

We are highly dubious of the overall benefits of overconfidence in general and positive illusions in particular. Our cynicism is shared by a number of scholars, who caution that positive illusions are likely to have a negative impact on learning and on the quality of decision making, personnel decisions, and responses to crises (such as the argument that "global warming isn't that bad"). Moreover, positive illusions can contribute to conflict and discontent (Brodt, 1990; Dunning, Heath, & Suls, 2004; Kramer, 1994; Tyler & Hastie, 1991). Positive illusions lead organizational members to claim an inappropriately large proportion of the credit for positive outcomes, to overestimate their value to the organization, and to set objectives that have little chance of success. Self-enhancing interpretations of negative outcomes, such as blaming bad luck or other people rather than yourself, also prevent managers from learning from their poor decisions (Morris & Moore, 2000).

Overconfidence and positive illusions can lead people to behave in ways that are arrogant, careless, and self-centered (Anderson, Srivastava, Beer, Spataro, & Chatman, 2006; Baumeister, Campbell, Krueger, & Vohs, 2003). Those who engage in the most self-serving reasoning are also more likely to cheat on tasks, in part because they are better at justifying the behavior to themselves than are others (von Hippel, Lakin, & Shakarchi, 2005). And as we have discussed, people who are overconfident about their abilities, their traits, and their future are often sure that these opinions are accurate. Being too sure that you will succeed— whether at mountain climbing, taking your company public, or getting a good grade—can set you up for failure. And while displaying confidence in your knowledge and abilities will give you credibility as a leader, that confidence can backfire if it turns out that you were wrong.

Positive illusions are hazardous when they cause us to temporarily fool ourselves into believing that we are better than we are. In a study of college students, Robins and Beer (2001) found that positive illusions are associated with higher levels of self-reported well-being and self-esteem in the short term. But, over time, individuals become frustrated as they encounter evidence that their academic performance is not as good as they had thought (see also McGraw et al., 2004). In areas where performance depends on effort, confidence in one's performance can actually undermine future performance (Vancouver & Kendall, 2006). We have noticed that the students in our classes who are most confident that they will do well, and who therefore believe that they do not need to study hard, are not those who get the highest test scores and grades. While it may feel good to savor a positive future, contrary to the "secrets" of success offered in some popular self-help books, simply visualizing or fantasizing about a desired outcome is not sufficient to produce success.

Interestingly, the extent to which people can maintain unrealistically positive beliefs about themselves on various dimensions may be constrained to some degree by the objectivity and credibility of these beliefs and the potential to disconfirm them (Allison, Messick, & Goethals, 1989; Kunda, 1990). For example, it is easier for individuals to maintain the view that they are more honest than others than to believe that they are better tennis players or wittier cocktail party conversationalists: we can easily find evidence of the latter, but it's much harder to measure the former. As Allison et al. (1989) reason, it is tough to hold optimistic illusions that are inconsistent with easily available, objective data. For the same reason, it may be easier for negotiators to maintain the belief that they are fairer than other negotiators than to believe that they are more skillful at reaching profitable agreements. Similarly, Wade-Benzoni, Li, Thompson, and Bazerman (2007) find that people rate themselves more highly on the overall dimension of being environmentally friendly than on specific behaviors such as recycling, reusing paper, or turning off lights.

As we have noted, it is easy to identify circumstances in which people underestimate and underplace themselves. Sometimes we are too cautious and too modest, reporting ourselves to be worse than we actually are or worse than others on a given task, when in fact we are not. These instances are of great scientific interest, as they help us understand why people are overconfident in other circumstances. From a practical standpoint, they help us anticipate when we will likely underestimate ourselves and also help us identify times when we might forgo opportunities at which we would succeed if only we had the courage to try.

Summing up the evidence from the overconfidence literature, we argue that, when making decisions, you should strive to be well calibrated. That is, you should try to match your private beliefs to reality. This basic prescription is surprisingly difficult to achieve. As the coming chapters will document, we all see the world through our own unique perspective, which includes simplifying assumptions, coping mechanisms, and biases that operate in ways that we often misunderstand.

CHAPTER THREE

Common Biases

T he modern world is a big, complicated, messy place. The number of people, the amount of knowledge, and the degree of complexity are all expanding rapidly. Despite the sophistication of our corporations and the speed of our technological development, the capabilities of the human brain have not changed dramatically in the last ten thousand years. As we noted in Chapter 1, individuals rely on rules of thumb, or heuristics, to lessen the information-processing demands of making decisions. Heuristics reduce the effort people must put into making decisions by allowing them to examine fewer pieces of information, simplify the weights of different information, process less information, and consider fewer alternatives in making decisions (Shah & Oppenheimer, 2008). By providing managers with efficient ways to deal with complex problems, heuristics frequently produce effective decisions. However, heuristics also can lead managers to make systematically biased judgments. Biases result when an individual inappropriately applies a heuristic.

The inappropriate application of heuristics can be difficult to avoid. We often make decisions in contexts that are drastically different from one another, and we may incorrectly apply the same decision processes that we successfully used in the past to a completely different context in the future (Kahneman & Klein, 2009). Furthermore, because we often do not receive clear signals about the quality of our decisions, we may rely excessively on our own intuitions in determining whether to use a particular problem-solving strategy in the future. The inherent difficulty of understanding the appropriateness and effectiveness of a particular heuristic may explain why even some of the most intelligent people are susceptible to biases that result from the inappropriate use of heuristics (Stanovich & West, 2008).

The three sections in this chapter correspond to three of the general heuristics we introduced in Chapter 1: the availability heuristic, the representative heuristic, and the confirmation heuristic. (We will discuss a fourth general heuristic, the affect heuristic, in Chapter 6.) The three heuristics covered in this chapter encompass 11 specific biases that we will illustrate using your responses to a series of problems. The goal of the chapter is to help you "unfreeze" your decision-making patterns by showing you how easily heuristics become biases when improperly applied. Once you can spot these biases, you will be able to improve the quality of your decisions by learning to consciously override some of the faulty heuristics that you automatically use on a regular basis (Morewedge & Kahneman, 2010).

Before reading further, please take a few minutes to respond to the problems presented in Table 3.1.

TABLE 3.1 Chapter Problems

Respond to the following problems before reading the rest of the chapter.

Problem 1. Please rank order the following causes of death worldwide in 2008, placing a 1 next to the most common cause, a 2 next to the second most common, etc.

___ War and civil conflict

___ Nutritional deficiencies, including starvation

___ Cancers of the trachea, bronchus, and lung

___ Chronic obstructive lung diseases, including emphysema

___ Respiratory infections, including pneumonia

Now estimate the number of deaths per 100 people caused by each of these five causes in 2008. The world population was approximately 6.7 billion people in 2008.

Problem 2. Estimate the percentage of words in the English language that begin with the letter "a."

Problem 3. Estimate the percentage of words in the English language that have the letter "a" as their third letter.

Problem 4. Lisa is 33 and is pregnant for the first time. She is worried about birth defects such as Down syndrome. Her doctor tells her that she need not worry too much because there is only a 1 in 1,000 chance that a woman of her age will have a baby with Down syndrome. Nevertheless, Lisa remains anxious about this possibility and decides to obtain a test, known as the Triple Screen, which can detect Down syndrome. The test is moderately accurate: When a baby has Down syndrome, the test delivers a positive result 86% of the time. There is, however, a small "false positive" rate: 5% of babies produce a positive result despite not having Down syndrome. Lisa takes the Triple Screen and obtains a positive result for Down syndrome. Given this test result, what are the chances that her baby has Down syndrome?

    a. 0–20% chance

    b. 21–40% chance

    c. 40–60% chance

    d. 61–80% chance

    e. 81–100% chance

Problem 5. A certain town is served by two hospitals. In the larger hospital, about 45 babies are born each day. In the smaller hospital, about 15 babies are born each day. As you know, about 50 percent of all babies are boys. However, the exact percentage of boys born varies from day to day. Sometimes it may be higher than 50 percent, sometimes lower (from Tversky & Kahneman, 1974).

For a period of one year, each hospital recorded the days in which more than 60 percent of the babies born were boys. Which hospital do you think recorded more such days?

    a. The larger hospital

    b. The smaller hospital

    c. About the same (that is, within 5 percent of each other)

Problem 6. You and your spouse have had three children together, all of them girls. Now that you are expecting your fourth child, you wonder whether the odds favor having a boy this time. What is the best estimate of your probability of having another girl?

    a. 6.25% (1 in 16), because the odds of getting four girls in a row is 1 out of 16.

    b. 50% (1 in 2), because there is roughly an equal chance of getting each gender.

    c. A percentage that falls somewhere between these two estimates (6.25–50%).

Problem 7. You are the manager of a Major League Baseball team, and the 2010 season has just ended. One of your most important jobs is to predict players' future performance. Currently, your primary interest lies in predicting batting averages for nine particular players. A measure of a player's performance, batting averages ranges from 0 to 1. Larger numbers reflect better batting performance. You know the nine players' 2010 batting averages and must estimate each one's 2011 batting average. Please fill in your guesses in the right-hand column.

Player	2010	Estimated 2011 batting average
1	.284	
2	.265	
3	.359	
4	.291	
5	.318	
6	.286	
7	.277	
8	.155	
9	.212	

Problem 8. Linda is 31 years old, single, outspoken, and very smart. She majored in philosophy. As a student, she was deeply concerned with issues of discrimination and social justice, and she participated in antinuclear demonstrations.
Rank the following eight descriptions in order of the probability (likelihood) that they describe Linda:

    ___ a. Linda is a teacher in an elementary school.

    ___ b. Linda works in a bookstore and takes yoga classes.

    ___ c. Linda is active in the feminist movement.

    ___ d. Linda is a psychiatric social worker.

    ___ e. Linda is a member of the League of Women Voters.

    ___ f. Linda is a bank teller.

    ___ g. Linda is an insurance salesperson.

    ___ h. Linda is a bank teller who is active in the feminist movement.

Problem 9. Take the last three digits of your phone number. Add the number one to the front of the string, so now you have four digits. Think of that number as a year.

    Write that number here: _____

(continued)

Now try to estimate the year that the Taj Mahal was completed. Was it before or after the date made by your phone number?

_____ Before _____ After

On the line below, please make your best estimate of the actual year in which the Taj Mahal was completed:

_____

Problem 10. Which of the following instances seems most likely? Which seems second-most likely?

    a. Drawing a red marble from a bag containing 50 percent red marbles and 50 percent white marbles.

    b. Drawing a red marble seven times in succession, with replacement (a selected marble is put back into the bag before the next marble is selected), from a bag containing 90 percent red marbles and 10 percent white marbles.

    c. Drawing at least one red marble in seven tries, with replacement, from a bag containing 10 percent red marbles and 90 percent white marbles.

Problem 11. If you had to describe the relationship between baseball players' batting averages in one season and their batting averages in the subsequent season, which of the following four descriptions would you pick?

    1. Zero correlation: Performance is entirely unpredictable, in the sense that knowing how well a player hits one year does not help you predict how well he is going to hit the next year.

    2. Weak correlation of about .4: Performance from one season to the next is moderately predictable, but there are also a lot of random, unpredictable influences on how well a particular player hits in a particular season.

    3. Strong correlation of about .7: Performance is quite predictable from one season to the next, but there is a small random component in how well a player hits.

    4. Perfect correlation of 1.0: Performance stable from one year to the next. The player with the highest batting average in one season always has the highest batting average the next year.

BIASES EMANATING FROM THE AVAILABILITY HEURISTIC

Bias 1: Ease of Recall (Based on Vividness and Recency)

    Problem 1. Please rank order the following causes of death worldwide in 2008, placing a 1 next to the most common cause, a 2 next to the second-most common, and so on.

    _____ War and civil conflict

    _____ Nutritional deficiencies, including starvation

    _____ Cancers of the trachea, bronchus, and lung

    _____ Chronic obstructive lung diseases, including emphysema

    _____ Respiratory infections, including pneumonia

Now estimate the number of deaths per 100,000 people caused by each of these five causes in 2009.

It may surprise you to learn that, according to data published by the World Health Organization, the causes of death above are listed in the reverse order of frequency, with respiratory infections causing the most deaths and war causing the fewest. Even if you got the order right, you probably under-estimated the magnitude of difference between the first three causes and the last two causes. The leading cause of death in the group, respiratory infections, caused 3.5 million deaths, while war and starvation caused 182,000 and 418,000 deaths, respectively. Vivid deaths such as those resulting from civil war, drought, and famine, all of which kill young people, tend to get more press coverage than common afflictions such as emphysema and pneumonia, which are more likely to kill the elderly. The availability of vivid stories in the media biases our perception of the frequency of events toward the first two causes over the last three causes. As a result, we may underestimate the likelihood of death due to lung diseases while overestimating the commonness of death by war or starvation.

Many life decisions are affected by the vividness of information. The require-ment of removing one's shoes at airport security checks is one example. In December 2001, on American Airlines Flight 63 from Paris to Miami, so-called "shoe-bomber" Richard Reid attempted to ignite explosives in his shoes, only to be subdued by other passengers. The plastic explosives in his shoes could have done real damage to the plane, but the fuse was too wet to ignite. Since then, travelers have had to take off their shoes and put them through the X-ray machines despite the fact that shoes are just one of innumerable ways in which a terrorist could hide plastic explosives on his or her body. There are good reasons for governments to take protective action against terrorist attacks, but there can be little doubt that air travelers have Richard Reid to thank for their having to go barefoot through the metal detector.

The availability heuristic describes the inferences we make about event commonness based on the ease with which we can remember instances of that event. Tversky and Kahneman (1974) cite evidence of this bias in a lab study in which individuals were read lists of names of well-known personalities of both genders. Different lists were presented to two groups. One group was read a list in which the women listed were relatively more famous than the listed men, but the list included more men's names overall. The other group was read a list in which the men listed were relatively more famous than the listed women, but the list included more women's names overall. After hearing their group's list, participants in both groups were asked if the list contained the names of more women or men. In both groups, participants incorrectly guessed that the gender that included the relatively more famous personalities was the more numerous. Participants apparently paid more attention to vivid household names than to less well-known figures, leading to inaccurate judgments.

While this example of vividness may seem fairly benign, it is not difficult to see how the availability bias could lead managers to make potentially destructive workplace decisions. One of our MBA students shared this anecdote: As a purchasing agent, he had to select one of several possible suppliers. He chose the firm whose name was the most familiar to him. He later found out that the name was familiar to him because the firm had recently received adverse publicity for extorting funds from client companies!

Managers conducting performance appraisals often fall victim to the availability heuristic. Vivid instances of an employee's behavior (either positive or negative) will be most easily recalled from memory, will appear more numerous than commonplace incidents, and will therefore be weighted more heavily in a performance appraisal. The recency of events is also a factor: Managers give more weight to an employee's performance immediately prior to the evaluation than to the previous nine months of the evaluation period. This is even true when the most recent period is no more relevant or diagnostic but simply more available in memory.

In one clever experiment that illustrates the potential biasing effect of availability, Schwarz and his colleagues (1991) asked their participants to assess their own assertiveness. Some participants were instructed to think of six examples that demonstrate their assertiveness—a fairly easy assignment. Other participants were instructed to come up with 12 instances of their own assertiveness—a tougher task. These participants had more trouble filling up their list than those who only needed to think of six. Consistent with the predictions of the availability heuristic, those who were asked to generate *more* examples actually ended up seeing themselves as *less* assertive, despite the fact that they actually listed more instances of their own assertiveness. Because it was more difficult for them to come up with examples demonstrating their assertiveness, they inferred that they must not be particularly assertive.

Many of us are guilty of committing the availability heuristic through our internal feelings about tempting of fate. In one study of this phenomenon, Risen and Gilovich (2008) had participants rate the likelihood of negative outcomes occurring for individuals involved in different scenarios. One scenario involved a student who either had or had not done the required reading for class. Participants rated the student as being more likely to be called on in class when he did not do the assigned reading than when he did. Risen and Gilovich (2008) argued that actions that "tempt fate" lead us to think of negative outcomes rather than positive ones and that this differential availability biases our predictions.

Along these lines, research shows that people are more likely to purchase insurance to protect themselves from a natural disaster that they have just experienced than to purchase such insurance before this type of disaster occurs. This pattern may be sensible for some types of risks. After all, the experience of surviving a hurricane may offer solid evidence that your property is more vulnerable to hurricanes than you had thought or that climate change is increasing the frequency or severity of hurricanes. This explanation cannot account, however, for trends in the purchase of earthquake insurance. Geologists tell us that that the risk of future earthquakes subsides immediately after a large earthquake occurs. Nevertheless, those who lived through the earthquake were more likely to purchase earthquake insurance immediately afterward (Lindell & Perry, 2000; Palm, 1995). The risk of experiencing an earthquake becomes more vivid and salient after one has experienced an earthquake, even if the risk of another earthquake in the same location diminishes.

Perhaps it ought not surprise us that our memories and recent experiences have such a strong impact on our decisions. Nevertheless, it can be fascinating to discover just how unaware we are of our own mental processes and of the powerful influence of availability on our recollections, predictions, and judgments.

Bias 2: Retrievability (Based on Memory Structures)

Problem 2. Estimate the percentage of words in the English language that begin with the letter "a."

Problem 3. Estimate the percentage of words in the English language that have the letter "a" as their third letter.

Most people estimate that there are more words beginning with "a" than words in which "a" is the third letter. In fact, the latter are more numerous than the former. Words beginning with "a" constitute roughly six percent of English words, whereas words with "a" as the third letter make up more than nine percent of English words. Why do most people believe the opposite to be true? Because we are better at retrieving words from memory using the word's initial letter than the word's third letter (see Tversky & Kahneman, 1973), something you'll see for yourself if you attempt both tasks. Due to the relative ease of recalling words starting with "a," we overestimate their frequency relative to words that have "a" as a third letter.

Tversky and Kahneman (1983) demonstrated this retrievability bias when they asked participants in their study to estimate the frequency of seven-letter words that had the letter "n" in the sixth position. Their participants estimated such words to be less common than seven-letter words ending in the more memorable three-letter "ing" sequence. However, this response pattern must be incorrect. Since all words with seven letters that end in "ing" also have an "n" as their sixth letter, the frequency of words that end in "ing" cannot be larger than the number of words with "n" as the sixth letter. Tversky and Kahneman (1983) argue that "ing" words are more retrievable from memory because of the commonality of the "ing" suffix, whereas the search for words that have an "n" as the sixth letter does not easily generate this group of words.

Sometimes the world structures itself according to our search strategies. Retail store location is influenced by the way in which consumers search their minds when seeking a particular commodity. Why are multiple gas stations at the same intersection? Why do "upscale" retailers want to be in the same mall? Why are the biggest banks in a city often located within a couple blocks of each other? An important reason for this pattern is that consumers learn the location of a particular type of product or store and organize their minds accordingly. To maximize traffic, the retailer needs to be in the location that consumers go to when they want this type of product or store.

Other times, the most natural search strategies do not serve us as well. For instance, managers routinely rely on their social networks to identify potential employees. While this approach has the distinct benefit of eliminating the need to review the hundreds of resumes that may arrive in response to a broader search, it results in a highly selective search. The recommendations that come through people in a manager's network are more likely to be of a similar background, culture, and education as the manager who is performing the search. Thus, the seemingly efficient time-saving strategy of finding qualified employees through social networks can have far-reaching consequences for the diversity of a firm (Pager & Shepherd, 2008). One consequence is that, without intending to discriminate, an organization led by white, college-educated males ends up hiring more of the same (Petersen, Saporta, & Seidel, 2000).

As these first two biases (ease of recall and retrievability) indicate, the misuse of the availability heuristic can lead to systematic errors in managerial judgment. We too easily assume that our available recollections are truly representative of the larger pool of events that exists outside of our range of experience. As decision makers, we need to understand when intuition will lead us astray so that we can avoid the pitfall of selecting the most mentally available option.

BIASES EMANATING FROM THE REPRESENTATIVENESS HEURISTIC

Bias 3: Insensitivity to Base Rates

Problem 4. Lisa is 33 and is pregnant for the first time. She is worried about birth defects such as Down syndrome. Her doctor tells her that she need not worry too much because there is only a 1 in 1,000 chance that a woman of her age will have a baby with Down syndrome. Nevertheless, Lisa remains anxious about this possibility and decides to obtain a test, known as the Triple Screen, that can detect Down syndrome. The test is moderately accurate: When a baby has Down syndrome, the test delivers a positive result 86% of the time. There is, however, a small "false positive" rate: 5% of babies produce a positive result despite not having Down syndrome. Lisa takes the Triple Screen and obtains a positive result for Down syndrome. Given this test result, what are the chances that her baby has Down syndrome?

How did you reach your answer? If you are like most people, you decided that Lisa has a substantial chance of having a baby with Down syndrome. The test gets it right 86% of the time, after all.

The problem with this logic is that it ignores the "base rate"—the overall prevalence of Down syndrome. For 1,000 women Lisa's age who take the test, an average of only one will have a baby with Down syndrome, and there is only an 86% chance that this woman will get a positive test result. The other 999 women who take the test will have babies who do not have Down syndrome; however, due to the test's 5% false positive rate, just under 50 (49.95) of them will receive positive test results. Therefore, the correct answer to this problem is that Lisa's baby has only a 1.7% (.86/(.86 + 49.95)) chance of having Down syndrome, given a positive test result. Due to the simplifying guidance of the representativeness heuristic, specific information about Lisa's case and her test results causes people to ignore background information relevant to the problem, such as the base rate of Down syndrome.

This tendency is even stronger when the specific information is vivid and compelling, as Kahneman and Tversky illustrated in a study from 1972. Participants were given a brief description of a person who enjoyed puzzles and was both mathematically inclined and introverted. Some participants were told that this description was selected from a set of 70 engineers and 30 lawyers. Others were told that the description came from a list of 30 engineers and 70 lawyers. Next, participants were asked to estimate the probability that the person described was an engineer. Even though people admit that the brief description does not offer a foolproof means of distinguishing lawyers from engineers, most tended to believe that the description came from an engineer. Their assessments were relatively impervious to differences in base rates of engineers (70% versus 30% of the sample group).

Participants do use base-rate data correctly when no other information is provided (Kahneman & Tversky, 1972). In the absence of a personal description, people used the base rates sensibly and believed that a person picked at random from a group made up mostly of lawyers was most likely to be a lawyer. Thus, people understand the relevance of base-rate information, but tend to disregard such data when individuating data are also available.

Ignoring base rates has many unfortunate implications, three of which we mention here. First, prospective entrepreneurs typically spend far too much time imagining their success and far too little time considering the base rate for business failures (Moore, Oesch, & Zietsma, 2007). Entrepreneurs think that the base rate for failure is not relevant to their situations; many of them lose their life savings as a result. Second, graduate school admissions decisions tend to favor applicants who have come from institutions with lenient grading. Ignoring the base rates of grading leniency and toughness at different institutions, admissions committees treat high grades as evidence of high achievement, even when they come from a school where everyone gets high grades because of lenient grading (Moore, Swift, Sharek, & Gino, 2010; Swift, Moore, Sharek, & Gino, 2009). Third, people punish others for behavior that ultimately led to bad outcomes, even when the outcomes were largely a function of chance (Gino, Moore, & Bazerman, 2009). Thanks to the representativeness heuristic, we tend to assume that causes (choices) and consequences (outcomes) are related, even when they are not.

Bias 4: Insensitivity to Sample Size

Problem 5. (from Tversky & Kahneman, 1974). A certain town is served by two hospitals. In the larger hospital, about 45 babies are born each day. In the smaller hospital, about 15 babies are born each day. As you know, about 50 percent of all babies are boys. However, the exact percentage of boys born varies from day to day. Sometimes it may be higher than 50 percent, sometimes lower.

For a period of one year, each hospital recorded the days in which more than 60 percent of the babies born were boys. Which hospital do you think recorded more such days?

a. The larger hospital
b. The smaller hospital
c. About the same (that is, within 5 percent of each other)

Most individuals choose C, expecting the two hospitals to record a similar number of days in which 60 percent or more of the babies born are boys. People seem to have some basic idea of how unusual it is to have 60 percent of a random event occurring in a specific direction. However, statistics tells us that we are much more likely to observe 60 percent of male babies in a smaller sample than in a larger sample. This effect is easy to understand. Think about which is more likely: getting more than 60% heads in three flips of a coin or getting more than 60% heads in 3,000 flips of a coin. Half of the time, three flips will produce more than 60% heads. However, 10 flips will only produce more than 60% heads about 17% of the time. Three thousand flips will produce more than 60% heads only .000001% of the time (odds of one in a million). However, most people judge the probability to be the same in each hospital, effectively ignoring sample size.

Although the importance of sample size is fundamental in statistics, Tversky and Kahneman (1974) argue that sample size is rarely a part of our intuition. Why? When responding to problems dealing with sampling, people often use the representativeness heuristic. For instance, they think about how representative it would be for 60 percent of babies born to be boys in a random event. As a result, people ignore the issue of sample size—which is critical to an accurate assessment of the problem.

Consider the implications of this bias for advertising strategies. Market research experts understand that a sizable sample will be more accurate than a small one, but use consumers' bias to the advantage of their clients: "Four out of five dentists surveyed recommend sugarless gum for their patients who chew gum." Without mention of the exact number of dentists involved in the survey, the results of the survey are meaningless. If only five or ten dentists were surveyed, the size of the sample could not justifiably be generalized to the overall population of dentists.

Bias 5: Misconceptions of Chance

Problem 6. You and your spouse have had three children together, all of them girls. Now that you are expecting your fourth child, you wonder whether the odds favor having a boy this time. What is the best estimate of your probability of having another girl?

a. 6.25% (1 in 16), because the odds of getting four girls in a row is 1 out of 16.

b. 50% (1 in 2), because there is roughly an equal chance of getting each gender.

c. A percentage that falls somewhere between these two estimates (6.25–50%).

Relying on the representativeness heuristic, most individuals have a strong intuitive sense that the probability of having four girls in a row is unlikely; thus, they assume that the probability of having another girl in this instance ought to be lower than 50%. The problem with this reasoning is that the gender determination of each new baby is a chance event; the sperm that determines the baby's gender does not know how many other girls the couple has.

This question parallels research by Kahneman and Tversky (1972) showing that people expect a sequence of random events to "look" random. Specifically, participants routinely judged the sequence of coin flips H–T–H–T–T–H to be more likely than H–H–H–T–T–T, which does not "appear" random, and more likely than the sequence H–H–H–H–T–H, which does not represent the equal likelihood of heads and tails. Simple statistics, of course, tell us that each of these sequences is equally likely because of the independence of multiple random events.

Problem 6 triggers our inappropriate tendency to assume that random and nonrandom events will balance out. Will the fourth baby be a boy? Maybe. But your earlier success producing girls is irrelevant to its probability.

The logic concerning misconceptions of chance provides a process explanation of the "gambler's fallacy." After holding bad cards on 10 hands of poker, the poker player believes he is "due" for a good hand. After winning $1,000 in the Pennsylvania State Lottery, a woman changes her regular number—after all, how likely is it that the same number will come up twice? Tversky and Kahneman (1974) note: "Chance is commonly viewed as a self-correcting process in which a deviation in one direction induces a deviation in the opposite direction to restore the equilibrium. In fact, deviations are not corrected as a chance process unfolds, they are merely diluted."

In the preceding examples, individuals expected probabilities to even out. In some situations, our minds misconstrue chance in exactly the opposite way. Our construal of chance often seems to rely on how controllable, intentional, and simple a goal appears (Oskarsson, Van Boven, McClelland, & Hastie, 2009). For outcomes that are obviously due to chance, such as coin flips or sperm arrival times, the representativeness heuristic leads us to expect a self-correcting process that more closely resembles the chance process. For outcomes driven by an intentional actor, we see streaks as intentional, or at least representative of the actor's abilities. If your favorite player has made his last four shots, is the probability of his making his next shot higher, lower, or the same as the probability of his making a shot without the preceding four hits? Most sports fans, sports commentators, and players believe that the answer is "higher." And so a basketball player who hits a few shots in a row has a "hot hand" or is "on fire."

There are many biological, emotional, and physical reasons why this answer could be correct. However, exhaustive analyses show that it is gloriously, emphatically wrong! In one analysis of the shooting of the Philadelphia 76ers and the Boston Celtics, Gilovich, Vallone, and Tversky (1985) found that immediately prior shot performance did not change the likelihood of success on the upcoming shot.

Out of all of the findings in this book, this effect is one of the hardest for our managerial students to accept. We can all remember sequences of five hits in a row; streaks are part of our conception of chance in athletic competition. However, our minds do not think of a string of "four in a row" shots as a situation in which "he missed his fifth shot." As a result, we have a misconception of connectedness when, in fact, chance (or the player's normal probability of success) is actually in effect.

The belief in the hot hand arises from the human mind's powerful ability to detect patterns. We can recognize a face, read distorted writing, or understand garbled language far better than even the most sophisticated and powerful computer. But this ability often leads us to see patterns where there are none. Despite many sports fans' fervent beliefs, thousands of analyses on innumerable sports datasets have shown again and again that there is no such thing as a hot hand, only chance patterns and random streaks in performances that are partially influenced by skill and partially by luck (Reifman, 2011).

The belief in the hot hand has interesting implications for how players compete. Passing the ball to the player who is "hot" is commonly endorsed as a good strategy. Similarly, the opposing team often will concentrate on guarding the "hot" player. But consider that another player, who is less hot but equally skilled, may have a better chance of scoring. Thus, the belief in the "hot hand" is not just erroneous, but also can be costly if people allow it to influence their decisions.

Misconceptions of chance are not limited to gamblers, sports fans, or laypersons. Research psychologists Tversky and Kahneman (1971) found that research psychologists themselves fall victim to the "law of small numbers": They believe that sample events should be far more representative of the population from which they were drawn than simple statistics would dictate. Putting too much faith in the results of initial samples, scientists often grossly overestimate the degree to which empirical findings can be generalized to the general population. The representativeness heuristic may be so well institutionalized in our decision processes that even scientific training and its emphasis on the proper use of statistics may not eliminate its biasing influence.

Bias 6: Regression to the Mean

Problem 7. You are the manager of a Major League Baseball team, and the 2010 season has just ended. One of your most important jobs is to predict players' future performance. Currently, your primary interest lies in predicting batting averages for nine particular players. A measure of a player's performance, batting averages ranges from 0 to 1. Larger numbers reflect better batting performance. You know the nine players' 2010 batting averages and must estimate each one's 2011 batting average. Please fill in your guesses in the right-hand column.

Player	2010	Estimated 2011 batting average
1	.284	
2	.265	
3	.359	
4	.291	
5	.318	
6	.286	
7	.277	
8	.155	
9	.212	

How do you think a prediction like this should be made, absent more specific information about each player? Your answer will depend on how predictable you think batting averages are, which is the question that you answered in Problem 11. If you think that batting averages hold constant from year to year, then you probably would predict that players will repeat their previous year's performance exactly. If you think that last year's performance is worthless for predicting this year's, then you might predict that each player would do about as well as the team's average in 2010 (.276).

Most people understand that there is an imperfect relationship between the performance of a baseball player—or a corporation, for that matter—from one year to the next. Specifically, the basic principles of statistics tell us that any extreme performance is likely to regress to the mean over time. A player or a business that is lucky one year cannot expect to be lucky in just the same way the following year. When it comes time to apply this knowledge to performance expectations, however, most people do not do so systematically. Most people who respond to Problem 8 predict that a player's 2011 performance will be almost identical to his 2010 performance.

In fact, statistics show that the correlation between Major League Baseball players' batting averages from one year to the next is around .4. The nine players listed in Problem 8 actually played for the Texas Rangers in 2010 and 2011. Here are the players' names and batting averages for the 2010 and 2011 seasons:

Player	2010	2011
Michael Young	.284	.338
Elvis Andrus	.265	.279
Josh Hamilton	.359	.298
David Murphy	.291	.275
Nelson Cruz	.318	.263
Ian Kinsler	.286	.255
Andres Blanco	.277	.224
Taylor Teagarden	.155	.235
Craig Gentry	.212	.271

The correlation from 2010 to 2011 among these nine players is roughly the same as in the league overall (.41). You will note that exceptional performances tend to regress to the mean—the worst performances improve and the best performances decline from one year to the next. For example, Josh Hamilton, who led all qualifying Major League Baseball players with a .359 batting average in 2010, saw his average drop to .298 in 2011. Hamilton's 2011 average, while still quite respectable, only managed to rank him 30th in the Major League in 2011.

Accordingly, your estimates in Problem 8 would have been pretty good if you had simply predicted that each player's 2011 batting average would have been equal to the team's 2010 average. Your 2011 predictions would have been *more* accurate for each player if you had equally weighted the team's average with that player's 2010 batting average and taken the average of the two.

Such instances of regression to the mean occur whenever there is an element of chance in an outcome. Gifted children frequently have less successful siblings. Short parents tend to have taller children. Great rookies have less impressive second years (the "sophomore jinx"). Firms that achieve outstanding profits one year tend to perform less well the next year. In each case, individuals are often surprised when made aware of these predictable patterns of regression to the mean.

Why is the regression-to-the-mean concept, a fundamental principle of statistics, counterintuitive? Kahneman and Tversky (1973) suggest that the representativeness heuristic accounts for this systematic bias in judgment. They argue that individuals typically assume that future outcomes (for example, this year's sales) will be directly predictable from past outcomes (last year's sales). Thus, we tend to naively develop predictions based on the assumption of perfect correlation with past data.

In some unusual situations, individuals do intuitively expect a regression-to-the-mean effect. In 2001, when Barry Bonds hit 73 home runs in a single season, few expected him to repeat this performance the following year. When Wilt Chamberlain scored 100 points in a single game, most people did not expect him to score 100 points in his next game. When a historically 3.0 student gets a 4.0 one semester, her parents do not expect a repeat performance the following semester. When a real-estate agent sells five houses in one month (an abnormally high performance), his fellow agents do not expect equally high sales from him the following month. Why is regression to the mean more intuitive in these cases? When a performance is extreme, we know it cannot last. Thus, under unusual circumstances, we expect performance to regress, but we often miss the regression effect in less extreme cases.

Consider Kahneman and Tversky's (1973) classic example in which misconceptions about regression led people to overestimate the effectiveness of punishment and underestimate the power of reward. In a discussion about flight training, experienced instructors noted that praise for an exceptionally smooth landing was typically followed by a poorer landing on the next try, while harsh criticism after a rough landing was usually followed by an improvement on the next try. The instructors concluded that verbal rewards were detrimental to learning, while verbal punishments were beneficial. Obviously, the tendency of performance to regress to the mean can account for the results; verbal feedback may have had absolutely no effect. However, to the extent that the instructors were prone to biased decision making, they were liable to reach the false conclusion that punishment is more effective than positive reinforcement in shaping behavior.

What happens when managers fail to acknowledge the regression principle? Consider an employee who performs extremely well during one evaluation period. He (and his boss) may inappropriately expect similar performance in the next period. What happens when the employee's performance regresses toward the mean? He (and his boss) will begin to make excuses for his failure to meet expectations. Managers who fail to recognize the tendency of events to regress to the mean are likely to develop false assumptions about future results. Consequently, they make inappropriate plans and have unrealistic expectations for employee performance.

Bias 7: The Conjunction Fallacy

Problem 8. Linda is 31 years old, single, outspoken, and very smart. She majored in philosophy. As a student, she was deeply concerned with issues of discrimination and social justice, and she participated in antinuclear demonstrations.

Rank the following eight descriptions in order of the probability (likelihood) that they describe Linda:

    a. Linda is a teacher in an elementary school.

    b. Linda works in a bookstore and takes yoga classes.

    c. Linda is active in the feminist movement.

    d. Linda is a psychiatric social worker.

    e. Linda is a member of the League of Women Voters.

    f. Linda is a bank teller.

    g. Linda is an insurance salesperson.

    h. Linda is a bank teller who is active in the feminist movement.

Examine your rank orderings of descriptions C, F, and H. Most people rank order C as more likely than H and H as more likely than F. Their rationale for this ordering is that C–H–F reflects the degree to which the descriptions are representative of the short profile of Linda. Linda's profile was constructed by Tversky and Kahneman to be representative of an active feminist and unrepresentative of a bank teller. Recall from the representativeness heuristic that people make judgments according to the degree to which a specific description corresponds to a broader category within their minds. Linda's profile is more representative of a feminist than of a feminist bank teller, and is more representative of a feminist bank teller than of a bank teller. Thus, the representativeness heuristic accurately predicts that most individuals will rank order the items C–H–F.

The representativeness heuristic also leads to another common systematic distortion of human judgment—the conjunction fallacy (Tversky & Kahneman, 1983). This is illustrated by a reexamination of the potential descriptions of Linda.

One of the simplest and most fundamental laws of probability is that a subset (for example, being a bank teller and a feminist) cannot be more likely than a larger set that completely includes the subset (for example, being a bank teller). In other words, a conjunction (a combination of two or more descriptors) cannot be more probable than any one of its descriptors; all feminist bank tellers are also bank tellers. By contrast, the "conjunction fallacy" predicts that a conjunction will be judged more probable than a single component descriptor when the conjunction *appears* more representative than the component descriptor. Intuitively, thinking of Linda as a feminist bank teller "feels" more correct than thinking of her as only a bank teller.

The conjunction fallacy can also be triggered by a greater availability of the conjunction than of one of its unique descriptors (Yates & Carlson, 1986). That is, if the conjunction creates more intuitive matches with vivid events, acts, or people than a component of the conjunction, the conjunction is likely to be perceived falsely as more probable than the component. Here's an example. Participants in a study by Tversky and Kahneman (1983) judged the chances of a massive flood somewhere in North America, in 1989, in which one thousand people drown, to be less likely than the chances of an earthquake in California, sometime in 1989, causing a flood in which more than a thousand people drown. Yet, note that the latter possibility (California earthquake leading to flood) is a subset of the former; many other events could cause a flood in North America. Tversky and Kahneman (1983) have shown that the conjunction fallacy also is likely to lead to deviations from rationality in judgments of sporting events, criminal behavior, international relations, and medical decisions. The obvious concern arising from the conjunction fallacy is that it leads us to poorly predict outcomes, which makes us ill-prepared to cope with unanticipated events. We have examined five biases that emanate from the use of the representativeness heuristic: insensitivity to base rates, insensitivity to sample size, misconceptions of chance, regression to the mean, and the conjunction fallacy. The representativeness heuristic can often serve us well. After all, the likelihood of a specific occurrence is usually related to the likelihood of similar types of occurrences. Unfortunately, we tend to overuse this simplifying heuristic when making decisions. The five biases we have just explored illustrate the systematic irrationalities that can occur in our judgments when we are unaware of this tendency.

BIASES EMANATING FROM THE CONFIRMATION HEURISTIC

Bias 8: The Confirmation Trap

Imagine that the sequence of three numbers below follows a rule, and that your task is to diagnose that rule (Wason, 1960). When you write down other sequences of three numbers, an instructor will tell you whether or not your sequence follows the rule.

$$2 - 4 - 6$$

What sequences would you write down? How would you know when you had enough evidence to guess the rule? Wason's study participants tended to offer fairly few sequences, and the sequences tended to be consistent with the rule that they eventually guessed. Commonly proposed rules included "numbers that go up by two" and "the difference between the first two numbers equals the difference between the last two numbers."

In fact, Wason's rule was much broader: "any three ascending numbers." This solution requires participants to accumulate disconfirming, rather than confirming, evidence. For example, if you think the rule is "numbers that go up by two," you must try sequences that do not conform to this rule to find the actual rule. Trying the sequences 1–3–5, 10–12–14, 122–124–126, and so on, will only lead you into the "confirmation trap." Similarly, if you think the rule is "the difference between the first two numbers equals the difference between the last two numbers," you must try sequences that do not conform to this rule to find the actual rule. Trying the sequences 1–2–3, 10–15–20, 122–126–130, again would only bring you feedback that strengthens your hypothesis. Only six out of Wason's twenty-nine participants found the correct rule on their first guess. Wason concluded that obtaining the correct solution necessitates "a willingness to attempt to falsify hypotheses, and thus to test those intuitive ideas that so often carry the feeling of certitude" (1960, p. 139).

As teachers, we have presented this task hundreds of times in classes. The first volunteer typically guesses "numbers going up by two" and is quickly eliminated. The second volunteer is often just as quick with a wrong answer. Interestingly, at this stage, it is rare that a volunteer will have proposed a sequence that doesn't conform to the rule. Why? Because people naturally tend to seek information that confirms their expectations and hypotheses, even when disconfirming or falsifying information is more useful.

When we encounter information that is consistent with our beliefs, we usually accept it with an open mind and a glad heart. If we scrutinize it at all, we ask, in Gilovich's (1991) words, "May I believe it?" We accept information uncritically unless there is an unavoidable reason to doubt it. Yet when we discover facts that force us to question our beliefs, we ask a very different question: "*Must* I believe it?" In other words, we wonder whether we can dismiss this troublesome tidbit or whether the evidence is so overwhelming that we must accept it.

There are two reasons that we fall prey to the confirmation trap. The first has to do with the way the human mind is designed to retrieve information from memory. The mere consideration of certain hypotheses makes information that is consistent with these hypotheses selectively accessible (Gilbert, 1991). Indeed, research shows that the human tendency to entertain provisional hypotheses as true even makes it possible to implant people with false memories. In one study, Loftus (1975) had participants watch a film of an automobile accident. Half of them were asked, "How fast was the white sports car going when it passed the barn while traveling along the country road?" There was, in fact, no barn in the film. Those asked about the non-existent barn were substantially more likely to subsequently recall having seen it than those who were not asked about a barn.

We also succumb to the confirmation trap due to how we search for information. Because there are limits to our attention and cognitive processing, we must search for information selectively, searching first where we are most likely to find the most useful information. One consequence is the retrievability bias we discussed earlier. Another consequence is that people search selectively for information or give special credence to information that allows them to come to the conclusion they desire to reach (Kunda, 1990). Casual observation tells us that political conservatives are the most likely group to listen to conservative talk-show host Rush Limbaugh on the radio and also most likely to avoid watching liberal commentator Rachel Maddow on TV. It seems equally likely that political liberals are the group that most enjoys Maddow's show and that avoids listening to Limbaugh. Political partisans, like all of us, prefer to have their beliefs affirmed rather than undermined.

The biased search for and interpretation of evidence is particularly striking when it comes to political partisanship. Those who were most outraged by President Bill Clinton's false statements about his relationship with Monica Lewinsky were less outraged when it emerged that President George W. Bush and his administration had falsely led the nation to believe that Saddam Hussein possessed weapons of mass destruction. Similarly, those most outraged by Bush's misstatements found it easier to forgive Clinton's.

Here's another example of the confirmation trap. Lord, Ross, and Lepper (1979) asked participants in their study to review evidence for and against the effectiveness of the death penalty in deterring crime. Those who identified them-selves as supporters of the death penalty were completely unpersuaded by research evidence that the death penalty was ineffective at deterring crime. They criticized the studies as poorly designed and the findings as unreliable. Meanwhile, partic-ipants who entered the study as opponents of the death penalty found the same evidence to be valid and persuasive. These participants criticized research showing the effectiveness of the death penalty at deterring crime and came up with plenty of reasons to disregard the evidence. In the end, those on both sides of the issue left the experiment even more solidly assured of their opening opinions.

Once you become aware of the confirmation trap, you are likely to find that it pervades your decision-making processes. When you make a tentative decision (to buy a new car, to hire a particular employee, to start research and develop-ment on a new product line, etc.), do you search for data that supports your decision before making the final commitment? Most of us do. However, the search for disconfirming evidence will provide the most useful insights. For example, when you are seeking to confirm your decision to hire a particular employee, you probably will have no trouble finding positive information about the individual, such as enthusiastic recommendations from past employers. In fact, it may be more important for you to determine whether negative informa-tion about this individual such as a criminal record also exists, as well as positive information about another potential applicant. Now consider the last car you purchased. Imagine that the day after you drove your new car home, your local newspaper printed two lists ranking cars by performance—one by fuel efficiency and one by crash-test results. Which list would you pay more attention to? Most of us would pay more attention to whichever list confirms that we made a good purchase.

Our colleague Dick Thaler has identified a business opportunity to help managers avoid the confirmation trap. Thaler's idea is to form two new consulting firms. One of them, called "Yes Person," would respond to all requests for advice by telling the clients that all their ideas are great. In fact, to speed service and ensure satisfaction, Yes Person would allow clients to write the consulting report themselves if they liked. The other consulting firm, called "Devil's Advocate," would disapprove of any plans currently being considered by a client. Reports by Devil's Advocate would consist of a list of the top ten reasons the client should not pursue the plan under consideration.

Which consulting style would be more useful to the client? Thaler insists that Devil's Advocate would provide a much more important service than Yes Person, and it is hard to disagree. In reality, however, consulting engagements often bear a closer resemblance to the Yes Person format than to that of Devil's Advocate, in part because consulting firms know that clients like to hear how good their ideas are. Our desire to confirm our initial ideas is so strong that we will pay people to back us up! When pressed, Thaler conceded that he wouldn't start either consulting firm, since neither could succeed. After all, he pointed out, no client would ever hire Devil's Advocate, and Yes Person already has too much competition from established consulting firms.

We all fall victim to the tendency to process information in a biased manner, consistent with prior beliefs. Avoiding it requires careful monitoring. Fischer, Greitemeyer, and Frey (2008) demonstrated that individuals who had just finished a tiring task preferred an article consistent with their own viewpoint to a greater extent than did individuals who were not tired. This finding suggests that our natural tendency is to believe the things that confirm our expectations, and that preventing the confirmation trap takes a lot of effort.

Bias 9: Anchoring

Problem 9. Take the last three digits of your phone number. Add the number one to the front of the string, so now you have four digits. Think of that number as a year.

Write that number here: _____

Now try to estimate the year that the Taj Mahal was completed. Was it before or after the date made by your phone number?

_____ Before _____ After

On the line below please, make your best estimate of the actual year in which the Taj Mahal was completed: _____

Was your answer affected by your phone number? Most people who answer this question are influenced by this obviously irrelevant information. Reconsider how you would have responded if your phone number resulted in the year 1978 or the year 1040. On average, individuals whose final three digits are high give more recent estimates for the Taj Mahal's completion than do individuals with lower phone numbers. In fact, the Taj Mahal was completed in 1648 in Agra, India, after 15 years of construction.

Why do we pay attention to irrelevant "anchors" such as digits in a phone number? There are at least two reasons that anchors affect our decisions. First, we often develop estimates by starting with an initial anchor that is based on whatever information is provided and adjust from the anchor to yield a final answer (Epley & Gilovich, 2001). Adjustments away from anchors are usually not sufficient (Tversky & Kahneman, 1974). Second, Mussweiler and Strack (1999) show that the existence of an anchor leads people to think of information that is consistent with that anchor (reasons why the Taj Mahal may have been completed around the year formed by the end of your telephone number) rather than accessing information that is inconsistent with the anchor (reasons why the Taj Mahal's completion date was different from the number formed by your phone number). This phenomenon occurs even when anchors are presented subliminally (Mussweiler & Englich, 2005).

In their classic demonstration of anchoring, Tversky and Kahneman (1974) asked participants to estimate the percentage of countries represented in the United Nations that were African. For each participant, a random number (obtained by a spin of a roulette wheel, observed by the participant) was given as a starting point. From there, participants were asked to state whether the actual quantity was higher or lower than this random value and then develop their best estimate. The arbitrary values from the roulette wheel had a substantial impact on participants' estimates. For example, among those who started with the number ten from the roulette wheel, the median estimate was 25 percent African countries in the U.N. Among those who started with the number 65 from the wheel, the median estimate was 45 percent. Thus, even though participants were aware that the anchor was random and unrelated to the judgment task, the anchor had a dramatic effect on their judgment. Interestingly, paying participants according to their accuracy did not reduce the magnitude of the anchoring effect.

Mussweiler and Strack (2000) have shown that the power of anchoring can be explained by the confirmation heuristic and by the selective accessibility in our minds of hypothesis-consistent information. In one experiment, they asked participants to estimate the average price of a new car in Germany. Half of the participants were provided with a high anchor (40,000 German marks) and half were provided with a low anchor (20,000 German marks). Participants who received the high anchor were quicker to recognize words (such as "Mercedes" and "BMW") associated with expensive cars. Participants who got the low anchors, on the other hand, were quicker to recognize words (such as "Golf" and "VW") associated with relatively inexpensive cars, suggesting that concepts that related to the anchors provided were more active in their minds and more mentally accessible. In fact, simply exposing an individual to an extreme price can increase the price that the individual is willing to pay for a product (Janiszewski, Lichtenstein, & Belyavsky, 2008), even if the focal product is in a different category than the product with an extreme price (Adaval & Wyer, 2011). Additionally, Oppenheimer, LeBoeuf, and Brewer (2008) demonstrated that seemingly arbitrary actions can influence the magnitude of anchors. For example, participants who were asked to draw long lines provided higher estimates of the length of the Mississippi River than did participants who were asked to draw short lines.

Graduating MBA students routinely complain about the effect of anchoring on their salary negotiations. Hiring organizations typically are interested in knowing these students' pre-MBA salaries. Inevitably, these figures influence the post-MBA offers that the students receive, despite the fact that these figures are only marginally relevant to their future performance. A more informative figure would be what a student could earn elsewhere with her MBA experience, perhaps as measured by the offers that her classmates are receiving. Once students accept jobs, future pay increases usually come in the form of percentage increases based on current salary. Those MBA students who negotiate aggressively upfront tend to obtain higher salaries, which then serve as anchors for future years' salaries. Their propensity to negotiate from the start may be quite unrelated to their performance on the job. For instance, evidence suggests that women are less inclined to bargain in situations such as salary negotiations than are men (Bowles, Babcock, & McGinn, 2005). Furthermore, the research findings suggest that when an employer is deciding what offer to make to a potential employee, any anchor that creeps into the discussion, such as an off-hand comment by an uninformed spouse or secretary, is likely to affect the eventual offer, even if the employer tries to ignore the anchor as being irrelevant.

There are numerous examples of anchoring in everyday life. For example:

- In education, children are tracked by a school system that may categorize them by ability at an early age. One study showed that teachers tend to expect children assigned to the lowest group to achieve little and expect those assigned to the top group to achieve much more (Darley & Gross, 1983). These expectations influence actual performance in profound ways, as revealed by studies in which students were randomly assigned to groups of varying levels. Teachers who were unaware that the assignment was random treated students differently depending on which group they belonged to (Rosenthal, 1974; Rosenthal & Jacobson, 1968).

- We have all fallen victim to the first-impression syndrome when meeting someone for the first time. We often place so much emphasis on initial impression anchors that we fail to adjust our opinion appropriately at a later date when we have the chance to do so (Dougherty, Turban, & Callender, 1994).

- A person's race serves as an anchor with respect to our expectations of their behavior, and we tend to adjust insufficiently from that anchor. Due to deeply ingrained stereotypes about people of African descent, Americans perceive the very same behavior as more aggressive when exhibited by an African American than when exhibited by a European American (Duncan, 1976). Our tendency to react more aggressively to individuals who are dissimilar to us (Pedersen, Bushman, Vasquez, & Miller, 2008) exacerbates this problem, as white Americans are not only more likely to perceive African Americans as being more aggressive than other white Americans, but are more likely to react with hostility to perceived aggression by African Americans. Hostile behavior may incite actual aggressive behavior that affirms false views about the aggression of African Americans.

Joyce and Biddle (1981) have provided empirical support for the presence of the anchoring effect among practicing auditors of major accounting firms. Auditors participating in one condition were asked the following questions (adapted from the original version to keep the problem current):

It is well known that many cases of management fraud go undetected even when competent annual audits are performed. The reason, of course, is that Generally Accepted Auditing Standards are not designed specifically to detect executive-level management fraud. We are interested in obtaining an estimate from practicing auditors of the prevalence of executive-level management fraud as a first step in ascertaining the scope of the problem.

1. Based on your audit experience, is the incidence of significant executive-level management fraud more than 10 in each 1,000 firms (that is, one percent) audited by Big Four accounting firms?
   a. Yes, more than 10 in each 1,000 Big Four clients have significant executive-level management fraud.
   b. No, fewer than 10 in each 1,000 Big Four clients have significant executive-level management fraud.
2. What is your estimate of the number of Big Four clients per 1,000 that have significant executive-level management fraud? (Fill in the blank below with the appropriate number.)

   _____ in each 1,000 Big Four clients have significant executive-level management fraud.

The second condition differed from the first only in that participants were asked whether the fraud incidence was more or less than 200 per 1,000 firms audited, rather than 10 per 1,000. Prior to the auditing scandals that started to emerge in 2001, participants in the first condition estimated a fraud incidence of 16.52 per 1,000 on average, compared with an estimated fraud incidence of 43.11 per 1,000 in the second condition! In our own use of these problems with executive classes, answers to both versions have roughly doubled since the fall of Enron, but the differences between the two versions of the problem remain large. It seems that even seasoned experts, including professional auditors, can be affected by anchors. In fact, Englich and her colleagues (Englich & Mussweiler, 2001; Englich, Mussweiler, & Strack, 2006) show that judges' sentencing decisions are influenced by anchors as irrelevant as a roll of the dice.

Epley (2004) discusses two different processes that lead to the anchoring bias. Specifically, he shows that when an anchor is externally set (not set by the decision maker), the anchor leads to a biased search for information compatible with the anchor (Mussweiler & Strack, 1999, 2000, 2001). For example, when you view a house whose list price is dramatically above its market value, the high anchor is likely to lead you to see the positive features of the house that are consistent with a high valuation. In contrast, when someone develops her own anchor, she will start with that anchor and insufficiently adjust away from it (Epley & Gilovich, 2001). For example, when considering the question of when George Washington was elected president of the United States, most Americans begin with the year in which the country declared its independence from England (1776) and adjust up to arrive at an estimate.

Findings from Nisbett and Ross (1980) suggest that the anchoring bias itself dictates that it will be very difficult for this book to convince you to change your decision-making strategies. They would argue that the heuristics we identify here are cognitive anchors that are central to your judgment processes. Thus, any cognitive strategy that we suggest must be presented and understood in a manner that will force you to break your existing cognitive anchors. The evidence presented in this section suggests that this should be a difficult challenge—but one that is important enough to be worth the effort.

Bias 10: Conjunctive and Disjunctive Events Bias

Problem 10. Which of the following instances appears most likely? Which appears second most likely?

    a. Drawing a red marble from a bag containing 50 percent red marbles and 50 percent white marbles.

    b. Drawing a red marble seven times in succession, with replacement (a selected marble is put back into the bag before the next marble is selected), from a bag containing 90 percent red marbles and 10 percent white marbles.

    c. Drawing at least one red marble in seven tries, with replacement, from a bag containing 10 percent red marbles and 90 percent white marbles.

The most common ordering of preferences is B–A–C. Interestingly, the correct order of likelihood is C (52 percent), A (50 percent), B (48 percent)—the exact opposite of the most common intuitive pattern! This result illustrates a general bias to overestimate the probability of conjunctive events, or events that must occur in conjunction with one another (Bar-Hillel, 1973), and to underestimate the probability of disjunctive events, or events that occur independently (Tversky & Kahneman, 1974). Thus, when multiple events all need to occur (choice B), we overestimate the true likelihood of this happening, while if only one of many events needs to occur (choice C), we underestimate the true likelihood of this event.

As we discussed in Chapter 2, the overestimation of conjunctive events offers a powerful explanation for overestimation of future productivity and the planning fallacy. Individuals, businesses, and governments frequently fall victim to the conjunctive-events bias in terms of timing and budgets for projects that require multistage planning. Home remodeling, new product ventures, and public works projects seldom finish on time or on budget. Why are we so optimistic in our assessments of a project's cost and time frame? Why are we so surprised when a seemingly unlikely setback occurs? Because of the human tendency to under-estimate disjunctive events. "A complex system, such as a nuclear reactor or the human body, will malfunction if any of its essential components fails," argue Tversky and Kahneman (1974). "Even when the likelihood of failure in each component is slight, the probability of an overall failure can be high if many components are involved."

An awareness of our underestimation of disjunctive events sometimes makes us too pessimistic. Consider the following scenario:

> It's Monday evening (10:00 P.M.). Your boss calls to tell you that you must be at the Chicago office by 9:30 A.M. the next morning. You call all five airlines that have flights getting into Chicago by 9:00 A.M. Each has one flight, and all the flights are booked. When you ask the probability of getting on each of the flights if you show up at the airport in the morning, you are disappointed to hear probabilities of 30 percent, 25 percent, 15 percent, 20 percent, and 25 percent. Consequently, you do not expect to get to Chicago on time.

In this case, the disjunctive bias leads you to expect the worst. In fact, if the probabilities given by the airlines are unbiased and independent, you have a 73 percent chance of getting on one of the flights (assuming that you can arrange to be at the right ticket counter at the right time).

Bias 11: Hindsight and the Curse of Knowledge

Imagine yourself in the following scenarios:

- You are an avid football fan, and you are watching a critical game in which your team is behind 35–31. With three seconds left and the ball on the opponent's three-yard line, the quarterback calls a pass play into the corner of the end zone. When the play fails, you shout, "I knew that was a bad play."
- You are driving in an unfamiliar area, and your spouse is behind the wheel. When you approach an unmarked fork in the road, your spouse decides to go to the right. Four miles and 15 minutes later, it is clear that you are lost. You blurt out, "I knew you should have turned left at the fork."
- A manager who works for you hired a new supervisor last year. You were well aware of the choices she had at the time and allowed her to choose the new

employee on her own. You have just received production data on every supervisor. The data on the new supervisor are terrible. You call in the manager and claim, "There was plenty of evidence that he was the wrong man for the job."

• As director of marketing in a consumer-goods organization, you have just presented the results of an extensive six-month study on current consumer preferences for the products manufactured by your company. At the conclusion of your presentation, a senior vice president responds, "I don't know why we spent so much time and money collecting these data. I could have told you what the results were going to be."

Do you recognize any of your own behaviors in these scenarios? Do you recognize someone else's remarks? Each scenario exemplifies "the hindsight bias" (Fischhoff, 1975), which often occurs when people look back on their own judgments and those of others. We typically are not very good at recalling or reconstructing the way an uncertain situation appeared to us before finding out the results of the decision. What play would you have called? Did you really know that your spouse should have turned left? Was there truly evidence that the selected supervisor was a bad choice? Could the senior vice president actually have predicted your study's results? While our intuition is occasionally accurate, we tend to overestimate what we knew beforehand based upon what we later learned.

Fischhoff (1975) examined the differences between hindsight and foresight in the context of judging the outcomes of historical events. In one study, participants were divided into five groups and asked to read a passage about the war between the British and Gurkha forces in 1814. One group was not told the result of the war. The remaining four groups of participants were told either that: (1) the British won, (2) the Gurkhas won, (3) a military stalemate was reached with no peace settlement, or (4) a military stalemate was reached with a peace settlement. Obviously, only one group was told the truthful outcome—in this case, (1)—that the British won. Each participant was then asked what his or her subjective assessments of the probability of each of the outcomes would have been without the benefit of knowing the reported outcome. Participants tended to believe that even if they had not been told the outcome, they would have judged the outcome that they were told happened as being most likely. Based on this and other varied examples, it becomes clear that knowledge of an outcome increases an individual's belief about the degree to which he or she would have predicted that outcome without the benefit of that knowledge.

The processes that give rise to anchoring may also be at work in producing the hindsight bias (Fiedler, 2000; Koriat, Fiedler, & Bjork, 2006). According to this explanation, knowledge of an event's outcome works as an anchor by which individuals interpret their prior judgments of the event's likelihood. Because confirmatory information is selectively accessible to us during information retrieval, our adjustments to anchors are inadequate (Mussweiler & Strack, 1999). Consequently, hindsight knowledge biases our perceptions of what we remember knowing in foresight. Furthermore, to the extent that various pieces of data about the event vary in support of the actual outcome, evidence that is consistent with the known outcome may become cognitively more salient and thus more available in memory (Slovic & Fischhoff, 1977). This tendency will lead an individual to justify claimed foresight in view of "the facts provided." Finally, the relevance of a particular piece of data may later be judged important to the extent to which it is representative of the final observed outcome.

In the short run, the hindsight bias can offer a number of advantages. For instance, it can be flattering to believe that your judgment is far better than it actually is. In addition, hindsight allows us to criticize other people's apparent lack of foresight. However, the hindsight bias reduces our ability to learn from the past and to evaluate decisions objectively. In general, individuals should be judged by the process and logic of their decisions, not just on their results. A decision maker who makes a high-quality decision that does not work out should be rewarded, not punished. Why? Because results are affected by a variety of factors outside the direct control of the decision maker. When the hindsight bias leads our knowledge of a result to color our evaluation of decision makers' logic, we will make worse evaluations than we would otherwise.

Closely related to the hindsight bias is the "curse of knowledge," which argues that when assessing others' knowledge, people are unable to ignore knowledge that they have that others do not have (Camerer, Loewenstein, & Weber, 1989). Available knowledge is hard to forget when you try to imagine how much others know about something; your sophistication stands in the way of a fair assessment. This "curse" explains the difficulty that teachers often have adjusting their lessons to students' level of knowledge and the tendency of product designers to over-estimate the average person's ability to master high-tech devices. Indeed, evidence suggests that as many as half of high-tech devices that consumers return as malfunctioning are, in fact, in perfect working order: consumers just couldn't figure out how to use them (den Ouden, 2006). Interestingly, Hoch (1988) found that marketing experts are generally *worse* at predicting the beliefs, values, and tastes of other consumers than are non-expert consumers. This is the case because the marketing experts assume and behave as if non-expert consumers understand as much about the products being marketed as the experts do.

Have you ever given someone what you believed were very clear directions to your home, only to find out that he got lost? Keysar (1994) argues that when an individual sends an ambiguous message (which is clear to her) to another individual, based on information that the receiver does not possess, she assumes that the other party will magically understand her intent. Keysar (1994) had people read scenarios that provided them with privileged information about "David." They read that David had dinner at a particular restaurant based on a friend's recommendation. Half the participants in the experiment learned that David really enjoyed his meal, and the other half learned that he disliked it very much. All the participants read that David wrote his friend the following note: "About the restaurant, it was marvelous, just marvelous." The participants who knew that David enjoyed the restaurant had a strong tendency to believe that the friend would take the comment as sincere. In contrast, participants who knew that David disliked the restaurant had a strong tendency to believe that the friend would take the comment as sarcastic. This result occurred despite the fact that both groups of participants knew that the friend had access to the same note and no additional information about David's dining experience.

In organizations, a great deal of disappointment results from the failure to communicate clearly. This disappointment is caused in part by our false belief that people understand our ambiguous messages. It should come as no surprise that communication by e-mail, lacking the cues of intonation and body language, only makes this problem worse (Kruger, Epley, Parker, & Ng, 2005). One potential remedy for the curse of knowledge is to adopt a mindset of perceiving differences in people and objects as opposed to similarities. Todd, Hanko, Galinsky, and Mussweiler (2011) found that after people focused on differences, they were better at taking the visual perspective of others and were less likely to project their privately held information onto others. Arguing that a mindset of acknowledging differences could be induced by having participants interact with out-group members, Todd and colleagues also demonstrated that after arbitrarily assigning individuals to groups, those who interacted with out-group members were better at navigating a blindfolded partner through a maze than were those who interacted with in-group members. These findings not only suggest that thinking in terms of differences can reduce the curse of knowledge, but also that diversity in the workplace can reduce the curse as well.

If we can learn to overcome the confirmation heuristic and to consider a range of alternative explanations to originally considered explanations, we can improve the quality of our decisions. Evidence suggests that when presented with multiple pieces of information, people often do a surprisingly good job choosing the most useful information, rather than the information that confirms their expectations (Nelson, McKenzie, Cottrell, & Sejnowski, 2010). This encouraging evidence suggests that once we can overcome the tendency to think in a confirmatory fashion and generate a large number of alterative explanations for events, we can rely on our intuition to a reasonable extent in attending to these alternative explanations. Research to date suggests that our intuition can actually be helpful in selecting the information that best improves our probability of accurately identifying the cause of an event (Crupi, Tentori, & Lombardi, 2009).

INTEGRATION AND COMMENTARY

Heuristics, or rules of thumb, are the cognitive tools we use to simplify decision making. The preceding pages have described 12 of the most common biases that result when we over-rely on these judgmental heuristics. These biases, along with their associated heuristics, are summarized in Table 3.2. Remember that more than one heuristic can operate on your decision-making processes at any given time.

Reliance on heuristics is actually wise when the loss in decision quality is outweighed by time saved. And, indeed, such "shortcuts" often lead to adequate

TABLE 3.2   **Summary of the 12 Biases Presented in Chapter 3**

Bias	Description
Biases Emanating from the Availability Heuristic	
1. Ease of recall	Individuals judge events that are more easily recalled from memory, based on vividness or recency, to be more numerous than events of equal frequency whose instances are less easily recalled.
2. Retrievability	Individuals are biased in their assessments of the frequency of events based on how their memory structures affect the search process.
Biases Emanating from the Representativeness Heuristic	
3. Insensitivity to base rates	When assessing the likelihood of events, individuals tend to ignore base rates if any other descriptive information is provided—even if it is irrelevant.
4. Insensitivity to sample size	When assessing the reliability of sample information, individuals frequently fail to appreciate the role of sample size.
5. Misconceptions of chance	Individuals expect that a sequence of data generated by a random process will look "random," even when the sequence is too short for those expectations to be statistically valid.
6. Regression to the mean	Individuals tend to ignore the fact that extreme events tend to regress to the mean on subsequent trials.
7. The conjunction fallacy	Individuals falsely judge that conjunctions (two events co-occurring) are more probable than a more global set of occurrences of which the conjunction is a subset.
Biases Emanating from the Confirmation Heuristic	
8. The confirmation trap	Individuals tend to seek confirmatory information for what they think is true and fail to search for disconfirmatory evidence.
9. Anchoring	Individuals make estimates for values based upon an initial value (derived from past events, random assignment, or whatever information is available) and typically make insufficient adjustments from that anchor when establishing a final value.
10. Conjunctive and disjunctive events bias	Individuals exhibit a bias toward overestimating the probability of conjunctive events and underestimating the probability of disjunctive events.
11. Hindsight and the curse of knowledge	After finding out whether or not an event occurred, individuals tend to overestimate the degree to which they would have predicted the correct outcome. Furthermore, individuals fail to ignore information they possess that others do not when predicting others' behavior.
12. Overconfidence	Individuals tend to be overconfident of the correctness of their judgments, especially when answering difficult questions.

decisions. However, as we have demonstrated in this chapter, a blanket acceptance of heuristics is unwise. First, as illustrated by the quiz items, there are many instances in which the loss in decision quality far outweighs the time saved by heuristics. Second, the "wise" logic of reliance on heuristics suggests that we voluntarily accept tradeoffs on quality when we decide to employ a heuristic. In reality, we do not: Most of us are unaware of their existence and their pervasive impact upon our decision making. Consequently, we fail to distinguish between situations in which heuristics are beneficial and situations in which they are potentially harmful.

Why do we fail to apply heuristics selectively? In good part because our minds are wired to make reliance on these heuristics natural and comfortable. For instance, the biases related to the availability heuristic appear to be a natural function of the selectiveness of human memory. Our brains are better at remembering information that is interesting, emotionally arousing, or recently acquired. The human brain evolved over millennia using strategies that helped our ancestors survive and reproduce. Humans seem to be more self-aware than any other animals. Nevertheless, we remain profoundly ignorant of the internal workings of our minds and of the processes, such as recall from immediate memory and confirmatory hypothesis testing, that can have such important and negative consequences.

When the stakes are high and decision quality is important, it is worth engaging in more effortful thought processes that can avoid biases. The key to improved judgment lies in learning to distinguish between appropriate and inappropriate uses of heuristics, when your judgment is likely to rely on heuristics, and how to avoid them. This chapter gives you the foundation you need to make these distinctions.

CHAPTER FOUR

Bounded Awareness

Over the course of three decades, Bernard Madoff intentionally stole from his investors. In December 2008, he confessed to his crimes, and his Ponzi scheme cracked, wiping out $64.8 billion in paper profit. Madoff sold most of his investments through feeder funds—that is, other funds that either marketed their access to Madoff to potential investors or claimed they had access to some exotic investment strategy. The feeder funds often did nothing more than turn the money they collected over to Madoff. These intermediaries were extremely well paid, often earning a small percentage of the funds invested plus 20% of any investment returns. As Madoff claimed a consistent record of success, the feeder funds profited handsomely.

This chapter is not about Madoff's deeds but rather is about our amazing ability to not notice things that happen right under our noses. There is no actual investing strategy that could have produced the returns that Madoff claimed. Did the managers of the feeder funds know that Madoff was running a Ponzi scheme, or did they simply fail to notice that Madoff's performance reached a level of return and stability that was impossible? While some may have noticed (Markopolos & Casey, 2010), ample evidence suggests that many feeder funds had hints that something was wrong but lacked the motivation to see the evidence that was readily available. Beyond the managers of the feeder funds, professional investors, government regulators, and investment bankers failed to notice that something was wrong. When they got hints, they ignored them. Rene-Theirry Magon de la Villehuchet, the CEO of Access International Advisors and Marketers, invested his own money, his family's money, and money from his wealthy clients with Madoff. He was repeatedly warned about Madoff and received ample evidence that Madoff's returns were not possible, but he did not investigate. Two weeks after Madoff was arrested and the truth came out, de la Villehuchet killed himself in his office by slitting his wrist and taking sleeping pills.

This chapter is about our systematic and predictable failures to notice critical information that is available to us. Just as we rely on the decision-making heuristics we discussed in Chapter 3, we also limit our search for information to simplify complex decisions. Simplifying complex situations is a problem that human beings must deal with from their first moments of life. When we first enter the world as infants, we experience it, in William James's (1890) words, as "one great buzzing, blooming confusion" (p. 488). The constant process of learning to navigate our way through the world—from learning to understand language to learning to do our jobs—largely involves figuring out what is worth paying attention to and what we can ignore. As human beings, we lack the attention and brain power we would need to pay attention to every potentially relevant fact or piece of information in our environment when making a decision. Even if we did possess such brain power, we would also need to do better at determining the relative importance of various pieces of information.

To avoid the problems associated with information overload, people constantly engage in information filtering. Much of it is carried out unconsciously, automatically, and inefficiently. We end up ignoring or neglecting useful information while paying attention to irrelevant information. In this chapter, we illustrate some of the ways our minds are likely to filter out key pieces of information. We also explore the consequences of this selective attention for our perceptions and our decisions. Before reading this chapter, please respond to the problems presented in Table 4.1.

TABLE 4.1 Chapter Problems

Please respond to the following problems before reading the rest of the chapter.

Problem 1. MBA students from a prestigious university read the following problem and played one of the six roles—A, B, C, D, E, and F:

In this exercise, six people will be randomly assigned to the roles A, B, C, D, E, and F. A will be randomly selected and given $60 to allot among A, B, C, D, E, and F. The amounts given to B, C, D, E, and F must be equal, but this amount may be different from the amount that A allocates to A (herself/himself). B, C, D, E, and F will be asked to specify the minimum amount that they would accept. If the amount offered by A to each of B, C, D, E, and F is equal to or greater than the largest amount specified by B, C, D, E, or F, the $60 will be divided as specified by A. If, however, any of the amounts specified by B, C, D, E, and F are larger than the amount offered by A, all six parties will receive $0.

Please estimate the allocation from A that would maximize A's average dollar payoff (use whole numbers, not decimals/fractions):

A: $_____ B: $_____ C: $_____ D: $_____ E: $_____ F: $_____

Problem 2. In a recent study, college students were presented with the following question:

In this problem, you will be given a choice of boxes X, Y, or Z. One of these three boxes has a valuable prize in it. The other two boxes are empty. After you pick one of the boxes, the computer will open one of the other two boxes, show you that this unchosen box does not have the prize, and offer you to trade your chosen box for the unopened, unchosen box. For example, if you were to choose box X, the computer would open one of the two other boxes (e.g., Y) and show you that it is empty. The computer would then offer you the opportunity to switch your choice from X to Z.

A student who participated in the study picked box Y. The computer then opened box Z, showed the student it was empty, and offered the student to trade box Y (which the student originally chose) for box X (the remaining unopened, unchosen box).

Please state whether the student should have traded box Y for box X or not, in order to have the best chance of winning the prize.

    Answer: Yes   No

Problem 3. In this exercise you represent Company A (the acquirer), which is currently considering acquiring Company T (the target) by means of a tender offer. You plan to tender in cash for 100 percent of Company T's shares but are unsure how high a price to offer. The main complication is this: The value of Company T depends directly on the outcome of a major oil exploration project it is currently undertaking. Indeed, the very viability of Company T depends on the exploration's outcome. If the project fails, the company under current management will be worth nothing—$0 per share. But if the project succeeds, the value of the company under current management could be as high as $100 per share. All share values between $0 and $100 are considered equally likely.

By all estimates, the company will be worth considerably more in the hands of Company A than under current management. In fact, whatever the ultimate value under current management, *the company will be worth 50 percent more under the management of A than under Company T*. If the project fails, the company is worth $0 per share under either management. If the exploration project generates a $50 per share value under current management, the value under Company A is $75 per share. Similarly, a $100 per share value under Company T implies a $150 per share value under Company A, and so on.

The board of directors of Company A has asked you to determine the price they should offer for Company T's shares. This offer must be made now, before the outcome of the drilling project is known. From all indications, Company T would be happy to be acquired by Company A, provided the price is profitable. Moreover, Company T wishes to avoid, at all cost, the potential of a takeover bid by any other firm. You expect Company T to delay a decision on your bid until the results of the project are in, then accept or reject your offer before the news of the drilling results reaches the press. Thus, you (Company A) will not know the results of the exploration project when submitting your price offer, but Company T will know the results when deciding whether or not to accept your offer. In addition, Company T is expected to accept any offer by Company A that is greater than the (per share) value of the company under current management.

As the representative of Company A, you are deliberating over price offers ranging from $0 per share (this is tantamount to making no offer at all) to $150 per share. What price offer per share would you tender for Company T's stock?

    My tender price is $_____ per share.

Problem 4. MBA students from a prestigious university read the following problem and played one of the six roles—A, B, C, D, E, and F:

In this exercise, six people will be randomly assigned to the roles A, B, C, D, E, and F. A will be randomly selected and given $60 to allot among A, B, C, D, E, and F. The amounts given to B, C, D, E, and F must be equal, but this amount may be different from the amount that A allocates to A (herself/himself). B, C, D, E, and F will be asked to specify the minimum amount that they would accept. If the amount offered by A to each of B, C, D, E, and F is equal to or greater than the smallest amount specified by B, C, D, E, or F, the $60 will be divided as specified by A. If, however, all of the amounts specified by B, C, D, E, and F are larger than the amount offered by A, all six parties will receive $0.

Please specify the allocation from A that would maximize A's average dollar payoff (use whole numbers, not decimals/fractions):

    A: $_____ B: $_____ C: $_____ D: $_____ E: $_____ F: $_____

Problem 5. In a recent study, college students were given the following question:

In this problem, you will be given a choice of boxes X, Y, or Z. One of these three boxes has a valuable prize in it. The other two boxes are empty. After you pick one of the boxes, the computer may open one of the other two boxes, show you that this unchosen box does not have the prize, and offer you to trade your chosen box for the unopened unchosen box. The computer will make its decision whether to open a box and offer you a switch with the goal of minimizing the likelihood that you get the prize. For example, if you were to choose box X, the computer might decide to open one of the two other boxes (e.g., Y), show you it's empty, and offer you the opportunity to switch your choice from X to Z.

A student who participated in the study picked box Y. The computer then opened box Z, showed the student it was empty, and offered the student to trade box Y (which the student originally chose) for box X (the remaining unopened, unchosen box).

Please state whether the student should have traded box Y for box X or not, in order to have the best chance of winning the prize.

Answer: Yes   No

Problem 6. Without lifting your pencil (or pen) from the paper, draw four (and only four) straight lines that connect all nine dots shown here:

· · ·

· · ·

· · ·

Chapter 1 introduced the concept of bounded rationality, which describes the fact that our thinking is limited and biased in systematic, predictable ways. Descriptions of these bounds, or limitations, tend to concern how people process and make decisions using the information of which they are aware. In this chapter, we argue that people have *bounded awareness* (Bazerman & Chugh, 2005) that prevents them from noticing or focusing on useful, observable, and relevant data. Our minds are constantly making choices about what to pay attention to and what to ignore, but our information filters make some predictable mistakes. Bounded awareness often leads people to ignore accessible, perceivable, and important information, while paying attention to other equally accessible but irrelevant information (Bazerman & Chugh, 2005). The availability heuristic, discussed in Chapters 1 and 2, offers some evidence for this idea. But bounded awareness goes well beyond the availability heuristic. Within specific domains, we can identify useful information that, due to bounded awareness, is systematically left outside the awareness of most decision makers. The misalignment between the information needed for a good decision and the information included in awareness results in a focusing failure.

One well-known problem that illustrates the concept of bounded awareness is Problem 6 from Table 4.1. Were you able to solve the problem? Most intelligent people fail to solve it, even those who remember seeing the problem before. Most people attempt to apply their logical decision-making skills to the problem that is in focus: connecting all nine dots without going outside the bounds imposed by the nine dots. Common attempts look like the following:

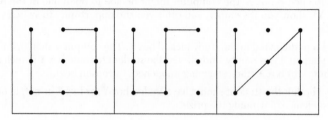

People naturally create a boundary that frames the problem and constrains them from finding a solution. But note that the problem does not tell you to keep your pencil within the bounds imposed by the nine dots. Once people become aware of the space outside the area bounded by the nine dots, the following solution is fairly easy to achieve:

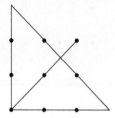

As you can see, the solution is simple. However, many bright people could look at this problem for hours and not solve it. Why? Because bounds created by our minds eliminate the solution. Creativity problems frequently make people feel tricked. A common "trick" of such problems is to misdirect our attention by causing us to psychologically see bounds on the problem. These bounds prevent discovery of the solution. After the teacher breaks the psychological bound, the solution seems obvious. The most critical barriers to creative decisions are our assumptions, or the information we allow into the defined problem space. To fit problems into our previously established decision-making processes, we make assumptions about them. Creativity problems may not seem to be representative of common real-world decisions, but the tendency to place false perceived bounds is a common aspect of decision-making.

The phenomenon of bounded awareness is captured by the familiar exclamation, "How could I have missed that?" Many of us have this response after seeing important information that we previously overlooked. Offering an intriguing approach to idea innovation, Nalebuff and Ayres (2003) encourage us to ask

"Why not?" For example, they argue that the "anticipation" problem posed by the slow flow of ketchup out the top of its bottle was solved by a new design that allows the bottle to be stored upside down, a design later extended to a broad array of products. Nalebuff and Ayres encourage product developers to imagine the products they would want to create if resources were not a constraint. Once you know what you want in an unbounded world, these researchers suggest, you can explore whether it is viable in our real, constrained world.

This chapter examines the prevalence of bounded awareness in a variety of realms: (1) inattentional blindness to obvious information, (2) the failure to notice obvious changes in one's environment, (3) the tendency to focus on only a part of the problem at hand, as well as bounded awareness in (4) groups, (5) strategic decisions, and (6) auctions.

INATTENTIONAL BLINDNESS

Over 30 years ago, Neisser (1979) asked people to watch a video of two visually superimposed groups of players passing basketballs. One group wore white shirts, and the other group wore dark shirts. Participants were instructed to count the number of passes made between members of one of the two groups. The superimposed video made the task moderately difficult, and participants had to give it their full attention. The interesting result is that only 21 percent of Neisser's participants reported seeing a woman who clearly and unexpectedly walked through the basketball court carrying an open umbrella.

Our repeated experience, using this video in the classroom, is that far fewer than 21 percent of our students notice the woman. After showing the video, we ask our students whether anyone saw anything unusual. In a large room, it is common for just a few people to mention seeing a woman with an umbrella. When they offer this observation, the others in the room scoff at it. Yet, when we show the video again to demonstrate what most of the class missed, everyone sees the woman. By focusing on one task—in this case, counting passes—people miss very obvious information in their visual world.

Using a video in which a person in a gorilla costume walks through a basketball game, thumping his chest, and is clearly and comically visible for more than five seconds, Simons and Chabris (Chabris & Simons, 2010; 1999) have replicated Neisser's findings. Simons provides a series of such demonstrations on a video that can be purchased at www.viscog.com.

We find the failure to see the obvious (including our own failures the first time we saw the video) so remarkable because it violates common assumptions about our visual awareness. This phenomenon has captured the interest of cognitive and perceptual psychologists and has become known as *inattentional blindness* (Simons & Levin, 2003). Mack and Rock (1998) provide broader evidence in perceptual experiments that people have a tendency not to see what they are not looking for, even when they are looking directly at it. Mack (2003) points out that inattentional blindness might cause an airplane pilot who is attending to his controls to overlook the presence of another airplane in his runway. Similarly, many car accidents undoubtedly result from drivers focusing on matters other than driving, such as talking on their cell phones (Levy, Pashler, & Boer, 2006). We believe that research on inattentional blindness provides ample evidence against the use of cell phones while driving.

Recent work connects inattentional blindness to neural regions in the brain (C. M. Moore & Egeth, 1997) and identifies many key independent variables that affect the probability of not seeing the obvious (Mack, 2003). Beyond our own fascination with this basic research, we are interested in making an analogy from this work in the visual realm to the inattentional blindness that leads most decision makers to overlook a broad array of information that is readily available in the environment. For instance, we are struck by the many times our spouses have claimed to have told us something of which we have absolutely no recollection. Like many people would, we tend to conclude that our spouses must have imagined the interaction. But if we could miss seeing the woman with the umbrella in Neisser's video, we must accept the possibility that our spouses did indeed provide the information that they claimed and that our minds were focused elsewhere.

CHANGE BLINDNESS

Researchers have provided evidence that, in a surprisingly large number of cases, people fail to notice obvious visual changes in their physical environments (Simons, 2000). For example, Simons, Chabris, Schnur, and Levin (2002) had an experimenter who was holding a basketball stop a pedestrian and ask for directions. While the pedestrian was giving directions, a group of people walked between the experimenter and the pedestrian, and one member of the group surreptitiously took the basketball from the experimenter. After the pedestrian finished providing directions, he or she was asked if he or she noticed anything unexpected or noticed a change. Most of the pedestrians did not report noticing the removal of the basketball.

In a parallel study, Angelone, Levin, and Simons (2003) showed people a videotape of an interaction in which clearly visible clothing or objects were changed during a cut in the camera position.[1] It is not simply the case that people failed to perceive these changes. In a series of studies, Mitroff, Simons, and Franconeri (2002) confirmed a pattern in which people failed to explicitly notice a change, despite having an implicit representation in their mind of the information that was available pre- and post-change. This suggests that at some level they perceived the change but somehow screened it out of their conscious awareness. Evidence suggests people are even more prone to missing changes that occur gradually (Simons & Rensink, 2005).

Are people any better at detecting changes in realms outside of visual perception? Probably not. Imagine that you are an accountant who is in charge of the audit of a large, well-respected corporation. After you have seen and

[1] For an example, visit http://www.youtube.com/watch?v=voAntzB7EwE

approved of high-quality, highly ethical financial statements for one year, the corporation begins stretching the law in a few places but commits no clearly unethical behaviors. The third year, the firm stretches the ethicality of its returns a bit further; some of the company's accounting decisions may in fact violate federal accounting standards. By the fourth year, the corporation is stretching the law in many areas and occasionally breaking them. In this situation, would you ever notice the unethical aspects of the reporting? And if so, at what point, if any, would you refuse to sign a statement affirming that the financial records are acceptable according to government regulations?

We predict that you would be much more likely to notice and refuse to sign the statements if the ethical lapse occurred abruptly from one year to the next. This prediction is based on the notion of a "slippery slope" of unethical behavior (Gino & Bazerman, 2009), which posits that one small step away from high ethical standards puts you on a downward slide into larger ethical lapses. Such lapses are more likely to occur through tiny slips than in one fell swoop. When our behavior becomes unethical one step at a time, we are less likely to notice what we are getting ourselves into and more likely to be able to justify the behavior than if we abruptly drop our ethical standards (Tenbrunsel & Messick, 2004).

In this sense, ethical degradation is like the (false) folk wisdom regarding boiling frogs: If you throw a frog in boiling water, it will jump out. But if you put a frog in warm water and slowly raise the temperature, by the time the frog realizes the water has become too hot, it will already be cooked. Even if this isn't true of frogs, it does appear to be the case for humans and ethical judgment. Studies of ethical decision-making confirm that people are more willing to accept ethical lapses when they occur in several small steps than when they occur in one large step (Gino & Bazerman, 2009).

To avoid taking the second wrong step down the slippery slope of ethical lapses after an initial misstep, we need to recognize when our moral standards have been compromised. In order to do this, we need to recognize that we have, in fact, taken an ethical misstep. The research on change blindness presented above suggests that noticing these differences is a difficult task, but we may be able to use the confirmation heuristic to our advantage. If we begin with the self-critical assumption that we are prone to ethical lapses, and actively searching to find them, we will be attuned to cues suggesting that our ethical standards may have slipped. We may be more capable of identifying information that reveals that we have taken an ethical misstep.

FOCALISM AND THE FOCUSING ILLUSION

Gilbert, Wilson, and their colleagues (2000; Wilson, Wheatley, Meyers, Gilbert, & Axsom, 2000) coined the term *focalism* to describe the common tendency to focus too much on a particular event (the "focal event") and too little on other events that are likely to occur concurrently (Wilson et al., 2000). As a consequence, people tend to overestimate both the degree to which their future thoughts will be occupied by the focal event and the duration of their emotional response to the event. For example, we tend to overestimate the impact of positive and negative events, such as the wins and losses of our preferred sports team or political candidate, on our overall happiness. We even dramatically overestimate the effects on our happiness of being afflicted by a major medical condition (Ubel et al., 2001).

One form of focalism is manifested as affective forecasting errors. Affective forecasting, or the act of predicting one's future emotional state, is often seriously flawed: namely, we overestimate the extent to which a current emotional state will persist into the future. In a study on television viewing preferences, Nelson, Meyvis, and Galak (2009) demonstrated that although people say they prefer their television without commercial interruptions, these breaks actually enhance the degree to which people enjoy television programs. Why? Because the commercial breaks intensify our enjoyment of programming that follows them. Thus, it may be that people who watch television without commercial breaks may fail to account for the degree to which their interest in the program declines over an uninterrupted commercial-free sitting.

Schkade and Kahneman (1998) define the *focusing illusion* as the tendency of people to make judgments based on their attention to only a subset of available information, to overweight that information, and to underweight unattended information. Using logic similar to Gilbert, Wilson, and colleagues, Schkade and Kahneman (1998) asked college students in the Midwest and in Southern California about their own life satisfaction and the perceived life satisfaction of others. Californians and Midwesterners reported a similar level of life satisfaction, yet both groups rated Californians as having greater life satisfaction than Midwesterners. Essentially, differences between California and the Midwest, such as climate, strongly influenced nonresidents' judgments of residents' life satisfaction. However, these factors did not predict the experienced life satisfaction of citizens of the two locales. Schkade and Kahneman argue that when students imagined how a move to the other location would affect them, the obvious difference of weather became a salient factor, and all other life events affecting satisfaction were out of focus.

Imagine that eight teams in any game or sport are engaged in a single elimination tournament. Now imagine that eight people are each assigned to each team and asked the probability that "their" team will win the tournament. Of course, some teams would be better, and some would be worse, but the probabilities of the eight teams winning should roughly add up to 100 percent.

Now let's see what really happens in such a situation. When the 1995 National Basketball Association championship was down to eight teams, Fox and Tversky (1998) recruited basketball fans as research participants. Participants were asked either (1) the probability that each team (Chicago, Indiana, Orlando, New York, Los Angeles, Phoenix, San Antonio, and Houston) would win the championship; (2) the probability that the winning team would come from each of the four divisions (Central [Chicago and Indiana], Atlantic [Orlando and New York], Pacific [Los Angeles and Phoenix], and Midwestern [San Antonio and Houston]); or (3) the probability that the winning team would come from either the Eastern conference (comprising the Central and Atlantic divisions) or the Western conference (comprising the Pacific and Midwestern divisions). If the participants were well calibrated, the sum of the probabilities for the eight teams, the sum of the probabilities for the four divisions, and the sum of the probabilities for the two conferences each should have added up to 100 percent.

The combined probabilities for the two conferences were close to the expected 100 percent; the sum added up to 102 percent. However, the sum of the probabilities of the four divisions was 144 percent, and the sum of the probabilities of the eight teams was 218 percent. Fox and Tversky argue that when participants focus on an individual team, they can find reasons to support that team winning the tournament; meanwhile, the data that supports other teams winning is out of focus. Similarly, Tversky and Koehler (1994) found that medical doctors, when asked to assess the probabilities of four mutually exclusive prognoses for a patient, gave probabilities for the four prognoses that totaled far in excess of 100 percent. The specific team or prognosis was in focus, and the others teams and other prognoses were out of focus.

Finally, perhaps the most memorable example of focalism has been the *Challenger* space shuttle disaster (see Vaughn (1996) for an excellent overall analysis). As many readers know, the space shuttle *Challenger* exploded in 1986 after being launched at the lowest temperature of any prior launch. The explosion was caused by the failure of the shuttle's O-rings to seal, due to the low temperatures. When the potential problem of low temperatures was brought up in a prelaunch meeting, the decision makers examined the temperatures and magnitude of O-ring problems in the seven prior launches that had had some O-ring failure. Looking at the seven temperatures in these seven launches showed no clear pattern regarding the O-rings, so those involved made the decision to go ahead with the launch.

Unfortunately, no one at the meeting pointed out the relevance of the 17 past launches without O-ring failure. This was a critical oversight: an examination of all 24 launches shows a clear connection between temperature and O-ring failure. Indeed, a logistic regression using the full data set suggests that the *Challenger* had a greater than 99 percent chance of malfunction. The failure of NASA engineers to look outside the boundaries of the analysis in front of them caused seven astronauts to lose their lives and perhaps the worst setback in the space program's history. More broadly, we argue that many decision-makers and groups err by limiting their analysis to the data in the room, rather than asking what data would best answer the question being asked. In this case, decision makers' failure to look for more data was probability facilitated by the confirmation heuristic. In other words, when they wanted to know whether O-ring failures were due to low temperatures, they looked only at launches with O-ring failures. A full analysis, however, would have required the examination of launches with and without O-ring problems at both low and high temperatures.

BOUNDED AWARENESS IN GROUPS

As we move from considering the role of bounded awareness in individual decision-making to its effects on groups, consider the fact that the information *discussed* by a group has a key influence on any final decision it makes. Conversely, information mentally *considered* by individual members, but not mentioned, will have little influence on the eventual decision. Thus, while individuals' awareness is bounded by the information they mentally consider, the awareness of groups is also bounded by the information that becomes part of the discussion.

One of the advantages of groups over individuals is that they collectively possess more information than any individual member does. In organizations, one of the reasons to create groups is to pool information from different divisions (Mannix & Neale, 2005). Thus, sharing unique information is a critical source of group potential, both in an absolute sense and in comparison to individual decision-making. Yet Stasser and his colleagues (Stasser, 1988; Stasser & Stewart, 1992; Stasser & Titus, 1985), as well as others (e.g., Gruenfeld, Mannix, Williams, & Neale, 1996), show a consistent tendency of groups to focus more on shared information (information group members already have) than on unique or unshared information (information known by only one group member).

In an early example of this pattern, Stasser and Titus (1985) asked college students to choose between three candidates running for student council president. Data on the candidates was created with the intention of making Candidate A the preferred choice when individuals or groups had access to all of the information about all of the candidates. Accordingly, Candidate A was the preferred option, at 67 percent, by individuals when they had all of the information available. When these fully informed individuals were combined into groups, 83 percent chose Candidate A.

In an alternative version of the exercise intended to simulate the nature of information in most real-world groups, some of the information about the candidates was shared by all group members and some of it was unshared, including much of the positive information about Candidate A. This unshared information was known only to one member of the group. Thus, before interacting in their groups, individuals had little reason to support Candidate A, since they were missing most of the positive information about this candidate. In this instance, only 23 percent of the individuals in the unshared condition chose Candidate A. Now consider the decisions made by these individuals with unshared information when they were put into groups. Collectively, the group had access to the same information as the shared groups, but the information was diffused among various members. Interestingly, in this case, only 18 percent of the groups with unshared information chose Candidate A.

Why didn't the groups capture the unshared information and make the same decision as the groups in which all members had all of the information? Stasser and Titus (1985) have shown consistently that groups discuss more shared information than unshared information. This is true despite the fact that groups are brought together for the very purpose of pooling information. An interesting paradox exists: groups are created to share information, yet they end up spending their time discussing already shared knowledge. Our conclusion from this literature is that groups have bounded awareness regarding their unique or unshared information.

To help groups overcome their bounded awareness, Stasser, Vaughn, and Stewart (2000) propose a number of strategies based on encouraging members to share information, particularly unique information. These strategies include forewarning the group in advance of the unique knowledge of different members and identifying expertise present in the group before the discussion begins. The overall goal is to recognize the tendency of groups to have bounded awareness of unshared information and to create structures to overcome this tendency.

BOUNDED AWARENESS IN STRATEGIC SETTINGS

This section explores the five problems from Table 4.1 that we have not yet discussed. As you probably noticed, Problems 1 and 4 were similar, and Problems 2 and 5 were similar. In fact, Problems 1 and 4 are two variations of what is known as the "multiparty ultimatum game," and Problems 2 and 5 are two variations of the "Monty Hall problem." For each problem, we will provide evidence that minor changes in the decisions of others and the rules of the game can create huge differences in the optimal strategy for a negotiator. Thanks to bounded awareness, however, most people miss this information. Problem 3 is the "Acquiring a Company" problem; again, the common failure to optimally answer this question results from the failure to think appropriately about the decisions of others and the rules of the game. We will analyze these three problems and discuss related strategic problems. Then we will offer behavioral evidence of our boundedness regarding the decisions of others and the rules of the game.

Multiparty Ultimatum Games

How would it affect your bidding on a house if you learned that the sellers were three siblings? Would the three use majority rule, or was unanimity necessary? As you will see, the decision rules matter a great deal, a fact we often fail to appreciate.

Chapter 8 discusses ultimatum games in some detail. As a quick preview, suppose that Player 1 divides a known, fixed sum of money any way he chooses by filling out a form stating, "I demand X." Player 2 either accepts the offer and receives her portion of the money as allocated by Player 1 or rejects the offer, leaving both parties with nothing. Concerns for fairness often lead Player 1s to be more generous and Player 2s to demand more than economic models suggest. In this section, we examine multiple-party ultimatum games, typified by Problems 1 and 4 (Messick, Moore, & Bazerman, 1997). In the multiparty version of the ultimatum game, six participants are assigned to the roles of A, B, C, D, E, and F. Player A is given $60 dollars to allocate to the six parties. The offers to B, C, D, E, and F must be equal and must be an integer. B, C, D, E, and F each record the minimum amount that they would accept.

Problems 1 and 4 differ only in the decision rule for the game. In Problem 1, also known as the "dividing the pie—largest" condition, if the amount that A offers to B–F is equal to or greater than the largest amount requested by B, C, D, E, or F, then A's allocation is distributed. If it is not, all parties receive $0. By contrast, in problem 4, the "dividing the pie—smallest" condition, if the amount that A offers to B–F is equal to or greater than the smallest amount requested by B, C, D, E, or F, then A's allocation offer is distributed; if it is not, all parties receive $0. Consistent with the two-party ultimatum game, a bimodal response pattern emerges from the demands of players B–F. While many B–F players will take $1, since $1 is better than the $0 they would receive from turning the offer down, another large group of players B–F demand $10—they want their "fair" share. As we know from Chapter 3, individuals underestimate disjunctive events (those that can occur independently) and overestimate conjunctive events (those that must occur in conjunction with one another). In the present context, this implies that player As will underestimate the likelihood of how easy it is to get at least one out of five people to accept $1, but will overestimate the likelihood of all five individuals accepting anything less than $10. But you, the reader, were asked to estimate the profit-maximizing strategies for the two different problems. Let's see how you did.

Messick, Moore, and Bazerman (1997) had MBA students at Northwestern University's Kellogg School of Management play this game and calculated which strategy did best on average across all of the trials of each game. The researchers found that the profit-maximizing strategy for player A would be to divide the money 55-1-1-1-1-1 in Problem 4 and to divide it 10-10-10-10-10-10 in Problem 1. In fact, in Problem 1, any allocation less than 10 invariably led to player A receiving $0. To help you evaluate your own decisions, note that players that offered anything less than 10-10-10-10-10-10 in Problem 1 were bound to get $0 themselves (because the probability of getting even 15-9-9-9-9-9 was quite small). In addition, players that offered anything more than $1–2 to the other players in Problem 4 were doing so because they wanted to be "fair" or because they made a bad decision; the expected payoff by player As falls dramatically as they increase their offers to B–F.

To players who do not attend to the nuances of the rules of the game and the likely heterogeneity of the other actors, Problems 1 and 4 would look very similar. Bounded awareness keeps negotiators from failing to differentiate the problems. But those who note the important difference between these two versions of the multiparty ultimatum game are likely to do much better. Negotiators often overgeneralize from one situation to another, even when the generalization is inappropriate. They assume that what worked in one context will work in another. But the rational negotiator is attuned to the important differences that exist, particularly regarding the rules of the game and the likely decisions of other parties.

The Monty Hall Game

For those too young to have seen him, or for those with limited exposure to American television, Monty Hall was the host of the television game show *Let's Make a Deal*. On the show, Monty would ask contestants to pick one of three doors, knowing that one of the doors led to the grand prize and that the other two doors were "zonks" leading to small prizes or gag gifts. Once a contestant picked a door, Monty would often open one of the other two doors to reveal a zonk, then offer the contestant the chance to trade their chosen door for the remaining unchosen and unopened door. A common but false analysis is that with only two doors remaining following the opening of one door by the host, the odds are 50–50. Most contestants on the actual show preferred to stick with the door they originally chose.

Years after the show ceased production, statisticians, economists, and journalists (Nalebuff, 1987; Selvin, 1975; vos Savant, 1990a, 1990b, 1991) had some fun critiquing contestants' choices. They argued that contestants should have switched to the remaining unchosen door, assuming that Monty always opened an unchosen door (known as the "Monty always opens" condition) and then offered a switch. Their logic is simple: when they first chose their door, the contestants had a one-in-three chance of winning the prize. When Monty opened one door to reveal a zonk, which he could always do, this probability did not change. Thus, there was still a one-in-three chance that the contestant had the winner to start with and a two-in-three chance that the big prize was behind one of the other two doors. When Monty reveals the zonk, he has provided useful information. Now the contestant knows which of the two doors to open to collect the two-in-three chance of winning. The contestant should therefore always have switched doors, thereby doubling the chance of winning.

Assuming that Monty always opened an unchosen door that did not contain the grand prize is, of course, a critical element in this analysis. Yet on *Let's Make a Deal*, Monty Hall did not always open one of the three doors to reveal a zonk. Problem 5 posits a "Mean Monty": one who knew where the grand prize was located and who wanted to minimize the contestant's chances of winning. So, after the contestant picked a door, "Mean Monty" could either declare the game over or open one door and offer a switch. If Monty wanted to minimize the contestant's chances of winning the grand prize, the contestant should never have accepted an offer from Monty to switch. In fact, since Monty wanted the contestant to lose, the fact that Monty makes the offer indicated that the contestant had already picked the winning door.[2]

Thus, you should always switch doors in the "Monty always opens" condition (Problem 2), but never switch in the "Mean Monty" condition (Problem 5). But if people's awareness of the rules of the game and of Monty's decision processes is bounded, they will likely fail to differentiate the two problems. Did you distinguish between the two versions of the multiparty ultimatum game and the two versions of the Monty Hall game?

Acquiring a Company

In Problem 3, the "Acquiring a Company" problem, one firm (the acquirer) is considering making an offer to buy out another firm (the target). However, the acquirer is uncertain about the ultimate value of the target firm. It knows only that its value under current management is between $0 and $100, with all values

[2] In a dynamic game-theoretic equilibrium, the contestant would not know that she won, but should still keep her original choice.

equally likely. Since the firm is expected to be worth 50 percent more under the acquirer's management than under the current ownership, it appears to make sense for a transaction to take place. While the acquirer does not know the actual value of the firm, the target knows its current worth exactly. What price should the acquirer offer for the target?

The problem is analytically quite simple, yet intuitively perplexing. Consider the logical process that a rational response would generate in deciding whether to make an offer of $60 per share:

> If I offer $60 per share, the offer will be accepted 60 percent of the time— whenever the firm is worth between $0 and $60 to the target. Since all values between $0 and $60 are equally likely, the firm will, on average, be worth $30 per share to the target and $45 to the acquirer, resulting in a loss of $15 per share ($45 to $60). Consequently, a $60 per share offer is unwise.

It is easy to see that similar reasoning applies to any positive offer. On average, the acquirer obtains a company worth 25 percent less than the price it pays when its offer is accepted. If the acquirer offers $X and the target accepts, the current value of the company is worth anywhere between $0 and $X. As the problem is formulated, any value in that range is equally likely, and the expected value of the offer is therefore equal to $X/2. Since the company is worth 50 percent more to the acquirer, the acquirer's expected value is 1.5($X/2) = 0.75($X), only 75 percent of its offer price. Thus, for any value of $X, the best the acquirer can do is not make an offer ($0 per share). The paradox of the situation is that even though in all circumstances the firm is worth more to the acquirer than to the target, any offer above $0 generates a negative expected return to the acquirer. The source of this paradox lies in the high likelihood that the target will accept the acquirer's offer when the firm is least valuable to the acquirer—that is, when it is a "lemon" (Akerlof, 1970).

Imagine that while traveling in a foreign country, you meet a merchant who is selling a very attractive gemstone. Although you have purchased a few gems in your life, you are far from an expert. After some discussion, you make the merchant an offer that you believe, but that you are not certain, is on the low side. He quickly accepts, and the transaction is completed. How do you feel? Following this quick acceptance, most people would feel uneasy about the purchase, sensing that they got a rotten deal. This sensation is known as the "winner's curse." But if you were comfortable with your voluntary offer, why would you suddenly wish it had not been accepted?

Groucho Marx understood the tendency to ignore the decisions of others when he famously declared that he didn't want to belong to any club that would have him as a member. If a club's standards were so low that they would accept *him*, he didn't want any part of it! In the context of bargaining, the key feature of the "winner's curse" is that one side often has much better information than the other side; the party with the better information is usually the seller. A knowledgeable gem merchant will accept your offer only when the gem is worth less than your estimate.

Similarly, a structural inefficiency is built into the Acquiring a Company exercise: A rational buyer will bid $0 despite the fact that the buyer values the company at a price higher than the seller's valuation. The problem is that the strategic seller will not provide the buyer with information about the company's true value, especially when the company is of low value. As a result, game theory recommends that buyers not make an offer in order to avoid an expected value loss.

What Do People Actually Do?

Across Problems 1 through 5, people make consistent errors due to the failure to think rationally about the game. Specifically, an overly narrow focus on their own thoughts and actions causes negotiators to ignore the rules of the game and the decisions of the opposing party. Tor and Bazerman (2003) have shown that these errors existed and led to failure across three seemingly different tasks—the multiparty ultimatum game, the Monty Hall problem, and the Acquiring a Company problem.

In the multiparty ultimatum game, the best strategy for player A diverges dramatically between the two conditions (offers of $1 versus $10). Yet, in studies, the actual behavior of player As has been much closer across the two conditions (Messick et al., 1997). On average, player As allocated $8.15 to the other players in the "dividing the pie—smallest" condition (Problem 4), while allocating $8.47 to the other players in the "dividing the pie—largest condition" (Problem 1). Many player As in Problem 1 miss an easy opportunity to collect $10, while player As in Problem 4 also pass up a significant profit opportunity.

Turning to the Monty Hall problem, in the version in which Monty always opens a door (Problem 2), Friedman (1998) has found substantial failure among

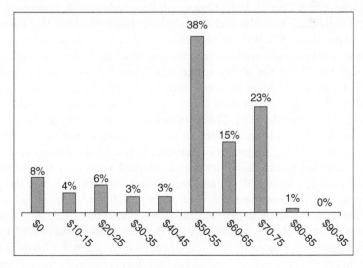

Figure 4.1 The Distribution of Price Offers

study participants to make the correct decision and only limited learning through repeated trials. That is, most people keep the door originally chosen, giving them a one-in-three chance of winning, rather than trading for a two-in-three chance. Tor and Bazerman (2003) replicated this result, finding specifically that 41 percent of participants traded doors and 59 percent kept the inferior door. In the Mean Monty version (Problem 5), 79 percent made the right decision to keep the existing door, which is consistent with modal intuition in the other version. Finally, most people made the same decision in both versions of the game; only 24 percent answered both versions correctly.

The most extensive evidence on bounded awareness in negotiation comes from "Acquiring a Company," the problem that has been researched for the longest period of time. Substantial research on this problem suggests that bounded awareness leads decision makers to ignore or simplify the cognitions of opposing parties as well as the rules of the game (Carroll, Bazerman, & Maury, 1988). The first group to respond to this problem was comprised of 123 MBA students from Boston University (Samuelson & Bazerman, 1985). Their results are charted in Figure 4.1, which shows that the dominant response fell between $50 and $75. How did students reach this $50–to–$75 decision? One common, but wrong, explanation is that, "On average, the firm will be worth $50 to the target and $75 to the acquirer; consequently, a transaction in this range will, on average, be profitable to both parties."

In fact, the correct answer to the Acquiring a Company problem is so counterintuitive that only nine of 123 participants correctly offered $0 per share. Replications with accounting firm partners, CEOs, investment bankers, and many other skilled groups have produced similar results. Finally, even participants who were paid according to their performance and given many opportunities to learn through experience exhibited the same pattern of responses depicted in Figure 4.1 (Ball, Bazerman, & Carroll, 1991; Grosskopf, Bereby-Meyer, & Bazerman, 2007).

Most individuals have the analytical ability to follow the logic that the optimal offer is $0 per share. Yet, without assistance, most individuals do not see it. Thus, individuals systematically exclude information from their decision-making processes that they have the ability to include. They fail to recognize that their expected return depends on an acceptance by the other party, which in turn is affected by the rules, which state that they get to know the true value before accepting or rejecting the offer. This implies that acceptance by the target is most likely to occur when it is least desirable to the negotiator making the offer.

The overwhelming majority of respondents provided solutions that yield a negative expected return. However, in an adapted version of the Acquiring a Company exercise, Valley, Moag, and Bazerman (1998) found that if the parties talk face-to-face, the common result is a trade at a mutually beneficial value. Thus, social interaction creates a mechanism to overcome the inefficient outcomes predicted by game theory and behavioral decision theory. Valley and her colleagues suggest that communication enhances positive utility for benefits gained by the other party, creates trust, and allows for information exchange not expected by game-theoretic models.

Auctions

Consider the following auctions:

> Your consulting firm is trying to hire a young, highly regarded MBA student from a prestigious university. Many other organizations are also interested in this apparently talented individual. In fact, your firm seems to be competing against these other firms, motivating you to sweeten the deal with a big signing bonus. Finally, the MBA accepts your offer. As she signs on the dotted line, you wonder if her productivity will exceed the high price of hiring her.

> Your company has placed a bid on a firm that has suggested it will gladly be acquired by the highest bidder. The actual value of the target firm is highly uncertain; even the firm itself does not know its real worth. With at least a half-dozen firms pursuing the target, your bid turns out to be the highest. Your offer is accepted. Should you break out the champagne?

> You just purchased the most beautiful rug you have ever seen in an eBay auction. There were a lot of bids on the rug, showing that you were not alone in recognizing its value. As you anxiously await delivery of the rug, you start to wonder: Did you get a good deal?

In each of these scenarios, a naive analysis would suggest that you should be glad to have won the competitive situation. However, Bazerman and Samuelson (1983) argue that you may have just become the most recent victim of the winner's curse. In a two-party negotiation between buyer and seller, the winner's curse usually occurs when the buyer fails to consider the perspective of the seller. In auctions, the winner's curse typically results from the winning bidder's failure to consider the implications of bidding higher than his or her competitors—all of whom are at the same information disadvantage relative to the seller.

Bazerman and Samuelson (1983) argue that as the highest bidder, you may have significantly overestimated the actual value of the commodity being sold. Figure 4.2 provides a graphic depiction of what may have occurred. Curve E shows the distribution of bidder estimates for the true value of the commodity, and curve B depicts the distribution of bids. The depiction assumes that (1) the mean of the distribution is equal to the true value of the commodity—that is, no aggregate under- or overestimation is expected; and (2) bidders discount their estimates a fixed amount when making bids, which explains the leftward shift of the bid distribution. The figure suggests that a winning bid—that is, one from the right tail of the distribution—is likely to exceed the actual value of the commodity. The highest bidder is likely to have been one of the highest estimators, and unless they had reason to believe that they had better information than the other bidders, they likely overpaid. In fact, our research found that the winning bidder in auctions of highly uncertain commodities with a large number of bidders commonly pays more than the commodity is worth.

Why does the winning bidder fall prey to the winner's curse? Because of the information that is left out of his or her thought processes—in other words,

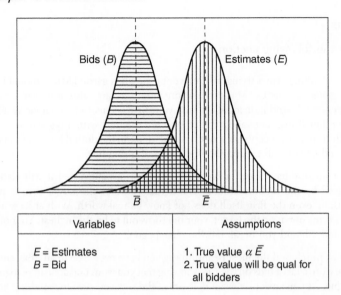

Figure 4.2 Graphic Illustration of the Winner's Curse

Source: Bazerman & Samuelson, 1983, "I Won the Auction But Don't Want the Prize." *Journal of Conflict Resolution* 27, pp. 618–634. Copyright © by Sage Publications, Inc. Reprinted by permission of Sage Publications, Inc.

because of bounded awareness. Bidders who think that their bids will win should infer that they are likely to have overestimated the value of the commodity in comparison to other bidders. Based on this reasoning, bidders on objects of uncertain value who are competing against other bidders should adjust their estimates of the object's value downward and lower their bids accordingly. Thus, if they do win, they are less likely to have overbid, or at least not by the same margin. Yet most people ignore the effects of uncertainty, even falsely viewing the presence of lots of bidders as a signal that they should be confident of the commodity's value and quality.

Corporate takeovers have provided ample evidence that acquiring companies often compete destructively against each other and pay too much for what they get. As many as one-third of all acquisitions have been failures, and an additional one-third have failed to live up to expectations. In addition, financial synergy created by mergers usually goes to the target, not the acquirer. Potential acquirers should temper their optimism by recognizing that the winning bidder is likely to acquire a company that is worth less than the winning bidder's estimate of its value.

As the Internet attracts more and more auction participants each day, the lessons of the winner's curse become more important. The good news is that eBay and other Web-based auction sites have created an excellent means of enabling efficient trades between a seller and a buyer, where the buyer potentially values a particular item more than the seller. The bad news is that among these buyers, there will be lots of suckers. Who will they be? They are most likely to be ill-informed buyers in auctions with lots of bidders; these buyers will have failed to consider the auction from the perspective of the seller or the other bidders. So the next time you place an online bid on a hot commodity, remember to ask what its popularity might tell you about your valuation.

Beyond Auctions, Ultimatums, and Monty's Three Doors

The problems we have considered above are particularly good examples of instances in which the rules of the game and the decisions of others—two absolutely central and often accessible pieces of information in a negotiation—are out of focus. However, these focusing failures explain decision failures far beyond our example problems. Ho, Camerer, and Weigelt (1998) examined a game in which each player was trying to anticipate the others' choices, as follows. Each player chooses a number from 0 to 100. The winning number is the one closest to one half of the mean of all of the entries. If the decisions of others and nuances of the rules of the game are out of focus, 50 emerges as a naive yet common submission. But even the simplest logic should lead people to think that if the average were 50, a better submission would be half the mean, or 25. Of course, this logic requires attention to the rules of the game. Yet when you consider the decisions of other players, it should become clear that others may follow this same logic; therefore, if the mean might be 25, you should submit 12.5. However, if others use this logic, you should submit 6.25, and so on, down to 0—the equilibrium solution. The winning answer is typically greater than 0. Simple numbers such as 50 and 25 are common in this game, and they come from not fully considering the rules of the game and the thoughts of other players.

Bounded awareness also affects our assessments of competitors. Camerer and Lovallo (1999) argue that people are insensitive to the quality of their competition, a phenomenon they label *reference group neglect*. Moore, Oesch, and Zietsma (2007) demonstrate that entrepreneurs are more focused on themselves and their strengths and weaknesses than on the competition. This self-focus makes them too eager to enter simple contests (which many other competitors also enter) and too reluctant to enter difficult competitions (which have few competitors) (see also D. A. Moore & Cain, 2007). This may in part help account for why the rate of entry into industries like restaurants, bars, hobby shops, liquor stores, and clothing retail is so persistently excessive. In order to succeed, a new venture depends on more than the founder's energy and the quality of the product or service. It also must be better than its competitors.

Radzevick and Moore (2007) observed a closely related effect in predictions regarding the outcomes of athletic contests. They reasoned that if people focused on their own team, they would be excessively confident of winning when their own team was strong, regardless of the strength of the competition. Indeed, that is what they found. Casino betting patterns suggested that people tended to bet on the home team primarily when the home team was good. This effect is largely attributable to the fact that people have better information about the home team than they do about the competition and don't bother collecting more balanced information before placing their bets (Massey, Simmons, & Armor, 2011).

To us, the most important example of this type of bounded awareness is the widespread failure of U.S. citizens to consider campaign-finance reform as a means of curbing the undue political influence of special-interest groups (Bazerman, Baron, & Shonk, 2001). When people are asked whether they support and care about the issue of campaign-finance reform, they say "yes." Yet, when asked to rank the importance of campaign-finance reform relative to other issues, they rank it very low. Bazerman et al. (2001) argue that voters undervalue campaign-finance reform because their awareness of the indirect impact of campaign finance reform is bounded. Yet we believe that people should care deeply about such reform, since it affects virtually every other issue (and its effects could be enormous). People generally do not think through this process. They value issues that are more clearly seen as end states or outcomes (such as tax cuts or education) rather than using a broader awareness that would direct their attention toward a set of outcomes that would have a large, positive effect on many issues (Bazerman et al., 2001).

Understanding the Bounds of Others

We need not only understand our own bounded awareness but also the bounded awareness of others. One domain where this becomes clear is the question of how much choice to give one's customers. Most people assume that more choice is good, but recent books question that conclusion (Iyengar, 2010; Schwartz, 2005). When people feel overwhelmed, they often entirely avoid deciding. The act of choosing uses up scarce mental resources that are necessary for self-regulation, which is needed to implement decisions (Vohs et al., 2008). Thus, when faced with too many choices, people may find the act of choosing to be mentally exhausting. Even if they do make a choice, they may lack the motivation to act on it. And when they do act on it, the numerous unchosen options leave them at greater risk of feeling regret over forgone opportunities (Epstude & Roese, 2008).

Iyengar and Lepper (2000) presented grocery store shoppers with a sample of either 6 or 24 different gourmet jams. Those who were offered the larger set were more likely to try them but less likely to buy them. Similarly, when people are offered too many investment options for their savings, they have more difficulty choosing and often end up not saving at all (Iyengar, Jiang, & Huberman, 2004). This type of "choice overload" even holds in the case of bank loans: when fewer examples of loans are provided in advertisements, loan demand has been demonstrated to increase (Bertrand, Karlan, Mullainathan, Shafir, & Zinman, 2010). Essentially, we may have preferred choices and courses of action. Yet, when faced with too many options, we may not act on our preferences even when additional options are inferior to our preferred option (Bernheim & Rangel, 2009).

DISCUSSION

Bazerman and Chugh (2005) coined the term "bounded awareness" to describe the narrowing of attention and focus in negotiation. The concept of bounded awareness overlaps to a degree with the concept of availability (Tversky & Kahneman, 1974) introduced in Chapter 1 and illustrated in Chapter 3. Both concepts confront the fact that important information often remains unavailable to the decision maker. However, the two concepts have different foci. Unlike bounded awareness, availability is a general cognitive heuristic. That is, availability explains the tendency for decision makers to assume that across contexts, information that is most readily available, such as vivid data, is more common than less available information. In contrast, the concept of bounded awareness concerns the specific groups of variables that are likely to be in or out of focus in particular domains. Your knowledge of the specific contexts and consequences of your bounded awareness will make you better able to avoid the pitfalls that have contributed to disasters such as the Madoff scandal.

CHAPTER FIVE

Framing and the Reversal of Preferences

The following is one of the most famous problems in the decision-making literature. Please make the best choice possible (Tversky & Kahneman, 1981):

Problem 1. Imagine that the United States is preparing for the outbreak of an unusual Asian disease that is expected to kill 600 people. Two alternative programs to combat the disease have been proposed. Assume that the exact scientific estimates of the consequences of the programs are as follows.

Program A: If Program A is adopted, 200 people will be saved.

Program B: If Program B is adopted, there is a one-third probability that 600 people will be saved and a two-thirds probability that no people will be saved.

Which of the two programs would you favor?

There are a number of factors you might consider when evaluating these options. For example, what will be the impact of each program on the broader society? Who is most at risk for the disease? Which option would provide the greatest benefit? There are many other questions you might ask. But if you had to pick Plan A or Plan B based only on the information given in the problem, which program would you choose? Most people choose Program A.

Let's consider how you might think through this decision. One simple rule for making decisions is always to select the alternative with the highest expected value—the strategy that provides the best outcome, on average. But, as you can see, the expected values of the two programs are equal. Program A will definitely save 200 lives. Program B has a one-third chance of saving 600 lives or, on average, 200 lives.

The simple argument for an expected-value decision rule is that decisions made according to this rule will, in the aggregate, be optimal. But consider the following scenarios:

Big positive gamble: You can (a) receive $10 million for sure (expected value $10 million) or (b) flip a coin and receive $22 million for heads but nothing for tails (expected value = $11 million). An expected-value decision rule would require you to pick (b). What would you do?

Lawsuit: You are being sued for $500,000 and estimate that you have a 50 percent chance of losing the case in court (expected value = −$250,000). However, the other side is willing to accept an out-of-court settlement of $240,000 (expected value −$240,000). An expected-value decision rule would lead you to settle out of court. Ignoring attorneys' fees, court costs, aggravation, and so on, would you (a) fight the case, or (b) settle out of court?

Most people would choose (a) in both cases. As these scenarios show, we do not always pick the option with the highest expected value. To explain why people depart from the expected-value decision rule, Daniel Bernoulli (1738/1954) first suggested replacing the criterion of expected monetary value with the criterion of expected utility. Expected-utility theory suggests that each level of an outcome is associated with an expected degree of pleasure or net benefit, called utility. The expected utility of an uncertain choice is the weighted sum of the utilities of the possible outcomes, each multiplied by its probability. While an expected-value approach to decision-making would treat $1 million as being worth twice as much as $500,000, a gain of $1 million does not always create twice as much expected utility as a gain of $500,000. Most individuals do not obtain as much utility from the second $500,000 as they did from the first $500,000.

The reason for this has to do with the "declining marginal utility of gains": in other words, the more we get of something, the less pleasure it provides us. For instance, while winning half a million dollars is nice, and winning an entire million is nicer, winning one million is not twice as nice as winning half a million. Likewise, the second piece of pizza is tasty, but not as tasty as the first. Thus, in terms of utility, getting $500,000 for sure is worth more to most people than a 50 percent chance at one million ($1,000,000).

We can also describe decisions that deviate from expected value according to their implications about risk preferences. When we prefer a certain $480,000 over a 50 percent chance of $1 million, we are making a risk-averse choice, since we are giving up expected value to reduce risk. Similarly, in the Big Positive Gamble problem above, taking the $10 million is a risk-averse choice, since it has a lower expected value and lower risk. In contrast, fighting the lawsuit would be a risk-seeking choice, since it has a lower expected value and a higher risk. Essentially, expected utility refers to the maximization of utility rather than simply a maximization of the arithmetic average of the possible courses of action. While expected utility departs from the logic of expected value, it provides a useful and consistent logical structure—and decision researchers generally view the logic of expected utility as rational behavior.

Now consider a second version of Kahneman and Tversky's Asian Disease Problem:

Problem 2. Imagine that the United States is preparing for the outbreak of an unusual Asian disease that is expected to kill 600 people. Two alternative programs to combat the disease have been proposed. Assume that the scientific estimates of the consequences of the programs are as follows.

Program C: If Program C is adopted, 400 people will die.

Program D: If Program D is adopted, there is a one-third probability that no one will die and a two-thirds probability that 600 people will die.

Which of the two programs would you favor?

Close examination of the two sets of programs in Problems 1 and 2 shows that they are objectively the same. Saving 200 people (Program A) offers the same objective outcome as losing 400 people (Program C), and programs B and D are also objectively identical. However, informal empirical investigation demonstrates that most individuals choose Program A in the first set and Program D in the second set (Tversky & Kahneman, 1981). While the two sets of choices are objectively identical, changing the description of outcomes from lives saved to lives lost is sufficient to shift prototypic choice from risk-averse to risk-seeking behavior.

Individuals treat risks concerning perceived gains (for example, saving lives—Programs A and B) differently from risks concerning perceived losses (losing lives—Programs C and D). Kahneman and Tversky's (Kahneman and Tversky, 1979) prospect theory describes the fact that even perceived differences based on a change in the "framing" of choices—in this case, from losses to gains—can dramatically affect how people make a decision. We use the term framing to refer to alternative wordings of the same objective information that significantly alter the decisions that people typically make, even though differences between frames should have no effect on the rational decision.

In the case of Problems 1 and 2, the key framing manipulation involves the implicit reference point against which outcomes are supposed to be evaluated. Note that the two problems are objectively the same. Problem 1 is framed in terms of saving lives, where the implied reference point is a worst outcome of 600 deaths. Most of us, when we make decisions about gains, are risk averse—hence our tendency to take the sure $10 million in the Big Positive Gamble problem.

In contrast, Problem 2 is framed in terms of losses. Here, the implicit reference point is the best outcome of no deaths due to the Asian disease. Most of us, when we make decisions regarding losses, are risk seeking. Thus, many would fight the lawsuit in the example above, despite the lower expected value relative to Problem 1. Kahneman and Tversky's key insight was that it is possible to take the same objective problem, change the frame, and get predictably different results.

The typical decision maker evaluates outcomes relative to a neutral reference point. Consequently, the location of the reference point has a critical effect on whether the decision is positively or negatively framed and affects the resulting risk preference of the decision maker. The Asian Disease Problem illustrates the importance of reference points. In the positively framed case, the implicit question is: How many lives can be saved from the possible loss of all 600 lives? Thus, the loss of 600 lives is the neutral reference point. In contrast, in the negatively framed case, the implicit question is: How many lives will be lost from the existing state of having all 600 people alive?

For another example of the importance of this reference point shift, consider the following scenario:

Problem 3. You were given 100 shares of stock in XYZ Corporation two years ago, when the value of the stock was $20 per share. Unfortunately, the stock has dropped to $10 per share during the two years that you have held the asset. The corporation is currently drilling for oil in an area that may turn out to be a big "hit." On the other hand, they may find nothing. Geological analysis suggests that if they hit, the stock is expected to go back up to $20 per share. If the well is dry, however, the value of the stock will fall to $0 per share. Do you want to sell your stock now for $10 per share?

What is your reference point in this problem? Is it the amount you can gain (the amount that you receive for the stock above $0 per share), or is it the amount you can lose (the amount that the stock has fallen from $20 per share when you sell it)? If you cognitively adopt $0 per share as your reference point, you will be risk-averse and will likely take the sure "gain" by selling the stock now. If your reference point is $20 per share, however, you will likely be risk seeking and hold onto the stock rather than accept a sure "loss."

Rational decision makers should be immune to the framing of choices, yet we now know that frames can strongly affect our decisions. In recent years, there have been important discoveries in the way in which frames produce profound effects. The concept has helped researchers develop a more thorough understanding of errors and inconsistencies in human judgment. Framing has generated a great deal of excitement in the fields of decision theory, psychology, marketing, law, medicine, finance, organizational behavior, and economics.

This broader definition of framing is the focus of this chapter. We will examine preference reversals in the following contexts: (1) how framing can lead to a portfolio of decisions that few of us would want, yet are likely to choose; (2) how the perception of "pseudocertainty" can affect judgment; (3) how framing causes us to purchase more insurance than we need; (4) how we evaluate the quality of a transaction; (5) how ownership creates a different frame for valuation; (6) how our mental accounts affect how we frame decisions; (7) the differences between calling something a "bonus" versus calling it a "rebate"; and (8) whether we evaluate options separately or simultaneously.

FRAMING AND THE IRRATIONALITY OF THE SUM OF OUR CHOICES

Tversky and Kahneman (1981) asked 150 people the following questions.

Problem 4. Imagine that you face the following pair of concurrent decisions. First, examine both decisions, and then indicate the options you prefer.

Decision A

Choose between:
  a. a sure gain of $240
  b. a 25 percent chance to gain $1,000 and a 75 percent chance to gain nothing

Decision B

Choose between:

  c. a sure loss of $750

  d. a 75 percent chance to lose $1,000 and a 25 percent chance to lose nothing

In Decision A, 84 percent of respondents chose (a) and only 16 percent chose (b). In Decision B, 87 percent of respondents chose (d) and only 13 percent chose (c). The majority chose "a sure gain of $240" in Decision A because of our tendency to be risk averse concerning gains and positively framed questions. By contrast, the majority chose "a 75 percent chance to lose $1,000" in Decision B because of our tendency to be risk seeking concerning losses and negatively framed questions. Combining the responses to the two problems, 73 percent of respondents chose (a) and (d), while only three percent chose (b) and (c).

Now consider the following problems presented by Tversky and Kahneman (1981) to 86 people (who were not previously exposed to Problem 4):

Problem 5. Choose between:

  e. a 25 percent chance to win $240 and a 75 percent chance to lose $760

  f. a 25 percent chance to win $250 and a 75 percent chance to lose $750

Not surprisingly, all 86 respondents chose (f) over (e). In fact, (f) dominates (e) in all respects. Why is this problem interesting? When you combine (a) and (d) (the preferred choices) in Problem 4, (e) results, whereas when you combine choices (b) and (c) (the choices not preferred), (f) results.

$$\text{Adding choices (a) and (d)} = \text{(e):}$$
$$(100\%)(\$240) + [(75\%)(-\$1,000) + (25\%)(\$0)] = (25\%)(\$240) + (75\%)(-\$760)$$

$$\text{Adding choices (b) and (c)} = \text{(f):}$$
$$[(25\%)(\$1,000) + (75\%)(\$0)] + (100\%)(-\$750) = (25\%)(\$250) + (75\%)(-\$750)$$

The sum of the undesirable choices *dominates* the sum of the desirable choices! Thus, the framing of the combined problem in two parts results in a reversal of preferences.

Why should this finding interest managers? Many interconnected decisions in the real world, such as portfolio selection, budgeting, and funding for new projects, can occur one decision at a time or in groups of decisions. This finding suggests that the sequential nature of the decision-making process in organizations is likely to enhance the potential for inconsistency and nonrational choice. Managers may go along making individual decisions that each seem sensible, but when viewed as a whole are obviously suboptimal. For example, sales departments are encouraged to think in terms of the acquisition of corporate gains, while credit offices are encouraged to frame decisions in terms of avoiding corporate losses. To arrive at a coherent strategy for making judgments under uncertainty, individuals and organizations need to become more aware of this bias and develop procedures for identifying and integrating risky decisions across organizations.

By being risk averse some of the time and risk seeking at other times, we are likely to adopt a decision portfolio that is just as inferior as selecting the preceding choices (a) and (d). To override our intuitive tendency for our risk preferences to be highly affected by the problem frame, Kahneman and Lovallo (1993; see also Rabin & Thaler, 2001) have argued that we would be generally better off following an expected-value rule for most decisions. This can be seen in the famous story of Nobel Prize–winning economist Paul Samuelson (1963), who offered a colleague a coin-toss gamble. If the colleague won the toss, he would receive $200, but if he lost, he would lose $100. Samuelson was offering his colleague a positive expected value with risk. The colleague, being risk averse, refused the single bet, but said that he would be happy to toss the coin one hundred times! The colleague understood that the bet had a positive expected value and that across lots of bets, the odds virtually guaranteed a profit. Yet with only one trial, he had a 50 percent chance of regretting taking the bet.

Notably, Samuelson's colleague doubtless faced many gambles in life, such as whether to invest extra money from his paycheck in stocks, bonds, or money markets. He would have fared better in the long run by maximizing his expected value on each decision, as his preference for running the bet one hundred times suggests. All of us encounter such "small gambles" in life, and we should try to follow the same strategy. Risk aversion will likely tempt us to turn down each individual opportunity for gain. Yet the aggregated risk of all of the positive expected-value gambles that we come across would eventually become infinitesimal, and the potential profit large.

In the real world, deviations from risk neutrality should probably be reserved for critically important decisions such as job acceptances, house buying, or corporate acquisitions, after careful consideration of the problem from multiple frames. By contrast, most of us tend to be risk averse toward some choices and risk seeking toward others, leading to a suboptimal group of decisions. Unless the decision is very important, a simple and effective strategy is to use expected value as the basis for decision making.

WE LIKE CERTAINTY, EVEN PSEUDOCERTAINTY

As you probably know, Russian Roulette is a rather unpleasant game in which a single bullet is placed into one of six chambers of a revolver. The barrel is then spun, and the game's players take turns pointing the gun to their heads and pulling the trigger.

The very thought of playing this game makes most of us queasy, as well it should. What if you were forced to play the game, but had the option, before putting the gun to your head, of paying some amount of money to remove the bullet and reduce your chance of impending death from about 17 percent (one sixth) to zero? If you're like most people, you would be ready to pay a handsome sum to get rid of that bullet.

Now consider an even nastier version of Russian Roulette in which the revolver has two bullets in it. How much would you pay to remove one of the bullets, reducing your chances of imminent death by 17 percent (from one third to one sixth)? Most people see that as a much less satisfying change, and consider it to be less valuable than the certainty of reducing the chance of imminent death to zero. This is true despite the fact that your probability of death is reduced by the same amount in both instances.

Kahneman and Tversky (1979) were the first to document the human tendency to underweight high-probability events (such as the 83 percent chance of living to tell about your adventure playing the one-bullet version of Russian Roulette) but appropriately weight events that are certain (such as the certainty of living to tell about the zero-bullet version of the game). If an event has a probability of 1.0 or zero, we tend to accurately evaluate the event's probability. However, if the event has a high probability (say, 83 percent), we tend to respond as the expected-utility framework would expect us to respond to a probability of less than .83. As a result, Slovic, Fischhoff, and Lichtenstein (Slovic et al.,1982) observe that "any protective action that reduces the probability of harm from, say, .01 to zero will be valued more highly than an action that reduces the probability of the same harm from .02 to .01" (p. 24). In other words, people value the creation of certainty over an equally valued shift in the level of uncertainty.

Interestingly, the perception of certainty (that is, the perception that the probability of an event is zero or 1.0) can be easily manipulated. Slovic et al. (1982) considered the best way to advertise a disaster insurance policy that covers fire but not flood. The policy can be accurately advertised either as "full protection" against fire or as a reduction in the overall probability of loss from natural disasters. The researchers found that the full-protection advertisement makes the policy most attractive to potential buyers. Why? Because the full-protection option reduces perceived uncertainty for loss from fire to zero, whereas the overall disaster policy reduces uncertainty some incremental amount to a value that is still above zero. The perceived certainty that results from the full-protection framing of the advertisement has been labeled "pseudocertainty" because it provides certainty regarding a subset of the relevant uncertainties (Slovic, Fischhoff, et al., 1982).

Slovic et al. (1982) provided empirical evidence of the strength of the pseudocertainty effect in the context of disease vaccination. The researchers created two versions of a questionnaire. Version 1 described a disease that was expected to afflict 20 percent of the population. Research participants in this condition were asked if they would receive a vaccine that protected half of the individuals vaccinated. Version 2 described two mutually exclusive and equally probable strains of the disease, each of which was expected to afflict 10 percent of the population. In this case, vaccination was said to give complete protection (certainty) against one strain and no protection against the other. Would you take the vaccine described in Version 1? What about the vaccine described in Version 2? In either case, the vaccine would objectively reduce one's overall risk from 20 percent to 10 percent. Slovic et al. found that Version 2 (pseudocertainty) was more appealing than Version 1 (probabilistic). Some 57 percent of participants who were given Version 2 said that they would get the vaccination, compared with only 40 percent of the participants who received Version 1.

In the following problems, Tversky and Kahneman (1981) simultaneously investigated the impact of certainty and pseudocertainty:

Problem 6. Which of the following options do you prefer?

   a. a sure win of $30

   b. an 80 percent chance to win $45

Problem 7. Consider the following two-stage game. In the first stage, there is a 75 percent chance to end the game without winning anything and a 25 percent chance to move into the second stage. If you reach the second stage you have a choice between:

   c. a sure win of $30

   d. an 80 percent chance to win $45

Decide whether you prefer (c) or (d). Your choice must be made before the game starts—that is, before the outcome of the first stage is known.

Problem 8. Which of the following options do you prefer?

   e. a 25 percent chance to win $30

   f. a 20 percent chance to win $45

Tversky and Kahneman (1981) presented each of these problems to a different group of people. In Problem 6, 78 percent of the respondents chose the more-likely small win (a) and 22 percent took the risk on the larger win (b). In Problem 7, 74 percent of the respondents chose the more-likely small win (c) and 26 percent took the risk (d). In Problem 8, 42 percent of the respondents chose the more-likely small win (e) and 58 percent took the risk on a larger win (f).

Some interesting contrasts result. Consider Problem 7: By combining the first and second part of the problem, it becomes evident that (c) offers a .25 chance to win $30 and (d) offers a $.25 \times .80 = .20$ chance to win $45. This is the same choice offered in Problem 8! Yet the modal choice has shifted. In Problem 7, if you lose in the first stage, it does not matter what choice you made. If you win in the first stage, Problem 7 reduces to Problem 6. Consequently, there seems to be no reason to respond differently to Problems 6 and 7. Since Problem 7 is equivalent to Problems 6 and 8, it can be inferred that Problems 6 and 8 should also be treated similarly. However, people responded similarly to Problems 6 and 7, but differently to Problem 8. Why this discrepancy in response to Problem 8?

The difference between Problems 6 and 8 illustrates what Tversky and Kahneman (1981) called the certainty effect: "A reduction of the probability of an outcome has more importance when the outcome was initially certain than when it was merely probable" (p. 455). The discrepancy, in response to objectively identical Problems 7 and 8, illustrates the pseudocertainty effect described earlier (Slovic, Lichtenstein, & Fischhoff, 1982; Tversky & Kahneman, 1981). The prospect of winning $30 is more attractive in Problem 7 than in Problem 8 because of the perceived certainty ("a sure win") associated with choice (c). However, this potential "certainty" is contingent upon reaching the second stage of the game, which still makes the outcome uncertain. The certainty and pseudocertainty effects lead to judgmental inconsistencies. The certainty effect makes us more apt to be interested in reducing the likelihood of certain events than uncertain events. Under the pseudocertainty effect, we are more likely to favor options that assure us certainty than those that only reduce uncertainty. Rationally, any constant reduction of risk in an uncertain situation should have the same value for the decision maker. For example, reducing the risk of cancer from 20 percent to 10 percent should have the same value as a reduction from 10 percent to 0 percent. But pseudocertainty has a special value to most people. Manipulations of pseudocertainty have important implications for the design of communications about medical treatments, personal insurance, corporate liability protection, and a variety of other forms of protection. The data suggest that individuals may buy insurance not only to protect against risk, but also to eliminate the worry caused by any amount of uncertainty (Tversky & Kahneman, 1981).

FRAMING AND THE OVERSELLING OF INSURANCE

What is an insurance premium? It is a certain loss (the premium) that you accept in exchange for the reduction of a small probability of a large loss. Virtually all insurance provides customers with negative expected value—that's how insurance companies make a profit.

Interestingly, Schoemaker and associates (Hershey & Schoemaker, 1980; Schoemaker & Kunreuther, 1979) and Slovic et al. (1982) have found that describing a sure loss as an insurance premium makes the loss more attractive, even when the objective amount of loss is the same. Slovic et al. (1982) asked study participants to pick between a sure loss (insurance premium) versus a risky option that had a small probability of a significant loss. For half of the participants, the risk-free option was called a certain loss. For the other half, the risk-free option was called an insurance premium. Study participants were much more likely to choose the risk-free loss when it was called an insurance premium than when it was called a certain loss.

Kahneman and Tversky (1979) and Hershey and Schoemaker (1980) argue that the word "insurance" triggers pervasive social norms: "How can you not carry insurance?" and "All good citizens carry insurance." Buying insurance is something most of us do without considering an alternative strategy. When was the last time you considered dropping your auto insurance (assuming that you live in a state where it is legal to drive uninsured)?

The framing of insurance and warranties may explain a very strange set of consumer decisions. After agreeing to buy a new automobile, consumers are typically offered the option of purchasing an extended warranty. The salesperson typically notes that, "For just a few dollars more per month, you'll never have to worry about repairs." Why do nearly half of new car buyers purchase extended warranties? It is certainly not because they are a good deal. Extended warranties are mostly profit for car dealers. Documents in a lawsuit filed against Nissan revealed that at that time, the typical extended warranty cost $795. A mere $131 went toward covering repairs, $109 went to Nissan for administrative costs, and the remaining $555 was straight dealer profit. It seems that the vividness of a costly repair, coupled with a social norm favoring insurance and warranties, leads many consumers to make a risk-averse choice that they would probably not make if they considered their options more carefully. As we have seen, people are more likely to accept a certain loss if they view it as insurance rather than as a sure monetary loss. Consumers would be better off if they said "no" to all extended warranties, put the money saved in the bank, and used it to pay for necessary repairs. Across their life span, they would keep more of their money.

WHAT'S IT WORTH TO YOU?

Please read the following scenario from Thaler (1985) twice—first with the words in parentheses and excluding the words in brackets, and second with the words in brackets and excluding the words in parentheses.

> You are lying on the beach on a hot day. All you have to drink is ice water. For the last hour you have been thinking about how much you would enjoy a nice cold bottle of your favorite brand of beer. A companion gets up to go make a phone call and offers to bring back a beer from the only nearby place where beer is sold (a fancy resort hotel) [a small, rundown grocery store]. He says that the beer might be expensive and asks how much you are willing to pay for it. He says that he will buy the beer if it costs as much as or less than the price you state. But if it costs more than the price you state, he will not buy it. You trust your friend, and there is no possibility of bargaining with the (bartender) [store owner]. What price do you tell him?

Notice some of the features of this dual problem. First, in both the hotel and the grocery store versions, you get the same product. Second, there is no possible negotiation on price. Third, there will be no advantage to the resort hotel "atmosphere," since you are going to drink the beer on the beach. According to expected-utility theory, people should be willing to pay the same amount in both versions of the scenario. In fact, Thaler found that participants in an executive development program were willing to pay significantly more if the beer was purchased from the "fancy resort hotel." Decades ago, the results for the problem were medians of $2.65 for a beer bought at the resort and $1.50 for a beer bought at the store.

Why does this contradiction occur? Thaler suggests the reason is that while "paying $2.50 for a beer at a fancy hotel would be an expected annoyance, paying $2.50 at a grocery store would be an outrageous 'rip-off.'" This leads to the conclusion that something else matters besides the value you place on the commodity acquired. Did you ever buy something because it was "too good a deal to pass up," despite the fact that you had no need for the product? Or have you ever refused to buy something that you could afford, simply because it was a rip-off? Thaler explains this phenomenon by suggesting that purchases are affected by both acquisition utility and transactional utility. *Acquisition utility* describes the value you place on a commodity (in this case, the beer). *Transactional utility* refers to the quality of the deal that you receive, evaluated in reference to "what the item should cost." Obviously, overpaying for a beer at a grocery store leads to a greater negative transactional utility than at a fancy resort hotel. One can argue that the inclusion of transactional utility in decision making is not rational, but it does describe our behavior.

Now consider two other problems, adapted from Tversky and Kahneman (1981):

Problem 9. Imagine that you are about to purchase a high-tech mouse for $50. The computer salesperson informs you that the mouse you wish to buy is on sale at the store's other branch, located a 20-minute drive away. You have decided to buy the mouse today, and will either buy it at the current store or drive 20 minutes to the other store. What is the highest price that the mouse could cost at the other store such that you would be willing to travel there for the discount?

Problem 10. Imagine that you are about to purchase a laptop computer for $2,000. The computer salesperson informs you that this computer is on sale at the store's other branch, located a 20-minute drive from where you are now. You have decided to buy the computer today, and will either buy it at the current store or drive to the store a 20-minute drive away. What is the highest price that you would be willing to pay at the other store to make the discount worth the trip?

What is a rational way of deciding whether to buy the mouse or the laptop in the current store or to drive 20 minutes to the other store? Most people quickly conclude that you should compare the value of 20 minutes of your time plus the cost of travel versus the expected savings. This would mean that the minimum discount demanded for each of the two products should be similar. In contrast, most people demand a greater discount in absolute dollars to make the computer trip than to make the mouse trip. Why? The issue of transactional utility enters into our assessments of the value of our time. Most people will be willing to travel the 20 minutes only to get a "very good deal." A $40 (2 percent) savings is not a big discount on the computer, but it is an outstanding deal on the mouse (you would be saving 80 percent). Normatively, however, the difference in percentage reduction is irrelevant. One should simply compare the savings obtained to the value of the time spent, and this value should remain consistent across decisions.

Personally, we find Tversky, Kahneman, and Thaler's insights informative regarding how we use our own time. The items described in this section forced us to think about how we, people who grew up in families that taught us to clip coupons, trade off time and money. We noted that, due to System 1 thinking, even decision researchers can develop patterns of behavior that are inconsistent with their preferred values. These problems clarify the importance of spending more time on a search when significant amounts of money are at stake and spending less time on a search for items of small value. Far too many people go to multiple grocery stores to save $10 or $12 but fail to search thoroughly when making large purchases, such as a house or car.

THE VALUE WE PLACE ON WHAT WE OWN

Imagine that you purchased a painting from an up-and-coming artist five years ago for $1,000. The artist has since become very famous, and the painting is now worth about $10,000. Consider the minimum amount for which you might willingly sell this painting. Now also think about how much you would be willing to pay for a similar-quality painting.

Most people would demand far more to sell the painting than the amount they would be willing to pay for a similar painting or the amount they would pay for the exact same painting if they did not own it. This pattern is called the *endowment effect* (Thaler, 1980). There are numerous other examples of the endowment effect. Home sellers think their houses are worth more than most buyers do, and many homes sit on the market for a long time as a result. Sellers believe their used cars are more valuable than most buyers do. In fact, fully one-third of items put up on eBay, the Internet auction house, fail to sell because no buyer bids more than the seller's reserve price—the lowest price the seller would consider accepting (Null, 2007).

In any exchange, a buyer must be willing to pay at least the minimum amount that a seller is willing to accept; otherwise, no agreement takes place. Objectively, the valuation of a commodity should be based on its true worth. However, the value that a seller places on a commodity often includes not only its intrinsic worth, but also value that is based on his or her attachment to the item.

In a clever experiment, Kahneman, Knetsch, and Thaler (1990) placed mugs in front of one-third of the participants in their study. These "sellers" were told that they owned the mug and had the option of selling it if a price, to be determined later, was acceptable to them. They were then given a list of possible selling prices, ranging from $0.50 to $9.50 (in 50-cent increments) and were told to indicate for each possible price whether they would sell the mug for that amount or keep it. Another third of the participants, the "buyers," were told that they would be given a sum of money which they could keep or use to buy a mug. They were also asked their preferences between a mug and sums of money ranging from $0.50 to $9.50. The remaining third of the participants, the "choosers," were given a questionnaire indicating that they would be given a choice between either a mug or a sum of money. They also marked their preferences between the mug and sums of money ranging from $0.50 to $9.50. All three groups were assured that their answers would not influence either the predetermined price of the mug or the amount of money to be received in lieu of the mug.

The results reveal a great deal about how our role in a buyer-seller relationship affects our value assessments. Sellers required a median value of $7.12 for the mug, the buyers $2.87, and the choosers $3.12. The buyers and choosers had very similar evaluations of the worth of the mug. In contrast, ownership made the mug much more valuable for the sellers; differences of 2:1 are common in such endowment experiments.

The implication of this endowment effect is that people tend to overvalue what they own. The frame of ownership creates value that is inconsistent with a rational analysis of the worth that the commodity brings to the individual. This inconsistent valuation partially explains why so many home sellers set an inappropriately high value on their homes and find themselves without any bidders for extended periods of time. An understanding of the endowment effect is critical to making wise assessments of the value of your commodities.

Dick Thaler gave his University of Chicago MBA students the following pair of hypothetical problems, which were realistic at the time:

Problem 11. It is 1998, and Michael Jordan and the Bulls are about to play their final championship game. You would very much like to attend. The game is sold out, and you won't have another opportunity to see Michael Jordan play for a long time, if ever. You know someone who has a ticket for sale. What is the most you would be willing to pay for it?

Problem 12. It is 1998, and Michael Jordan and the Bulls are about to play their final championship game. You have a ticket to the game and would very much like to attend. The game is sold out, and you won't have another opportunity to see Michael Jordan play for a long time, if ever. What is the least that you would accept to sell your ticket?

Thaler reports that while his students were willing to pay only $330, on average, in Problem 11, they demanded $1,920, on average, in Problem 12. We can identify with this behavior, yet we also find it problematic. How much is the ticket worth? Without knowing the answer, it is far too likely that you will hold onto it long after it makes sense to give it up for a great price. The same holds true for anything you or your company owns—cars, houses, stocks, divisions of a firm, and so on.

MENTAL ACCOUNTING

The previous two sections are consistent with Thaler's (1999) work on mental accounting, which shows that people have a variety of "mental accounts" that they use to organize, evaluate, and keep track of a variety of financial activities, such as money for vacation, a renovation, this month's budget, etc. Interestingly, we apply strikingly different decision rules to different mental accounts. The previous two sections highlighted specific aspects of mental accounting in action. This section adds other interesting components of our mental accounts.

Thaler (1999) relates a story of traveling to Switzerland to give a paid talk to a group of executives. After the talk, Thaler and his spouse traveled around the country, at a time when the dollar was weak and travel costs were high. Thaler notes that, knowing that the travel expenses would total far less than his speaking fee, he had no trouble spending money on the trip. He then offers a mental comparison between this story and a similar story in which he earns the same speaking fee in New York, then travels with his spouse to Switzerland. In the latter story, the high costs of Swiss travel would be more bothersome. Essentially, when costs come out of the same account (the Swiss trip account), they seem less important than when they come out of a different account (the New York talk account).

In a parallel story that is more common, imagine that, as you arrive at the grocery store with a plan to do your food shopping for the week, a store employee hands you a $10 certificate that you can use at the store on that day only. Will the certificate affect the amount that you spend in the store? From a rational perspective, you are now simply $10 wealthier than you were before being given the coupon, and the coupon should have no effect on how much you spend. Thus, if your net wealth was $100,000 before receiving the coupon, it is now $100,010. We would not predict systematically higher spending from someone with $100,010 net wealth than from someone with $100,000 net wealth. Yet Milkman, Beshears, Rogers, and Bazerman (2008), working with an online grocery ordering and delivery service, find people spend more at the grocery store after they have just received a "$10 off" certificate. To be specific, $2 of the $10 goes to increased purchases. The ease with which people spent their newfound wealth is consistent with Thaler's behavior, though on a more mundane scale.

Similarly, Shafir and Thaler (2006; Thaler, 1999) asked a group of subscribers to a wine newsletter to consider the following problem:

Problem 13. Suppose that you bought a case of a good 1982 Bordeaux in the futures market for $20 a bottle. The wine now sells at auction for about $75 per bottle. You have decided to drink a bottle.

Which of the following best captures your sense of the cost of your drinking this bottle?

    a. $0

    b. $20

    c. $20 plus interest

    d. $75

    e.   −$55 (you're drinking a $75 bottle for which you paid only $20)

Shafir and Thaler (2006; Thaler, 1999) report that the percentages for each of the answers were (a) 30 percent, (b) 18 percent, (c) 7 percent, (d) 20 percent, and (e) 25 percent. The authors note that the newsletter was published by an economist, Orley Ashenfelter, and that most of respondents who answered "d" were also economists—the answer consistent with economic analysis. The rest of us do not think about the value of our assets based on what they are currently worth. Rather, we either treat costs as something that we have already expensed away (option a), as the cost that we paid (option b), or in terms of the value of the transaction (option e—you made money by making a good purchase).

Your mental accounts can also affect your satisfaction with outcomes that you did not choose. Consider the following two outcomes (adapted from Thaler, 1985):

Outcome A. You receive a letter from the IRS saying that you made a minor arithmetic mistake in your tax return and must send them $100. You receive a similar letter the same day from your state tax authority saying you owe them $100 for a similar mistake. There are no other repercussions from either mistake.

Outcome B. You receive a letter from the IRS saying that you made a minor arithmetic mistake in your tax return and must send them $200. There are no other repercussions from the mistake.

Which situation would be more upsetting? Most people are more upset by Outcome A, the two small losses, than by Outcome B, the one large loss, despite the fact that the two outcomes are equal in financial terms. This emotional reaction is consistent with the nature of our reactions to losses. Specifically, when assessing each loss that hits us, the first dollars lost hurt us more than additional dollars lost. So, just as you learned earlier that most people do not perceive losing $200 to be twice as bad as losing $100, two losses of $100 from two different mental accounts feel worse than one larger loss of $200. The reverse occurs with gains. The benefit of a given amount of money would be perceived as greater if it were given in smaller discrete payments rather than all at once, since we value $100 as more than half of what we value $200. The lesson? Do not give your significant other many gifts at once. Doling them out over time will create more total joy!

Finally, Thaler (1999) tells an interesting story about how a colleague uses mental accounting to avoid becoming annoyed by the small losses that he, like all of us, incurs on a moderately regular basis. At the beginning of each year, this colleague sets up a fund that he will use to pay for annoying losses, such as parking tickets and library fines. When those minor annoyances occur, he simply pays the cost from the account. At the end of the year, he gives the balance in the account to the United Way.

Apparently, this form of mental accounting reduces the man's annoyance about unexpected and petty expenditures. We are not sure what the net impact of the story is on charitable giving, but we like the idea. Once you have set some money aside, the details of how you spend it become less bothersome.

REBATE/BONUS FRAMING

In September 2001, the United States government paid $38 billion to tax-paying U.S. citizens—$300, $500, or $600 per individual, depending on annual income. Government officials and the media used the term "rebate" to describe these payments, which the Bush administration argued would fuel spending and energize the flagging economy. Epley, Mak, and Idson (2006) have conducted a trio of studies showing that the way the government framed the program—specifically, through the use of the term "rebate"—dramatically limited its effectiveness. These researchers provide fascinating evidence that if the government had described the payments as "bonuses" instead of "rebates," more citizens would have immediately spent the money instead of saving it, creating a greater stimulus to the economy.

In their first study, Epley et al. showed that the terms "rebate" and "bonus" create very different mental states within taxpayers concerning how they feel the money should be used. The researchers reminded participants, all of whom were taxpayers, that the federal government had issued checks to all taxpayers approximately six months earlier. One group of participants, the "rebate" participants, read this statement: "proponents of this tax cut argued that the government collected more tax revenue than was needed to cover its expenses, resulting in a tax surplus" that should be returned to taxpayers "as withheld income." In contrast, the "bonus" participants read: "proponents of this tax cut argued that the costs of running the government were lower than expected, resulting in a budget surplus" that should be returned to taxpayers "as bonus income."

Both groups of participants were then asked to recall what percentage of their checks they spent and what percentage they saved. "Rebate" participants remembered spending 25 percent and saving 75 percent, while "bonus" participants remembered spending 87 percent and saving 13 percent. Due to random assignment, there is no reason to believe that participants in the two conditions actually spent substantially different amounts. Rather, the data suggest that people associate "bonus" with spending and "rebate" with saving. Epley et al. argue that the word "bonus" creates the image of surplus cash, while "rebate" conveys the image of money that simply returns you to the appropriate status quo.

In their second study, Epley et al. gave Harvard undergraduate student participants $50, described as either a tuition rebate or a bonus. In a follow-up a week later, the researchers asked the students how much of the $50 they saved and how much they spent. On average, "rebate" participants reported spending $10 and saving $40, while "bonus" participants reported spending $22 and saving $28; bonus participants spent more than twice as much as rebate participants. Because the students' reports could have been inaccurate, the researchers conducted a third study in which they gave Harvard undergraduates a $25 windfall framed either as "bonus money" or "rebate money." Epley et al. then set up a "lab store" and offered products for sale at about 20 percent off standard prices. On average, rebate participants spent only $2.43, while bonus participants spent $11.16, or more than four times as much.

These studies show the amazing power of framing, the importance of knowing how you can be affected by framing, and the relevance of framing to important decisions. Clearly, the U.S. government could have stimulated the economy far more in 2001 with a bonus campaign instead of a rebate plan.

JOINT-VERSUS-SEPARATE PREFERENCE REVERSALS

Imagine that you independently assess two options and place a higher value on Option A than on Option B. You might logically infer that if you then chose between the two options, you would select Option A over Option B. This section focuses on a set of preference reversals that violate the very simple condition of logical consistency.

An extensive literature on separate versus joint preference reversals now exists. Here, we examine a selective set of examples in which people place a higher value on one option than another when looking at them individually, but reverse their preference when considering two or more options at the same time (Bazerman, Loewenstein, & White, 1992). We will provide at least two explanations for these reversals, which can help clarify when we can expect them to occur.

Consider two salary packages: Package A pays $27,000 in year 1, $26,000 in year 2, $25,000 in year 3, and $24,000 in year 4. Package B pays $23,000 in year 1, $24,000 in year 2, $25,000 in year 3, and $26,000 in year 4. Hsee (1996) found that when undergraduate participants were asked to report how likely they would be to accept each of the offers, Package B was more likely than Package A to be acceptable when participants evaluated just one of the two options. But when they consider the two options together, Package A was much more acceptable. When assessing one option at a time, participants did not like to see pay go down over time. But when assessing both simultaneously, it was easy for them to see that Package A provides more money, more quickly.

In a very different context, Hsee (1998) asked participants to imagine that they were in the market for a music dictionary and then to evaluate either one or two music dictionaries. The Large Dictionary had 20,000 words and a torn cover. The Intact Dictionary had 10,000 words and an intact cover. Participants examined either one dictionary or both and reported the highest amount they were willing to pay for each. When participants assessed their willingness to pay for both, they valued the Large Dictionary more than the Intact Dictionary ($27 versus $19, on average). By contrast, participants who assessed only one of the two dictionaries valued the Intact Dictionary more than the Large Dictionary ($24 versus $20, on average). The torn cover mattered more when participants assessed only one option, but the number of words mattered more when they assessed the dictionaries jointly.

Kahneman and Ritov (1994) showed similar inconsistencies for different types of environmental or social issues. Participants were presented with headlines that highlighted specific problems and were asked either to report their level of support for government intervention in one particular cause (separate condition) or to choose between two causes by stating which one they would support more (joint condition). In separate evaluations, consistent with the affect heuristic (Slovic, Finucane, Peters, & MacGregor, 2002), people leaned toward "affectively arousing" environmental causes (those that triggered strong emotions), such as spotted owls, coral reefs, and toxic spills. When choosing between causes, however, participants tended to prefer causes directly relevant to people, such as skin cancer, multiple myeloma, and lead-based paint. For example, while the cause of improving the plight of a "threatened Australian mammal species" was slightly more important to people than "skin cancer in farm workers" when participants assessed them one at a time, "skin cancer in farm workers" won by more than a 2-to-1 margin when participants selected between the two causes.

In some political opinion polls, citizens are asked whether or not they approve of a particular candidate. In other polls, citizens are asked which of two candidates they would vote for. Sometimes the inferences that pollsters make from approval polls do not match up with voting intentions. Lowenthal (1996) provides some clarity on how this can occur. She found that separate evaluations of individual candidates reversed themselves in pair evaluations and voting behavior. Specifically, she examined voter preference for two hypothetical candidates. One candidate was expected to deliver 10,000 new jobs but was rumored to have evaded paying personal taxes. The other candidate would probably deliver 5,000 new jobs and had no rumors of misconduct. When participants assessed the candidates individually in an approval poll, the clean candidate received much more favorable assessments. But when asked to vote between them, the candidate expected to deliver more jobs won by almost a 2-to-1 margin.

These examples document a growing body of evidence that demonstrates inconsistencies in preferences across joint versus separate evaluations (Bazerman, Moore, Tenbrunsel, Wade-Benzoni, & Blount, 1999; Hsee, Loewenstein, Blount, & Bazerman, 1999). In interpreting these examples, note that they all involve outcome pairs distinguished along two attributes. One attribute is preferred in separate evaluation, and the other attribute is preferred in joint evaluation. There are at least two explanations for these effects: the "want/should" explanation and the "evaluability" explanation.

Bazerman, Tenbrunsel, and Wade-Benzoni's (1998) want/should explanation views a tension between what an individual wants to do versus what the individual thinks he or she should do. Consistent with the affect heuristic (Slovic et al., 2002), Bazerman et al. (1998) essentially argue that the more affectively arousing option, or the "want" option, will be valued more highly in separate evaluations, while the more logical and reasoned option, or the "should" option, will be valued more highly in joint evaluations. Supporting the face validity of the want/should distinction, O'Connor, De Dreu, Schroth, Barry, Lituchy, and Bazerman (2002) show that people think of the affectively arousing option as the option that they want and think of the more logical option as the option they believe they should choose. Essentially, Bazerman et al. (1998) argue that we often act on our affective preferences when assessing one option at a time, but that joint assessment triggers more reasoned analysis. In other words, System 1 thinking will be comparatively more prevalent in separate evaluations, and System 2 thinking will be comparatively more prevalent in joint evaluations.

The *evaluability hypothesis* (Bazerman et al., 1992; Hsee, 1996; Hsee et al., 1999) offers a more cognitive explanation of joint-versus-separate preference reversals. This argument suggests that separate versus joint reversals are driven by differences in the ability of attributes to be evaluated, or their "evaluability."

When two options require a tradeoff between a hard-to-evaluate attribute (such as the number of words in a dictionary) and an easy-to-evaluate attribute (such as a torn cover), the hard-to-evaluate attribute will have less impact in separate evaluation than in joint evaluation. In separate evaluation, people often have difficulty assessing the desirability of an option based on a hard-to-evaluate attribute (is 10,000 words a good amount?); as a result, the hard-to-evaluate attribute has little influence on decision making. In joint evaluation, having comparison data on the hard-to-evaluate attribute for both options provides additional information and increases the attribute's evaluability. Thus, the number of words in a dictionary has much more meaning when you can compare the number of words to the number in another dictionary. In contrast, you do not need to have comparative information to know that a torn cover is bad.

The task of separate evaluation is complex. In this section, we have highlighted two processes that can lead to changes in the weight that attributes receive between joint and separate evaluations. First, based on the affect heuristic, people will go with their gut response, paying primary attention to the attribute that creates emotional arousal. Second, attributes that are hard to evaluate will be underweighted in separate evaluations. Clearly, both processes are at work in creating separate versus joint preference reversals. We will return to these reversals in Chapter 7, where we explore the conditions under which people obsess about social comparison processes.

CONCLUSION AND INTEGRATION

The categories of framing effects and reversals of preference covered in this chapter demonstrate some of the key findings in the field of behavioral decision research. The Asian disease problem that opened the chapter is a particularly important one in the history of the field. Prior to this result and the development of Kahneman and Tversky's (1979) prospect theory, the behavioral decision literature was largely ignored by economists. Simon's concept of bounded rationality, discussed in Chapter 1, was explained away as a rational strategy, adapting for the costs of search. The heuristics and biases explored in Chapter 2 were discounted for similar reasons. But the framing effects described in this chapter showed people making dramatically different decisions based on what even economists had to agree was normatively irrelevant information.

The Asian disease problem, which challenged the dominant economic paradigm more than 25 years ago, is a cornerstone of the type of data that creates a productive dialogue between psychologists and economists. The numerous other framing effects that have been documented continue this tradition and have contributed to the growth of the fields of behavioral economics and behavioral finance.

One question that often emerges from these studies is whether or not these effects generalize to the real world. Five editions ago, Max was optimistic about this question but did not have the data he required to make a convincing case. Since then, numerous excellent studies have used framing effects to explain why taxi drivers drive more hours on slow days than on busy ones (Abeler, Falk, Goette, & Huffman, 2011; Camerer, Babcock, Loewenstein, & Thaler, 1997), why so many people pay for line insurance on their telephones (Thaler & Ziemba, 1988), why professional golfers are more likely to leave their putts short when shooting for birdie as compared to shooting for bogey (Pope & Schweitzer, 2011), why football bettors are more likely to bet on favorites than underdogs against a point spread (Simmons, Nelson, Galak, & Frederick, 2011), the conditions under which negotiators are most likely to reach an impasse (see Chapter 11), and a wide variety of investment mistakes (the topic of Chapter 9), including the tendency to sell winners and to hold losers (Odean, 1998). Indeed, framing effects even appear to extend to other species, such as capuchin monkeys (Chen, Lakshminarayanan, & Santos, 2006). Camerer (2000) also does an excellent job of summarizing the strong evidence of the relevance of framing effects in the real world.

Now that you understand reference points and framing, how should this understanding affect your decisions? First, when facing a risky decision, you should identify your reference point. Next, consider whether other reference points exist and whether they are just as reasonable. If the answer is yes, think about your decision from multiple perspectives and examine any contradictions that emerge. At this point, you will be prepared to make your decision with a fuller awareness of the alternative frames in which the problem could have been presented.

Why does framing exert such a powerful effect on our judgments? The answer cannot be the same one that we used to explain the biases covered in Chapters 3 and 4. The biases in those chapters result from heuristic shortcuts in judgment. By comparison, the striking aspect about framing and reference point effects is that they suggest the presence of underlying mental processes that are *more* complicated than a rational decision maker would employ. Rational decision makers would simply seek to maximize the expected value of their choices. Whether these outcomes represented gains or losses would be irrelevant, and consideration of the outcome relative to the status quo would be a superfluous consideration.

Rayo and Becker (2007) present a persuasive explanation for why evolution would have programmed us with extra machinery that impairs our decisions. According to their explanation, our reliance on frames and reference points to assess outcomes is an elegant solution to a problematic biological constraint. The constraint is that our "subjective utility scale"—our ability to experience pleasure and pain—is not infinitely sensitive. Was Bill Gates's 50th billion dollars as satisfying as his first? Certainly not. The limited sensitivity of our subjective utility scale is precisely the reason why we experience declining marginal utility for both gains and losses, as we discussed earlier in this chapter.

Given this biological constraint on the sensitivity of our subjective utility scale, we need to readjust our reference point by getting used to what we have and then taking it for granted. If we didn't adjust our reference point, we could quickly hit the maximum of our utility scale and realize that nothing we could ever do would make us happier. That would effectively kill our motivation to work harder, become richer, and achieve more. In reality, of course, we get used to our current level of wealth, status, and achievement, and are then motivated to seek more, believing that it will make us happier.

The irony of this motivational system is that for it to keep working, we have to habituate to our new condition but not anticipate this habituation. Evidence does indeed confirm that people adjust to both positive and negative changes in circumstances with surprising speed and then promptly forget that they did so (Brickman, Coates, & Janoff-Bulman, 1978; Gilbert, Pinel, Wilson, Blumberg, & Wheatley, 1998). Thus, we find ourselves on a hedonic treadmill in which we strive for an imagined happiness that forever slips out of our grasp, beckoning us onward (Brickman & Campbell, 1971; Gilbert, 2006; Kahneman, Krueger, Schkade, Schwarz, & Stone, 2006).

CHAPTER SIX

Motivational and Emotional Influences on Decision Making

$\mathbf{Y}$ou are standing on a footbridge spanning some trolley tracks. Below, you see that a runaway trolley is bearing down on five hapless people. Next to you on the bridge is a railway worker wearing a large backpack. (See Figure 6.1.) The only way to save the people is to push this man off the bridge and onto the tracks below. The man will die, but his body will stop the trolley from reaching the others. (You can't jump yourself because you aren't carrying enough weight to stop the trolley, and there's no time to put on the man's backpack.) Legal concerns aside, would *you* push this stranger to his death?

The situation that we have just described is a famous philosophy problem known as the "footbridge dilemma" (Foot, 1978). It pits two different philosophical approaches to ethical decision-making against each other: a utilitarian approach and a *deontological* approach. Utilitarianism is often described by the phrase, "doing the greatest good for the greatest number of people." From a utilitarian perspective, you add up the costs and benefits of each choice and choose the option that yields the best balance of costs and benefits for all involved—which, in this case, would be to save five lives at the expense of one.

A very different form of ethical thinking, what Immanuel Kant (1964) referred to as a *deontological* approach, judges the morality of an action based on the action's adherence to rules or duties. Kant argued that judgments of whether an act is right or wrong should be determined by a consideration of people's rights and duties in society. From Kant's point of view, the act of pushing someone off of a bridge would violate his rights and is therefore immoral. Notice that Kant's perspective is linked to the negative emotional response that most of us have to the idea of pushing the stranger to his death. In such cases, our emotions tend to win the debate; most people do not believe it would be ethically acceptable to push the railway worker off the bridge in order to save five lives. If you ask them why they will not push the man off the bridge, common answers include, "That would be murder!" "The ends don't justify the means!" or "People have rights!" (Greene, forthcoming). People's emotional reactions are an undeniable factor in this decision.

We realize that most readers are currently on the side of the deontologists. But before you put yourself firmly in that camp, consider a philosophical problem that

Figure 6.1 The Footbridge Dilemma

was posed before the footbridge dilemma, the "trolley dilemma": This time, a runaway trolley is headed for five railway workmen who will be killed if it proceeds on its present course. The only way to save these people is to hit a switch that will turn the trolley onto a side track where it will run over and kill one workman instead of five. (See Figure 6.2.) Again, ignoring legal concerns, would you turn the trolley by hitting the switch in order to save five people at the expense of one person?

Most people who have not previously been exposed to the footbridge dilemma say that they would hit the switch in the trolley problem. They explain their behavior by focusing on the belief that having five people die would be worse than having one person die—standard utilitarian thinking (Greene, forthcoming).

When people are exposed to both of these problems, some are bothered by the arguable inconsistency of deciding to flip the switch to turn the trolley (in the trolley dilemma) contrasted with the decision not to push the man over the bridge (in the footbridge dilemma). Those who are bothered by the inconsistency generally made

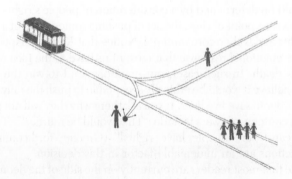

Figure 6.2 The Trolley (Switch) Problem

the footbridge decision intuitively; later exposure to the trolley dilemma leads them to greater reflection consistent with utilitarian reasoning.

As these two stories illustrate, sometimes we follow our emotions, and sometimes we do not. More importantly, we do not necessarily apply our emotions to our decisions in the manner that we would choose upon greater reflection.

It used to be that most behavioral decision research, like the economic research that it so often criticizes, viewed decision making as a cognitive process. More recently, however, researchers have begun to attribute many of the errors that people make to motivational and emotional influences. This chapter covers situations in which we make decisions that are inconsistent with our long-term interests because of a temporary emotional or motivational impulse to pursue some tempting alternative, whether due to addiction, hunger, sexual arousal, or some other transitory passion.

Specifically, we will focus on three categories of motivational and emotional influences on decision making. The first section describes the tension between doing what we want to do and doing what we think we should do. The second section discusses self-serving ways in which people interpret fairness. The third section explores precisely how our emotional states influence our judgment.

WHEN EMOTION AND COGNITION COLLIDE

In Homer's *The Odyssey*, Ulysses was confronted with a problem during his long voyage. He knew that he would soon encounter the Sirens, female enchanters who lured seafaring men to an island—and to their subsequent deaths—by singing sweetly to them. No man had ever been able to resist the Sirens, and their beach was "piled with boneheaps of men now rotted away." Ulysses instructed his men to sail past the Sirens without stopping and to put wax in their ears to block out the Sirens' sweet song. Because Ulysses wanted to hear the Sirens, he told his men to tie him with ropes to the ship's mast and ordered them not to release him, no matter how much he begged, until they had sailed safely by the Sirens. As his ship set sail, he warned his men: "If I supplicate you and implore you to set me free, then you must tie me fast with even more lashings." Ulysses' plan worked, and his ship passed the Sirens unscathed.

Each one of us faces internal conflicts between what we want to do and what we think we should do. While Ulysses knew that he should not follow the Sirens' song, when he heard them sing he wanted desperately to go to them. Compulsive gamblers want to visit the casino but know that they should avoid it because of the difficulty they have knowing when to stop. Alcoholics want to drink but know that they should abstain because of the likely negative consequences. Students want to relax and socialize in the evenings, but know they should study. Consumers must often decide whether to buy the product they want or a product they think they should purchase for health, environmental, or budgetary reasons.

In Chapter 1, we introduced the affect heuristic (Slovic, Finucane, Peters, & MacGregor, 2002), which argues that decision makers have an automatic affective, or emotional, reaction to most options. Bazerman et al. (1998) argue that this emotional response is often in disagreement with the decision that an individual would make after more thoughtful reasoning. We use the terms "want" and "should" to categorize these two types of preferences. How do individuals come to have preferences that put them in disagreement with themselves? When does emotion win, and when does reason?

Multiple Selves

Schelling (1984) argues that people frequently behave like two individuals: "one who wants clear lungs and long life and another who adores tobacco, or one who wants a lean body and another who wants dessert" (p. 58). The "multiple-selves" theory has been used to account for a variety of dysfunctional behaviors, such as alcohol and drug abuse (Ainslie, 1975), as well as common consumer errors, including the decision to spend money rather than save it (Loewenstein, 1996). In almost all of these cases, one of our "selves" is in favor of a decision that provides immediate gratification rather than an alternative that would provide greater future rewards.

Cognitive neuroscience research suggests that we may actually be able to identify our multiple selves in different brain regions. Different brain areas are activated when we consider either immediate rewards we want or larger delayed rewards we feel we should choose (McClure, Laibson, Loewenstein, & Cohen, 2004). These different brain regions may also be associated with automatic (System 1) and deliberative (System 2) thought. System 1, composed of the amygdala, basal ganglia, and lateral temporal cortex, is associated with automatic thought; System 2, composed of the anterior cingulate cortex, prefrontal cortex, and medial-temporal lobe, is associated with more deliberative thought (Evans, 2008). In particular, the prefrontal cortex seems to be key in the integration of information and decision making (Bechara, Damasio, Damasio, & Lee, 1999). People with damage to the prefrontal cortex have trouble weighing the immediate and long-term benefits necessary for deciding between what they want to do and what they should do (Bechara, Damasio, Tranel, & Damasio, 1997). A major reason for this difficulty is that people with a damaged prefrontal cortex have trouble encoding information relevant to emotions (G. Loewenstein, Rick, & Cohen, 2008). Notably, people who have suffered injuries to emotional regions of the brain sometimes become *more* rational decision makers, such that they are more likely to select options with higher expected value because they are less frightened by potential losses and thus take more sensible risks (Shiv, Loewenstein, Bechara, Damasio, & Damasio, 2005). In sum, the neuroscience evidence suggests that emotional brain areas impel us toward desires that are not in our long-term interests and that higher brain areas in the prefrontal cortex can override these desires and select options with higher expected utility.

Whatever the source of our clashing internal preferences, Schelling (1984) points out that they have substantial economic consequences. Indeed, the multiple-selves theory helps to explain otherwise perplexing phenomena, including:

- The prevalence of large industries supporting both smoking products and treatments to help people quit smoking.

- The simultaneous increase in obesity and the increasing popularity of diet books and diet fads.
- The popularity of drinking and the need for programs like Alcoholics Anonymous.
- The popularity of both illegal drugs and clinics to treat drug addiction.
- The prevalence of pornography and prostitution in the face of strong social and legal taboos regarding sexual behavior.
- The frequency of procrastination and the popularity of books, programs, and motivational systems designed to help people get things done.

As we have noted, internal inconsistencies between transient concerns and long-term self-interest reflect natural tensions between what people *want* to do and what they think they *should* do. Evidence suggests that emotional appeal (and the "want" self) is stronger when we evaluate options one at a time and that the more reasoned, reflective "should" self will be stronger when we confront multiple options at the same time and can weigh them against each other. Standards of comparison clarify differences between alternatives and promote more rational decision making (Hsee, 1996). By contrast, when considering a single option, decision makers are often driven by the question, "Do I want it?" In this situation, emotional and visceral motives are stronger.

Thus, when someone is given the option of a short-term reward (recreational drugs, skipping work, etc.) that has long-term costs, the "want" self may make an immediate assessment that the option seems appealing. Yet when that person explicitly compares the short-term desire against the choice to resist the indulgence, the "should" self is empowered by the ability to evaluate and compare the relative value of each. It is the "should" self that methodically makes New Year's resolutions and the "want" self that breaks them one at a time (Khan & Dhar, 2006, 2007), while the "should" self is tired or distracted (Danziger, Levav, & Avnaim-Pesso, 2011; Shiv & Fedorikhin, 1999).

The Impact of Temporal Differences

One way to describe the behavior produced by internal conflicts is by applying the economic concept of *discounting*, which states that any choice that involves a tradeoff between current and future benefits should discount the future to some extent. For example, a can of your favorite soda should be more valuable to you tonight than if you were to receive it 10 years from now, if for no other reason than you might not be around to enjoy it in 10 years. A rational decision maker would discount the future using *exponential discounting*, which means discounting each future time period by the same percentage. Say, for instance, that your chance of death is about 1 percent per year. You might then discount the value of the soda by 1 percent for a delay of one year. If you had been willing to pay $1 to receive it immediately, you would only be willing to pay $.99 now in order to guarantee delivery a year from now. To guarantee delivery in 10 years, you would be willing to pay $1 \times .99^{10}$ or about $.90.

By contrast, self-control problems such as procrastination, laziness, and addiction can produce choices that reflect *hyperbolic discounting*. The intuition behind this theory, first formally employed by Laibson (1994), is quite simple. Relative to the present time period, we view all gains and losses in the future to be worth less than they would be in the present. Returning to the soda example, a soft drink would be worth subjectively more to you today than it would be tomorrow *or* a year from now. Note that the difference between getting it in 365 days or 366 days seems miniscule, while the same one-day delay between today and tomorrow is likely to matter much more. As O'Donoghue and Rabin (1999) put it, we are biased towards the present.

Milkman, Rogers, and Bazerman (2007) examined the temporal component of the conflict between the "want" self and the "should" self in the context of movie rentals. They found that when people are ordering movies that they will receive days later from their online DVD rental service, they focus more on what they think they should see (such as documentaries and art films). In contrast, once the movies arrive, the movies that they want to see (such as comedies and action movies) are more likely than the "should" movies to wind up in the DVD player. As a result, "should" movies stay in customers' homes without being played significantly longer than "want" movies. Essentially, when customers are making decisions about the future, they focus on what they should do. But when making decisions in the present, they are more likely to do what they want to do.

The same researchers (Rogers, Milkman, & Bazerman, 2007) examined ordering choices in the context of an online grocery delivery service, in which customers place an order online and it arrives within a few days. In general, as the time between the order and the requested delivery increases, customers spend a higher percentage of their order on "should" items (such as vegetables) than on "want" items (such as ice cream).

Rogers and Bazerman (2008) explore the support that citizens have for policies that pit what they think they should support versus what they want to support. An example of this conflict is a gas tax, which most people do not want yet believe that they should support. Rogers and Bazerman (2008) find that support for such "should" policies goes up significantly if the policy will be implemented in the future rather than immediately. When people think of the distant future, they adopt a more abstract view of their goals; when they think of the near future, they tend to focus on the specific, concrete details of their goals (Fujita & Roberts, 2010). Such contradictions between decisions made at different time periods can be traced to the vividness of present concerns. Obviously, we care most about what is happening to us in the present moment, since that is what we are actually experiencing. If you're craving Ben & Jerry's ice cream, you want it now, not later, and certainly not in a couple of days. Notably, our differing temporal preferences are rooted in our biology. When we consider an immediate reward, the emotional centers in our brains are activated. When we consider a delayed reward, it is the more rational and reflective prefrontal cortex that is most active (McClure et al., 2004).

The result of this neural wiring is preferences that dramatically overweight the present, neglecting both future pain and future pleasure. People are willing to pay to enjoy rewards immediately. However, when people indicate their willingness to pay to accelerate an outcome, they become much less willing to pay when the anticipated outcome is farther in the future than when it is closer to the present, even though the amount of time is the same in both instances (Zauberman, Kim, Malkoc, & Bettman, 2009). This type of hyperbolic discounting may be explained by our overweighting of the present. Emotionally, the near future is more interesting, motivating, and compelling than the hazy, uncertain someday.

Hyperbolic discounting affects our treatment of many valuable resources, including environmental resources. People generally believe that we ought to leave the natural environment in as good a state as we inherited it and that we should not treat the earth and its natural resources "as if it were a business in liquidation" (Herman Daly, cited in Gore, 1992, p. 191). These explicit values concern future generations. In contrast, we often make decisions that are inconsistent with our explicit views. Rather than making decisions aimed at sustainability, we choose to consume environmental resources at an ever-increasing rate. Our explicitly stated concern for the future collides with our implicit desire to consume and, too often, our implicit desires win out. We discount the future, as well as future generations, in ways inconsistent with our explicit environmental attitudes.

Research documents extremely high discount rates regarding the future (Bazerman, Wade-Benzoni, & Benzoni, 1996; Loewenstein & Thaler, 1989). Most homeowners do not sufficiently insulate their attics and walls. They also fail to buy more expensive, energy-efficient appliances, even when they would recoup the extra costs in less than a year. Organizations are also guilty of discounting the future. Many institutions fail to use building materials that would be the most cost-efficient over the long term thanks to a shortsighted concern for immediate costs of construction (Hawken, 1993). Investments in efficient building materials can pay off handsomely (Ager & Dawes, 1965), yet many institutions seek to minimize the short-term cost of construction to the long-term detriment of their maintenance costs and the planet's scarce resources.

The crash of the U.S. housing market, which triggered the global financial crisis in 2008, stands as a vivid illustration of the tendency to overly discount the future (Bazerman & Tenbrunsel, 2011). During a boom in the real estate industry, developers built more and more homes, and lenders offered increasingly attractive mortgages to an ever-expanding group of citizens. Low-income borrowers, previously shut out of the housing market, suddenly were being pursued by real estate brokers offering low-interest, adjustable rate mortgages. President Bill Clinton pursued his goal of increasing home ownership by promoting "paper-thin down payments" and urging lenders to give mortgages to unqualified buyers, according to *BusinessWeek* editor Peter Coy (2008). As the housing bubble expanded, lenders lowered their standards and began bundling and selling off what came to be known as subprime mortgages. More and more borrowers were able to realize their dreams of home ownership thanks to minimal down payments and, in some cases, no concrete evidence that they would be able to repay their loans. When their monthly payments inevitably shot up, these "subprime borrowers" fell behind and succumbed to an epidemic of mortgage delinquencies and foreclosures. Borrowers, lenders, and politicians alike failed to anticipate the long-term negative consequences of their short-term decision making.

Reconciling Internal Conflicts

The research on internal inconsistency raises important questions. For our own long-term health and safety, should we try to allow the "should" self to completely control our decisions? Or does the "want" self have something valuable to add to improve the decisions of the "should" self? We offer advice on this issue from three areas: economics, Raiffa's decision-analysis perspective (see Chapter 1), and a negotiation framework (developed further in Chapter 10).

Advice from economists. Economists such as Schelling (1984) and Thaler (1980) argue that the key to resolving our internal conflicts is to create means of controlling the destructive impulses of the short-term decision maker. Because the "should" self is the planner, it can develop advance schemes to corral, co-opt, or control the "want" self. Thaler and Shefrin (1981) compare the multiple-selves problem to the agency problem faced by the owner of a firm who employs a clever but self-interested manager. The owner's challenge is to structure the manager's job in a way that makes the manager want to act in the owner's best interest. In this metaphor, the firm's owner is the "should" self, planning to control the impulses of the "want" self.

Specifically, the "should" self could search for ways to bring the interests of the two selves into alignment. For someone on a diet, this might mean finding enjoyable forms of physical exercise and making sure that healthful food is available when the "want" self gets hungry. The "should" self might also anticipate situations in which passion tends to overcome reason and avoid those situations entirely. Some casinos offer self-exclusion lists for problem gamblers, but casino managers, facing their own want/should problem of sorts, have proven quite accommodating to gamblers who change their minds and arrive with money to spend (Holt, 2006).

For precisely this reason, inflexible pre-commitment can increase the effectiveness of such rules. For example, alcoholics can take a drug called Antabuse, which produces violent nausea if they subsequently consume alcohol. Similarly, paternalistic outside parties (such as parents, an employer, or the government) sometimes try to help people avoid succumbing to the "want" self. Many states try to protect consumers from short-term impulses by legislating revocability periods for high-priced items (e.g., condominium share purchases).

Advice from decision theorists. The multiple-selves problem implies that, in the words of Walt Whitman (1855/2001), we each "contain multitudes." Acknowledging this complexity represents a challenge for decision analysts, who usually assume decision makers have coherent and internally consistent preferences. Howard Raiffa's (1968) approach to the problem is particularly intriguing. He advocates acknowledging both these internal inconsistencies as well as the fact that two competing preferences cannot *both* be in an individual's interest. Specifically, Raiffa recommends questioning each self to find out which one is making the error. Perhaps the "should" self can confront the "want" self with its limited perspective—for example, the danger of ignoring long-term implications of a decision. Alternatively, it could be that the "want" self can elucidate for the "should" self some of the more elusive feelings that have been neglected by its formal analysis. Raiffa suggests that this communication should take place until reconciliation occurs.

Raiffa's approach recognizes the importance of giving voice, opportunity, and input to the emotional and visceral needs of the want self. As Loewenstein (1996) notes, the "want" self can provide valuable input: "Hunger signals the need for nutritional input, pain indicates the impingement of some type of potentially harmful environmental factors, and emotions serve a range of interrupting, prioritizing, and energizing functions."

Advice from negotiation researchers. Raiffa's approach assumes that the two parts of the self can negotiate a settlement to their differences, given their mutual dependence on each other. Yet we can all think of instances in which the "should" self made a decision with the logic of self-interest, only to be overruled later by the impulsive behavior of the "want" self. For example, a diet or exercise regime could be sabotaged by an individual's failure to reconcile the "want" self to the "should" self's new agenda. For this reason, we recommend the development of a rational negotiation strategy for dealing with the "want" self. Our modification of Raiffa's advice grants the "want" self more autonomy and a stronger voice in the decision-making and negotiation process. By treating the "want" self as a negotiator who has the power to declare an impasse, we aim to bypass both the domination of the "should" self in the decision-making stage and the "want" self in the implementation stage.

We suggest that you impose several criteria on your negotiation between the "want" and "should" selves. First, require the two sides to reach an agreement, as ongoing conflict would lead the "should" self to continue to make a variety of decisions that the "want" self sabotages. Second, the agreement should be Pareto efficient (see Chapter 10); that is, there should be no other arrangement that the "want" self and the "should" self both prefer over the created agreement. This agreement might be reached through "discussions" and compromises between the two selves about key issues—for example, how often the "want" self will get to eat ice cream, how many days a week the "should" self will exercise, and so on. By agreeing to reasonable times and limits, the "want" self will likely be more willing to follow the agreement. Third, the "should" self must not push for an agreement that is outside the bargaining zone; that is, the terms must not be unacceptable to the "want" self, either currently or in the future. The "should" self must remember that there is no court of law for suing yourself for a contract violation—the "want" self can void the contract at any time.

SELF-SERVING REASONING

- The West blames the Third World for burning the rain forests and for overpopulation. At the same time, the Third World blames the West for pollution caused by industrialization and excessive consumption.

- A *U.S. News and World Report* survey asked, "If someone sues you and you win the case, should he pay your legal costs?" Eighty-five percent of respondents answered "yes." However, only 44 percent answered "yes" to this question: "If you sue someone and lose the case, should you pay his costs?" (Budiansky, Gest, & Fischer, 1995, p. 52)

- The use of tall smokestacks to reduce local air pollution contributes to the regional problem of acid rain. The higher the air pollution, the farther it travels from its source (Gore, 1992). When Northeastern Canada is affected by acid rain, citizens blame the industrialization of the Northeast and Midwest United States. The United States denies responsibility, claiming acid rain may be caused by the local burning of coal.

Perceptions and expectations are often biased in a self-serving manner (Babcock & Loewenstein, 1997; Diekmann, Samuels, Ross, & Bazerman, 1997). When presented with identical information, individuals perceive a situation in dramatically different ways, depending on their roles in the situation (Babcock, Loewenstein, Issacharoff, & Camerer, 1995). Evidence suggests that individuals first determine their preference for a certain outcome on the basis of self-interest and then justify this preference on the basis of fairness by changing the importance of attributes affecting what is fair (Messick & Sentis, 1983). While people frequently have the goal of reaching a fair solution, their assessments of what is fair are often biased by self-interest. For example, it is common for all parties in a conflict to suggest differing viable but self-serving solutions, which each party justifies based on abstract fairness criteria. Self-serving reasoning allows people to believe that it is honestly fair for them to have more of a given resource than an independent advisor would judge. The problem lies not in a desire to be unfair but in our failure to interpret information in an unbiased manner (Diekmann et al., 1997; Messick & Sentis, 1983).

Hastorf and Cantril (1954) asked student football fans from Princeton and Dartmouth to view a short film of a particularly rough football game between the two schools. Although both sides watched the same film, each side thought the opposing team played less fairly and engaged in more aggressive and unsportsmanlike conduct. The researchers observed that the two groups of students "saw a different game." Similarly, the United States and China, which together are responsible for 42 percent of human-caused greenhouse gas emissions, tend to blame each other for the problem of climate change. During a July 2009 visit to China, U.S. energy secretary Steven Chu and commerce secretary Gary Locke called on China to reverse the increase in its greenhouse-gas emissions. Chu claimed that if China refused to act, the country would emit more greenhouse gases in the next 30 years than the United States had emitted in its entire history. "Fifty years from now, we do not want the world to lay the blame for environmental catastrophe at the feet of China," said Locke (as quoted in Bradsher, 2009). Notably, China's official news agency, Xinhua, failed to mention China's role in climate change or the Americans' criticisms when reporting on the Chu and Locke speeches; instead, Xinhua focused on Locke's acknowledgment that the United States had been emitting greenhouse gases for 150 years.

As we discussed in our review of the confirmation heuristic in Chapter 3, when people encounter favorable information, they are likely to accept it uncritically. Negative information, however, produces more critical and suspicious evaluation. Dawson, Gilovich, and Regan (2002) nicely document our tendency to select standards of evidence in self-serving ways. They note that it sounds completely reasonable to accept an argument when the available data are consistent with the argument. On the other hand, it also seems reasonable to require the data to be overwhelmingly supportive. Dawson *et al* (2002) argue that when we want to believe an argument, we tend to ask "Can I believe this?" This is a far lower standard than we demand when we do not want to believe an argument: "*Must* I believe this?"

Illustrating this phenomenon, Ditto and Lopez (1992) told their research participants that they had to pick a colleague with whom they would work on a collaborative project. Each participant was told to pick the more intelligent of two potential coworkers. The participants were given information about the performances of the two coworkers on several tasks and were told to review the information until they were satisfied that they had picked the more intelligent partner. Participants were led to believe that one of the two coworkers was friendly and helpful and that the other was rude and inconsiderate. When the evidence seemed to suggest that the friendly coworker was the smarter one, people stopped searching for information and quickly chose him. When the evidence favored the jerk, however, people kept seeking more and more information, hoping to justify the choice they wanted to make.

Evidence for the automatic nature of biased perception comes from Balcetis and Dunning (2006). They told participants that they would be taking a taste test of one of two drinks standing before them: either (1) freshly squeezed orange juice or (2) a gelatinous, chunky, green, foul-smelling, somewhat viscous concoction labeled as a "veggie smoothie." Which drink they would have to taste would be determined by the random appearance of either a farm animal or a sea creature on a computer screen. For some participants, seeing a farm animal meant that they had a veggie smoothie in their future; for others, the sea creature had the same ominous significance. Participants were then shown an ambiguous picture that had features of both a horse and a seal. Balcetis and Dunning found that those who were hoping to see a farm animal saw only a horse and never registered the possibility of interpreting the same picture as a seal, and vice versa. The findings suggest that the filters and choices driving their selective perception may have occurred at a pre-conscious level.

If these biases occur at an unconscious level, then it ought to come as no surprise that people are unaware of their own vulnerability to bias (Pronin, Gilovich, & Ross, 2004). Intelligent, well-intentioned people come to biased conclusions even as they continue to believe in their own fairness and objectivity. In fact, this faith in objectivity often leads people to conclude that anyone who challenges their well-considered beliefs must himself be biased (Pronin et al., 2004). Auditors may find ways to excuse the questionable accounting practices of a valuable client, yet believe that their conclusions are consistent with generally accepted accounting practices (Moore, Tetlock, Tanlu, & Bazerman, 2006). CEOs can find ways to grant themselves huge bonuses while believing they are acting in best interests of the company's shareholders. Medical doctors can accept gifts from pharmaceutical manufacturers while believing that their clinical judgment has not been biased. And politicians can accept generous campaign contributions that they believe have not influenced their votes. For unethical behavior to legally qualify as fraud, the person engaging in such crimes must know at the time that she is behaving unethically. As always, the most effective lies are those we tell ourselves (von Hippel & Trivers, 2011). In Chapter 8, we will discuss the ethical implications of decision-making biases in greater detail.

EMOTIONAL INFLUENCES ON DECISION MAKING

In recent decades, researchers have made important progress toward understanding how specific emotions influence our judgments. This research began by examining the effects of generalized positive and negative moods. For instance, evidence suggested that a good mood increases reliance on heuristics and results in more biased judgments (Bodenhausen, Kramer, & Suesser, 1994). Researchers speculated that bad moods may trigger more deliberative (System 2) thought processes that could reduce biases in judgment (Forgas, 1995). However, too much contradictory evidence has emerged for this general claim to be true. For instance, sad people are more affected by anchors than are those in a more neutral state, and sad people make worse decisions as a result (Bodenhausen, Gabriel, & Lineberger, 2000). To examine these complications, we turn to the study of specific emotions.

Specific Emotions

Researchers have identified a small set of basic emotions, including happiness, sadness, fear, disgust, and anger, whose expressions are the same across cultures (Ekman, 1992). Each of these emotions activates a set of feelings and "appraisal tendencies" that prepare us to respond to the world in a certain way. For instance, fear makes our minds sensitive to risks and prepares our bodies to flee (Lerner & Keltner, 2001). Disgust focuses our attention on physical contamination and motivates us to purge our bodies and our minds of contaminating agents (Horberg, Oveis, Keltner, & Cohen, 2009; Rozin, Haidt, & McCauley, 1999). Sadness focuses attention on the self, leading people to ruminate more and motivating them to seek change (Cryder, Lerner, Gross, & Dahl, 2007). Anger is a particularly interesting emotion: although it is negative, it shares many features with happiness, including increased confidence, increased feelings of power, and decreased sensitivity to risk (Lerner & Tiedens, 2006). Social emotions such as compassion and pride are more complex, yet are still associated with a distinctive mindset (Oveis, Horberg, & Keltner, 2010).

Each of these emotions can influence judgment. For instance, Lerner, Small, and Loewenstein (2004) have found that one's emotional state can have a significant effect on the nature of the endowment effect. The endowment effect, which we introduced in Chapter 5, describes the fact that the value people place on a commodity is greater if they own the commodity than if they do not (Kahneman, Knetsch, & Thaler, 1990). Lerner and her colleagues (2004) explored what happens to selling prices of a commodity (the prices set by those who own it) and choice prices (the prices set by those who are choosing between the commodity and money) if sellers are in a sad or disgusted state rather than in a more neutral state. They induced disgust by showing participants a film clip depicting intimate use of an unsanitary toilet (from the film *Trainspotting*). They induced sadness by showing participants a film clip dramatizing the death of a boy's mentor (from *The Champ*). The results showed that disgust triggered the desire to expel, making people more eager to get rid of things they owned and avoid acquiring new things. Consequently, disgust led sellers to be willing to sell at lower prices and led potential buyers to lower how much they would be willing to pay. In contrast, sadness triggered the goal to change one's circumstances, thereby increasing people's willingness to pay to buy and decreasing the price they demanded to sell.

With this study, Lerner and her colleagues (2004) show how emotions can affect financial decisions. More interestingly, by manipulating emotion in a separate task that occurred prior to the buying and selling decisions, they show how emotional influences bleed over from one context to another, unrelated context. Even more important, this research demonstrates the need for a clear and precise understanding of how emotion affects decision making. Many scholars have assumed that emotions could be categorized simply into positive and negative emotions. But Lerner et al. (2004) show that two different negative emotions can create two very different patterns of effects.

Emotions are tightly wound up with our perception of risk (Slovic & Peters, 2006). Happy people are more optimistic; sad people are more pessimistic (George Loewenstein, Weber, Hsee, & Welch, 2001). In addition, fear and anxiety create risk-averse behavior (Lerner & Keltner, 2000). By contrast, angry people are especially willing to endure risk, and even appear quite optimistic with respect to risk (Leith & Baumeister, 1996; Tiedens & Linton, 2001). Angry people think that they are less susceptible to a wide variety of career and health risks (Lerner & Keltner, 2001). Angry people even believe their risk of heart disease is lower than do others (Taylor, Lerner, Sage, Lehman, & Seeman, 2004). This is ironic, because those who experience more anger actually put themselves at heightened risk of heart disease (Williams et al., 2000).

Mood-Congruent Recall

Depressed people often report that the bleakest aspect of their depression is that they cannot remember what it felt like to be happy. Similarly, when people are happy, they might have trouble recalling how they felt during more difficult times. Human resource consultants advise that it is best to ask the boss for a raise when he or she is in a good mood. The happy boss will find it easier to recall times when you performed well and is also more likely to feel optimistic about the company's ability to afford a raise for you.

The weather can also influence people's moods in ways that affect their perceptions. When pollsters call to ask how happy they are, people report being less satisfied with their lives overall on cloudy than on sunny days (Schwarz, 2001). This effect even extends to stock-market prices (Saunders, 1993): prices on the New York Stock Exchange are more likely to go up when it is sunny in New York than when it is cloudy. The pervasiveness of mood-consistent judgments may well be due to the same mental processes that generate the confirmation heuristic discussed in Chapter 3. We are simply better at remembering information consistent with our state of mind than information inconsistent with it.

Regret Avoidance

Another area in which emotions drive behavior is the anticipation of regret. Consider the following story:

> Imagine that you are at an out-of-town business meeting that runs late. As soon as you can break away, you head to the airport to catch the last flight home. If you miss the flight, which is scheduled to leave at 8:30 P.M., you will have to stay overnight and miss an important meeting the next day. You run into traffic and do not get to the airport until 8:52 P.M. You run to the gate, arriving there at 8:57 P.M. When you arrive, either:
>
> **a.** You find out that the plane left on schedule at 8:30 P.M., or
> **b.** You see the plane depart, having left the gate at 8:55 P.M.

Which is more upsetting, (a) or (b)? Most people quickly agree that (b) is more upsetting. Yet, both possibilities create the same net outcome for you—you've missed your flight, and will have to spend the night. Choice (b) simply highlights the counterfactual thought that, with any minor change in schedule, you could have made the flight (Kahneman & Miller, 1986; Kahneman & Tversky, 1982).

The impact of counterfactual thinking and feelings of regret have been central to the work of Medvec, Madey, and Gilovich (1995), who discovered the interesting fact that silver-medal winners at the Olympics are less happy with their achievement than bronze-medal winners. Obviously, any athlete would choose to win silver over bronze. However, when these researchers coded the initial reactions and the facial expressions of athletes as they received their medals, they found that the bronze-medal winners appeared to be happier. Medvec et al. concluded that while the bronze-medal winners are thrilled simply to be medalists, silver-medal winners can't forget that they almost won the gold.

The motivation to minimize the opportunity for regret can lead people to make decisions that are suboptimal with respect to actual outcomes. For instance, one of the reasons people are reluctant to switch doors in the Monty Hall Problem we discussed in Chapter 4 is that they fear the sting of regret if they switch to an empty door and learn that the prize was behind the door they chose initially (Gilovich, Medvec, & Chen, 1995). Larrick (1993) provides evidence that decision-makers will distort their decisions to avoid such negative feedback, and he identifies two ways in which they can do so. First, they can choose options that shield them from feedback on foregone alternatives. Second, when feedback on the decision not chosen is inevitable, they can make choices that are likely to compare favorably to foregone options. In this context, it may be useful to have your "should" self compare the various outcomes. The two selves also will need to negotiate with each other over the relative value of better outcomes (such as winning a silver rather than a bronze medal) compared with the pain of regret.

SUMMARY

Too often, people view their emotions as uncontrollable. The fact is, even if we can't stop ourselves from feeling, we may be able to limit the negative effects of our emotions on the quality of our decisions. Johnson and Tversky (1983) and Lerner, Goldberg, and Tetlock (1998) note that people are typically unaware of the influence of their emotions on their decisions. Thus, though we may feel that we are angry, we may falsely believe that anger will not influence our judgment. Or perhaps even more dangerously, we incorrectly infer that our righteous fury is a consequence of our well-considered judgment (Haidt, 2001). Perhaps a better appreciation of the literature can help create the knowledge that, just like everyone else, you will be affected by your emotional state. It may simply help to be more aware of the ways in which emotion can bias our judgment.

To neutralize the negative impact of our emotions on our decisions, we must begin by identifying our emotions and their sources. Labeling our emotions in itself can be an effective means of reducing their strength (Lieberman et al., 2007). Emotion researchers know, for instance, that asking research participants to explicitly identify their emotional state can often eliminate the effect of an emotion manipulation. But unpleasant emotions are sometimes even more effectively neutralized by identifying the *source* of the emotion. This allows people to react to the causal stimulus with System 2's more cognitive assessments, rather than with System 1's impulsive and emotional reactions. Earlier we noted that the weather influences people's reports of life satisfaction. But consider what happens when, just before asking about a question about life satisfaction, a pollster asks a respondent, "So how's the weather where you are?" This question eliminates the effect of weather on responses to the life satisfaction question (Schwarz & Strack, 1999).

Another strategy for managing the negative impact of emotions is to make decision makers accountable for their choices. Lerner and Tetlock (1999) have found that study participants who must in some way justify their decisions learn to hold their emotions in check and move toward more systematic, System 2 thinking. This may be because such articulation is itself a System 2 process or because verbalization can neutralize an emotion. To create such accountability for yourself, you might report your rationale for a decision to your boss or simply write down an explanation for your decision for yourself. Logically and empirically, the simple cognition of accountability has the ability to reduce the likelihood of acting on emotions in ways that you will later regret.

Finally, it may be possible to institutionalize controls on emotion. It is widely known that government policies can be overly influenced by the vividness of various issues (see Chapter 3). As a society, we tend to allocate scarce resources to vivid concerns rather than to the issues where scarce resources would do the most good. Why? Vivid stories create emotional reactions; these emotions, in turn, lead us to misallocate scarce resources. Sunstein (2002) argues, "Just as the Senate was designed to have a 'cooling effect' on the passion of the House of Representatives, so cost–benefit analysis might ensure that policy is driven not by hysteria or alarm, but by a full appreciation of the effects of relevant risks and their control." Essentially, Sunstein suggests that institutionalizing the use of logical decision-making processes would protect our society from being overly influenced by temporary emotions. Unfortunately, in the U.S. Congress, Democrats too often have rejected the use of cost-benefit analysis out of hand, while Republicans have conducted biased cost-benefit analyses to support their viewpoints. Congress should use cost-benefit analysis to make wise decisions rather than rejecting it outright or using it to push for partisan policies.

This chapter has offered a different perspective on decision biases than was offered in the first five cognition-oriented chapters. Specifically, it focused on biases that emanate from motivational and emotional influences within the individual. We have reviewed the motivational pressures of momentary desires, the need to view ourselves in a positive manner, the tendency to view events according to how we would like them to turn out, and the systematic influence of emotions on our decisions. Certainly, other motivational and emotional influences exist. This chapter simply highlights the additive role of motivation and emotion, beyond the role of cognition, in helping us understand unusual patterns in our decision-making processes. While it may be difficult for us to control our emotional responses, a fuller understanding of how they influence our choices is likely to improve our decisions.

CHAPTER SEVEN

The Escalation of Commitment

If at first you don't succeed, try, try, again. Then quit. No use being a damn fool about it.

—*W. C. Fields*

In the previous chapters, we examined single decisions and the ways in which judgmental and motivational biases and the framing of information can influence our responses to them. However, many critical managerial decisions concern a series of choices rather than an isolated decision. We are prone to a particular type of bias when approaching decisions serially—namely, a tendency to escalate commitment to our initial decision. This chapter opens with an explanation of the individual tendency to escalate commitment. In the second section, we show how a competitive environment increases the tendency to escalate commitment. The third section provides a taxonomy of explanations for the psychological tendency to escalate and offers recommendations for eliminating nonrational escalation behavior.

Consider the following examples of situations that invite escalation:

- You personally decided to hire a new manager to work for you. Although you had expected excellent achievement, early reports suggest that she is not performing as you had hoped. Should you fire her? You have invested a fair amount of time and money in her training, and you wonder if she's just in the process of learning the ropes. You decide to invest in her success a bit longer and provide additional resources to help her achieve. Two months later, her performance is still subpar. Although you have even more reason to "cut your losses," you also have a greater investment in this employee. When should you give up on your "investment"?

- You accept a position with a prestigious consulting firm, believing that the job offers an excellent career opportunity in an organization that has room for you to grow. Two years later, you have not progressed as rapidly as you had expected. Anxious to demonstrate your worth to the company, you decide to invest large amounts of unpaid overtime to get ahead. Still you fail to get the recognition you think you deserve. By now, you have been with the organization for several years and would lose numerous benefits, including stock options, if you decide to leave. You are in your late thirties and feel you have invested some of your best years with this company. Do you quit?

- You work for a private equity firm and make a decision to invest $2 million in a start-up venture. You personally argued for this investment against some skeptics in your firm. One year later, the CEO from the start-up appears in your office and says: "I have bad news, and I have good news. The bad news is that the company is running out of cash. Without additional funds, we will definitely go under, and you will lose the $2 million. The good news is that I am quite confident that if you invest another $1 million, we can work out the bugs in our invention and still be a great success." Do you invest the additional $1 million?

Although each of these decisions represents a very different situation, they share a number of common elements. In each case, you have to make a decision as a result of a previous decision. You hired the employee. You took the job. You made the investment. In each case, you have invested a great deal of time, effort, and resources in your selected course of action, and now things are not working out as you had hoped.

We frequently face similar decisions of varying importance. Should you sink more money into that old wreck of a car? How long should you stay on hold with an airline before hanging up? When the price of a stock that you own goes down, how far should you let it go before selling it? Inertia frequently leads us to continue on our previously selected course of action, or we may feel we have "too much invested to quit." How do you know when to quit? At what point does continuing on the same course of action become irrational? And why, when such behavior becomes irrational, is it so common? These are the central questions of this chapter.

Although we are taught from an early age to "try, try again," the fact is that misdirected persistence can lead us to waste a great deal of time, energy, and money. However, directed persistence can lead to commensurate payoffs. The key to making intelligent decisions in dynamic contexts such as those presented above is being able to discriminate between situations in which persistence will pay off and those in which it will not.

A variety of authors from different fields have presented ideas relevant to the three hypothetical situations described above, using a number of different terms (such as escalation, entrapment, and persistence) to describe commitment to a previously selected course of action. In this chapter, we define nonrational escalation as the degree to which an individual escalates commitment to a previously selected course of action to a point beyond that which a rational model of decision making would prescribe.

Accountants and economists provide insight into how to handle these scenarios. Experts from these areas tell us that in such situations we need to recognize that the time and expenses that we have already invested are "sunk costs." That is, these costs are historical, irrecoverable, and should not be considered in any future course of action. Our reference point for action should be our current state, and we should consider all alternative courses of action by evaluating only the future costs and benefits associated with each alternative. For example, if you are considering whether to quit a doctoral program, it is irrelevant whether it took you six months or four years to get to the point you are at now; the key decision involves the future costs and benefits of exiting versus the future costs and benefits of continuing.

Accounting professors teach their students to recognize sunk costs in accounting contexts, yet the decisions of managers trained in accounting suggest that the textbook advice to ignore sunk costs seldom translates to wise solutions to real-world problems. Why is it so hard for managers to truly absorb the sunk-cost concept? In part, because typical training of the concept lacks a clear description of the reasons that we intuitively tend to include sunk costs in our calculations. To eliminate escalatory behavior from our repertoire, we need to identify the existing nonrational behavior within ourselves, "unfreeze" that behavioral pattern, and prepare for change.

Decision makers who commit themselves to a particular course of action tend to make subsequent decisions that continue that commitment beyond the level suggested by rationality. As a consequence, they often allocate resources in a way that justifies previous commitments, whether or not those initial commitments now appear valid. The following section examines the components of this behavior in more detail.

THE UNILATERAL ESCALATION PARADIGM

Put yourself in the equity firm officer's predicament again. Our description of the escalation situation has probably biased you to assume that it would be "bad" for you to escalate your commitment to the first investment by granting another one. The fact is, it might be economically rational to continue your investment in the start-up. After all, it is not always wise to quit at the first sign of failure. Many would argue that doing so is a sign of a serious psychological deficiency.

How do you separate the rational from the nonrational tendency to escalate? One body of knowledge suggests that you should try to determine the rational course of action, ignoring the fact that you personally made the initial monetary commitment. A number of studies have attempted to separate the effect of being the person who made the initial commitment from a later decision. Specifically, these studies have investigated the difference between how two groups of decision makers make a second decision that follows an initial failure. One group has already made the initial decision, while the other group inherits the initial decision and thus has less of a stake in it.

In Staw's initial study of this type (1976), one group of participants (labeled the high-responsibility participants) was asked to allocate research-and-development funds to one of two operating divisions of an organization. The participants were then told that, after three years, the investment either had proven successful or unsuccessful and that they were now faced with a second allocation decision concerning the same division. A second group (labeled the low-responsibility participants) was told that another financial officer of the firm had made a decision that had been either successful or unsuccessful (the same content information about success or failure was provided to this group as to the previous one) and that they were to make a second allocation of funds concerning that division. When the outcome of the previous decision was negative (an unsuccessful investment), the high-responsibility participants allocated significantly more funds to the original division in the second allocation than the low-responsibility participants did. In contrast, for successful initial decisions, the amount of money allocated in the second decision was roughly the same across participants. Given that the greater escalation of commitment occurred only for the participants who had made a previously unsuccessful decision, Staw concluded that the mechanism underlying escalation is self-justification. That is, once an individual makes an initial decision to embark on a course of action, negative feedback is dissonant with the initial decision. One way to eliminate this dissonance is to escalate commitment to the initial action in the belief that it will eventually lead to success.

We also know a fair amount about the conditions that tend to lead people to escalate commitment to a chosen course of action. Staw and Ross (1978) found that the tendency to escalate commitment was more pronounced when the failure could be explained away with a causal account unrelated to the individual's initial decision (e.g., a shift in the economy instead of poor market appeal). Bazerman, Giuliano, and Appelman (1984) found that groups are less likely than individuals to escalate commitment; however, groups that escalate tend to do so to a greater degree than individuals. Apparently, the presence of multiple members increases the likelihood that the group will recognize the irrationality of escalating commitment to previous unsuccessful actions. If this realization does not occur, however, the group dynamic reinforces support for the initial decision and increases the level of rationalization to escalate commitment. Schoorman (1988) found that supervisors who participate in a hiring or promotion decision, and who agree with the eventual decision to hire or promote, positively bias that employee's subsequent performance appraisals. In addition, supervisors who participate in such a decision and disagree with the actual decision to hire or promote bias subsequent performance appraisals that employee in a negative direction.

Staw and Hoang (1995) found that National Basketball Association teams escalate their commitment to their draft choices. The sunk costs that teams incur are the use of draft choices and money to select and sign players. Staw and Hoang found that draft order had strong effects on playing time, likelihood of being traded, and survival in the league, even after taking into account the performance of players. Friedman's (1996) account of the decisions of mountain climbers to go for the peak provides chilling insight into the role of escalation in vivid life-and-death situations. Interestingly, Friedman presented his paper at a conference in memory of Jeffrey Z. Rubin, a noted escalation scholar and mountain climber who died in a 1995 climbing accident. Rubin's climbing partner had turned around earlier, believing the weather conditions were too dangerous.

Taken together, the foregoing evidence suggests that managers should beware of the difficulty of separating initial decisions from related future decisions. Managers can take steps within their organizations to combat nonrational escalation of commitment. Some hedge funds rotate portfolios on a regular basis so that the same trader who bought a commodity does not also make the decision to sell. Of course, mechanisms such as this are not amenable to situations where it is necessary for one person to make a string of related decisions. In general, we should try to be cognizant of the fact that our decisions will tend to be biased by our past actions and that we have a natural individual tendency to escalate commitment, particularly after receiving negative feedback.

THE COMPETITIVE ESCALATION PARADIGM

In the unilateral escalation paradigm we have just described, justifications for nonrational escalation lie within the individual; we escalate because of our own previous commitments. In the competitive escalation paradigm, additional competitive forces feed the escalatory process. This section examines the process of escalation in competitive situations.

Imagine that two companies, A and B, are the most important in a given industry. Company C, an important third player, is their potential target: either a key supplier or a key buyer. C is worth $1 billion as a stand-alone company and would be worth $1.2 billion if managed by A or B, as a result of the synergy in the possible combination of A and C or of B and C. If A were to acquire C, B would be at a catastrophic disadvantage and would lose $0.5 billion. It would be similarly destructive to A if B were to acquire C; A would also lose $0.5 billion. Finally, if either A or B makes an offer on C, the other company will learn of the offer. Question: As the head of Company A, what do you do?

A typical response by executives to whom we have posed this problem is to offer $1.1 billion to Company C, which, if accepted, would create a $100 million benefit to A and C. However, this offer, once made, creates a problem for B: if B does not act, B loses $0.5 billion. So, rather than suffering a $0.5 billion loss, B offers $1.2 billion to break even. Now A has a problem: If A does not act, A loses $0.5 billion. So, A offers $1.3 billion to limit its losses to $100 million and avoid suffering a $0.5 billion loss. The problem is now B's, and we can easily see the auction escalating to an amount around $1.7 billion, where both A and B end up losing $0.5 billion in this competition. Any party quitting below that amount would still suffer a $0.5 billion loss.

This story is consistent with the lack of profit obtained by buyers in the merger mania of the 1980s: in the aggregate, the synergy that was obtained in acquisitions went to the sellers. This story is also consistent with a classroom auction that we have run many times. It works as follows. The instructor at the front of the classroom takes a $20 bill out of his/her pocket and announces the following:

> I am about to auction off this $20 bill. You are free to participate or just watch the
> bidding of others. People will be invited to call out bids in multiples of $1 until no

further bidding occurs, at which point the highest bidder will pay the amount bid and win the $20. The only feature that distinguishes this auction from traditional auctions is a rule that the second-highest bidder must also pay the amount that he or she bid, although he or she will obviously not win the $20. For example, if Bill bid $3 and Jane bid $4, and bidding stopped, I would pay Jane $16 ($20 – $4), and Bill, the second-highest bidder, would pay me $3.

Would you be willing to bid $1 to start the auction? (Make this decision before reading further.)

We have run this auction with undergraduate students, graduate students, and executives. The pattern is always the same. The bidding starts out fast and furious until it reaches the $12 to $16 range. At this point, everyone except the two highest bidders drops out of the auction. The two bidders then begin to feel the trap. One bidder has bid $16 and the other $17. The $16 bidder must either bid $18 or suffer a $16 loss. The uncertain option of bidding further (a choice that might produce a gain if the other guy quits) seems more attractive than the current sure loss, so the $16 bidder bids $18. This continues until the bids are $19 and $20. Surprisingly, the decision to bid $21 is very similar to all previous decisions: You can accept a $19 loss or continue and reduce your loss if the other guy quits. Of course, the rest of the group roars with laughter when the bidding goes over $20—which it almost always does. Obviously, the bidders are acting irrationally. But which bids are irrational?

Skeptical readers should try out the auction for themselves. The bidding typically ends between $20 and $70, but hits $100 with some regularity. In total, the two of us have earned over $30,000 running these auctions in classes over the last twenty years. (Note: While we win this money fair and square, we do not keep it. The money either has been used to provide food and beverage for the class or immediately given to charity.)

Shubik (1971) introduced the dollar auction. Max adjusted the auction from $1 to $20 for inflation and to sharpen the impact. Teger (1980) has used the paradigm extensively to investigate the question of why individuals escalate their commitment to a previously selected course of action. Teger argues that participants naively enter the auction not expecting the bidding to exceed $1 (or $20); "After all, who would bid more than a dollar for a dollar?" The potential gain, coupled with the possibility of "winning" the auction, is enough reason to enter the auction. Once an individual is in the auction, it takes only a few extra dollars to stay in the auction rather than accept a sure loss. This "reasoning," along with a strong need to justify entering the auction in the first place, is enough to keep most bidders bidding for an extended period of time. Recently, with more senior executive groups, we have shifted to $100 auctions, in $5 increments. The basic pattern remains unchanged.

Thoughtful examination of the dollar auction suggests that individuals who choose to bid are entering a trap. While it is true that one more bid may inspire the other party to quit, if both bidders hold this belief, the result can be catastrophic. Yet, without knowing the expected bidding patterns of the opponent, we cannot conclude that continued bidding is clearly wrong. What is the right course of action? Successful decision makers must learn to identify traps, and the key to the problem lies in identifying the auction as a trap and never making even a very small bid. One strategy for identifying competitive traps is to try to consider the decision from the perspective of the other decision maker(s). In the dollar auction, this strategy would quickly tell you that the auction looks just as attractive to other bidders as it does to you. With this knowledge, you can accurately predict what will occur and stay out of the auction.

You can also develop strategies that discourage escalatory behavior by your competitors. In the $20 bill auction, one class member could organize the class to collude against the auctioneer. That class member could arrange for one member to bid $1 and for everyone else to refrain from bidding, and the class could later divide the $19 profit—communication can be a very effective tool.

The same is true of the earlier scenario involving companies A, B, and C. In 1995, the basic pattern of this story played out with American Airlines, United Airlines, and USAir. USAir, the nation's fifth largest airline, announced in 1995 that it was for sale at the right price. Analysts quickly speculated that the two industry leaders, United and American Airlines, were likely to be interested. However, their analyses were limited to the expectation that the value of USAir was higher to United or American as an acquisition than as a stand-alone company. These analyses ignored information suggesting that United and American would be extremely motivated to avoid losing a bidding war, since the sale of USAir to American would be a major setback for United, and the sale of USAir to United would be a similarly damaging blow to American. As the head of American or United, what would you do?

American developed a strategy aimed at avoiding the escalatory war described above. Robert Crandall, the chairperson of American, wrote an open letter to his company's 118,000 employees that stated:

> We continue to believe, as we always have, that the best way for American to increase its size and reach is by internal growth—not by consolidation. . . . So we will not be the first to make a bid for USAir. On the other hand, if United seeks to acquire USAir, we will be prepared to respond with a bid, or by other means as necessary, to protect American's competitive position (Ziemba, 1995).

Although the letter was addressed to American Airlines employees, it was obvious that the most important target of this message was United. The message was clear: Keep things as they are, or we will both end up in a money-losing battle. Crandall's letter was effective in avoiding an escalatory war (no offers were made on USAir in 1995). Five years later, when United made a preemptive bid on USAir for 232 percent of the company's stand-alone value, both United and American stock prices fell sharply.

Failing to learn from Crandall's successful strategy, Johnson & Johnson (J&J) got into a bidding war for Guidant, a medical products manufacturer. J&J began with a bid of $25.4 billion for Guidant in December 2004 (Feder, 2006).

Initially, this appeared to be a profitable deal for both Guidant stockholders and for J&J. About six months later, however, before the deal closed, the *New York Times* uncovered a scandal involving one of Guidant's products. For three years, Guidant had failed to tell doctors that its implantable defibrillator contained a flaw that had caused it to malfunction in some instances. The FDA opened an investigation into Guidant, and soon the company announced a product recall of its defibrillator.

In fall 2005, J&J indicated that it wanted to renegotiate the terms of its deal with Guidant, citing concerns about the federal investigation and Guidant's "short-term results and long-term outlook" (Feder & Sorkin, 2005). New York Attorney General Eliot Spitzer announced a lawsuit against Guidant on the same day that the FTC conditionally approved the J&J/Guidant merger. J&J chose not to execute the deal, and Guidant sued J&J to force the acquisition (Feder, 2006). As negative press surrounding Guidant mounted (Meier, 2005), J&J entered a revised $21.5 billion bid for Guidant on November 16.

A third firm, Boston Scientific, a key J&J competitor, realized that they would be at a strategic disadvantage if J&J were to acquire Guidant. Indeed, in the time between J&J's initial offer for Guidant and its revised bid, Boston Scientific's stock price fell from $35.88 to $25 per share. On December 5, 2005, Boston Scientific offered $24.7 billion for Guidant. Meanwhile, Guidant's problems worsened; on December 27, the FDA released a warning letter that it had sent to Guidant about problems with its products (Bajaj, 2005).

Nonetheless, negotiations among the three companies continued into 2006. Guidant tentatively accepted J&J's raised bid of $23.2 billion on January 11. The next day, Boston Scientific upped its bid to $25 billion. The following day, Guidant provisionally accepted J&J's newly revised bid of $24.2 billion. On the 17th, Boston Scientific offered to buy Guidant for $27 billion, more than J&J's initial bid prior to Guidant's legal troubles (Feder & Sorkin, 2005). On January 25, J&J decided to bow out of the race, and Guidant accepted Boston Scientific's bid (Harris & Feder, 2006; Saul, 2006).

The next day, Boston Scientific's share price fell to $23.15—almost $2 lower than it had been prior to the company's first bid for Guidant. (Notably, J&J's share price had fallen every time it announced a bid on Guidant.) Months later, in June 2006, Boston Scientific was forced to recall 23,000 Guidant pacemakers. The company's share price had fallen below $17 per share.

Both J&J and Boston Scientific aggressively pursued the takeover of a company that had obvious technological, legal, financial, and public-image liabilities. These decisions caused the two companies' stock prices to fall. This outcome is not surprising. In takeover contests where the losing bidder faces a loss in market share or competitive position, the natural outcome can be overpayment for target firms. Bidders become indifferent between winning the auction by overpaying and losing the auction and suffering a loss in competitive position.

Escalation can also occur in reverse-bid auctions where many sellers compete with one another to offer the lowest price to a buyer. These types of auctions are common in the procurement, legal, construction, and consulting industries, as several firms will often compete for one potentially profitable client by submitting a series of bids that progressively decline in estimated cost to the buyer. In both the $20 auction and in corporate bidding wars, bidders typically fail to consider the perspective of the other party and continue to bid to justify their initial strategy. The auction ultimately leads to dramatic levels of financial loss when the two parties forget their original objective of earning money and switch to the objective of beating the other party. This is when the auctioneer does especially well!

The competitive-escalation paradigm has much in common with Staw's unilateral-escalation paradigm. In both cases, the decision maker makes an initial decision that he or she feels a need to justify through future decisions and reaches a point where he or she has "too much invested to quit." However, there is one major difference between the two paradigms: in the dollar auction, competition with the other party—that is, the desire to "win"—serves as added motivation to escalate commitment.

WHY DOES ESCALATION OCCUR?

The previous sections have provided some clues about the conditions under which escalation of commitment occurs. The first step toward eliminating nonrational escalation from our decisions is to identify the psychological factors that feed it. The existing literature clearly suggests that there are multiple reasons for escalation. Building on findings presented in earlier chapters, this section provides a taxonomy of these reasons. The first three classes of explanations—perceptual biases, judgmental biases, and impression management—are general to all of the examples of escalation presented. The fourth class of explanations, competitive irrationality, differentiates the unilateral-escalation paradigm from the competitive-escalation paradigm. After presenting each class of explanation, we consider the implications for eliminating escalation.

Perceptual Biases

Consider the case at the beginning of this chapter, in which you made the decision to hire the employee who subsequently performed below your expectations. Evidence presented in this chapter suggests that your perception of the employee's performance may be biased by your initial decision. That is, you may notice information that supports your hiring decision and ignore information that contradicts your initial decision. Similarly, in the start-up venture case, after making the initial investment decision, you may have a greater tendency to notice positive information about the start-up than negative information about it.

This phenomenon can be predicted by the common tendency, discussed in Chapter 2, to pay more attention to confirming than disconfirming information. Similarly, Staw (1980) suggests that administrators often protect their initial decisions by actively seeking out information that supports these decisions—for example, information that suggests an employee is performing well. Caldwell and O'Reilly (1982) empirically show that participants who freely choose a particular course of action will then filter information selectively to maintain commitment to that course of action.

The perceptual biases that result from our commitment to a particular course of action suggest a number of corrective procedures. As recommended in Chapter 2, when we are making a decision, we need to search vigilantly for disconfirming information to balance out the confirming information that we intuitively seek. This need is particularly pronounced in serial decisions, where we have a natural tendency toward escalation. In addition, establishing monitoring systems that help us check our perceptions before making subsequent judgments or decisions could prove useful. For instance, by having an objective ider evaluate our openness to disconfirming information, we could reduce or inate our perceptual barrier to nonescalatory behavior.

One way to teach ourselves to look for disconfirming information is to consider possibility that we may be vulnerable to escalating commitment before even ring a situation. If we merely imagine how regretful we would be if we _____lated commitment, we may be less likely to do so in the future. Ku (2008) demonstrated the importance of regret in reducing escalation by having participants consider a hypothetical situation where they escalated commitment in an auction and experienced a bad outcome. Just by considering how regretful they would be in such a situation, people became less likely to escalate their commitment in a future auction.

Judgmental Biases

After we filter the information we need to make a subsequent decision, it becomes time to make that decision. In this section, we argue that any loss from an initial investment (such as bidding more than $20 in a $20 bill auction, or more than the initial research-and-development funding in Staw's unilateral escalation paradigm) will systematically distort our judgment toward continuing the previously selected course of action. The logic of this prediction lies in the framing concepts developed in Chapter 5. As you will recall, individuals tend to be risk averse to positively framed problems and risk seeking to negatively framed problems.

In 1995, Nick Leeson showed the dramatic consequences that can result from escalation of commitment to avoid losses. Leeson was an up-and-coming young manager at Barings Bank when he was assigned to manage the bank's Singapore office. As Leeson recounts in his 1997 book, *Rogue Trader*, he engaged in some unlucky trades using bank money. The risk-averse option would have been to accept his small losses at the outset and move on to less risky investments. Instead, he hid his losses and continued to gamble on risky investments with ever-larger sums of money, always hoping to dig himself out of the hole that he had created. From Chapter 5, we know that most of us tend to be risk seeking in the domain of losses. Leeson's luck did not turn. By the time his losses were discovered, they had mounted to $1.4 billion. The result was the collapse of the venerable 233-year-old Barings Bank. Leeson himself was caught trying to flee the country and was sent to prison.

Now reconsider how the situation might have turned out if a different manager at Barings had been given the choice of whether to continue to pursue Leeson's risky investment strategies after he had lost a few million dollars. This person would have been likely to evaluate the potential consequences from a different reference point. Without having made the initial decision or having attempted to hide it, this manager would have been more likely to choose against continued risky investment.

Impression Management

Let's return to the hiring decision from the beginning of this chapter. Even if your perception and judgment led you to conclude that the underachieving employee should be fired, you might not choose to fire her. Why not? Firing the employee would be tantamount to a public announcement that your earlier decision was a mistake. You might decide to keep the employee on simply to "save face." Managing the impressions of others serves as a third reason for escalating commitment.

In addition to not wanting to admit failure, we also try to appear consistent to others. Increasing our commitment to our previous actions is one sign of consistency. Staw and Ross (1980) suggest that our society perceives administrators whose actions are consistent as better leaders than those who change their behavior or opinions. As we mentioned in Chapter 2, John Kerry's failed bid for the U.S. presidency in 2004 ran up against this perception. Many voters expressed grave misgivings about Kerry's "waffling" over the Iraq war. Kerry had voted for a resolution in the U.S. Senate giving President Bush the authority to go to war in Iraq but later was heavily critical of the war in his own presidential campaign. Kerry's now-infamous explanation for his stance on the Iraq war—"I voted for it before I voted against it"—was cited as evidence of his indecisiveness. News stories with headlines such as "Kerry's Top Ten Flip-flops" became common (CBS News, 2004).

George W. Bush's campaign skillfully used Kerry's apparent inconsistency to imply hypocrisy and fuel concerns that voters could not rely on him to stick to his convictions. By contrast, Bush's campaign ads heralded him as offering "Steady leadership in times of change." Bush's consistency seemed to matter more than the fact that his stance on many issues, from the Iraq war to the Patriot Act to domestic spying, were not particularly popular with voters. Bush's unwillingness to revise his position on key issues, regardless of their unpopularity or their impracticality, was regarded as evidence of strength of character and steadfast determination. "You may not always agree with me, but you know what I stand for," Bush proudly announced (Webb, 2004). Obviously, public expectations of consistency can lead to what looks like overprecision in judgment.

In his book *Profiles in Courage*, John F. Kennedy (1956) wrote that the most courageous decisions that politicians must make are those favoring an action that they believe to be in the best interests of their constituency, yet that they know will be disfavored by that very same constituency. Staw and Ross's (1980) findings suggest that this conflict is particularly severe when an actic⟨ning one's back on a previously supported course of action.

An interesting paradox results: To make the best decision for your organization, you should focus on future costs and benefits, ignoring any previous commitments. Yet empirical evidence shows that you are more likely to be rewarded for escalating commitment than for changing course (Ross & Staw, 1986). From an organizational standpoint, this suggests that we need to replace systems that encourage impression management with those that reward good decisions. To do this, managers must convey to all members of the organization that impression management at the expense of high-quality decisions will not be tolerated. Second, organizations should strive to match employees' values to those of the organization by modifying reward systems. The organization wants managers to make smart organizational decisions; managers want to make decisions that will further their careers. When rewards are based on results, employees will hide bad results by escalating commitment to their initial decisions. When management determines rewards by looking at the decision process, not at the outcome, employees will be motivated to make the best possible decisions at different stages, whether or not their initial decisions have been judged to be correct (Staw & Ross, 1987).

Competitive Irrationality

The previous three explanations for escalation can be generalized to both the unilateral and competitive paradigms. Research on competitive irrationality, however, adds an additional insight that distinguishes between the two paradigms. Specifically, competitive irrationality refers to a situation in which two parties engage in an activity that is clearly irrational in terms of the expected outcomes to both sides, despite the fact that it is difficult to identify specific irrational actions by either party.

Many people would argue that getting involved in the dollar auction is an irrational decision. While this is a very reasonable perspective, the argument is not completely valid. If it makes sense for you not to bid, then it does not make sense for anyone else to bid. If no one else plays, then one person can bid a small amount and get a bargain. This reasoning sounds logical, but it depends on a strong assumption: that everyone else will have reasoned through the problem and will decide to stay out. If this assumption does not hold—and it has never held in the hundreds of times we have played this game in our classes—then you find yourself as the second bidder, stuck in an escalation trap.

We argued earlier that continuing to bid then depends on your estimation of the likelihood that the other party will quit. Obviously, the same reasoning applies to the other party. If it is possible for someone to get $20 cheaply (for $1, for example), then it must be rational for one individual to be able to bid. Thus, in many ways, competitive irrationality presents an unresolved paradox rather than an explanation of escalation. The main recommendation offered by research on escalation and competitive irrationality is that many situations may look like opportunities but prove to be traps when you have fully considered the likely actions of others.

Perhaps the most dangerous trap is the competitive motive to "win" rather than to seek one's own gain. Winning involves besting others in the competition. It leads our students to continue bidding for the $20 bill after the bidding has passed $20. It leads bidders at art auctions to bid more than they thought a piece of art was worth before the bidding began (Ku, Malhotra, & Murnighan, 2005). And it can drive the final price higher at auctions with lots of bidders, even when that same product is available more cheaply elsewhere (Ku, Galinsky, & Murnighan, 2006). When two parties become determined to beat the other side—be it companies battling for market share, ethnic groups battling for dominance, or estranged spouses jockeying for a more advantageous divorce settlement—the stage is set for an escalatory battle in which both lose.

INTEGRATION

This chapter has suggested four additive causes that contribute to our tendency to escalate commitment to a previously selected course of action. Each one can trigger escalation independently, but they more often act together to increase a decision maker's nonrational tendency to continue a previous mistake. To reduce escalation, we must attack each cause at the individual and organizational levels.

Overall, the findings on the tendency to escalate suggest that managers need to take an experimental approach to management. That is, as a manager, you should make a decision and implement it, but be open to dropping your commitment and shifting to another course of action if the first plan does not work out. This means constantly reassessing the rationality of future commitments and learning to identify failures early.

Finally, a caveat: While this chapter has dealt with situations in which people take commitment too far, it is also important to consider the other side of the spectrum. In certain scenarios, you should maintain or even escalate your commitment to a chosen course of action, primarily to keep your options open. In business and personal relationships, you may feel as if you should give up when a situation becomes difficult. It is important to realize, however, that by ending a commitment, you may lose out on all future benefits of the relationship. Often, maintaining a relationship provides you with more options as you move forward. This advice may seem to run contrary to the discussion of escalation of commitment: one argument seems to urge caution while the other supports taking chances. In fact, they can be reconciled. The key is to make decisions without regard to sunk costs and instead with a focus on the future benefits and costs of your choices.

CHAPTER EIGHT

Fairness and Ethics in Decision Making

You are graduating from a good MBA program. Subsequent to your discussions with a number of firms, one of your preferred companies makes you an offer of $110,000 a year, stressing that the amount is not negotiable. You like the people. You like the job. You like the location. However, you find out that the same company is offering $120,000 to some graduating MBAs from similar-quality schools. Will you accept the offer?

Hurricane Katrina hits southern Louisiana, leaving many people homeless. For commodities such as building materials, demand is up and supply is down. This is a condition that leads economists to predict an increase in prices. In fact, in the aftermath of the hurricane, a small building-supply company more than doubles its prices on many items that are in high demand, such as lumber. Are the price increases ethical? Are they rational?

*I*n the first story, many of our students are very bothered by the difference between their salary offer and the salary offers of others, even if they learn that the difference does not predict how the company will treat them in the future. In the second story, most people believe that it is not ethical for the company to raise its prices on high-demand items. Since many customers can be predicted to react negatively to the perceived unfairness of the price increase, it may not even be rational for retailers to raise their prices in response to temporary increases in demand, regardless of what economists tell us ought to happen in efficient markets.

Issues of fairness and ethics are essential to a complete understanding of decision making. The first half of this chapter focuses on how individuals perceive the fairness of the actions of others. As we will discuss, people care passionately about fairness despite the fact that economic theory dismisses such concerns as superfluous to our decisions. The second half of the chapter focuses on ethics and considers the ways in which our ethical judgments can be biased, usually in self-serving ways, and often without our awareness.

PERCEPTIONS OF FAIRNESS

Research on fairness has focused on either the distribution of scarce resources (Messick, 1991) or the fairness of distribution procedures (Lind & Tyler, 1988). Most fairness research has avoided making evaluative statements about the rationality of fairness judgments. This silence has inhibited our understanding of how our cognitive processes create anger, jealousy, and inefficiency. If we are to reduce or eliminate our dysfunctional perceptions of fairness, we need to confront the rationality of fairness perceptions.

Fairness considerations may account for some of the limitations of the explanatory power of economic models. Kahneman, Knetsch, and Thaler (1986) argue that fairness considerations inhibit employers from cutting wages during periods of high unemployment despite changes in supply and demand, and also explain particular inflexibility in consumer prices. Here, we examine three systematic ways in which fairness considerations lead our decisions to deviate from a rational model. First, we describe situations in which individual judgment deviates from the expectations of supply-and-demand considerations. Second, we examine the ultimatum bargaining problem and what it reveals about why we make choices inconsistent with our own economic self-interest. Third, we consider how social-comparison processes lead to decisions that may clash with our underlying preferences. We conclude this section with a discussion of why fairness judgments matter.

When the Consequences of Supply and Demand Seem Unfair

In a provocative set of experiments, Kahneman et al. (1986) demonstrated that fairness considerations can dominate economically rational choices in decision making. Consider the action of the hardware store owner in the following scenario, which mirrors one of our opening stories:

> A hardware store has been selling snow shovels for $15. The morning after a large snowstorm, the store raises the price to $20.

Would you rate this action as fair or unfair? From an economic perspective, the price should go up. When demand increases relative to supply, an increase in price is the logical consequence. If the store does not increase its prices, there will be a surplus of people who would buy shovels at the higher price but who cannot get them because they were snatched up by people at the lower price. Those who want the shovels may have to spend time and energy standing in long lines before the store opens. Under some circumstances, the imbalance could result in a secondary market in which individuals can re-sell their shovels to others at higher prices.

Despite the economic rationality of raising the prices of snow shovels, 82 percent of respondents viewed raising the price of snow shovels to be unfair. And even among the individuals who said it was fair, many would not think it fair for a hardware store to raise the price of generators after a hurricane, even though the logic is the same. Thus, fairness considerations are often inconsistent with economic models.

An interesting reversal of the snow-shovel problem emphasizes the importance of thinking about others' fairness concerns. Assume that you own the hardware store and have 25 shovels remaining after a blizzard. Should you raise the price by $5? Even if you are economically rational, the answer may be no. If you ignore your customers' concerns for fairness, you might end up raising the price and collecting an additional $125 on the shovels. However, the loss of future business from angry customers may cost you more than $125. Providing your customers with a brief lesson on the laws of supply and demand is unlikely to help your cause. If they think the price increase is unfair, they probably will react negatively. Thus, businesses that act in an economically rational manner (e.g., increasing the price of the shovels) may underperform those that consider norms of fairness, because customers may punish retailers for the perceived unfairness of an economically rational action.

These facts raise important questions about how people arrive at fairness judgments. If you are a hardware store trying to set prices for shovels, you need to know when price increases will be perceived as unfair. It would be useful to know, for instance, that fairness judgments seem to be susceptible to the effects of framing (see Chapter 5). Consider Kahneman et al.'s (1986) following two problems:

Problem A. A company is making a small profit. It is located in a community experiencing a recession with substantial unemployment but no inflation. Many workers are anxious to work at the company. The company decides to decrease wages and salaries 7 percent this year.

Sixty-two percent of respondents thought the company's behavior was unfair.

Problem B. A company is making a small profit. It is located in a community experiencing a recession with substantial unemployment and inflation of 12 percent. Many workers are anxious to work at the company. The company decides to increase wages and salaries 5 percent this year.

In this case, only 22 percent of the participants thought the company's behavior was unfair. Despite the similar changes in real income, judgments of fairness were strikingly different. A wage cut was perceived as an unfair loss, while a nominal gain that does not cover inflation was more acceptable. We seem to hold certain rules of fair behavior, such as the rule that wages should go up and not down. Thus, when economic conditions change for the worse, it is difficult for employers to reduce wages. Our tendency to rely on nominal quantities, known in the economics literature as the "money illusion," makes Problem B seem fair, even though it is essentially equivalent to the wage change in Problem A. It is logical to think about money in terms of its actual buying power (real dollars), rather than the arbitrary unit of a dollar (nominal dollars), which changes in value as a result of inflation. In contrast, our assessments of fairness are largely built around whether the nominal dollar amount of our salary is increasing and decreasing. Instead of rationally adjusting for inflation before making the judgment, we follow our intuitive social rules.

Consumers show similar inconsistencies when thinking about discounts and price increases. Consider the following scenarios from Kahneman et al. (1986):

Scenario 1: A shortage has developed for a popular model of automobile, and customers must now wait two months for delivery. A dealer has been selling these cars at list price. Now the dealer prices this model at $200 above list price.

Scenario 2: A shortage has developed for a popular model of automobile, and customers must now wait two months for delivery. A dealer has been selling these cars at a discount of $200 below list price. Now the dealer prices this model at list price.

The majority of individuals view the action in the first scenario to be unfair (71 percent), yet only a minority considers the action in the second scenario to be unfair (42 percent). Consumers seem to grant special status to the manufacturer's list price, even if they do not expect to pay that amount. The list price acts as a critical anchor for assessments of fairness, such that it is unacceptable to exceed that amount. Yet, there is no normative basis for the manufacturer's list price having this special value.

The pattern that emerges is that individuals are concerned with departures from the status quo and that economically justifiable actions will often be perceived as unfair. We seem to rely on list prices and current prices to set a reference point against which we assess changes. When prices change, interpretations of fairness are clearly influenced by the framing effects we discussed in Chapter 5. It is hard to argue that the resulting fairness judgments are rational. Nevertheless, managers ought to be concerned about the way their actions are likely to be perceived by employees, colleagues, business partners, and customers.

Thaler (2004) documents multiple examples in which consumers' emotions, rather than market forces, decide what is fair: Delta's attempt to charge $2 per ticket extra for tickets not purchased on the Internet, First Chicago's idea of a $3 charge for doing business with a human teller, Coke's development of vending machines that change price based on demand level. We could add to the list the large bonuses AIG paid to generously compensated bankers in 2009 at the same time as it was accepting large government bailouts. In each case, there was no evidence that these actions violated market pricing. However, most of us sense intuitively that these were bad business ideas because most people would perceive them to be "unfair."

WHEN WE RESIST "UNFAIR" ULTIMATUMS

Consider the following situation:

You are traveling on an airplane, sitting in an aisle seat next to an eccentric-looking woman in the middle seat (Vivian). Next to her, in the window seat, is a rather formal-looking businessperson (Mark). About 30 minutes into the flight, Vivian interrupts you and Mark. She explains that she is quite wealthy, that she becomes bored on flights, and that she likes to pass the time by playing games. She then pulls 50 $100 bills out of her wallet and makes the following proposition. "I will give the two of you this $5,000 provided that you can agree on how to split the money. In splitting up the money, however, I will impose two rules. First, Mark must decide how the $5,000 is to be split between the two of you. Then, you [the reader] will decide whether to accept the split. If you do accept, then you and Mark will receive the portion of the $5,000 based on Mark's allocation. If you do not accept the split, then you and Mark will each receive nothing." Both you and Mark agree to play the game. Mark thinks for a moment and then says, "I propose that the $5,000 be split as follows: I get $4,900 and you get $100." Now it is up to you: Will you agree to this split?

If you are like most people, you will probably reject this split. Why? Obviously, rejecting such a deal is inconsistent with traditional notions of economic rationality, because each party would be better off (+$4,900 for Mark and +$100 for you) if you were to accept it. However, you might choose to reject this offer for a variety of reasons that lie outside self-interested wealth maximization. Reasons for rejecting the $100 include not wanting to accept an unfair allocation and not wanting Mark to benefit from your acceptance. Alternatively, some may argue that you are doing society as a whole a favor by punishing Mark for making an unfair offer. Any of these possibilities show that fairness concerns factor into your decision. If you were unaffected by fairness considerations, you would accept the $100. After all, $100 is better than nothing. If Vivian had instead offered to hand you $100, you likely would take it.

This story points out the importance of understanding the role of fairness and equality in decision making. Assume that the roles were reversed: You could determine the allocation, and Mark would have the option of accepting or rejecting it. What would you decide? If you did not factor in fairness considerations, it would be easy to conclude that the other party would accept the $100 or even less. However, this proposal would very likely leave you with $0 because Mark would probably reject your offer. In contrast, a consideration of fairness and emotion would lead you to anticipate the likely response of the other party and consequently improve the expected value that you would receive from this transaction by offering the other party significantly more than $100.

This airplane story may seem to be an implausible and contrived situation, but we play a game with this underlying structure every day. Any time we consider buying something at a store with a posted price, we are put in the position of deciding whether to accept the store's ultimatum offer. The store has chosen a sale price that is, presumably, above the store's cost. If you value the item more than what it costs, then you may choose to buy it. But you are not invited to negotiate with the clerk at the grocery store about whether you think the celery is really worth what the store is charging. The store has given you an ultimatum: "Here is our price. Take it or leave it."

A number of researchers have systematically studied how people respond to ultimatums that are similar to the fictitious airplane story (Güth, Schmittberger, & Schwarze, 1982). In these studies, a proposer divides a known, fixed sum of money any way he chooses by filling out a form stating, "I demand X." The responder either accepts the offer and receives her portion of the money as allocated by the proposer or rejects the offer, leaving both parties with nothing. Traditional models of rational actors predict that the proposer will offer the responder only slightly more than zero and that the responder will accept any offer greater than zero. The results, however, show that individuals incorporate fairness considerations into their offers and choices. The average demand by the proposer was for less than 70 percent of the pie, both for first-time players and for players repeating the game one week later. In fact, the most frequent offer from the proposer was an even split of the money. In addition, individuals in the role of the responder rejected profitable but unequal offers routinely; offers for less than 20 percent were usually rejected.

People often rely on attaining what they consider to be a fair or justifiable result. As a result, they are often willing to pay to punish their opponent if he or she asks for too much. Ochs and Roth (1989) studied a situation in which the responder could reject the allocation offer of the proposer, then counterpropose an allocation. However, the amount of money shrank if the responder rejected the first offer. The researchers found that in such ultimatum games, 81 percent of rejected offers were followed by disadvantageous counteroffers in which parties who rejected the initial offer demanded less than they had just been offered. Ochs and Roth argue that players' utilities for fairness can explain the results. However, they also argue that a simple notion of equality does not explain the data, since in most cases the proposer asks for more than 50 percent of the resources in the first stage. Rather, parties realize that the other side may very well refuse offers perceived as unfair despite the economic rationality of accepting them.

Fair dictators? Ochs and Roth had participants play either an ultimatum game like the one just described or a "dictator" game in which the proposer could simply decide how the resources would be split without the responder's acceptance. They found that while many proposers chose a 50:50 split in the ultimatum game, none proposed a 100:0 split. By contrast, under the dictator format, 36 percent of all proposers took 100 percent. When acceptance was required, proposals became more equal. However, in the dictator game, when acceptance by the other party was not required, 64 percent still chose to give the other party some portion of the resources.

Pay-what-you-want pricing employs a real-life version of the dictator game. According to this concept, rather than paying a fixed price for a product as typically occurs, consumers have the opportunity to pay any price of their choosing. Thus, a consumer could theoretically purchase a product for $0 and "free ride." In this situation, the consumer has all the power. However, even though consumers could theoretically free ride in a pay-what-you-want pricing situation, not all take this chance. In a study of photo sales from an amusement park ride, Gneezy, Gneezy, Nelson, and Brown (2010) provide evidence that pay-what-you-want pricing can actually be more profitable than a normal pricing scheme, particularly when the choice to pay appears virtuous because a portion of the proceeds will go to a charitable cause. Refreshingly, it appears that feeling a sense of social obligation can go a long way toward encouraging fair behaviors, even when selfishness is easy.

These results demonstrate that both a desire to be fair and the realization that being unfair can generate social sanctions led to choices that deviated from rational models in systematic and predictable directions.

The persistent desire for fairness. Many people intuit that it is not difficult to sacrifice a few dollars to punish an unfair allocation in the ultimatum game, but that people would behave more rationally if the stakes were sufficiently high. The evidence contradicts this intuition. A number of studies have varied the stakes in the ultimatum game and found no appreciable effect on behavior—even when the total pie was equal to several months' wages. An even split remains the most common offer from proposers, and responders routinely reject any offer less than 20 percent (Cameron, 1999; Hoffman, McCabe, & Smith, 1996; Straub & Murnighan, 1995).

Neuroimaging techniques pinpoint the role of emotional reactions in the ultimatum game. Functional magnetic resonance imaging technology (fMRI) allows scientists to see how blood flows to different parts of the brain in real time. Decision scientists who are interested in the mechanisms behind people's observed choices have used fMRIs to determine which part of the brain is activated under different conditions. Sanfey et al. (2003) scanned players' brains as they received ultimatum-game offers either from another person or from a computer. The researchers found different patterns in brain activation for unfair offers and for fair offers, and the differences were greater when these offers came from another person than when they came from a computer. A region associated with negative emotional states (the anterior insuala) was stimulated when players considered unfair offers, as was another region that the authors hypothesized was connected to the cognitive demands of the task (the dorsolateral prefrontal cortex), namely the desire to make as much money as possible. The greater emotional response for unfair offers provides concrete evidence that emotional processes are involved in this type of decision making.

There is surprising cross-cultural consistency in the way people play the ultimatum game. Henrich et al. (2001) conducted studies that included the game in 15 societies around the world. This research found little support for the classic economic view of self-interest; fairness was found to be an important factor in these economic games for each of the societies tested. However, the researchers did find that the patterns of everyday interaction explained variations between societies. Fairness appears to be a universal concept affecting decisions, but implementation of fairness depends on cultural norms.

Research by Brosnan and de Waal (2003) even offers a compelling demonstration of *cross-species* generality in fairness judgments. They showed that capuchin monkeys rebelled when they were given smaller rewards than their fellow monkeys for performing the same task, in much the same way that unequal payment undermines workers' motivation (Fehr, Kirchsteiger, & Reidl, 1993). These angry capuchins indignantly refused to work or even to eat their cucumbers if their neighbors received much tastier grapes in exchange for performing the same labor.

WHEN WE ARE CONCERNED ABOUT THE OUTCOMES OF OTHERS

Humans and capuchin monkeys both care about what happens to others. People may willingly pay in order to harm an adversary or forgo gains to help a loved one. In addition, people are concerned about how their own rewards compare to the rewards of others. Recognizing these concerns, organizations create elaborate job grade systems to specify the compensation available to employees at each level within the organization. Salaries, bonuses, and benefits are carefully calculated within these specified parameters so employees will believe they are being fairly compensated relative to others in comparable positions. In addition, organizations strive to conceal salary data to avoid social comparisons and perceptions of unfairness. This elaborate behavior is justified by research showing a positive correlation between the pay equity of corporations and the quality of their products (Cowherd & Levine, 1992). Similarly, Depken (2000) shows a negative relationship between the size of pay differentials within a Major League Baseball team and how well that team performs, judging by the objective standard of winning percentage. Namely, the smaller the gap between the highest-paid and the lowest-paid members, the better the team as a whole works together. Clearly, across a broad variety of situations, individuals exhibit concern for how their own rewards compare to those of relevant others and also show resulting changes in their own behavior.

Top executives in firms are also impacted by fairness considerations resulting from social comparison. In a study of S&P 500 firms, Fredrickson, Davis-Blake, and Sanders (2010) found that pay differences among the top executives within a firm were negatively correlated with firm performance. Top executives must work together as a team, and large pay disparities undermine this collaboration.

As recent college graduates entering the workforce learn, significant differences in payment exist across industries. Those who go into investment banking might earn $100,000 or more in their first year while their similarly qualified peers in publishing or architecture make less than half that amount. How can such seemingly unfair differences persist in the market? Two particularly interesting facts about this cross-industry wage differential can be explained by how we form fairness concerns (Thaler, 1991). First, there is an observed correlation between high-profit industries and high wages. Second, if one job within an industry is highly paid, other jobs in that industry also tend to be highly paid. Our perceptions of the fair comparison wage are related to the profitability of a given firm and what other individuals in closely related jobs can earn (Akerlof & Yellen, 1990). When oil companies or banks are highly profitable, they routinely share some of these profits with their workers, even if the profits are due to factors, such as currency exchange rates or global oil prices, that lie far outside the control of any of the firm's employees (Bertrand & Mullainathan, 2001). This suggests that people make comparisons within their firm and to other firms in their industry rather than across industries. This may account for the acceptance of differences in payment between industries such as banking and publishing.

Chapter 5 shows that people often compare what they have against a reference point. Sometimes the status quo, such as one's current wealth, serves as the reference point (Kahneman & Tversky, 1979). However, Loewenstein, Thompson, and Bazerman (1989) argue that the outcomes of others commonly act as a key reference point in interpersonal decision settings and that inter-personal comparisons can overwhelm concern for personal outcomes when people rate potential resolutions of a dispute. For example, in an experiment that asked participants to assess multiple outcomes to a dispute one at a time, individuals typically rated $500 for oneself and $500 for another person as a more satisfactory outcome than $600 for oneself and $800 for the other. Bazerman, Loewenstein, and White (1992) combined the logic on how concerns for others influence our decisions with the work on joint-versus-separate preference reversals from Chapter 5 to examine when people are concerned with the outcomes of others. In the first empirical demonstration of joint-versus-separate preference reversals, Bazerman et al. (1992) showed that while individuals care far more about social comparisons when rating a specific outcome, absolute individual outcomes are more important in actual choice behavior. Seventy percent rated the outcome of $400 for oneself and $400 for the other party as more acceptable than $500 for oneself and $700 for the other party when asked to evaluate these outcomes separately. However, only 22 percent chose $400 for oneself and $400 for the other party over $500 for oneself and $700 for the other party when asked to choose between the two. This basic pattern is consistent across many other comparisons and across a wide variety of contexts. When a series of joint outcomes are evaluated individually, the outcomes of others become the reference point. When choosing between two outcomes for oneself, the outcomes of others are not needed as a reference point, since the two outcomes can be easily compared. In this type of situation, the outcomes of others become less relevant. Instead, the salient attribute in a choice task is one's own outcome.

Blount and Bazerman (1996) extended this result to a real situation involving real payoffs. They agreed to recruit participants for a colleague's experiment. One group of potential participants was offered $7 to participate in a 40-minute experiment, knowing that all participants would be receiving $7. A second group was offered $8 to participate in a 40-minute experiment, knowing that some participants were arbitrarily (based on the last digit of their social security number) being offered $10. A third group was given an opportunity (1) to participate in a 40-minute experiment in which everyone was being paid $7; (2) to participate in a 40-minute experiment in which some participants, including themselves, would receive $8 and others would receive $10; or (3) not to participate. Although significantly more participants in the first group chose to participate (72 percent) than in the second group (55 percent), the majority of participants in the third group (56 percent) chose to participate in the experiment that gave them $8 while some others were given $10 (16 percent chose the experiment in which everyone received $7; 28 percent chose not to participate in either). Thus, when people evaluated whether to participate in one specific experiment, the outcomes of other potential participants were critical to their decisions. However, when multiple options were available, participants were able to compare what they would receive across the multiple experiments, and the outcomes of others became less important.

These findings are consistent with the affect heuristic introduced in Chapter 1, with the work on joint-versus-separate preference reversals introduced in Chapter 5, and with the want/should distinction developed in Chapter 6. When we assess one option at a time, social comparisons serve as reference points we use to assess our outcomes. But when multiple options exist, it becomes easier to compare across them and disregard the less useful comparison to others.

Perverse Consequences of Equality Norms

The responder's expectations in an ultimatum game are partially affected by a norm of equality. In the ultimatum game, expectations of fairness lead to the rejection of economically desirable offers, but it is also possible that the same norms of equality can cause us to accept "fair" situations too prematurely. Messick (1991) identifies many contexts in which individuals expect an even split, even when a rational analysis would not support such a split. The ease with which individuals accept an equal allocation of pleasure and pain probably accounts, in large measure, for the common use of compromise solutions in negotiation. Consider the following situation:

> You visit a car dealer and go on a test drive. You return to the salesperson's cubicle in the showroom, ready to do a deal. The car has a list price of $18,000. After a short discussion, you offer $15,500. The salesperson counters with $17,600, you counter with $16,000, he counters with $17,200, you counter with $16,400, and he reduces his price to $16,800. You act as if you will not make another move and threaten to visit another dealership. The salesperson then says earnestly, "You look like a nice person, and I can see that you really like the car. My main concern is that you get the car that you want. I assume that you are a reasonable person, and I want to be reasonable. How about if we split the difference—$16,600?"

Many of us would quickly accept the salesman's offer. After all, a 50:50 split sounds fair. Yet, careful consideration reveals that this 50:50 split, like most 50:50 splits, is quite arbitrary. The final two numbers on the table could have been $16,000 and $16,400, and the 50:50 split would have sounded just as fair, but the resulting price would have been $16,200, or $400 less. The fairness of a 50:50 split depends on the comparative fairness of the two numbers used as anchors for the split. A rational decision maker must be aware of the influence of a seemingly fair

50:50 split and realize that other 50:50 alternatives are easy to generate. Just because an offer can be considered fair does not mean that it is optimal. Other equally fair outcomes may exist that would be better for you.

Again, we see that fairness concerns do influence decisions and that ignoring others' fairness concerns can be costly. People are entitled to their own assessments of fairness. However, we must all realize that others may have very different standards about what is fair.

WHY DO FAIRNESS JUDGMENTS MATTER?

One reason we should care about whether others think our actions are fair is that they will punish us for behaving unfairly. People engage in such punishment even when doing so is not in their rational self interest. For example, when responders in the one-shot, anonymous ultimatum game reject offers, they are choosing to forego a monetary gain in order to punish the proposer for making an unfair allocation.

Indeed, research shows that observers who are not personally affected by unfair treatment are actually willing to pay money in order to punish others whom they observe behaving unfairly (Fehr & Fischbacher, 2003; Fehr & Gächter, 2000). Fehr and Fischbacher (2004) had participants in their experiment play a dictator game with a twist. In addition to the dictator and the recipient, there was also a third-party observer. The observer could see what the dictator provided the recipient and could decide whether to punish the dictator for the allocation. Such punishment was costly: For every $1 the observer paid to punish, the dictator's own payment was reduced by $3. Note that no purely self-interested observer would ever engage in such altruistic punishment, which is costly to both the dictator and the punisher, and provides no economic benefit. Nevertheless, 55 percent of observers chose to punish dictators who gave less than half of their money to their recipients. The less dictators gave, the more they were punished by the observers.

Fehr and his colleagues argue that their evidence shows that people actually derive measurable satisfaction from "altruistic punishment" that allows them to teach a lesson to a cheater. The researchers have shown that effective punishment of a cheater is anticipated by greater activity in the dorsal striatum, a brain region that delivers the satisfaction of attaining a desirable outcome (de Quervain et al., 2004).

Judgments of fairness permeate organizational life. Comparisons of pay raises, the distribution of scarce budgets, promotions, grades, and prices are just a few of the many situations in which we make fairness judgments that affect our emotions and behavior. It is probably not realistic to attempt to eliminate concerns for fairness and social comparisons from our decision-making repertoire. Nevertheless, when faced with the question of whether you should go to the effort to punish an individual or a firm that behaved unfairly, rational decision makers may want to consider the internal conflict that we explored in Chapter 6 between the "want" and the "should" self. You may be angry and want to punish someone, but should you? Would doing so truly be in your interest?

Even if you ignore fairness concerns in your own judgments, there is ample evidence that people will use fairness and social-comparison information to judge your actions. Thus, understanding how people judge fairness may help you make better decisions in both your personal and professional life. In the second half of this chapter, we turn from thinking about how people evaluate the fairness of others' actions to the issue of ethics. In contrast to fairness issues, ethical issues concern how we judge our own behavior and its consistency with our own values.

BOUNDED ETHICALITY

Following the many corporate scandals that coincided with the start of the new millennium, the media looked for the underlying cause of the unethical behavior. Popular targets of the media's blame included a handful of "bad" people within firms such as Enron and its auditor, Arthur Andersen, gatekeepers within these companies, and failed governmental regulation. Business leaders were blamed for their role in the presumed ethical decline, and business schools were criticized for failing to provide ethical training to future leaders.

The media implied that the key to stemming the tide of financial scandals was to stop managers from deciding to engage in unethical behavior. This approach is broadly consistent with the field of ethics, which focuses on deliberative decisions. In this section, we will challenge this ethical perspective on corporate scandals. We are in favor of changing the incentives of organizational actors to encourage more ethical behavior and would be pleased to see genuine corporate criminals serve time in prison. But recent research provides a compelling case that the vast majority of unethical behaviors occur without the conscious intention to behave unethically.

We focus on the cognitive biases that lead honorable people to engage in unethical behavior without realizing that they are doing so. The first half of this chapter examined the ways in which fairness judgments depart from standard economic models. This second half of the chapter considers how cognitive biases allow us to act in ways that contradict our own intended standard of ethics. These deviations from our intended standard are systematic and predictable, just as the biases from rationality discussed in Chapters 2 through 7 are predictable and systematic. Rather than concentrating on intentionally corrupt behavior, we will discuss recent research that identifies the types, magnitude, and causes of unethical behavior that occur without the awareness of the actor—what we refer to as *bounded ethicality* (Chugh, Bazerman, & Banaji, 2005). This perspective diverges from standard treatments of ethics, which assume the explicit analysis of appropriate action by the individual, yet complements this traditional view.

Our central argument is that understanding and changing the ethicality of human action requires going beyond the common assumption that ethically challenged behavior results from people choosing self-rewarding behavior over what is right. New evidence points to the limitations of the conscious mind and emphasizes the power of the unconscious mind to motivate us to engage in unethical behavior (Banaji & Bhaskar, 2000; Murnighan, Cantelon, & Elyashiv, 2004; Wegner, 2002).

We use the term "bounded ethicality" to refer to the psychological processes that lead people to engage in ethically questionable behaviors that are inconsistent with their own preferred ethics. Bounded ethicality comes into play when an executive makes a decision that not only harms others but also is inconsistent with his or her conscious beliefs and preferences. Managers develop protective cognitions that lead them to engage in behaviors that they would condemn upon further reflection or awareness. When they become aware of an ethically questionable situation that is not formally part of their responsibility, they may fail to get involved. They may have no trouble justifying their inaction as ethical; upon greater reflection, however, they might recognize inaction to be more harmful than many errors of action. Chugh (2004) argues that bounded ethicality is exacerbated by the pace of managerial life, which demands the speed and decisiveness that System 1 thinking (discussed in Chapter 1) provides. System 1 thinking allows the biases created by bounded ethicality to develop, which in turn lead to decisions that deviate from one's personal standards.

Like the other biases reviewed in this book, the biases emanating from bounded ethicality apply to all of us, even the best and the brightest. In March 2004, for example, Supreme Court Justice Antonin Scalia denied a motion from the Sierra Club to recuse himself from an upcoming case, Cheney v. U.S. District Court for D.C. Scalia had hunted ducks in Louisiana with Vice President Dick Cheney in January 2004, just three weeks after the Supreme Court agreed to consider whether Cheney should be forced to provide information about the energy task force he led as the Bush administration formulated its environmental policy. The Sierra Club argued that Scalia and Cheney's friendship compromised Scalia's objectivity. "If it is reasonable to think that a Supreme Court justice can be bought so cheap, the nation is in deeper trouble than I had imagined," Scalia wrote in defense of his decision (Janofsky, 2004). His friendship with the vice president would not intentionally distort his judgment, Scalia argued, and did not violate the Supreme Court's rules on conflicts of interest.

But the rules governing the Supreme Court, like most guidelines, rules, and laws that protect against conflict of interest, were generated to guard only against intentional corruption (Banaji, 2004). Scalia's comments indicate that he either chose to ignore or is unaware of the strong evidence of the psychological aspects of conflict of interest. In this section, we will provide evidence that even the strictest guidelines are generally insufficient to address conflicts of interest that escape the awareness of the professional being affected. For instance, psychologists have shown that a bond between two people can make it impossible for one to objectively assess issues involving the other (Murray & Holmes, 1994, 1997).

This chapter overviews six examples of bounded ethicality: overclaiming credit without realizing that you are doing so, in-group favoritism, implicit attitudes, indirectly unethical behavior, pseudo-sacred values, and the psychology of conflicts of interest. Regarding conflicts of interest, we examine both how they affect our decisions and how they motivate us to be blind to the ethical infractions of others. For each type of bounded ethicality, we present research showing that such behaviors occur beyond conscious awareness.

OVERCLAIMING CREDIT

Ross and Sicoly (1979) asked married couples to estimate the percentage of household activities, such as washing the dishes or taking out the trash, they each personally performed. When the percentages offered by husbands and wives were added, the per-couple average was close to 140 percent. Since this original demonstration by Ross and Sicoly, overclaiming of credit for work performed has been demonstrated in academia (Caruso, Epley, & Bazerman, 2006), athletics (Brawley, 1984; Forsyth & Schlenker, 1977), and fundraising (Zander, 1971), just to name a few fields (see Caruso, Epley, & Bazerman, 2005 for a review). The roots of overclaiming are the self-serving biases reviewed in Chapter 6. Even honest people tend to believe they contributed more to an enterprise than they actually did.

Overclaiming can also be a factor at the organizational level. Researchers have puzzled over the question of why joint ventures so often end in disappointment (Epley, Caruso, & Bazerman, 2006). One possible drawback of strategic partnerships is that parties are often skeptical that the other side is doing its share. It is a widely known problem that joint venture partners often contribute mediocre talent to the enterprise, rather than their firms' best talent. Why? In part because each party has an incentive to save its best talent for projects that the firm is fully invested in rather than on projects of which it owns only half. When we factor in the tendency of each side to overclaim credit for its own contribution, it becomes apparent that each side will feel entitled to reduce its contribution. Consequently, each side views the other side's behavior to be unfair and its own behavior to be justified, and the escalation of sinister attributions about the other party spirals downward.

Can anything be done to stop individuals and organizations from overclaiming credit? Caruso, Epley, and Bazerman (2007) asked Harvard MBA students to estimate how much of the work done in their study groups they personally had completed. When the researchers added up members' claims by group, the average total was 139 percent. In other words, the members of the average group believed that they were responsible for 139 percent of the 100 percent of work completed. However, when the researchers first asked group members to think about the contribution of each member, including themselves, the average total of the claimed work done by the group fell to 121 percent. While "unpacking" individuals' contributions to the group effort did not cause the overclaiming of credit to disappear, it did at least reduce the magnitude of the bias. Furthermore, in a study of academic authorship of articles that had between three and six authors, the same researchers found that overclaiming was rampant and that unpacking reduced overclaiming. In addition, the greater the magnitude of overclaiming, the less parties wanted to work together in the future.

Essentially, improving the perspective-taking skills of group members can help reduce overclaiming and raise group performance. In addition, overclaiming may have important implications for the longevity of groups. The next time a colleague makes a claim that you view to be outrageous, before arguing, consider that you yourself might also be guilty of the tendency to overclaim credit. In addition, remember that it is far more likely that your colleague is biased than dishonest.

IN-GROUP FAVORITISM

Think about some of the favors you've been asked to perform in recent years, whether for a friend, a relative, a friend of a friend, or a friend of a relative. Have you helped someone get concert tickets, an apartment rental, admission to a school, or a job? Most of us are glad to help out with such favors. More often than not, we have done them for people like ourselves—people who went to the same college, people we work with, or people who happen to be of the same race. A basic psychological finding is that we tend to identify with people who are a lot like us. In addition, we are more comfortable doing favors for those with whom we identify than for those noticeably different from us. Thus, we tilt toward helping people who share our nationality, religion, race, gender, or alma mater.

This all sounds rather innocent. What's wrong with asking your neighbor, the admissions officer at the nearby college, to check up on a coworker's son's college application? Isn't it just "networking" to recommend a former sorority sister for a job or to talk to your banker cousin when a friend from church gets turned down for a home loan? A favor is a favor no matter who you're helping, right?

Few people set out to exclude underrepresented minorities through such acts of kindness. But when those in the majority tend to favor people who are similar to them when allocating scarce resources (such as jobs, college admissions, and mortgages), they effectively discriminate against those who are different from them. Consistent with the work on implicit attitudes that we will discuss later in the chapter, Dasgupta (2004) has reviewed almost 100 research studies that show that people have a greater tendency to associate positive characteristics with their "in-groups" (groups they belong to) than with "out-groups" (groups they do not belong to) and to more easily associate negative characteristics with out-groups than with their in-groups. Moreover, Bernhard, Fischbacher, and Fehr (2006) have shown that people's willingness to enforce social norms by punishing those who treat others unfairly is much greater when those treated unfairly are similar to themselves with respect to ethnic, racial, or language group. These discriminatory patterns can result from both automatic, implicit processes and thoughtful, explicit processes.

People often regard the favors they do for in-group members as virtuous, without recognizing the harm that these favors may create for out-group members. Even as we congratulate ourselves for doing something nice for a member of our "community," we overlook the ethical implications of the favoritism we perpetuate in the process. In-group favoritism, or giving "extra credit" for shared demographic traits, is equivalent to punishing people for being different from you. Yet helping people who are like us is viewed by society as a nice thing to do, while discriminating against those who are different is viewed as unethical.

Over the last decade, studies have repeatedly shown that banks are much more likely to deny a mortgage to an African American than to a Caucasian, even after controlling for a variety of factors, including income, house location, and so on. The common view is that banks are overtly hostile to the African-American community. For some banks and some loan officers, this may be the case. But Messick and Bazerman (1996) argue that a much more common—and insidious—cause of discriminatory mortgage lending is likely to be in-group favoritism. That is, white loan officers may be making too many loans to unqualified whites. Given a limited pool of resources, fewer funds remain available for nonwhite applicants.

The leading form of affirmative action at many top-ranked U.S. colleges and universities is legacy admissions, or the policy of admitting unqualified or marginally qualified children of alumni, donors, and other well-connected individuals, according to Peter Schmidt, the deputy editor of the *Chronicle of Higher Education* (2007). At many of the nation's most prestigious colleges, less capable applicants from privileged social groups are favored over more qualified, unconnected applicants. In fact, "legacies" make up 10–15 percent of freshman classes at most Ivy League schools. Yet according to a 1990 Department of Education report, the typical Harvard University legacy student is "significantly less qualified" than the average non-legacy student in every relevant area but sports (*The Economist*, 2004). Just as mortgage lenders are probably unaware that they are disadvantaging minority borrowers when they favor Caucasians, university officials likely are blind to the fact that their legacy policies discriminate against less-connected but more qualified applicants.

IMPLICIT ATTITUDES

Most people think of their attitudes, including their attitudes toward various races, as being within the scope of their conscious awareness and under their control. This view is challenged by research on *implicit attitudes*, which shows, for instance, that when we meet someone, our minds automatically activate stereotypes of the person's race, sex, and age (Macrae & Bodenhausen, 2001). Even people who believe strongly in egalitarian values cannot help but have unflattering stereotypes come to mind without conscious awareness or intent. For example, Bargh, Chen, and Burrows (1996) had participants in their experiment work on a boring computer task. Meanwhile, the computers flashed subliminal images of either white or black faces, so quickly that participants were not consciously aware of them. When the computers "broke down" and the participants were informed that their work had been lost, those who had been shown black faces responded with significantly more aggression than those shown white faces, consistent with the common stereotype of African Americans as aggressive and violent.

The existence of automatic or unconscious attitudes and their effects on our judgments can place important bounds on the degree to which we can assure that our own behavior is consistent with the ethical values we want to express. Unconscious attitudes influence the information that is immediately accessible to us, which interacts with situational demands to shape our decision making (Jefferis & Fazio, 2008). Again, evidence shows that human ethicality is bounded. People often provide sincere and strenuous denials that they intended to behave in ways consistent with negative racial stereotypes. Nevertheless, their explicit intentions are contradicted by the implications of their actions.

Research by Jennifer Richeson and her colleagues shows that Americans of European ancestry are often less comfortable interacting with Americans of African ancestry than with Americans of European ancestry (Richeson & Shelton, 2005; Shelton, Richeson, & Vorauer, 2006). Those of European ancestry do not intend to behave poorly toward African Americans, but they display clear psychological signals of discomfort. Indeed, those people whose automatically activated stereotypes are the most negative suffer the most discomfort in inter-racial interactions (Richeson & Trawalter, 2005). In fact, the hard work of suppressing their negative racial stereotypes produces measurable cognitive impairments on other tasks (Richeson & Shelton, 2003).

Psychologists have developed a useful tool for examining our implicit attitudes regarding race, gender, and other human differences that are weighted with stereotypes: the Implicit Associations Test, or IAT (Greenwald, McGhee, & Schwartz, 1998). The IAT is one of the most interesting and controversial psychological tests ever developed because it offers the potential to assess attitudes that most people would rather not reveal. Unlike most psychological testing tools, it is very difficult to consciously manipulate one's IAT scores. The IAT cannot reveal whether or not someone is racist, sexist, and so on. Rather, it measures the strength of an individual's implicit association between two pairs of categories, such as White/Black and Good/Bad.

The IAT, which is usually administered via computer, works as follows. The test-taker is instructed to categorize items that appear on the screen as quickly as possible by striking keys on the keyboard. The items that appear on the screen might come from one of four categories, such as "White," "Black," "Good," and "Bad." If you were shown a series of pictures of people's faces, you might be asked to press one key to indicate that the face belongs to a "Black" person and to press a different key to indicate that the face belongs to a "White" person. You might also be shown words such as "Hate," "Love," "Kill," and "Heal," which you would have to categorize by pressing the key for "Good" or the key for "Bad."

The typical test includes a series of rounds. In some rounds, "White" faces and "Bad" words belong to the same category and should be categorized using the same key; meanwhile, "Black" faces and "Good" words belong to the same category and should be categorized using the same key. In other rounds, "White" faces are assigned to "Good" words and "Black" faces to "Bad" words.

Research using the IAT to study stereotyping and prejudice has produced some interesting results. Nosek, Banaji, and Greenwald (2002) report that roughly three-quarters of the white Americans who visit their Web site (http://implicit.harvard.edu) exhibit pro-white implicit attitudes. (If you are wondering about your own implicit attitudes, you can take the IAT yourself by visiting the IAT Web site.) On average, both white and black Americans perform the test more quickly and accurately when they must associate "White" with "Good" and "Black" with "Bad" than when they must associate "White" with "Bad" and "Black" with "Good." These results imply that most of us have deeply ingrained, if unconscious, associations that lead us to favor whiteness over blackness when it comes to race.

Many people are surprised to discover how little control they have over the expression of implicit attitudes regarding race, gender, age, and so on (Banaji, Bazerman, & Chugh, 2003). Because implicit attitudes are rooted in ordinary mental processes of categorization, perception, memory, and judgment, Banaji (2001) has called the use of these attitudes "ordinary prejudice." She argues further that the word "ordinary" captures the likelihood that, if ordinary mental processes are involved in expressions of stereotypes and prejudice, then ordinary managers, executives, and other professionals will demonstrate them.

Blanton and Jaccard (2006) advise IAT test-takers to keep several factors in mind when interpreting their scores. Most importantly, the IAT reveals the *relative* strength of implicit attitude but not their *absolute* strength. In other words, if the test reveals that you associate goodness more with white faces than with black faces, that does not necessarily mean that, on a subconscious level, you love white people and hate black people. Instead, it could be that you feel favorably toward both white and black people, but that you have slightly more positive feelings toward white people; conversely, it could be that you hate both white and black people but that you hate white people slightly less than black people.

Psychologists have found that implicit attitudes predict certain forms of behavior. Rudman and Borgida (1995) have found that implicit stereotypes predicted discrimination against female job applicants. Rudman and Glick (2001) found that study participants who held strong implicit attitudes connecting women with communal traits (e.g., helpful) and men with "agentic," or individualistic, traits (e.g., ambitious) were more likely to view a female exhibiting ambition as having poor social skills than were participants with weaker implicit attitudes on this dimension. McConnell and Leibold (2001) found that implicit attitudes were highly predictive of nonverbal behaviors toward different groups of people. Finally, Asendorpf, Banse, and Muecke (2002) demonstrated that implicit attitudes are more predictive of spontaneous behaviors and that explicit attitudes are more predictive of thoughtful behaviors. This effect implies that implicit attitudes are more likely to occur when decision makers are using System 1 than System 2 thinking.

One possible real-world example of this phenomenon was the arrest of Henry Louis Gates Jr., an African-American Harvard University professor, by James Crowley, a white Cambridge, Massachusetts police sergeant on July 16, 2009 (Bazerman & Tenbrunsel, 2011). Upon returning home from an overseas trip,

Gates was unable to open his front door, so he forced his way inside with the help of his cab driver. After a neighbor reported a possible break-in to the police, Crowley arrived. Gates showed Crowley proof of his residence. Yet Crowley later said that he felt compelled to make an arrest after Gates reportedly became disorderly while the men were standing on Gates's front porch. Gates was held for four hours and charged with disorderly conduct. The charges were dropped several days later, but Crowley refused to apologize for his actions. The incident became a cause célèbre when President Barack Obama said at a press conference that the Cambridge policy had "acted stupidly" in arresting Gates. To defuse the public debates on race that followed, Obama convened a "beer summit" with Gates, Crowley, and Vice President Joe Biden at the White House Rose Garden.

Many people who condemned Crowley's decision to arrest Gates on the porch of his own home assumed that the officer must be an overt racist. But consider that Crowley actually teaches a course to police cadets on how to avoid racial profiling. It seems more plausible that Crowley, when required to make a snap judgment about Gates, may have fallen victim to the type of subconscious racial bias identified by the IAT. Crowley's System 1 thinking could have prompted unconscious racial attitudes that caused him to decide to arrest Gates. As noted above, the less time we have to think, the more likely we are to succumb to racial bias. In one study using a computer simulation, participants were instructed to shoot criminals that crossed the screen, but not the unarmed citizens or police officers; the participants incorrectly shot more black men than white men (Correll et al., 2007).

Some researchers have noted a societal shift over the last few decades from "old-fashioned racism" to "modern racism" (Brief, Dietz, Cohen, Pugh, & Vaslow, 2000; Chugh, 2004). Old-fashioned racism is explicit and accompanied by hostility. Modern racism is more subtle, but affects managers' professional judgments nonetheless. In 2004, Morgan Stanley paid $54 million to settle a sex discrimination lawsuit filed on behalf of some of its female executives by the Equal Employment Opportunity Commission. The EEOC argued that much of the problem at Morgan Stanley, and at other investment banks, is that the mostly white men who are in charge do not seem to recognize the existence of gender inequities in their operations (*New York Times*, July 14, 2004, p. C1). Hydie Summer, a plaintiff in a separate sex discrimination lawsuit at Merrill Lynch, commented, "[The brokerage managers] really don't believe they are discriminating. If you come in and you look like they want you to look—probably a white male profile—they'll project success for you. They have a specific view of what a successful broker or manager will look like, and it is not usually a woman or a black or Hispanic." We all need to be aware that racial attitudes can affect our judgment without our conscious awareness and in ways that are at odds with our intentions and values.

There is some evidence that as we become less prejudiced as a society, our tendency to implicitly employ stereotypes in our decision-making process may be reduced. One such example comes in the election of Barack Obama as the first African-American president of the United States. Plant and colleagues (2009) provide evidence that implicit attitudes about black people became less prejudiced after Obama's election than they were prior to his election. The authors also argue that this drop in implicit prejudice occurred due to increased exposure to a positive exemplar of African Americans. It appears that as more members of stigmatized groups have an opportunity to succeed in high-status positions, the less prejudiced we will become as a society.

INDIRECTLY UNETHICAL BEHAVIOR

Imagine that a major pharmaceutical company is the sole marketer of a particular cancer drug. The drug is not profitable, due to high fixed costs and a small market size, yet the patients who do buy the drug depend on it for their survival. The pharmaceutical company currently produces the drug at a total cost of $5/pill and only sells it for $3/pill. A price increase is unlikely to decrease use of the drug, but will impose significant hardship on many users. How ethical would it be for the company to raise the price of the drug from $3/pill to $9/pill?

Now imagine that, instead of raising the price, the company sold the rights to produce the drug to a smaller, lesser-known pharmaceutical company. At a meeting between the two companies, a young executive from the smaller firm says: "Since our reputation is not as critical as yours, and we are not in the public's eye, we can raise the price five fold to $15/pill." Would selling the manufacturing and marketing rights to the other firm be more or less ethical?

Paharia, Kassam, Greene, and Bazerman (2007) found that when evaluating each of these two options individually, participants found it more unethical to raise the drug price to $9 per pill than to sell off the product to another firm, knowing that the other firm would raise the price to $15 per pill. When another group of participants was directly asked to compare the two options, however, they found the behavior that led to a $15 per pill price to be more unethical. But as we discussed in Chapter 5, people typically observe only one behavior at a time rather than comparing and contrasting two options. Thus, as compared to simply raising the price of the drug, the sale of the drug to the smaller company is a disguised, ambiguous price-raising tactic that is less likely to raise concerns from the public—yet, at the same time, it may be more hazardous to the drug's users.

Could this type of indirect price increase happen in the real world? Yes— and, in fact, some firms seem to specialize in creating such opportunities. In August 2005, pharmaceutical manufacturer Merck, which had made a cancer drug by the name Mustargen, sold the rights to manufacture and market the product to Ovation Pharmaceuticals, a much smaller, less-recognized company that specializes in buying slow-selling medicines from big pharmaceutical companies. Ovation soon raised the wholesale price of Mustargen by roughly ten times, despite no investment in R&D or any other significant new costs. As in the study described above, Merck might have faced a public backlash if it had raised the price of the drug on its own. But because Ovation is so small, it was able to raise the drug price without attracting much attention, and Merck was able to avoid public accountability for effectively raising the price of the drug tenfold.

Dana, Weber, and Kuang (2007) present intriguing evidence on this issue of camouflaging the intentionality behind exploitative actions. Their study suggests that people who carry out such "indirect unethical behavior" may do so as much to protect their self-perceptions as to influence the perceptions of others. Participants in their study played a peculiar dictator game in which half of them had to choose between two options. One option gave them $5 and the other person $5. The second option gave them $6 but gave the other person $1. Participants in the "baseline" condition had all of this information. Seventy-four percent of them chose the first option over the second option, giving an equal $5 payment to each player. By contrast, participants in the "hidden payoff" condition saw that the first option would pay them $5 and that the second option would pay them $6; however, they would have to click on a box to learn what the consequence of their decision would be for the other party. Half of these participants chose not to click; among this half, all chose the second option, which gave them $6 and the other person $1. Remaining willfully ignorant of the larger consequences of their choices allowed them to choose selfishly. (One additional interesting result: recipients who were only given a dollar were more forgiving of the dictator's choice when they learned that the dictator had willfully chosen not to find out how the choice would impact the recipient than when the dictator knew the consequences of the action. It seems that keeping yourself ignorant about the possible negative repercussions of your selfish behavior might, at least in some circumstances, be in your selfish interest.)

More evidence that keeping others in the dark facilitates our selfish behavior comes from Dana, Cain, and Dawes (2006). They gave participants in their study a choice: either (1) play a standard dictator game in which they could allocate $10 between themselves and another person who would know about the game and their choice, or (2) exit the game silently and receive $9, knowing that the other person would receive nothing and would never even know about the existence of the game. Roughly one third of participants took the "silent exit" option, a choice that is difficult to justify as rational, as a self-interested person should play the standard dictator game and simply allocate the entire $10 to himself or herself. The people who chose the $9 silent exit apparently wanted to behave selfishly but felt more comfortable doing so when they could keep their selfishness secret.

WHEN VALUES SEEM SACRED

Many people have values that they claim to hold sacred. For instance, most ethical systems, including most religions, hold life to be sacred. However, as suggested by Tetlock's (1986) concept of *value pluralism*, the world rarely allows us to hold a single principle as sacred. Instead, life is full of difficult choices that demand that we balance one value against another. Some ethical systems that hold life sacred also maintain that people should not interfere with life's natural processes and therefore should not practice birth control. While both the

Roman Catholic Church and the Dalai Lama's Tibetan Buddhism subscribe to this view, the Dalai Lama (1999) acknowledges a tradeoff on this issue. The Dalai Lama argues that human population growth is endangering the lives of those already on the planet. We ought to worry not only about exceeding the Earth's ability to sustain human population, according to the Dalai Lama, but also about non-human forms of life. The percentage of plant and animal species that go extinct each year is as high today as it was during the great Permian extinction event, some 250 million years ago, when 90 percent of the Earth's living species went extinct (Benton, 2005). Such radical changes to the natural world will no doubt have repercussions for human life, although it can be difficult to anticipate all of them. The inference the Dalai Lama draws is that limiting human population growth is a responsible way to affirm the sacredness of the lives already on the Earth.

Tetlock, Peterson, and Lerner (1996) point out that, under some circumstances, people are usually willing to compromise on values that they regard as sacred. For instance, the Dalai Lama's concern for the living comes at the expense of the potential lives that birth control will prevent. It is also often the case that we must consider tradeoffs between "sacred issues" (such as the value of life) and what Tetlock, Kristel, Elson, Green, and Lerner (2000) call "secular issues" (such as the value of money). Tetlock et al. (2000) examine how people deal with the wrenching conundrum of considering tradeoffs that invite them to compromise on their sacred values. The most common responses are what the authors refer to as "moral outrage" and "cleansing." For instance, their respondents expressed moral outrage at the very idea of allowing markets in which human body parts, babies, or sexual favors would be bought and sold. In response, the participants engaged in mental cleansing rituals that involved distancing themselves from the reprehensible idea they had been asked to consider and agreeing to volunteer their time to work on more morally acceptable alternatives.

Without a doubt, moral judgments are often strongly associated with powerful emotional reactions. People usually assume that these emotions follow moral assessments. However, Haidt (2001, 2007) presents compelling evidence that, in fact, it is more common for the opposite to occur. In other words, our moral issues produce emotional reactions, which then drive our more cognitive assessments. Some of Haidt's strongest evidence comes from situations in which people react to an issue with emotions that they cannot explain or justify but that nevertheless guide their decisions.

For instance, Haidt, Björklund, and Murphy (2007) offered their participants $2 to sign a form (inspired by an episode of *The Simpsons*) that read "I hereby sell my soul, after my death, to Scott Murphy [the experimenter], for the sum of two dollars." At the bottom of the page, a printed note read: "This is not a legal or binding contract." Participants were told that they could keep the signed form as well as the $2 and that they could do whatever they liked with the form, including tearing it up, since it was meaningless and they were not actually selling their souls. Nevertheless, 77 percent of participants—even many of those who claimed not to believe in the existence of souls—refused the chance to make a quick $2. When asked to explain their refusal, participants could not articulate a sensible explanation beyond the fact that they simply didn't want to sign the contract. Here, as elsewhere, moral objections were driven primarily by emotion rather than reason.

THE PSYCHOLOGY OF CONFLICTS OF INTEREST

Financial advisers often earn fees based on the transactions they recommend to their clients. Surgeons typically earn more when they operate than when they don't operate, and doctors often receive payment for recommending patients for clinical trials. Commission-paid lawyers are more likely to recommend settling a case than are lawyers who are paid by the hour. Real-estate agents earn their living from our housing transactions. Merger-and-acquisition experts typically are paid only when a transaction occurs, and sometimes Supreme Court justices rule on cases involving their friends.

Most members of these professions would agree that a conflict of interest exists in many of these examples between receiving personal benefits (such as money or a hunting trip with friends) and doing what is best for their clients, their patients, or society at large. These same professionals, however, assume that they themselves are immune from such conflicts of interest. Likewise, it would be natural for the authors of this book to believe that the degree to which a job candidate's research affirms our own research never would affect our opinions in a faculty hiring decision. After all, we consider ourselves to be honest and objective people. Not only do we believe that we ourselves are immune from conflicts of interest, but we believe that the professionals giving us advice can overcome them as well.

This common belief in our own objectivity and the objectivity of our advisers belies the clear evidence that conflicts of interest are less likely to lead to conscious corruption than they are to distort our judgments in ways that we are not even aware are occurring. When a real-estate agent advises you to raise your offer beyond what a rational assessment would suggest, the point is not that she is corrupt, but simply that she is human and therefore implicitly motivated to maximize her own benefits from the deal. Because of this, she will focus on anecdotal evidence suggesting that buyers would prefer to overpay a bit for a house rather than run the risk of losing it. When we are motivated to interpret or alter data in a direction that will benefit us financially or otherwise, we are not capable of providing others with an objective assessment (Moore, Cain, Loewenstein, & Bazerman, 2005). This is true of doctors, lawyers, real-estate agents, professors, and other professionals.

Many people believe that disclosure is the best solution to conflicts of interest. In the words of former U.S. senator Phillip Hart, "Sunlight is the best disinfectant." Disclosure is attractive in part because it does little to disrupt the status quo: Parties need only report what they are doing. Consequently, disclosure is one of the most common responses to conflicts of interest. Disclosure of donations to politicians and political parties is the centerpiece of most campaign-finance legislation, including the McCain-Feingold Act of 1997. Most of Title IV of the Sarbanes-Oxley Act of 2001, which regulates auditing, is dedicated to issues of disclosure. Professional associations, including the American Medical Association and the Society for Professional Journalists, have codes of ethics that instruct their members to disclose potential conflicts of interest, as does the New York Stock Exchange.

But disclosure is not a panacea. In fact, Cain, Loewenstein, and Moore (2005) present evidence suggesting that disclosure can actually *increase* bias. In their study, the researchers assigned one member of each pair of participants to the role of "estimator" and the other to the role of "adviser." Both participants were asked to estimate the amount of money held in each of six jars filled with coins. Each adviser was able to inspect each jar closely and at length, while the estimators could only look at the jars briefly and from a long distance. The advisers were then asked to provide advice to his or her estimator about the amount of money in the jars. Estimators were always paid more when their estimates were more accurate. The advisers had a conflict of interest: the more their estimators overestimated how much money was in the jar, the more the advisers were paid; in other words, advisers had an incentive to mislead the estimators into guessing high. Cain et al. (2005) told some of the estimators about the advisers' pay arrangement but said nothing about it to the rest of the estimators.

The results showed that advisers whose conflicts of interest were disclosed provided more biased guesses (i.e., higher estimates of coin-jar values) than did advisers whose motives were not disclosed. In addition, disclosure did not cause estimators to discount their advisers' advice sufficiently. Thus, disclosure led advisers to make more money and estimators to make less than they would have without disclosure. This raises the real possibility that professionals who are forced to disclose conflicts of interest, such as auditors, might be more self-serving than those who do not make such disclosures.

Motivated blindness. Why did Arthur Andersen accept Enron's blatantly flawed accounting? We believe that the Andersen auditors were likely to have been guilty of the motivational bias of interpreting and searching for data favorable to maintaining the client relationship. Auditors have long claimed that they can make independent and unbiased judgments about their clients' books. At the same time, these auditors typically want to maintain these clients, to sell services to them, or even to seek jobs from them in the future. It is quite possible that most auditors are honest enough to avoid the incentives that could lead to intentionally corrupt audits. But as long as auditors are dependent on their clients for future contracts, it is not possible for them to be completely unbiased. Contrary to the focus of the media on finding and punishing the few bad apples damaging the U.S. financial system, the research evidence makes it clear that deeply ingrained institutional conflicts of interest that reward auditors for pleasing their clients were largely responsible for the crisis.

Virtually all humans tend to view data from a self-serving perspective. Accordingly, when an auditing firm depends on a client for financial or consulting business, it is not psychologically possible for the auditor to maintain true independence of judgment (Bazerman, Loewenstein, & Moore, 2002; Bazerman, Morgan, & Loewenstein, 1997). Creating true auditor independence would require funda- mental changes to the relationship between auditors and their clients, such that auditors do not have a motivation to please their clients. Our society has not yet confronted the challenges of creating true auditor independence.

In fact, this story illustrates a far broader problem that we refer to as *motivated blindness*. Namely, when people have an incentive not to notice data, they are able to overlook it. In several recent news stories, motivated blindness appears to lie behind the failure to notice the unethical behavior of others. Soon after the auditor scandals broke, the lack of analyst independence in investment banks became a focus of media attention and another vivid example of conflict of interest in the business world. Former acting SEC Chairperson Laura Unger cited a 2000 survey documenting that, at the same time that the NASDAQ was in a decline that decreased its value by 60 percent, 99.1 percent of brokerage-house analysts' recommendations were still "Strong Buy," "Buy," or "Hold." Brokerage firms often tied analyst compensation to the amount of business done by the firms they analyzed, a practice that obviously gives analysts an incentive to maintain positive relationships with these companies and overlook their unethical behavior.

To take another example, in December 2007, a report issued by former senator George Mitchell revealed the names of 80 Major League Baseball players, representing all 30 major league teams, who were alleged to have used performance-enhancing steroids and growth hormones. Stand-outs on the list included pitching great Roger Clemens; Barry Bonds, who in 2007 broke Hank Aaron's record to become the all-time leader in career home runs; and MLB superstars such as Miguel Tejada and Andy Pettitte. In 2009, the news leaked that the MLB had known of at least 100 players who had tested positive for using performance-enhancing drugs. In the face of accusations against him, New York Yankees star Alex Rodriguez admitted to using such drugs from 2001–2003. And in January 2010, Mark McGwire, who set the single-year home run record in 1998, admitted he had periodically used steroids over a period of ten years in his career.

In response to the steroids scandal, baseball fans tend to blame the players who cheated for damaging the sport's reputation. But several factors gave players strong incentives to engage in doping, including cutthroat competition, huge salaries for top performers, and perhaps most notably, the fact that MLB team owners and management turned a blind eye to steroid use for many years. Indeed, given the prevalence of doping the sport and the lack of penalties, players may have felt they would have been at an unfair disadvantage if they stayed clean (Bazerman & Tenbrunsel, 2011).

The widespread use of performance-enhancing drugs was an open secret in baseball during the 1990s and early 2000s. Sports journalists and even some former MLB players were vocal in calling the steroid problem a blight upon the sport. Yet MLB leaders appear not to have questioned rapid, dramatic changes in the physique and performance of players such as Bond. Why did they look the other way? It seems they may have succumbed to motivated blindness. Artificially pumped-up players were breaking performance records and boosting game attendance and TV viewership. Addressing steroid use would have jeopardized league revenues. These financial benefits prevented MLB management from noticing problems they had reason not to see. As we have noted, when people have a stake in a certain outcome, it is almost impossible for them to view relevant information without bias. That's why broad policy changes are usually needed to address motivated blindness. Amid the firestorm of the steroids scandal, the MLB instituted a strict policy of random drug testing; only then did steroid use by players appear to fall dramatically.

Motivated blindness can cause leaders throughout society to engage in unethical behaviors that they would condemn with greater awareness. The child sexual abuse scandals that have rocked the Catholic Church in the United States are one example. For decades, at direct odds with its mission of helping and protecting children, the Church's hierarchy allowed abuse to run rampant. To take one example, Cardinal Bernard F. Law, the archbishop of Boston, overlooked the huge amount of child abuse committed by priests under his watch. In court papers, he admitted he had returned John J. Geoghan to parish work despite knowing that the priest had been accused of child abuse. Geoghan, later convicted as a child molester, was just one of many criminals whom Law kept active in the priesthood (Bazerman & Tenbrunsel, 2011).

A former civil rights activist, Law had committed himself to a life of serving others, including children and other defenseless members of society. Law appears to have been an ethical person who made some extremely unethical and possibly illegal decisions in the course of this service. Why? Law testified that he allowed his decisions to be swayed by outdated medical and psychiatric advice concerning the ability of child abusers to curtail their behavior. He likely hoped that the abusers could be reformed. He also had an incentive to cover up the abuse, lest the Church's reputation be tarnished. These desires appear to have blinded Law to the clear evidence that the abusers would repeat their crimes.

Entire organizations, and even industries, can be susceptible to motivated blindness, as in the case of credit-rating agencies in the lead-up to the 2008 financial crisis. Credit-rating agencies are responsible for educating outside stakeholders of the creditworthiness of issuers of debt obligations, including for-profit and nonprofit organizations and governments, and the debt instruments these financial organizations sell to the public. During the housing bubble, many debt issuers began to bundle and sell subprime and other high-risk home loans as mortgage-backed securities. In their independent assessments, credit-rating agencies failed to accurately rate the riskiness of these securities. After the financial crisis struck, the House Oversight and Government Reform Committee found evidence that executives at the rating agencies were "well aware that there was little basis for giving AAA ratings to thousands of increasingly complex mortgage-related securities, but the companies often vouched for them anyway," according to the committee's chairman, Representative Henry Waxman (D-CA) (Swanson, 2008).

Here again, motivated blindness appears to have led to flawed decision making. Former credit-rating agency executives testified to the House committee that a conflict of interest makes it difficult for the U.S. credit-rating system to perform as intended. Specifically, the largest agencies (including Standard & Poor's, Moody's, and Fitch) are paid by the companies they rate rather than by the investors who have a true stake in the ratings. Credit-rating agencies exist to provide objective analyses, yet their compensation displays an inherent conflict of interest. Now consider that the agencies made huge profits during the housing bubble by giving top ratings to securities and debt issuers. The promise of these profits motivated them to turn a blind eye to the extreme levels of risk the debt issuers were promoting during this time. Despite the catastrophe that followed, the federal government has failed to act to address the credit-rating agencies' conflict of interest, leaving them susceptible to motivated blindness in the future.

What can we do about conflicts of interest? First, try to eliminate them by avoiding advice from biased sources. Second, recognize that honesty does not solve the problem of conflicts of interest, as even the most honest people are biased. Finally, do not make the mistake of viewing yourself or your adviser as immune from the pernicious effects of conflicts of interest.

CONCLUSION

Throughout the scandals that have scarred corporate America in recent years, policy makers and the press have consistently sought to pin the blame on the individuals at the heart of the crisis. Yet when we examine each scandal, it becomes clear that it would not have been possible for just a few people to create these problems if others around them had behaved ethically. From the classic experiments of Milgram (1963) on obedience to authority, to Latane and Darley's (1969) demonstrations of bystanders' inaction to cries of help, to the contemporary research on implicit attitudes reviewed in this chapter, social psychologists have shown again and again that humans make systemic errors, inconsistent with their own desired ethics, that can profoundly harm others.

Much of this book considers the systematic and predictable errors that we make against the criterion of rationality. In this chapter, we have focused on the ethical errors we make against the criterion of our intended ethicality. We have documented perceptual and cognitive errors that lead our ethicality to be bounded in ways that contradict our typical assumption of unbounded ethicality. Most of us hold a stable view of ourselves as moral, competent, and deserving, and thus immune from ethical failures (Banaji et al., 2003). This high self-regard keeps us from monitoring our own behavior and makes bounded ethicality all the more likely.

Can ethics training help people behave more consistently with their values? Some knowledgeable observers argue that the actual results of ethics training are disappointing (Badaracco & Webb, 1995). Like Tenbrunsel and Messick (2004), we believe that most ethics training focuses too narrowly on explicitly unethical behavior. The concept of bounded ethicality addresses unethical behavior that escapes the actor's conscious awareness. Most managers think of themselves as ethical people, and they do not intentionally engage in unethical behavior. They therefore question why they should waste their time listening to lessons that tell them to behave ethically. The concepts presented in this chapter highlight ethical concerns that are likely to have escaped the attention of honest and dishonest managers alike.

More than a decade and a half ago, Messick and Bazerman (1996) argued against the perspective that questions of executive ethics can be boiled down to explicit tradeoffs between ethics and profits. Rather, we asserted that a focus on psychological tendencies will lead to improved ethical decision making. We now believe that the unconscious aspects of these psychological tendencies offer the best hope for improving individual and organizational ethics.

CHAPTER NINE

Common Investment Mistakes

*B*ecause money managers are paid so handsomely for their work, investment banks often have their pick of the best and the brightest. It seems reasonable to assume that these smart, hard-working people—who are generously rewarded when their investments perform well—can find ways to invest your money that will perform better than a passive index-fund strategy of putting your money in an investment fund that tracks a broad market index of stock performances. Surely even a mediocre money manager ought to be able to hand-select stocks that would perform better than an index fund.

Well, let's look at the data. Over time, the Vanguard Index 500 fund, which tracks the S&P 500 (Standard & Poor's index of 500 large U.S. corporations), has outperformed about 75 percent of the actively managed mutual funds in each year. Of course, you personally would not plan to invest in one of the 75 percent of funds that performs worse than the market; you would choose from among the top 25 percent. The only problem is that substantial evidence demonstrates that past stock performance is not a good predictor of future performance. While some research suggests minor relationships between past and future performance, these relationships have been small and inconsistent. That makes it very difficult to identify which funds will be in the top 25 percent in the future.

There are a lot of mutual funds—approximately 8,000—and all of them are being managed by people who would like you to believe they can outperform the market, though only an average of 25 percent will succeed in any given year. In other words, each year approximately 2,000 of these 8,000 funds will outperform the market. Of these, 25 percent, or 500, will outperform the market again the next year. And among these winners, 25 percent, or roughly 125 funds, will again outperform the market for a third year in a row. The key lesson is that there will always be funds that outperform the market for multiple years in a row, but this trend will happen roughly at random, and past performance will still have little predictive power.

By contrast, index funds are certain to perform at the level of the overall market to which they are indexed, minus a small operating fee. One reason index funds outperform the majority of mutual funds is simply that their fees are so low—often below 0.2 percent. Actively managed mutual funds have far higher expenses—often as high as two percent annually, or up to ten times higher than some index funds. What's more, the actively managed funds usually engage in frequent buying and selling of stocks, leading to higher brokerage costs that are subtracted from their returns. By definition, the aggregate of active funds (in which managers choose stocks) is likely to match the market, before fees are subtracted (Sharpe, 1991). In the end, high expenses significantly reduce the returns of these actively managed funds.

Now consider the case of hedge funds, which exploded onto the investment scene in recent years. The amount of money under management by hedge funds has grown dramatically, from $240 billion in 1998 to about $2.4 trillion by the middle of 2011 (BarclayHedge, 2012). Hedge funds provide wealthy individuals and institutional investors an alternative to traditional investment vehicles. By restricting who can invest in them, hedge funds avoid certain governmental regulations and disclosures, thereby allowing their managers to maintain secrecy about their investment strategies. This secrecy, coupled with stories of spectacular gains from certain hedge funds, has built a mystique that has attracted substantial investment. Furthermore, thanks to the high fees that hedge funds charge, their managers tend to earn extremely high incomes, even by the impressive standards of the investment banking industry. For instance, CNNMoney estimated that hedge-fund manager John Paulson took home $4.9 billion in 2010. This sort of compensation has meant that hedge funds can attract the best talent away from investment banks. Has this talent translated into superior performance?

The evidence suggests not. Kat and Palaro (2006) examined the performance of nearly 2,000 hedge funds and concluded that only 18 percent outperformed the relevant market benchmarks. The problem? As with actively managed mutual funds, the high fees attached to hedge funds detract from any returns they might achieve. It is standard for hedge funds to charge their investors "two and twenty"—an annual fee equal to two percent of the total amount invested plus 20 percent of any investment gains (Cassidy, 2007). These fees are similar to those of the most expensive actively managed mutual funds. In fact, hedge funds perform even worse than Kat and Palaro's (2006) performance data suggest, as they only examined existing hedge funds. As with mutual funds, the losers go out of business and thus are not included in long-term performance data. If the analysis included these "ghost" funds, performance would look even worse (Malkiel & Saha, 2005).

No individual who buys an active mutual fund or invests in a hedge fund is seeking an investment that will perform far worse than average. Yet lots of people buy and continue to hold onto such investments long after receiving evidence of their failure. The cost of these mistakes adds up to billions of dollars. Why do people make these mistakes? While the answers can be found in the preceding chapters of this book, researchers have developed these insights into a new field of inquiry: behavioral finance.

Essentially, behavioral finance is an application of what we know about common judgment errors to the world of investment. In the 1980s and early 1990s, behavioral decision research was applied most extensively to the area of negotiation (which we will cover in Chapters 10 and 11). In recent years, the most active area for new insights has been in the area of financial decisions. This research gives us a better understanding of an important set of life decisions and also offers clear evidence that the decision errors described in this book are broad in scope. Behavioral finance focuses on how biases affect both individuals and markets. This chapter focuses on the former application; Shleifer (2000) and Shefrin (2000) are good sources on the latter.

In this chapter, we will specifically: (1) apply some of the core findings from earlier chapters to investment decisions, (2) explore the scary practice of day-trading that became popular in the late 1990s, and (3) close with some clear, common-sense investment advice. As you read, we encourage you to compare these insights to your own beliefs about investing and to your current investment portfolio. Behavioral finance is, after all, an application of basic principles to a specific decision domain. Consequently, you will notice that this chapter is more practical and implies more specific advice than most of the other chapters in this book.

THE PSYCHOLOGY OF POOR INVESTMENT DECISIONS

Investors love new books promising huge increases in stock market prices. Glassman and Hassett's (1999) wildly optimistic book *Dow: 36,000*, for example, received enormous media attention during the giddy days of the dot-com boom. *Flipping Houses for Dummies* (Roberts & Kraynak, 2006), which advised investors on how to buy and sell houses for a quick buck, was more emblematic of the real-estate boom of the 2000s. Such titles achieve their success by exploiting investor psychology. Motivated optimism and the confirmation bias are sufficient to convince people with money in the market that their investments have a bright future. This is great for the authors who get rich from these books, but their success does not usually translate into investing success for the books' readers. As we have shown in earlier chapters, even very bright people make poor decisions that cost time, profit, and, in some cases, their financial futures.

As you read this chapter, our arguments against active investing may sound strong. However, the evidence is overwhelming, and it contradicts the massive amount of money and advice changing hands in financial markets. Investors pay high fees to actively managed mutual funds and hedge funds, to brokers to pick stocks, and to electronic trading companies to trade their money. These fees are how funds, brokers, and companies make their money. Are all of these investors making mistakes? The great majority of them are. As Jason Zweig (2000) warned the readers of *Money Magazine*, "The folks who run mutual funds have always been good at cooking up clever ways to gouge you on fees, confuse you about performance, make you pay unnecessary taxes and goad you into buying funds you don't need."

The high rate of trading in the stock market has long been a mystery for economists. Rational economic agents should trade very little, and certainly nowhere near as much as real investors trade (Grossman & Stiglitz, 1980; Odean, 1999). The human biases we have reviewed in the preceding chapters do offer some answers. Moreover, the financial professionals whose incomes depend on the fees their clients pay are good at exploiting these biases. This section will document how investment decisions are affected by: (1) overconfidence; (2) optimism; (3) denying random events and the regression to the mean; (4) anchoring, the status quo, and procrastination; and (5) prospect theory.

Overconfidence Produces Excessive Trading

In Chapter 2, we offered evidence that people are generally overconfident with respect to the precision of their knowledge, beliefs, and predictions. In the area of investing, this overconfidence can translate into a tendency to be excessively sure that you know which direction the market is headed or that you can pick the right fund in which to invest. This overconfidence leads people to engage in more active investing. Why should you be concerned about overconfidence? Because the data strongly suggest that the stocks or actively managed mutual funds that you pick underperform the market, on average, despite your optimism.

Overconfidence is especially pertinent to stock-market investing strategies. The expenses associated with owning individual stocks are largely created by the costs of buying and selling them. These expenses, which include transaction costs and differences between buy-and-sell prices, are dramatically higher for investors who make frequent trades. Collectively, these expenses can add up to a surprisingly large amount of money over time. While we have argued that investing in an index fund is a better strategy than frequent stock trades, it is not your only good option. For an investor with a moderate amount of wealth, a low-cost alternative to an index fund would be to buy a diversified portfolio of stocks and hold them for many years. Thanks to the emergence of a variety of investment vehicles designed to help you build a portfolio cheaply and conveniently, this strategy is becoming easier and more commonplace (Zweig, 2000).

Unfortunately, many stock-market investors fail to recognize the advantages of following this approach. Barber and Odean (2000) studied 66,465 households that held an investment account with a large discount broker during the period 1991–1996. In contrast to the buy-and-hold strategy, the average account turned over 75 percent of its portfolio annually. That is, on average, investors with this brokerage house sold 75 percent of their investments in any given year. Similarly, Carhart (1997) reports that the average turnover of mutual funds is 77 percent annually, while the New York Stock Exchange determined that in 1999, its total turnover rate was 78 percent. These numbers mark a dramatic increase since 1970, when the turnover rate for the New York Stock Exchange was 19 percent, and in 1980, when it was 36 percent. This growing frenzy can be attributed in part to bright people thinking they can predict the moves of the market. Are they right?

The average investor in the Barber and Odean (2000) database earned a return of 16.4 percent during a booming market, just 1.5 percent lower than the overall market return of 17.9 percent for this same period. Most interesting are the 20 percent of accounts (more than 12,000 accounts) that had the highest turnover rates—those investors who actively traded stocks. Presumably, these investors believe they can assess the direction stocks will take and are willing to incur the costs of buying and selling stocks to own the "right" portfolio at the right time. On average, the 20 percent with the highest turnover earned a return of just 11.4 percent. Thus, in comparison to the overall market return, by spending time and money trying to track, buy, and sell stocks, investors *lost* 6.5 percentage points. If active trading is so hazardous to your wealth, why do so many people engage in it? One simple explanation is that they are overconfident in their ability to predict where the market is going next.

Overconfidence does not affect the genders equally. Examining 35,000 investment accounts at a large discount brokerage, Barber and Odean (2001) sorted the accounts by gender and found that women achieved better results than men. In comparison to the market as a whole, women underperformed the return that they would have obtained by holding the same portfolio for a year by 1.72 annual percentage points, while in a similar comparison, men lost 2.65 percentage points. Does this mean that women pick better stocks than men? No. Actual returns of stocks picked by men and women were not significantly different. Rather, turnover patterns differed; the men had a harder time sitting still. Women had average turnover rates of 53 percent annually, while male turnover rates were 77 percent annually. It was the added costs of these more frequent trades that led men to underperform women; with each trade, the brokers got richer while the investors themselves fell further behind. Barber and Odean conclude that over-confidence among men leads to increased turnover, which in turn leads to lower performance after brokerage costs are carved out of the returns. Before women readers become overly satisfied about these findings, it is important to note that Barber and Odean are describing men performing worse than women whose results are *already far behind* those of the market. In other words, women did less badly than men—hardly an achievement worth celebrating.

Optimism about Investment Decisions

If you have money invested in the stock market, what was the total percentage return of your portfolio last year? Did you beat the market—in other words, did your performance compare favorably to the S&P 500? Now, go check your answers based on the actual data: Look up your account statements or call your brokerage or fund adviser, and don't forget to ask for last year's return on the S&P 500. How did your memory of your performance compare to your actual performance?

Our guess is that your comparison will be consistent with evidence showing that people tend to be optimistic about a variety of behaviors, such as expected career advancement, driving ability, etc. (see Chapter 2). Once people make an investment, they tend to be overly optimistic about its future profitability and later maintain optimistic recollections of the investment's past performance. Optimism is closely related to overconfidence, yet distinct from it. When investors make overly confident decisions, they will hold unwarranted optimism regarding future success; retrospectively, they will maintain this optimism, even when the dis-appointing results of their investments are easily available.

Moore, Kurtzberg, Fox, and Bazerman (1999) created an investment simulation based on the actual performance of the nine largest mutual funds, plus one index fund, over a ten-year period, 1985–1994. MBA students received a computer program with an investment assignment. Starting with $100,000, for each six-month simulated period, participants were allowed to invest their balance in any of the ten funds or in a money market account, with the goal of maximizing their ending balance at the end of the simulated ten years. (The entire task took the typical student 45 minutes to complete.) After making a six-month investment decision, participants received extensive feedback on their return, the return of all funds, and the return on the overall market; they were then prompted to place their next six-month investment. Investing the entire account in the index fund for the entire ten-year period would have led the $100,000 initial portfolio to grow to $380,041. However, the average investor ended up with only $349,620 in his or her account—a return consistent with the evidence from real-world databases presented earlier. The typical investor chose too many actively managed funds that made too many trades and charged fees that were too high.

False optimism was clearly a factor in the participants' investment strategies. Despite the fact that the market performed very well overall during this ten-year period (1985–1994), participants consistently predicted that their portfolios would grow faster for the next six-month interval than they actually did. Specifically, participants predicted that their portfolios would rise 8.13 percent per six-month period; in fact, they grew by only 5.50 percent. Even more interesting, participants had optimistic illusions about their past performance: At the end of the game, most participants reported that they had matched the market's performance. In fact, participants obtained an average return 8 percent *below* the market. More specifically, Moore et al. (1999) asked participants whether they had performed (1) more than 15 percent below the market, (2) 10–15 percent below the market, (3) 5–10 percent below the market, (4) within 5 percent of the market, (5) 5–10 above the market, (6) 10–15 percent above the market, or (7) more than 15 percent above the market. On average, participants overstated their performance by one entire level.

In a parallel study, Goetzmann and Peles (1997) obtained very similar results. Participants remembered obtaining more favorable returns than they actually obtained. Goetzmann and Peles conclude that optimism helps investors justify their past behaviors, allowing them to maintain illusions about the superiority of their investment strategy. We argue that optimism also encourages investors to continue active trading rather than pursuing wiser, time-saving investments in index funds.

By the way, before reading this chapter, had you ever compared your investment decisions to the market? Most investors have not. Why not? We argue that most investors want to protect their overly optimistic view of their investments—and are willing to pay a high price to maintain their illusions. Similarly, if you use an investment adviser, have you ever instructed this "expert" to provide systematic follow-up on his or her recommendations? It might be instructive for you to ask the adviser to compare the returns on his or her advice to the market's performance during the same period of time. The psychological need to perceive good news may be insulating you and your hired experts from the truth about investing—and costing you a great deal of money in the long run.

Plenty of external sources encourage investors' natural optimism. Financial magazines remind us of the wise advice they provided in the past, but generally neglect to mention the advice that was flat-out wrong. These publications also tend to supply anecdotal evidence of past success rather than risking their reputation by tracking it in a systematic manner. Overall, we have to admit that this is a wise business strategy: If they revealed the true returns on their past advice, they would probably sell fewer magazines.

Denying that Random Events are Random

As we saw in Chapter 3, people tend to deny that random events are random and find patterns where none exist, such as having a "hot hand" in basketball. When investors are led to believe that a specific fund is "hot," they will become more willing to pay the fees associated with active investing. For example, when a fund outperforms the market two years in a row, investors rarely attribute its success to random variation. It is more likely that they will overgeneralize from these few data points and assume that the manager of the fund has great skill and is therefore worthy of their investment. As money manager Nassim Nicholas Taleb discusses in his book *Fooled by Randomness* (2001), there is a great deal of randomness in the investment arena and even more denial of this randomness by investors and investing professionals. In their eagerness to outperform the market, most investors are reluctant to settle for the index fund strategy of performing at the level of the market and minimizing expenses. The most important conclusion? Be wary of any advice that predicts specific investments' future based on past performance.

Consistent with research by Bogle (1994), Carhart (1997), and Thaler and DeBondt (1992), in the ten-year database used in the Moore et al. (1999) study (1985–1994), the performance of mutual funds tended to regress to the mean. Nevertheless, study participants expected their portfolios' future performance to be highly correlated with past performance. In fact, their expectations were negatively correlated with actual returns. Overall, participants expected "hot" funds to stay hot, just as they expect basketball players who are "hot" to perform especially well. Both of these expectations overestimate the influence of individual skill and underestimate the role of chance. This is the same false expectation that leads real-world investors to hold on to expensive funds.

There is some minor evidence that past performance of stocks predicts their future performance. Jegadeesh and Titman (1993) document a momentum effect in which stocks that have done well continue to do well the next year. The only problem is that this pattern then reverses itself in subsequent years (DeBondt & Thaler, 1985). Odean (1999) argues that biased investors who expect past patterns to continue in the future may influence a stock's performance. However, after the last of these momentum traders enter the market and push the value of the stock beyond the underlying value of the company, the price will begin to fall, causing the inevitable reversal.

DeBondt and Thaler (1985) compared the future performance of two groups of stocks: one group of extreme losers from the past three years and one group of extreme winners from the past three years. They found that over the following five years, the "loser" portfolio dramatically outperformed the "winner" portfolio. DeBondt and Thaler (1985) attribute reversals to the tendency of investors to assume that the past is a good predictor of the future, and thus to their penchant for overbuying winners and overselling losers. The market eventually adjusts, and owners of the underpriced "loser" portfolio will find themselves with a better set of investments than owners of the overpriced "winner" portfolio.

Inspired by Jegadeesh and Titman's (1993) results, you might be tempted to adopt the strategy of buying recent stock-market winners. On the other hand, DeBondt and Thaler's (1985) findings might motivate you to buy recent losers. Unfortunately, it is extremely difficult to predict when the last momentum buyers have entered the market. Once again, the past is not an accurate predictor of the future. Personally, we are more comfortable admitting that we have no way of knowing which stocks will do better in the future and sticking with index funds.

Anchoring, the Status Quo, and Procrastination

Much of this chapter suggests that many investors think too much about their investments, trading stocks too frequently and shifting mutual funds based on the most recent advice of too many experts. Evidence also suggests that most people think too *little* about the type of assets they want in their investment portfolios. Thinking through one's asset allocation and developing a long-term plan makes a great deal of sense. This is where investment advice (including free software programs provided by many mutual fund companies) may be helpful. For example, Shefrin (2000), Belsky and Gilovich (1999), and many other sources of good financial advice suggest that most people place too little of their *long-term* investments in stocks. This observation is based on the long-term superior performance of stocks over bonds and other standard investments. Yet people use fairly naive strategies for asset allocation, sticking with what they or others have decided in the past; in other words, their investment decisions tend to be fairly mindless.

In a study of scholars who enroll in retirement plans offered by TIAA-CREF, Benartzi and Thaler (2001) found that most professors, facing a choice between investing their retirement funds in either TIAA (bonds) or CREF (stock), commonly allocated their money 50:50 to the two accounts. In addition, the median number of changes that professors made to this allocation over their career was zero. That is, professors (maybe not the smartest of people, but also not the dumbest) made a fairly naive allocation and then never adjusted their decision— even as their life circumstances changed over time.

The professors' 50:50 allocation meshes with another of Benartzi and Thaler's (2001) findings: When firms offer a choice of investment options for retirement accounts, the percentage of stock funds offered is an excellent predictor of the percentage of dollars that employees will choose to invest in stocks. That is, if a company offers four funds, three stock and one bond, employees put about

75 percent of their money into the stock funds. In contrast, if the company offers one stock fund and three bond funds, then employees hold, on average, 75 percent of their retirement investments in bonds. Thus, people choose their investments the way many diners order food in a Chinese restaurant: one dish from the "Vegetables" column, one from "Chicken," one from "Beef," and so on. That may be a good way to pick a satisfying meal, but it's not the best investment strategy; history shows that if your money will remain invested in a retirement fund for decades, stock funds will offer the best return. The point is that people should think carefully about this allocation rather than being led naively by the choices their employers offer them.

By this point in the chapter, we hope that readers are reconsidering their investment decisions. However, there is a strong force competing against change: the status-quo bias. This is the effect that prevented Benartzi and Thaler's (2001) professors from making even one allocation change in a lifetime. Samuelson and Zeckhauser (1988) find that people tend to keep their investments as they are. In an experimental study, the researchers presented a thought exercise to a group of individuals with a working knowledge of economics and finance. The participants were asked to imagine that they had inherited a large amount of money from a great uncle and were asked which of four possible investments they would pick: (1) a stock with moderate risk, (2) a risky stock, (3) U.S. Treasury bills, and (4) municipal bonds. Each investment was described in a bit of detail. Four other randomly selected groups were told that they had inherited money from their great uncle in the form of one of the four investments listed above. (That is, one group was told they inherited a stock with moderate risk, a second group was told they inherited a risky stock, a third group was told they inherited a U.S. Treasury bill, and a fourth group was told they inherited a municipal bond.) These participants were asked whether they would keep the investment or trade it for one of the three other investments listed above. They overwhelmingly chose to keep the investment they received rather than picking the investment best suited to their unbiased preferences. Essentially, the study participants accepted the status quo rather than switching to the investments that best suited their particular needs.

Finally, the bias against action also leads many people to procrastinate making investments in the first place. Studies of automatic enrollment in 401(k) employee savings plans powerfully illustrate just how passive people can be about very important economic decisions. 401(k)s are attractive savings vehicles not only because they defer taxation until the money is withdrawn, but also because some organizations offer to match the contributions of their employees up to a certain amount. Most companies use an "opt-in" savings plan, which means that their employees must enroll in the 401(k) on their own initiative, usually by filling out a form or calling a phone number. Others use automatic enrollment, where the default is enrollment at a set contribution rate. In this scenario, an employee must make an extra effort if he or she does not want to contribute. The difference in employee enrollment rates between these two different types of enrollment schemes is striking. Madrian and Shea (2001) found that initial enrollments in 401(k)s jumped from 49 percent to 86 percent within the same company when it switched from an opt-in system to automatic enrollment. Choi, Laibson, Madrian, and Metrick (2003) found that a third alternative called "no default," which forces the employee to think about the decision, also increases enrollment, but not as much as automatic enrollment (Choi et al., 2003).

Similarly, it is not uncommon for people to hold a large amount of money in their checking, savings, or money market account with the intention of investing it soon. Months pass, and they find themselves facing the same decision—but suddenly the market has gone up in value by 6 percent, and they've missed out on a great opportunity. By procrastinating, you may be sacrificing your long-term financial well-being. Somewhat paradoxically, investors procrastinate on making allocation decisions while being overly active in moving funds within a category (e.g., stocks), thus putting too much effort into the less important financial decisions and not enough effort into the far more vital ones.

Prospect Theory, Selling Winners, and Keeping Losers

Odean (1998) found that investors have a strong preference to hold on to stocks that are selling below purchase price, so that they will avoid becoming "losers," and to sell stocks that are selling above the purchase price, so that they will come out "winners." Similarly, Barber, Odean, and Zheng (2005) show that investors tend to hold on to losing mutual funds and oversell winning mutual funds. If your goal is to make as much money as you can, then the choice of whether to buy or sell a fund should be based solely on how much you expect its value to increase in the future. Thus, the price at which you bought it is an arbitrary and meaningless reference point, except with regard to taxes. From a tax perspective, when you sell a winner, you must pay taxes on your earnings, and when you sell a loser, your taxes are reduced. Therefore, with respect to taxation, it makes sense to sell more losers than winners. In addition, Odean (1999) finds that the winners that investors sell end up outperforming the losers that they keep. In sum, when investors seek to become winners, stock selection and taxes actually increase their chances of being losers.

Calvet, Campbell, and Sodini (2009) have found that investors become more eager to sell their winners as the performance of these investments improves. Why are investors biased to sell their winners? As we learned from prospect theory in Chapter 3, decision makers tend to compare outcomes to a reference point. For most investors, the most common reference point is the price they initially paid for a stock. Investors holding stocks valued at a price higher than they paid for them are faced with a sure gain (selling now and becoming a "winner") or holding the stock and risking the current gain for an unknown return. With gains, we tend to be risk averse; investors tend to sell to guarantee the gain. Investors holding stocks valued lower than their initial purchase price, on the other hand, must choose between selling now—a sure loss—or holding the stock for an unknown return. With losses, we tend to be risk seeking; investors tend to take the risk of holding on to the loser in the hope of becoming a winner. This pattern is also consistent with a regret minimization strategy—that is, an effort to avoid "booking" a loss and feeling regretful. As long as you let the loss "ride," you can pretend it doesn't exist. Once you sell the stock, however, you have to enter it in your mental accounts on the loss side of the ledger. This pattern leads investors to lose money relative to the market's overall performance, for three reasons: the high costs associated with making trades, selling the wrong stocks, and paying too much in taxes. It also has other surprising implications, as Barberis and Xiong (forthcoming) have shown, including the fact that investors should do more trading in rising than falling markets, that individual investors will be drawn to volatile stocks, and that these volatile stocks will wind up having lower average returns than steadier stocks.

ACTIVE TRADING

Starting in the late 1990s, online trading became the growth area of the investment world. Electronic trading was, and still is, simply cheaper than trading through a stockbroker, and as more people began to trade online, the costs went down. From 1996 to 1998, the average online trading commission fell by 75 percent. In addition, the Internet has enabled regular people to have access to a vast amount of financial data, research, and tools, including up-to-date information, low-cost trades, and almost instantaneous transactions.

First the good news about online trading: If you are planning to invest in stocks, bringing your costs down will be a key to your success. So, for those investors who follow a long-term buy-and-hold strategy, investing online rather than through a full-service broker makes a great deal of sense. However, buy-and-hold is not the strategy of the typical online trader. Especially during the late 1990s bull market, online traders tended to be actively engaged in trading stocks. In the worst case, they quit their jobs to be professional traders. Many of them were headed for disaster.

The typical investor who engaged in online trading around this time was someone whose trades had recently beat the market (most likely because they were lucky). In a 1992–1995 sample of online trading, Barber and Odean (2002) found that the average new online trader outperformed the market by two percentage points the year before switching to online trading. Note that these investors' confidence was further bolstered by the fact that these were very good years for the stock market. Unfortunately, after switching, these traders' average performance regressed to the mean and was further lowered by the costs of frequent trades. As a result, these online traders lagged the market by three percentage points.

Lagging a very successful market by three percentage points is no disaster, particularly if you engage in online trading in your spare time. However, it was the most overconfident traders who did lots of active trading online. Many of them quit their regular professions to trade full-time, becoming members of the now notorious pseudo-profession called "daytrading." Under the strict definition of daytrading, individuals initiate and close out high-volume positions by the end of the same trading day, but the term refers to short-term trades in general. Daytraders try to capitalize on price fluctuations of highly volatile, usually technology-related, stocks.

The high frequency of their trades doomed these full-time traders to under-perform the market by even more than three percentage points. Jordan and Diltz (2003) studied records of 324 daytraders during 1998 and 1999, the time of an immense stock market bubble, and found that only 36 percent made money during this heady period. In addition, nearly all of these daytraders' profits were short-term capital gains, which were taxed as ordinary income (with a tax rate of up to 35 percent, depending on the investor's income bracket); more patient investors were taxed on long-term gains at a much lower 15 percent. Even before the market plummeted, one particularly distraught Atlanta daytrader went on a shooting spree after a streak of "bad luck." When the market went down, many more sad stories emerged about those who had quit their jobs and subsequently lost life savings by daytrading.

What caused reasonably smart people to decide to become daytraders? In Chapter 3, we presented evidence that people respond to vivid data. Barber and Odean (2000b) document the barrage of ads that made daytrading success stories vivid to Americans. In one commercial, Discover Brokerage introduced us to an intrinsically motivated tow-truck driver with a postcard on his dashboard. "Vacation?" his white-collar passenger asks. "That's my home," the driver responds. "Looks more like an island," comments the passenger. The driver explains, "Technically, it's a country." Where did the driver get his wealth? Online trading, of course—it was that easy. This type of commercial, as well as real-life stories of the lucky, inspired more and more people to trade online, leading in many cases to tragic consequences.

When Max used to run into daytraders (some were also taxi drivers), he liked to ask them why they thought they knew more than the party on the other side of the trade. Most of the daytraders Max met had never considered this question. When they asked him to clarify, he tried to explain: When a daytrader is buying a stock, it is because someone else has sold it. Similarly, when a daytrader sells a stock, someone else is buying it. Odds are that the other party is an institutional investor of some sort. Thus, most daytraders are typically paying fees to make an exchange with someone who has better information, more experience, and quicker hardware to make the trade than they do. Overall, we argue, this sounds like a bad bet. But, as we saw in Chapter 4, people are not very good at considering the other side of a transaction.

ACTION STEPS

More than any other chapter in this book, the ideas presented in this chapter have action implications for virtually all readers. We have reviewed the mistakes that many people make and explained the psychology behind those mistakes. Now that we have observed these mistakes in the investing context, we close with some specific thoughts to consider as you strive to reduce the biases that affect your investments. We begin with the issue of saving for retirement and close with broader investment advice.

Determine Your Investment Goals

In Chapter 1, we argued that a key aspect of making more rational decisions is to clearly identify your final goal. Many investors have never put much thought into this issue. Some may have the goal of "accumulating as much money as possible." But, if you are able to take this goal to the extreme—by earning a good income, living frugally, and investing your savings wisely—you could end up dying with mountains of money in your accounts. A different goal is to save what you need to buy what you need to live. This goal is the central theme of the investment bestseller *Die Broke* (Pollan & Levine, 1997). We have no objection to a mixed strategy of buying the goods you desire and providing funds for other people and charitable organizations. However, many of us fail to think even this far ahead about our monetary objectives.

The goal of investing to earn enough for a comfortable retirement seems straightforward. However, a 1997 survey found that only 6 percent of U.S. citizens felt they had surpassed their retirement savings goal, while 55 percent felt that they were behind (Laibson, Repetto, & Tobacman, 1998). Laibson et al. (1998) report that the median U.S. household retires with liquid wealth of $10,000 and net worth of $100,000 (including house equity and autos). This finding is consistent with a broad array of evidence that Americans are saving too little for retirement. Assuming that we are capable of saving more, why do we fail to do so? Perhaps the most direct answer comes from the want/should distinction developed in Chapter 6. People know that they *should* save more for retirement, but they *want* to consume more now (to buy a new TV, eat dinners out, etc.). The evidence in Chapter 6 suggests that our desires typically overcome what we think we should do, particularly when the benefits of listening to our "should self" are decades in the future.

U.S. tax policy and many employers provide incentives for people to save for retirement. Because of these incentives, virtually all readers should be investing as much money as they can to reduce their taxable income and maximize employer matching contributions. If you are not contributing the maximum percentage of your salary that your plan allows, then you are missing out on one of the best and safest ways to build your long-term wealth. Yet, among those who do participate in 401(k) plans, most are contributing too little.

Once you have allocated money to savings, decisions regarding where to place your retirement money should be based on a clear asset allocation plan. Benartzi and Thaler (2001) make a convincing case that most people have far too low a percentage of their retirement funds in stock. The fact that retirement funding is for the distant future means that it should be easier to accept the higher risk of stock in return for the higher returns that stocks achieve over a long period of time. A few bad years are unlikely to lead stocks to underperform bonds between now and the time most readers will retire. As you approach retirement, it may make more sense to move more money into bonds to reduce risk.

As retirement draws near, annuities also make a great deal of sense for those investors who have the goal of buying a desired bundle of life goods. In return for a lump sum of money, the investor gets a guaranteed amount of funds periodically for the rest of his or her life. If you die ahead of schedule, you lose—but then again, you won't need the money anyway. However, if you outlive expectations, you can get a great return, and you are more likely to need these additional funds. Annuities are underused in comparison to the financial benefits that they create. In addition, annuities are now provided by a number of charitable organizations, allowing you to obtain guaranteed income and tax benefits and to fund your preferred charity. These annuities create more total benefit than you could achieve privately while making a similarly valued contribution to society. Although annuities are logical for many investors, you need to choose them carefully. Some annuities, pushed by the sleaziest outfits in the financial business, come with a slick sales pitch and are wildly overpriced. We recommend sticking with a highly reputable, well-known mutual-fund family that charges low fees, such as T. Rowe Price, Schwab, or Vanguard.

Beyond retirement, the key argument of this chapter is that very bright people are currently paying billions of dollars per year for collectively useless advice. Why? Because they are committing the errors described throughout this book in the area of investing.

Why is the Stock Market so Difficult to Predict?

Even smart people have trouble correctly predicting changes in the stock market, probably because lots of other smart people are trying to do the exact same thing. The economist John Maynard Keynes highlighted the situation with a famous analogy (1936, p. 156):

> Professional investment may be likened to those newspaper competitions in which the competitors have to pick out the six prettiest faces from a hundred photographs, the prize being awarded to the competitor whose choice most nearly corresponds to the average preferences of the competitors as a whole; so that each competitor has to pick not those faces which he himself finds prettiest, but those which he thinks likeliest to catch the fancy of the other competitors, all of whom are looking at the problem from the same point of view. It is not a case of choosing those which, to the best of one's judgment, are really the prettiest, nor even those which average opinion genuinely thinks the prettiest. We have reached the third degree where we devote our intelligences to anticipating what average opinion expects the average opinion to be. And there are some, I believe, who practice the fourth, fifth and higher degrees.

To predict which stocks will rise, investors need to know which stocks other investors think will rise, just as those other investors are trying to do the same. Of course, if everyone stopped playing this game, gave up hope that they could beat the market, and invested solely in passive index funds, then there might be a chance for a very small number of well-informed investors to exploit their knowledge. But there is no prospect of that happening any time soon, thanks to investors' enduring faith in their ability to pick investments that will beat the market.

Putting This Chapter to Use

Now that you understand the psychology behind investment mistakes, you must learn to confront them and identify a better strategy for the future. This strategy should include taking the time to formulate an asset allocation plan. You should strive to achieve this allocation in a low-cost manner; avoid paying fees to people and companies who do not truly add value. While many investors now know to avoid "loads" (commissions paid when you buy a mutual fund), far too many are still buying funds with very high annual expense ratios (Barber et al., 2005). Once you have your plan in place, continue to invest on a regular basis. If you combine these three tasks—appropriate asset allocation, low-cost investing, and adding regular investments— you are well on your way to an excellent investment strategy. Then relax and go back to tasks that you enjoy, be it playing tennis, playing with your kids, or traveling the world—there is little reason to be thinking about your investments more than a few hours per year.

The advice in this chapter is consistent with that offered by Burton Malkiel (2003). Readers interested in more information and more detailed recommendations on investment, including helpful suggestions for portfolio allocation, should consider reading his clear-sighted and informative book *A Random Walk down Wall Street*.

We should also offer some final words of caution: Changing your allocation of funds according to the advice in this chapter does require some care, as it can have tax implications. Before selling securities that have appreciated in value, you must first seek to understand the taxable consequences of doing so; you may want to check with your accountant. The advice in this chapter is relevant to existing investments, but must be applied to them with care. It should be easiest to follow our advice when you are thinking about making new investments.

CHAPTER TEN

Making Rational Decisions in Negotiations

When two or more parties need to reach a joint decision but have different preferences, they negotiate. They may not be sitting around a bargaining table; they may not be making explicit offers and counteroffers; they may even be making statements that suggest they are on the same side. But as long as their preferences concerning the joint decision are not identical, they have to negotiate to reach a mutually agreeable outcome.

Up to this point in the book, we have focused on individual decision making. Yet many managerial decisions are made in conjunction with other actors, and it is common for the different parties to have different interests. In this respect, negotiation is central to organizational life. But just as our individual decisions are often irrational, so, too, are our negotiated decisions—and for many of the same reasons. Negotiation outcomes are affected not only by our decisions, after all, but also by the decisions of others. This fact can make decision making in negotiation even more complicated than individual decision making. When negotiators improve the rationality of their decisions, they increase the likelihood of reaching an agreement when it is wise to do so as well as the quality of their negotiated outcomes.

People often believe that the outcomes they reached in a negotiation were inevitable. In fact, in most negotiations, a wide variety of outcomes are possible. When teaching negotiations to MBA students and executives, we typically use simulations in which half of the participants play one role and the other half play another role. All dyads negotiate the same problem and have access to the same information. When the participants reach an agreement or an impasse, they record their results on the chalkboard. The amazing result is that even within fairly homogenous groups, the range of outcomes obtained is enormous. The lesson? The decisions and behaviors of each negotiator matter.

This chapter outlines a framework for thinking rationally in two-party negotiation contexts. In Chapter 11, we will use this framework to examine how individual biases and heuristics are manifested in the negotiation context. Chapter 11 also provides information on cognitive biases created by the competitive environment. Essentially, this chapter provides a structure for System 2 thinking in negotiated environments, and the next chapter highlights some of the biases that occur due to System 1 thinking.

The goals of this chapter are to give you a framework for thinking about two-party negotiations and to introduce prescriptive suggestions for improving decision making within this context. This chapter seeks to improve the quality of your outcomes as the "focal" negotiator. In addition, we will recommend ways to improve the total outcomes for all parties and, hence, increase societal gains. You can achieve these goals by learning how to reduce the likelihood of impasse when it is in the interest of all parties to reach a settlement and by expanding the total range of benefits that both parties can receive.

Economists were the first to provide prescriptive advice to negotiators. The best-developed component of this economic school of thought is game theory. Game theory develops mathematical models to analyze the outcomes that will emerge in multiparty decision-making contexts if all parties act rationally. Game theorists begin by outlining the conditions that define how decisions are to be made—for example, the order in which players get to choose their moves—and attach utility measures of outcomes for each player to every possible combination of player moves. The actual analysis of the game focuses on predicting whether or not players will reach an agreement and, if one is reached, what the specific nature of that agreement will be.

The primary advantage of game theory is that, given absolute rationality, it provides the most precise prescriptive advice available to negotiators. The disadvantages of game theory are twofold. First, it relies on the ability to completely describe all options and associated outcomes for every possible combination of moves in a given situation—a tedious task at its best, infinitely complex at its worst. Second, it requires that all players consistently act in a rational manner. As we have seen in earlier chapters, individuals often behave irrationally, in ways that are not easily captured within rational analyses.

A DECISION-ANALYTIC APPROACH TO NEGOTIATIONS

As an alternative to game-theoretical analyses of negotiations that take place in a world of "impeccably rational, supersmart people," Raiffa (1982; 2001) has developed a decision-analytic approach to negotiations. Such an approach focuses on how "erring folks like you and me actually behave" rather than "how we should behave if we were smarter, thought harder, were more consistent, were all knowing" (Raiffa, 1982, p. 21). Raiffa's decision-analytic approach seeks to give the best available advice to negotiators involved in real conflict with real people. His goal is to provide guidance for you as the focal negotiator, given the most likely profile of the other party's expected behavior. Thus, Raiffa's approach is prescriptive from the point of view of the party receiving advice but descriptive from the point of view of the competing party.

Raiffa offers an excellent framework for approaching negotiations. The analytical structure of this approach is based on assessments of three key sets of information:

- Each party's alternative to a negotiated agreement
- Each party's set of interests
- The relative importance of each party's interests

Together, these three sets of facts determine the structure of the negotiation game (Lax & Sebenenius, 1987). Negotiation analysis considers how a rational negotiator should think about the structure of the negotiation and the other negotiator (Raiffa, 2001), as well as the common errors that negotiators and their opponents make (Bazerman, Curhan, & Moore, 2000; Bazerman, Curhan, Moore, & Valley, 2000; Bazerman & Neale, 1992; Thompson, 2001).

Alternatives to a Negotiated Agreement

Before we begin any important negotiation, we should consider what we will do if we fail to reach an agreement. That is, we must determine our *Best Alternative To a Negotiated Agreement*, or BATNA (Fisher, Ury, & Patton, 1981). Why is this important? Because the value of a negotiator's BATNA provides a lower bound for determining the minimum outcome we require of a negotiated agreement. We should prefer any negotiated agreement that provides more value to us than our BATNA; likewise, we should decline any negotiated agreement that provides less than our BATNA. This assessment logically determines the negotiator's *reservation point* (also called an indifference point)—the point at which the negotiator is indifferent between a negotiated agreement and impasse.

Imagine that you believe the other side has made her final offer, and all you have to do is accept or reject it. How do you decide? The BATNA concept makes this a fairly clear decision. If the offer is better than your BATNA, accept it. If not, reject it. Yet many people say "no" to final offers that are better than their BATNAs and "yes" to offers that are worse than their BATNAs. Why? When you have failed to carefully consider your BATNA, it is easy for emotions to hold sway.

Alternatives to agreement take a variety of forms. For example, rather than buying a specific new car, you may decide to continue to use mass transit. Alternatively, your BATNA may be to buy the same car from another dealership at a price that you have been offered in writing. Notice that in the second situation, it is far easier to determine your reservation price. However, whether you have an easy-to-assess reservation price or whether you seem to be comparing apples and oranges, you should always determine your BATNA and your best estimate of the value of your opponent's BATNA. While this analysis may be difficult, it will provide a better basis for negotiation than your intuitive, unprepared assessments. The most fundamental leverage you have in any negotiation is your threat to walk away. You should never enter a negotiation without having a sense of what your BATNA is and when you would walk away from the bargaining table.

The Interests of the Parties

To analyze a negotiation, it is necessary to identify all of the parties' interests—yet negotiators often do not understand the other side's interests. There is a difference between the parties' stated positions and their underlying interests. Positions are what parties ask from the other side. Interests are the motives behind these positions. As the following sections highlight, sometimes a focus on deeper interests can suggest creative solutions that help each side get more of what they want.

Not too long ago, the chief purchasing officer for one of our consulting clients (a *Fortune* 100 organization) participated in negotiating contract terms for the firm's purchase of a new health-care product ingredient from a European company. Both sides agreed to a price of $18 per pound for a million pounds of product per year. However, conflict arose over exclusivity: the European firm would not agree to sell the ingredient exclusively to our client. Our client could not afford to invest in producing a new product based on this ingredient if competitors had access to the same ingredient.

When the chief purchasing officer arrived in Europe, the argument over exclusivity continued. Finally, he asked the producer *why* they would not provide exclusivity to a major corporation that was offering to buy as much of the ingredient as he could produce. The producer explained that exclusivity would require him to violate an agreement with his cousin, who currently purchased 250 pounds per year to make a locally sold product. Once this piece of information emerged, the purchasing officer was able to quickly wrap up an agreement that provided exclusivity, with the exception of a couple hundred pounds annually for the producer's cousin—and the celebration began.

The key to this agreement was the chief purchasing officer's decision to ask about the producer's interests (selling a small amount of the ingredient to his cousin), rather than staying focused on the producer's stated goal (not providing exclusivity). Interestingly, the chief purchasing officer is viewed within his corporation as a negotiation genius, and part of his reputation is based on his ability to resolve this dispute. Yet, as he puts it, "All I did was ask them why they didn't want to provide exclusivity."

Even negotiators who are aware of each side's interests have not always thought through the relative importance of each issue. To be fully prepared to negotiate, you should know how important each issue is to you and have a sense of how important each issue is to your counterpart. The best agreements are reached by trading off relatively unimportant issues for more important ones. For example, when negotiating a new job offer, you may realize that health benefits are more important to you than an extra three days of personal time, or you may be so interested in delaying your start date that you are willing to take fewer vacation days your first year. You make these sorts of smart, efficient trades possible when you show up to negotiate knowing how issues trade off against each other.

Summary

Together, these groups of information (each party's BATNA, each party's set of interests, and the relative importance of each party's interests) provide the building blocks for thinking analytically about a negotiation. You should assess all components of this information before entering any important bargaining situation. With this information in hand, you will be prepared for the two primary tasks of negotiation: creating and claiming value (Lax & Sebenius, 1986). As we develop each of these two themes, it is important to remember that creating and claiming value are processes that occur simultaneously in a negotiation. Many of us are good at one, but not at the other. Our goal is to make you comfortable with both aspects of the negotiation challenge.

CLAIMING VALUE IN NEGOTIATION

Consider the following example:

> A new MBA is being recruited for a highly specialized position. The organization and the employee have agreed on all issues except salary. The organization has offered $90,000, and the employee has counteroffered $100,000. Both sides believe they have made fair offers, but they both would very much like to reach an agreement. The student, while not verbalizing this information, would be willing to take any offer over $93,000 rather than lose the offer. The organization, while not verbalizing this information, would be willing to pay up to $97,000 rather than lose the candidate.

A simplified view of the bargaining zone concept describes the recruitment problem:

Bargaining Zone

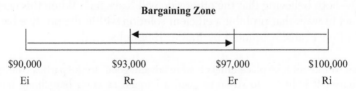

$90,000	$93,000	$97,000	$100,000
Ei	Rr	Er	Ri

Ei = Employer's initial offer
Rr = Recruit's reservation point (minimum limit)
Er = Employer's reservation point (maximum limit)
Ri = Recruit's initial offer

The bargaining zone framework assumes that each party has some reservation point below (or above) which the negotiator would prefer impasse to settlement. Reservation points are set at the value of the negotiator's BATNA. Notice that the two reservation points overlap. Thus, there is a set of resolutions that both parties would prefer over impasse—in this case, all points between $93,000 and $97,000. This area is known as a *positive bargaining zone*. When a positive bargaining zone exists, it is optimal for the negotiators to reach a settlement. When the reservation points of the two parties do not overlap, a *negative bargaining zone* exists. In such cases, no resolution should occur because there is no settlement that would be acceptable to both parties.

Many people find the notion of a bargaining zone to be counterintuitive. Having participated in a variety of negotiations throughout their lives, they have reached the conclusion that the reservation points of parties never overlap; they simply meet at the point of agreement. This reasoning is incorrect. In fact, at the point of agreement, when both parties choose a settlement rather than impasse, their actual reservation points overlap. This settlement point represents only one of what are often many points within the bargaining zone. Most people enter into negotiations with some notion of their target outcomes. However, most negotiators fail to think hard enough about their reservation prices and the reservation prices of other negotiators, which are determined by evaluating both parties' BATNAs.

Returning to our recruiting example, we can see that the bargaining zone falls between $93,000 and $97,000. If the employer could convince the recruit that an offer of $93,100 was final, the recruit would accept the offer, and the firm would minimize its settlement costs. Similarly, if the recruit could convince the employer that $96,900 was the lowest salary she would accept, the employer would accept this figure, and the recruit would maximize her settlement benefit. As this example shows, one of the key skills of negotiation is to determine the other party's reservation point and to aim for a resolution that is barely acceptable to the other party. This is a delicate process. If one or more parties were to misjudge the situation, they might rigidly demand a bargain that is beyond the other party's reservation point, leading to impasse. (Such would be the case if, for example, the recruit holds to a demand of $98,000 and the employer holds to the offer of $92,000—both believing that the other side will "cave in.") When this occurs, the parties act in ways that prohibit a efficient solution within the positive bargaining zone. As Ben Franklin (quoted by Raiffa, 1982) observed:

> Trades would not take place unless it were advantageous to the parties concerned. Of course, it is better to strike as good a bargain as one's bargaining position permits. The worst outcome is when, by overreaching greed, no bargain is struck, and a trade that could have been advantageous to both parties does not come off at all.

CREATING VALUE IN NEGOTIATION

The foregoing analysis dealt with a negotiation in which a single issue (salary) was under dispute. By definition, one-issue negotiations involve the claiming of value but not the creating of value. Most important negotiations are more complex, involving many disputed issues. Through the process of identifying and adding issues, the parties have the potential to create value, thereby increasing the amount of total benefit available.

Value Creation: The Case of the 1978 Camp David Accords

Consider the Camp David talks in 1978 (documented in Pruitt & Rubin, 1985).

> Egypt and Israel tried to negotiate the control of the Sinai Peninsula, a situation in which it appeared that the two sides had directly opposing goals. Egypt wanted the return of the Sinai in its entirety, while Israel, which had occupied the territory since the 1967 war, refused to return this land. Efforts at compromise failed. Neither side found the proposal of splitting the Sinai acceptable.

An initial examination of this conflict suggests that a negative bargaining zone existed and that a negotiated resolution would not be possible. That is, if we mapped the positions of the parties onto a single scale, the reservation points would not overlap, and impasse would be inevitable.

Who Gets the Sinai?

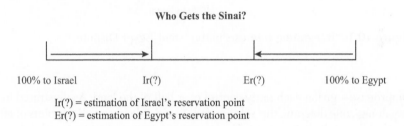

| 100% to Israel | Ir(?) | Er(?) | 100% to Egypt |

Ir(?) = estimation of Israel's reservation point
Er(?) = estimation of Egypt's reservation point

In contrast to this pessimistic and false prediction, the existence of multiple issues and the development of a creative trade explains the resolution that eventually developed at Camp David.

> As the Camp David negotiations continued, it became clear that while the positions of Egypt and Israel were incompatible, the interests of the two countries were compatible. Israel's underlying interest was security from land or air attack. Egypt was primarily interested in sovereignty over land that was part of Egypt for thousands of years. What emerged was the existence of two real issues, instead of one, with differential importance to the two parties: sovereignty and military protection. The solution that emerged traded off these issues. The agreement called for Israel to return the Sinai in exchange for assurances of a demilitarized zone and new Israeli air bases.

To analyze this agreement, examine the more complex diagram presented in Figure 10.1. The utility of an agreement to Israel is represented on the horizontal axis, and the utility of an agreement to Egypt is represented on the vertical axis. Point A represents the solution of giving the land and total control of it to Egypt. Notice that this solution would be completely acceptable to Egypt and completely unacceptable to Israel. Point B represents the solution of Israel keeping the land and maintaining total control over it. This solution would be completely acceptable to Israel and completely unacceptable to Egypt. Point C represents a straight

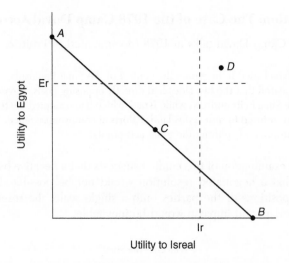

Figure 10.1 Integrating Interests in the Israel-Egypt Dispute.

compromise—giving each party control over half of the land. As illustrated in the bargaining-zone diagram, this solution fails to meet the reservation points of either Israel or Egypt. It does not give Egypt sovereignty over the Sinai, and it does not give Israel sufficient security guarantees. Point D (the eventual resolution), however, suggests a redefinition of the bargaining zone. In Figure 10.1, a positive bargaining zone exists to the extent that there are solutions that achieve the reservation points of both parties along the dimensions of sovereignty and security. The upper right-hand segment of the figure beyond the dotted lines represents the reservation points of the two parties.

What appears to have occurred in the Camp David accords is that the two parties realized the existence of a positive bargaining zone by considering each other's interests, not just their stated positions. With these interests in hand, they could develop an agreement by trading off the issue that each country cared less about for the issue that each country cared more about.

Trading on Issues to Create Value

The concept of trading off issues is not unique to this example. In fact, most important business transactions have the opportunity for value creation. Whenever one party weighs the issues differently than the other party, there is the opportunity to find tradeoffs across issues that make both parties better off than they would have been by simply compromising on both. In contrast to this advice, our experience teaching MBA students and executives has led us to believe that real-world negotiators frequently overlook opportunities to create value. In many cases, their failure to do so costs their firms millions of dollars.

When negotiators run into differences with other parties, the common response is to see this as a problem. In fact, differences are often opportunities. Negotiators should seize every opportunity to create value. And effective negotiators understand that the easiest way to create value is to trade issues of differential value. By identifying what you care about and assessing what the other side cares about, you will be equipped to create value based on these the differences. If the other party values something more than you do, let them have it. Don't *give* it away, but trade it for something that you care more about in return. If you *do* care about the other side, then you have all the more reason to create value. But creating value is not just what a "nice" negotiator does when she cares about the other side—it's what a rational negotiator does to increase the size of the pie that the parties have to divide.

The most common form of trade consists of one party making a concession on one issue in return for a concession on a different issue from the other party, such as a lower price in exchange for faster payment or a larger quantity of goods. Sophisticated trades often involve factors such as risk and time. In Chapter 4, we saw how individuals' differing tolerance for risk affects their decisions. Risk can play a critical role in negotiations as well. Imagine two partners in a new joint venture. One is risk averse and needs some income stability, while the other is more open to risk and needs less of the guaranteed income. The partners can make a tradeoff that gives one partner a higher salary and the other partner a higher percent of ownership in the firm, making both partners happier than a simple 50–50 split of their assets. Such risk-sharing strategies allow for trades that might not otherwise occur.

Differences in time preference might arise from individual, cultural, or situational preferences among the parties. The fluctuation of corporate budget cycles is one common real-world difference in time preferences. When a businessperson complains that her negotiating partner is fixated on meeting a certain budget cycle, we encourage her to view this as an opportunity—in all likelihood, the other side will be willing to make important concessions if she helps them solve their budget problems! Future consequences can often be rearranged in a way that gives earlier return to the more impatient party in exchange for concessions favored by the more patient party.

A multitude of differences between parties can enhance negotiation outcomes. Northcraft and Neale (1993) have pointed out that skill differences between parties collaborating on a project—such as a CEO and a COO, two researchers writing a book together, or partners in a strategic alliance—often contribute to the partnership's success. Effectively, complementary skills create the opportunity to make trades in work allocation, to the benefit of both parties. In their discussion of "dealcrafting," Lax and Sebenius (2002) cite a joint venture between auctioneer Butterfields and Internet auctioneer eBay as a successful partnership based on value creation. Butterfields' access to upscale commodities combined with eBay's new distribution mechanism to create value for both companies. Lax and Sebenius (2002) note a variety of other trades that can be enhanced by taking advantage of a wide range of differences, including differences in tax status, accounting treatments, and liquidity. By now, the overarching message of this section should be clear: To the well-informed negotiator, differences are not stumbling blocks, but opportunities.

Creating Value through Bets

While trading issues is the most common way to create value in a negotiation, you can also create value by betting on disagreements about the future, also known as *contingent contracts*. We have found that the answer to many stalled negotiations is to eliminate the need for parties to argue needlessly with the other side over their predictions about uncertain future outcomes. Instead, bets can be a very effective technique for dealing with differing predictions.

You will recall from the discussion of the endowment effect in Chapter 5 that people commonly overvalue what they own. It is important for sellers to recognize their susceptibility to this effect and adjust their expectations. If such adjustments fail to resolve the dispute, parties may be able to use their difference of opinion to craft a contingent contract that allows each side to bet on its opinion.

Malhotra and Bazerman (2007) give the example of a client who doubts her lawyer's ability to win in court. She might choose to sign a contingent contract with the lawyer, a common legal practice that would guarantee the lawyer a large payment if the client wins her case and nothing at all if she loses. Similarly, book publishers often pay authors a sum of money up front, followed by a fixed percentage of sales revenue, known as "royalties," if the publisher earns back the "advance." If the publisher is skeptical about the author's ability, it should be willing to pay the author a higher percentage of sales revenue in exchange for very little money up front. If the author is confident of her book's success, she will agree.

Now consider the case of a television production company negotiating the sale of syndication rights to one of its shows, a major sitcom that had just completed its prime-time run, with a major independent television station in one of the three leading television markets in the United States (Bazerman & Gillespie, 1999; based on a case by Tenbrunsel & Bazerman, 1995). The parties differed in their predictions of the ratings the sitcom would obtain in syndication: the seller argued that the show would receive at least a nine share rating (meaning nine percent of all American households with televisions would tune into the show), while the buyer countered that they expected the show would obtain no more than a seven share. Both parties agreed that each rating point was worth about $1 million in advertising revenue to the television station. After many heated debates about future ratings, the parties reached an impasse. The show was not aired in this market, and the television station bought a less attractive program. This negotiation failure resulted from an honest difference of opinion about how well the show would perform. Bazerman and Gillespie argue that the parties should have made the price that the station would pay the production company contingent on the show's perform-ance. That is, their disagreement about the expected quality of the show could have been resolved by an agreement in which the payment price went up with the ratings.

Bazerman and Gillespie (1999) describe a number of ways in which contingent contracts can improve the outcomes of negotiations for both sides, four of which are outlined here.

- **Bets build on differences to create joint value.** Bets can be extremely useful in short-circuiting debates over the likelihood of future uncertain events. Once parties have agreed to disagree, they will be able to design a contingent contract based on their differing predictions.
- **Bets help manage biases.** In previous chapters, we have documented a number of common decision-making biases, including overconfidence, the endowment effect, and egocentric interpretations of fairness. As we will discuss further in Chapter 11, these biases form strong barriers to negotiated agreements. Interestingly, contingent contracts allow agreements to be formed despite these biases. Rather than requiring the parties to be debiased, contingent contracts allow parties to bet on their own (biased) beliefs.
- **Bets diagnose disingenuous parties.** Contingent contracts are a powerful tool for identifying bluffs and false claims by one's negotiation opponent. When someone makes a claim, and you ask for a (costly) guarantee on that claim, if he is bluffing, he will typically back off of the claim. When you propose a bet, you do not need to know whether the other party's prediction is sincere. If it is, you have made a nice bet. If it isn't, his rejection of the bet reveals the bluff.
- **Bets establish incentives for performance.** Contingent contracts are also an excellent technique for increasing the parties' incentives to perform at or above contractually specified levels. Sales commissions are a common type of contingent contract designed to establish an incentive for high performance.

Summary

Getting a good deal in negotiation is not simply about claiming as much value as you can. Frequently, a much more important task is to increase the pool of resources to be divided between negotiators. Yet far too many negotiators focus only on claiming value and fail to create value. Having pummeled the other side effectively, they walk away pleased with themselves, but also lacking the value that could have been created. Would you rather claim 60% of a $1,000 pie, or 50% of a $2,000 pie? Even if you get a smaller portion of a large pie, this tradeoff may be profitable for you. Again, we are not preaching that negotiators have to be nice. The most self-interested negotiators should still want to create a bigger pie in order to claim more of that pie for themselves.

THE TOOLS OF VALUE CREATION

When we teach negotiation, our executive and MBA students often fail to find mutually beneficial trades in their negotiations. As we present data that clarifies that tradeoffs were possible, the students immediately respond by asking how they could have created optimal value when they lacked key information about the other side's interests and positions. This section reviews six strategies for collecting that information. While no single strategy is guaranteed to work in a specific situation, they collectively increase the likelihood of creating the biggest pie possible. The list begins with strategies that work best when you trust the other side. As we move down the list, we get to strategies that help create value when your relationship with the other side is competitive or even hostile.

1. Build Trust and Share Information

The easiest way for parties to create value is for the two negotiators to share information with each other about their preferences—specifically, the values that they place on different issues. Once this information comes to light, the parties can maximize joint benefit.

Unfortunately, information sharing is easier said than done. People are much more comfortable sharing information when they trust one another. Yet we often are reluctant to trust the other side in a negotiation because we believe that giving away information could prevent us from claiming value. In one negotiation simulation that we use in our teaching (El-Tek), for example, the two parties represent two different divisions of the same corporation. The vast majority of participants do not create the biggest pie possible. They fail to share information, despite being part of the same organization! Surprisingly, many executives note that it is harder to negotiate within their firm than with an outside supplier or customer. There is something wrong when negotiators in the same company fail to share information and destroy value as a result. Much more information sharing should occur within organizations, as well as between organizations.

In addition, Malhotra and Bazerman (2007) argue that it is useful to build trust when your cooperative behavior cannot be interpreted as self-serving. Even the untrustworthy appear nice when they are trying to get the deal. But rational negotiators maintain and strengthen relationships with others even when there is no obvious economic or political reason to do so. This relationship-building can increase the likelihood that your next negotiation will be with someone who happens to trust you. Finally, remember that the best way to build trust is to actually be trustworthy!

2. Ask Questions

Full information sharing will not always be to your advantage. You may have some information that will work against you if the other party obtains it; similarly, the other party also may be unwilling to fully disclose confidential information. What can you do? Ask questions! Most people have a tendency to see negotiating primarily as an opportunity to influence the other party. As a result, most of us do more talking than listening. Even when the other side is talking, we concentrate on what we are going to say next rather than listening for new information. This persuasion process is the basis of most sales training and assists the other party in collecting information from you. In negotiation, however, your goal must be to understand the other party's interests as well as possible.

By asking questions, you increase the likelihood of learning critical information that will allow you to find wise trades. Of course, it is usually not very helpful to ask the other party to tell you their reservation price; you are unlikely to get a useful response. However, there are important questions that they are much more likely to answer. For example:

- "How are you going to use our products?"
- "What would an ideal supplier do to make its products attractive to you?"
- "How can we make our offer better than that of our competitor?"

Too often, negotiators do not ask such questions because they are too busy trying to persuade the other side that their products and services are wonderful. The key insight of the chief purchasing officer in the procurement problem presented earlier in the chapter was to ask the European counterpart "why" when his colleagues had failed to do so.

Asking questions and listening actively are the keys to collecting important new information from the other side. Before you start to negotiate, assess the information that you need from the other side, then ask the questions necessary to collect this information. Some of our students have pointed out that, in the real world, the other side won't always answer your questions. That's true. However, the probability that they will answer is higher if you ask than if you do not!

3. Strategically Disclose Information

Your negotiation does not have a trusting atmosphere, and the other party is not answering your questions in any useful way. What do you do next? Give away some information of your own. Do not tell the other side your reservation price—this will only anchor your final outcome. Rather, reveal information of comparatively minor importance that focuses on the trades you are willing to make. The goal is to share information incrementally, back and forth. This technique minimizes your own risks: if the other party is still reluctant to discuss matters, you can decide to hold back as well.

The advice to give away information often surprises people because they assume that if they give away information, they are giving away their power. In fact, only giving away information about your reservation price gives away your power. Both parties can benefit as they learn about differing interests across issues.

One benefit of strategically disclosing information is that it can enable you and the other side to expand the pie. If they are smart, they will build on your information to help create mutually beneficial trades. An additional benefit is that behaviors in negotiation are often reciprocated. When you scream at people, they tend to scream back. When you apologize for a mistake or offense, they may do the same. And when you give them some information about your position, they may return some information of their own. This reciprocity can create the information sharing necessary to create mutually beneficial agreements.

4. Negotiate Multiple Issues Simultaneously

Executives often ask us, "What issue should we discuss first in a negotiation?" Some believe it is critical to get the most important issue resolved in the beginning, arguing that "any other strategy is simply procrastinating." Other negotiators believe that it is best to start with the easy issues, since this allows them time to build trust and gather momentum toward more difficult issues.

We disagree with both of these views. Instead, we strongly advocate negotiating multiple issues simultaneously. Consider what happens when you reach agreement on an issue before you know how the other issues are going to work out. If you have pushed hard and gotten what you wanted on one issue, you might leave the other side so little benefit that they become inflexible on all of the other issues, causing the entire deal to fall apart. By contrast, when people negotiate issues simultaneously, they can find favorable, value-creating trades across issues. While a buyer and seller may be in conflict on each issue, they are not equally passionate about each issue. The relative importance of each issue to each party only becomes apparent when the issues are discussed simultaneously.

How do you do this, given that it is usually not possible to talk about everything at once? When you negotiate, insist that nothing is settled until everything is settled. You can talk about different issues one at a time and even discuss tentative possible deals. But when it comes time to settle on definite outcomes, you should be considering packages of issues—deals that cover all the issues in the negotiation and that communicate your preferred outcome across all of the issues. Package offers help the other party isolate aspects of the offer that are particularly problematic and propose counter-offers that signal flexibility on some issues while making demands on others.

Our MBA students often ask us what they should say when a prospective employer asks them to specify a minimum salary requirement. Our advice is to tell the truth: that the answer to that question depends on lots of things, including the signing bonus, the yearly bonus, the job's benefits package, the job assignment, the job title, the promotion prospects, and more. It is impossible to specify a minimum acceptable salary without knowing the offer's other details. For the same reasons, it is a mistake to negotiate an agreement on the issue of salary before you move on to discussing other issues about the job. After all, if your new employer were prepared to offer a guaranteed annual bonus of at least a million dollars, you might be willing to work the rest of the year for no salary at all. Again, nothing is settled until everything is settled.

5. Make Multiple Offers Simultaneously

Many negotiators try to put an offer on the table early to "anchor" the discussion. Unfortunately, negotiators often make such offers before working hard to create additional value. Because anchors have such a strong impact, they can overshadow subsequent discoveries. Therefore, you should avoid putting an offer on the table before actively collecting information.

Sometimes, even after actively pursuing information, you may find that you cannot extend a single offer that creates value for both sides. When this happens, consider the possibility of presenting several package offers. Most of us put one offer on the table, and when the other side turns it down, we know little more than we did before we made the offer. If we had presented several alternatives, we might have learned more.

A better strategy is to make multiple package offers simultaneously, in which all of the offers are equally valuable to you. The other party might respond by saying that all three (or four or five) of your offers are unacceptable. Don't be discouraged. Instead, ask: "Which offer do you like the most?" or "If I were to rework one of the offers, which one is the best starting point? What do you like about it? What do you not like about it?" Her preferences will provide you with valuable hints about where to find trades that can create value.

Making multiple package offers simultaneously also allows you to come across as a flexible negotiator. Providing multiple options signals that you are willing to be accommodating and that you are interested in understanding the other party's preferences and needs. So, the next time you are preparing to make an offer, don't just make one. Rather, make several offers (of equal value to you) simultaneously.

6. Search for Post-Settlement Settlements

Imagine that you have just signed a complex deal. You are pleased with the outcome, and so is the other party. Most negotiators believe that their deal-making work is now concluded. Wise negotiators, however, continue to seek out ways to increase the size of the pie. After a contract is signed, consider asking the other side whether she would be willing to take another look at the agreement to see if it can be improved.

Raiffa (1985) suggests that after negotiators have found a mutually acceptable agreement, they should employ a third party to help them search for a *Pareto-superior* agreement—one that is potentially even better for both parties than the agreement they already reached. Under this scenario, each negotiator can reserve the right to veto any new settlement proposed by the third party and revert to the original agreement. Raiffa contends that, with this insurance in hand, negotiators may be more willing to allow a third party to create a superior agreement, which is known as a *post-settlement settlement* (PSS). Based on Raiffa's insight, negotiators should look for a PSS as a last step in creating value (Bazerman, Russ, & Yakura, 1987). This process does not necessarily require the help of a third party.

Typically, the last thing you want to do after a long negotiation is to reopen the discussion. Why, then, might you propose a PSS? After an agreement is reached, there is often ample opportunity to improve areas of the contract that may not be completely optimal for either party. The signed agreement confirms the parties' trust in each other and their ability to work together productively. If you are not confident that you have achieved a Pareto-efficient outcome, it may be in your best interest to propose to the other side a PSS process whereby both parties agree to be bound by the initial agreement if no better agreement is found. If you do find better agreement, however, you will share the surplus. A PSS is not an attempt to renege or squeeze last-minute concessions out of the other party, nor should it be perceived as such. To communicate that a PSS would be undertaken to benefit both sides, Malhotra and Bazerman (2007) suggest opening up a dialogue like this:

> Congratulations! I think that our hard work has really paid off in a great deal. We're probably both ready to call it a day. I'm wondering, though, whether you might be open to an idea. Though we're both satisfied with the agreement, there are inevitably aspects of the deal that I wish could have been better for me, and you probably feel the same way about other aspects. What if we spent a few more minutes talking about potential improvements to the deal that would make both of us better off? Maybe we've already exhausted those possibilities—but it might be a good idea to see if there are any stones left unturned. Of course, if we can't find ways to make both parties happier, we'll be even more confident that our signed agreement is the right one for everyone. If you're up for it, let's give it a try . . .

A PSS process offers a last attempt, with limited risk to either party, to ensure that a Pareto-efficient agreement has been found. This process can be initiated after an initial agreement by using any of the five previously defined information-building strategies. As Raiffa (1985, p. 9) writes:

> [W]e must recognize that a lot of disputes are settled by hard-nosed, positional bargaining. Settled, yes. But efficiently settled? Often not . . . they quibble about sharing the pie and often fail to realize that perhaps the pie can be jointly enlarged . . . there may be another carefully crafted settlement that both [parties] might prefer to the settlement they actually achieved.

Summary

The six strategies we have outlined provide the tools you need to create value in your important negotiations. Not all of these strategies will work in every situation. Collectively, however, they increase the potential joint benefit that parties will reach through negotiating.

How will you know that you captured all of the possible value in a negotiation? First, double-check to be sure you have considered all of the strategies listed above and attempted as many as possible. Next, think about how well you understand the interests and concerns of the other side. If you end a negotiation without knowing much about the other side's interests and priorities, you probably have left value on the table.

It is worth repeating that no strategy eliminates the need to eventually divide value; any negotiation advice is incomplete if it fails to deal explicitly with the claiming dimension. Armed with these strategies for creating and claiming value, negotiators should be able to improve their performance on both dimensions.

SUMMARY AND CRITIQUE

This chapter has introduced a number of methods for increasing the potential for successful negotiations. First, we outlined the decision-analytic approach, which focuses on information collection—namely, the importance of establishing reservation points, exploring the underlying interests of the parties, and weighting the relative importance of these interests. We discussed the need to think about creating and claiming value, and we introduced the concept of building on differences (such as estimates of future outcomes, risk preferences, and time preferences) as a strategy for uncovering trades. We also outlined six strategies for unlocking value in a negotiation. These include building trust, asking questions, strategically disclosing information, discussing multiple issues simultaneously, making multiple offers simultaneously, and searching for post-settlement settlements. Together, these techniques provide a prescriptive framework for thinking rationally about real-world negotiations.

As teachers of negotiation, we have noticed that students who fail to thoroughly prepare for a simulation are routinely clobbered by their opponent. The assumption that good intuition will allow you to sail through negotiation is simply wrong; preparation is critical. High-quality preparation requires you to reflect on a number of simple but important questions. This sample list of questions will not cover every negotiation situation, but it is a good place to start:

1. What is your BATNA?
2. What is your reservation price?
3. What are the issues in this negotiation?
4. How important is each issue to you?
5. What do you think the other party's BATNA is?
6. What do you think their reservation price is?
7. How important do you think each issue is to them?
8. Are there viable trades that create value?
9. Are you and the other party in disagreement about future events? If so, is a bet viable?
10. How will you go about identifying the information that you do not currently know?

Though answering these questions does not guarantee success, it will improve your odds.

As we saw in the first nine chapters, ours is not a fully rational world, particularly when it comes to our own decision-making processes. A central lesson of this book is that even when you are presented with rational advice, like the decision-analytic approach, your ingrained decision biases may limit your ability to follow this advice. In this sense, the decision-analytic approach is only a first step toward helping you to become a better decision maker in multiparty contexts. This approach cries out for additional descriptive models that allow you, as the focal negotiator, to better anticipate your own likely behaviors and those of the other party. If you or your opponent is not acting fully rationally, what systematic departures from rationality can be predicted? How can you better anticipate the actual behavior of your opponent, and how can you identify and overcome barriers that might prevent you from following decision-analytic advice? The decision-analytic approach tells us that we must consider the actual, but not necessarily rational, decisions of the other side. A useful addition to this advice is to identify the specific deviations from rationality that we can anticipate in our own and in other parties' decision making. This will be the focus of the next chapter.

CHAPTER ELEVEN

Negotiator Cognition

*T*he decision-analytic approach to negotiation presented in the previous chapter suggests that it is desirable for parties to strike an agreement whenever a positive bargaining zone exists. Why, then, do negotiators frequently fail to settle? The decision-analytic approach also provides strategies for reaching agreements of great value to both sides. Why, then, do even negotiators who have access to this advice fail to reach Pareto-superior outcomes?

This chapter explores the most common cognitive mistakes that people make in negotiation. Specifically, we will look at six key issues that affect negotiator cognition: (1) the mythical fixed pie of negotiation, (2) the framing of negotiator judgment, (3) the nonrational escalation of conflict, (4) overestimating your own value, (5) self-serving biases, and (6) anchoring biases. Each section illustrates how the decision-making processes of the typical negotiator diverge from a prescriptive model of behavior and discusses how we as negotiators can correct these deviations.

An understanding of these common mistakes will help improve your negotiating skills in two key ways. First, awareness is an essential step toward avoiding these errors in important negotiations. Second, once you have learned to identify these errors in your own behaviors, you will be better able to anticipate them in the decisions of other negotiators.

THE MYTHICAL FIXED PIE OF NEGOTIATION

Why do negotiators so often fail to reach agreements that create maximum value for both sides? One reason is the fixed-pie assumption. When individuals approach negotiations with a fixed-pie mentality, they assume that their interests conflict directly with the interests of the other side. Metaphorically, they believe they are both fighting for the biggest piece of a pie of fixed size.

Agreements in diplomatic conflicts, marital disputes, and the creation of strategic alliances are frequently blocked by the assumption that the parties' interests are diametrically opposed. Creative agreements occur when participants discover tradeoffs across issues—but individuals will not search for these trades if they assume the size of the pie is fixed.

The assumption of a fixed pie leads us to interpret most competitive situations as win–lose. Many contests are, in fact, win–lose: athletic competition, admission to academic programs, corporate battles for market share, and so on. Generalizing from these objective win–lose situations, people form similar expectations for situations that are not necessarily win–lose. When faced with a mixed-motive situation, such as a negotiation that requires both value creation and value claiming, the claiming component too often becomes salient, motivating most negotiators to develop a strategy for obtaining the largest possible share of the perceived fixed pie. Such a focus inhibits the search for creative solutions through mutually beneficial tradeoffs.

The destructiveness of the mythical fixed pie is captured in this Cold War–era declaration by Rep. Floyd Spence, R-South Carolina, regarding a proposed arms reduction treaty: "I have had a philosophy for some time in regard to SALT, and it goes like this: the Russians will not accept a SALT treaty that is not in their best interest, and it seems to me that if it is in their best interests, it can't be in our best interest" (originally cited in Ross & Stillinger, 1991). This kind of dangerously confused reasoning—that anything good for the Soviet Union must have been bad for the United States—defines the mythical fixed pie assumption. With the benefit of twenty-first century hindsight, we can easily recognize that treaties like SALT benefited both the United States and the Soviet Union by reducing wasteful defense spending and the specter of nuclear war. And yet, Thompson (2001) has found that even when two sides want the exact same outcome, such as ending the Cold War, negotiators often settle on a different outcome or reach an impasse. The mythical fixed pie can cause parties to fall prey to what Thompson calls the *incompatibility bias*—the assumption that one's own interests are at odds with the other party's.

The mythical fixed pie also leads us to "reactively devalue" any concession made simply because it is offered by an adversary (Stillinger, Epelbaum, Keltner, & Ross, 1990). In one study, Curhan, Neale, and Ross (2004) had negotiators estimate the value of various possible outcomes before and after taking part in a negotiation. Negotiators tended to like a possible outcome more after they proposed it in the negotiation. More to the point, they tended to like a possible outcome *less* after it was proposed by the other side. It seems that we are susceptible to viewing the same settlement terms as advantageous when we propose them but disadvantageous when our counterpart proposes them. As soon as the other party concedes on an issue, you might find yourself devaluing the concession with this faulty logic: "If she is willing to make this concession, the issue must not be very important."

When individuals make such assumptions about the other party's interests, they inhibit the search for mutually beneficial tradeoffs. The fact is, tradeoffs can be quite easy to find when negotiators actively look for them. But when we ask business students why they failed to make a tradeoff in a simulated negotiation, they commonly tell us that they did not know that the tradeoff was possible. Why not? The fixed-pie assumption prevented them from initiating the search.

THE FRAMING OF NEGOTIATOR JUDGMENT

Consider the following scenario:

> You bought your condo in 2005 for $250,000. You have just put it on the market for $299,000, with a real target of $290,000 (your estimation of the condo's true market value). An offer comes in for $280,000. Does this offer represent a $30,000 gain in comparison with the original purchase price or a $10,000 loss in comparison with your current target?

The answer to this question is "both." From a rational perspective, and based on our intuition, we can easily determine that the difference in the two points of view is irrelevant. However, as discussed in Chapter 5, Kahneman and Tversky (1982) have demonstrated that important differences arise from individuals' responses to questions framed in terms of losses versus gains. This difference is critical to describing negotiator behavior.

To understand the importance of framing in negotiations, consider the following labor–management situation. A trade union insists that management must increase the pay of union members from $16 to $18 per hour and that anything less, given current inflation, represents underpayment. Management argues that any raise above $16 per hour imposes an unacceptable expense. What if each side had the choice of settling for $17 per hour (a certain settlement) or going to binding arbitration (a risky settlement)? Since each side views the conflict in terms of what it has to lose, following Kahneman and Tversky's (1981) findings, we can predict that each side will be risk-seeking and therefore unwilling to accept the certain settlement. Changing the negotiators' framing from positive to negative, however, results in a very different predicted outcome. If the union views any raise above $16 per hour as a gain and management views any raise under $18 per hour as a gain, then both sides will be risk averse and a negotiated settlement will be likely. Neale and Bazerman (1985) found that negotiators with positive frames are significantly more likely to make concessions and to reach mutually beneficial outcomes than their negatively framed counterparts.

What determines whether a negotiator will have a positive or negative frame? The answer lies in the selection of a perceptual anchor. Consider some of the anchors available to a union leader negotiating a wage with management: (1) last year's wage, (2) management's initial offer, (3) the union's estimate of management's reservation point, (4) the union's reservation point, or (5) the bargaining position that the union publicly announced to its constituency. As the anchor moves from (1) to (5), a modest gain in comparison to last year's wage becomes a loss when compared to the higher goals touted publicly, thus moving the union negotiator from a positive to a negative frame. Specifically, for workers who are currently making $16 per hour and demanding an increase of $2 per hour, a proposed increase of $1 per hour can be viewed as a $1 per hour gain over last year's wage (anchor 1) or a $1 per hour loss when compared to the goals of the union's constituency (anchor 5).

Framing has important implications for the tactics used by negotiators. Framing effects suggest that, to induce concessionary behavior in an opponent, a negotiator should always create anchors that lead the opposition toward a positive frame. This means you will be negotiating in terms of what the other side has to gain, thereby increasing opportunities for tradeoffs and compromise. In addition, when you recognize that your counterpart has a negative frame, you should encourage him to recognize that he has adopted a risky strategy in a situation where a sure gain is possible.

Finally, the impact of framing has important implications for mediators. When the proposed goal is a compromise, the mediator should strive to convince both parties to view the negotiation with a positive frame. This is tricky, however, since the anchor that will lead to a positive frame for one negotiator is likely to lead to a negative frame for the other. This suggests that when mediators meet with each party separately, they need to present different anchors to create risk aversion in each party. Again, to affect the frame, mediators also must emphasize the realistic risk of the situation, thus calling attention to its uncertainty and leading both sides to prefer a sure settlement.

ESCALATION OF CONFLICT

Following decades of animosity, on March 18, 1990, baseball team owners and players reached a four-year agreement to avert a strike that threatened to cancel the 1990 baseball season. The agreement expired on December 31, 1993, and the 1994 baseball season began without a new contract in place. The first offer came from the owners on June 14, 1994, but it was well outside the bargaining range. Dysfunctional bargaining ensued, and on August 12, the players went on strike.[1]

The strike effectively ended the 1994 baseball season and destroyed approximately $1 billion worth of financial opportunity for the owners and players. Food vendors, retailers, baseball card companies, and fans also suffered in various ways during the strike. The strike's inefficiency was highlighted when the courts required the team owners to accept the preexisting structure for the 1995 season while negotiations for the future continued.

From 1986 to 1993, Major League Baseball operated at a profit; by 1993, annual profits had risen to $36 million. The strike changed that picture. The owners lost $375 million in 1994, $326 million in 1995, and between $100 million and $200 million in 1996 (Grabiner, 1996). Meanwhile, players lost money, status, and bargaining power. For at least several years, baseball's position as America's national pastime was tarnished. The strike was an extremely costly and vivid example of a conflict that entered an escalatory spiral.

---

[1] Many observations about the 1994 baseball strike in this section were prompted by the analysis of Chris Maxcy, Lisa Mroz, Keith Rakow, and Cynthia Safford in a course assignment for the MBA negotiations class at the Kellogg School of Management of Northwestern University.

In the midst of the controversy, Sebenius and Wheeler (1994) offered a potentially advantageous strategy for resolving the disagreement: Continue the baseball season, but do not allow the teams to receive revenue or the players to receive their pay. Rather, revenues and forgone pay would go into a pool until a resolution was reached. In the meantime, watching the funds pile up would be an impetus for both sides to agree on a settlement. Sebenius and Wheeler further argued that the parties could set aside a portion of the fund for charity (such as the Special Olympics) if they failed to reach agreement in a timely fashion—again encouraging compromise while creating positive rather than negative public relations. Overall, Sebenius and Wheeler outlined a very wise strategy that would have been far more efficient than the strike.

So, why didn't the parties follow this advice? Our answer is that because each party was focused almost exclusively on beating the other side, they were primed to escalate their commitment to their initial course of action. One sign that the parties were absorbed by inappropriate objectives was the team owners' gleeful reaction to the cancellation of the 1994 World Series. Too busy congratulating themselves for sticking together, they failed to notice that they were bonding over their destruction of $1 billion in profits.

Just four years later, it became apparent that National Basketball Association team owners had learned nothing from baseball's mistakes. Repeating this escalatory pattern, the NBA entered a 202-day lockout that cost the owners over $1 billion and the players more than $500 million in lost salaries. In 2011, the NBA again went down the same path of mutually destructive competition. As the professional basketball season approached, players and team owners were deadlocked on almost every major issue at stake, particularly salaries, a salary cap, and revenue sharing. Claiming it was losing about $300 million per year—a figure the players' union disputed—the league proposed slashing players' salaries by 40 percent. When the collective bargaining agreement expired on July 1, the league locked out the players. With the two sides still far apart on the most significant issues in September, the league cancelled training camp and preseason games. "The people who stand to have their livings impacted by a shutdown of our industry are going to have a negative view of both sides," commented NBA commissioner David Stern. "I think our fans will tend to have a negative view of why can't you guys work this thing out" (Chicago Tribune, 2011). In the end, the two sides came to agreement, but not before cancelling a fifth of the season and losing out on hundreds of millions of dollars in revenues from television, advertising, and product licensing.

Diekmann, Tenbrunsel, Shah, Schroth, and Bazerman (1996) explicitly studied escalation in the context of negotiation. They found both sellers and buyers of real estate to be affected by the price that the seller had earlier paid for the property. This "sunk cost" did not affect either party's assessment of the property's value, but it did affect their expectations, reservation prices, and final negotiated outcomes. An understanding of such escalation of commitment can be very helpful to a negotiator in anticipating an opponent's behavior. When will the other party really hold out, and when will he give in? The escalation literature predicts that the other side will hold out when he has "too much invested" in his position to quit. Announcement of one's position increases one's tendency to escalate nonrationally (Staw, 1981).

Strategically, the findings on escalation in negotiation suggests that you should avoid eliciting bold, firm statements from an opponent, lest your adversary later feel trapped in a corner. If your adversary has taken a rigid position on an issue, you may be able to find creative ways for him to concede to make a deal possible. For example, a colleague of ours was negotiating the purchase of a condominium in Chicago. The condo's seller announced a rigid position on price: "I'm not going to sell the condo for less than $350,000. That's my final offer." Our colleague, who also teaches negotiation, suggested other ways for the seller to concede. In the end, she paid the $350,000 that he was demanding, but got him to agree to make a number of changes and upgrades to the condo and to throw in a valuable parking space for "free."

OVERESTIMATING YOUR VALUE IN NEGOTIATION

As the 2006 baseball season ended, Matt Harrington, a 6-foot-4-inch, 210-pound, 22-year-old right-hander, was finishing his fourth season pitching for the Fort Worth Cats in the Central Baseball League. Over these four years, Harrington's baseball salary averaged less than $1,000 per month; during the off-season, he stocked shelves at Target. So far, Harrington probably sounds like a typical independent leaguer. But in 2000, at age eighteen, Harrington was pictured on the covers of *USA Today* and *Baseball America*. He was described in the press as a hard-working, modest young man who was probably the best pitcher available in the major-league draft.

That year, Harrington and his family hired Tommy Tanzer, a well-known player's agent, to represent him. To scare away teams with limited budgets, Tanzer told MLB teams with high draft choices that they would need to offer at least a $4.95 million first-year bonus to sign Harrington to a contract. The Colorado Rockies selected Harrington as the seventh pick in the draft but insisted they would not pay the price demanded by Tanzer. After the draft, the Rockies offered Harrington $4.9 million for eight years, then $5.3 million over eight years, and finally $4 million over only two years. Claiming to be insulted by the offers, Harrington, his parents, and Tanzer rejected each one— despite the fact that these figures were typical for a seventh-pick player. The tough negotiations extended for months before breaking down. Harrington could not play for a major-league team that year or for any of the high-level minor-league teams. He headed for the independent-league St. Paul Saints and hoped for a more successful negotiation the following year.

Harrington had a disappointing season with the Saints, but secured a new agent, Scott Boras, for the 2001 major-league draft. The San Diego Padres chose him as the 58th overall selection. This time, Harrington turned down an offer of $1.25 million over four years with a $300,000 signing bonus. The next year, 2002, Harrington was the 374th pick. He was offered (and refused) less than $100,000 from the Tampa Bay Devil Rays. In 2003, the Cincinnati Reds drafted him in the 24th round at number 711, but again talks fell through.

By this point, Harrington had become the longest holdout in baseball history, but his saga was not over. In 2004, The New York Yankees drafted him in the 36th round—he was player number 1,089—but did not make him a contract offer. None of the 30 MLB teams drafted Harrington in the 50 rounds of the 2005 draft. This made Harrington a free agent who could sign with any team that was interested in him. In October 2006, the Chicago Cubs signed Harrington to a minor-league contract. He was invited to spring training with the hope of finally entering the majors, but with no guaranteed payment. Harrington showed up to training camp, only to be released (fired) by the Cubs before the start of the 2007 season. He returned to the St. Paul Saints, his original independent-league team, which released him in June 2007.

In negotiation, it is useful to know when to hold out for a better outcome. At some point, however, wise negotiators know when it's time to accept the deal on the table. Year after year, Harrington, his parents, and his agents made a simple but critical mistake: they failed to say yes. Harrington's BATNA was risky at best, terrible at worst. Yet, along with the professional negotiators representing him, his overconfidence destroyed a tremendous amount of potential.

Overestimating the chances that the other side will give you what you want can be a devastating negotiation error. Matt Harrington's story is extreme, but all kinds of job seekers overestimate what the other side will pay. More broadly, negotiators who overestimate their value and consequently fail to reach agreement waste tremendous opportunities.

Research demonstrates that negotiators tend to overestimate the chances that their positions will prevail if they do not "give in." Similarly, negotiators in final-offer arbitration consistently overestimate the probability that their final offers will be accepted (Bazerman & Neale, 1982). (Each of the parties in final-offer arbitration submits a "final offer" to an arbitrator who must pick one of them. Unlike a judge or a mediator, the arbitrator cannot make another proposal.) In laboratory studies where there was, on average, only a 50 percent chance of a final offer being accepted, the average individual nonetheless estimated that there was a much higher probability (68 percent) that his or her offer would be accepted.

Negotiators who overestimate their value may miss out on a variety of settlements, despite the existence of a positive bargaining zone. Negotiators who are able to make more accurate assessments are likely to be more uncertain and uncomfortable about the probability of success and more likely to accept compromise. Neale and Bazerman (1985) found "appropriately" confident negotiators to exhibit more concessionary behavior and to be more successful than overly confident negotiators. You are most likely to overestimate your value in a negotiation when your knowledge is limited. As we learned in Chapter 2, most of us follow the intuitive cognitive rule, "When in doubt, be overconfident." One cure for overestimating your value is to seek objective value assessments from a neutral party. His or her neutral assessment is likely to be closer to your counterpart's position than you might have intuitively predicted.

SELF-SERVING BIASES IN NEGOTIATION

Overestimating your value is closely related to the concept of self-serving biases. While overestimating your value refers to the tendency to exaggerate your indispensability, self-serving biases refer to the tendency for people to define what is fair in ways that favor themselves. As a result of self-serving biases, even when two parties both sincerely claim to want an outcome that is "fair" to both sides, their different notions of fairness can lead to impasse.

Thompson and Loewenstein (1992) found that self-serving, biased attention to available information in a conflict affected the parties' perceptions of what constituted a fair settlement; in a simulated labor dispute, the magnitude of this bias affected the length of a strike. Similarly, Babcock, Loewenstein, Issacharoff, and Camerer (1995) presented participants with diverse materials (depositions, medical and police reports, etc.) from a lawsuit resulting from a collision between an automobile and a motorcycle. Participants were assigned the role of plaintiff or defendant and were instructed to attempt to negotiate a settlement. If they were unable to do so, they would pay substantial penalties; in addition, they were told that the amount paid by the defendant to the plaintiff would be determined by an impartial judge who already had made his decision based on exactly the same case materials. Before negotiating, the participants were asked to predict the judge's ruling. They were told that this estimate would not be communicated to the other party and would not affect the judge's decision (which already had been made). Nevertheless, plaintiffs' predictions of the judge's award amount were substantially higher than those of defendants, and the degree of discrepancy between the predictions of plaintiffs and defendants was a strong predictor of whether they settled the case (as opposed to relying on the judge's decision). The participants' fairness assessments were biased according to their assigned role. A number of follow-up experiments attempted to reduce the magnitude of the bias. Babcock and Loewenstein (1997) rewarded participants who accurately predicted the judge's ruling with cash and had them write an essay arguing the other side's point of view. Neither of these interventions had a measurable effect; participants consistently believed that the judge's own perceptions of fair judgments would match their own. Other findings from the same series of experiments point to a likely psychological mechanism underlying self-serving biases in negotiation. Participants were presented with eight arguments favoring the side to which they had been assigned (plaintiff or defendant) and eight arguments favoring the other side. They were asked to rate the importance of these arguments as perceived "by a neutral third party." There was a strong tendency to view arguments supporting one's own position as more convincing than those supporting the other side, suggesting that the bias operates by distorting one's interpretation of evidence. Consistent with this finding, when the parties were presented with their roles (plaintiff or defendant) only after reading the case materials, the magnitude of the bias was substantially reduced and almost all of the pairs reached rapid agreement on damages. Moreover, the effect only works when the information is complex or ambiguous enough for different parties to interpret it differently (Loewenstein & Moore, 2004).

Self-serving biases are just as pervasive and detrimental to negotiated settlements in disputes involving more than two parties. The inevitable tension between what is good for the individual negotiators and what is best for the group produces a *social dilemma*. In a vivid illustration of a social dilemma, Hardin (1968) offered a parable of a group of herdsmen grazing their cattle in a common pasture. Each herdsman knows that it is to his advantage to increase the size of his herd because each additional animal represents personal profit. However, the cost of grazing, measured by the damage done to the pasture, is shared by all of the herdsmen. If the total number of animals becomes too large, the pasture will be overpopulated and eventually will be destroyed. Thus, the herdsmen have a collective interest in setting individual limits on the number of cattle grazing in the pasture to a degree that matches the rate of pasture replenishment. At the same time, it is in each herdsman's interest to marginally expand his grazing cattle beyond his allotment. Hardin's parable has a parallel in negotiation. While each negotiator may suspect that overestimating what she deserves could improve her chances of getting more of what she wants, it also should be clear that as each person's demands increase, so does the probability of not reaching any deal at all. Many of the natural-resource and pollution issues that we face in contemporary society resemble Hardin's "tragedy of the commons." Wade-Benzoni, Tenbrunsel, and Bazerman (1996) created a social-dilemma simulation in which a group shares a common, scarce resource—in this case, ocean shark—from which individual members can harvest. This simulation is based on the real-life fishery crisis in the northeastern United States, where species of principal groundfish have been depleted by overfishing, resulting in considerable uncertainty as to when and how they will be brought back to a sustainable level. The two most critical issues facing fishery management are (1) who will pay the cost of reversing the crisis and (2) who will receive the subsequent benefits. Thus, the northeastern fishery captures the range of issues inherent in managing any commonly held resource. As in any social dilemma, individuals must choose between personal and group concerns. The group's best interest lies in limited harvesting, but personal interests may induce individual members to harvest excessively.

In our shark simulation, participants were assigned roles as representatives of organizations that relied on shark fishing for income. The representatives were gathering for a conference aimed at finding a solution to their common problem, the depletion of large coastal shark. All participants were told that they had two goals: (1) to maximize current profit without depleting the harvest pool to a level that would be too low to provide future harvests and (2) to maximize the net present value of the profit that their associations would receive. This profit would be broken up into two components: profit received from the current harvest and profit expected from future harvests. Participants were told that a given total harvest level was sustainable, enabling the species to reproduce itself at its current population level; if the total harvest rose above the given level, the species would suffer further depletion. Harvesting above the sustainable level decreased opportunities for future harvesting, resulting in a net decrease in total profit.

A characteristic of virtually all real-world social dilemmas is asymmetry in the parties' contribution to the problem and their willingness to cooperate with proposed solutions. Asymmetry allows negotiators to indulge in idiosyncratic self-serving biases about the fairness of resource distribution. To capture this asymmetry in the simulation, participants were told that their organizations placed different weights on the importance of future shark harvests. Specifically, those participants who represented commercial fishing groups harvested relatively large numbers of sharks and had a relatively low interest in the future health of the resource. By contrast, the representatives of recreational fishing groups harvested fewer sharks and had a very strong interest in the resource's future. Consistent with the real-world situation, participants were told that the commercial groups were better equipped than the recreational groups to switch to a different kind of fish should the shark resource be depleted.

After receiving the information just described, but before their simulated conference, the participants recorded what they personally believed to be a fair solution to the crisis. During the 30-minute conference that followed, participants discussed the issues and potential solutions, but did not make binding commitments. Participants were again asked to make individual fairness judgments following the conference. Self-serving interpretations of fairness were the common pattern in this asymmetric resource dilemma. In addition, we found that the amount of harvesting carried out by each group was positively related to the strength of the level of self-serving biases. Discussion of the issues reduced the magnitude of self-serving biases, thereby increasing cooperation.

This research strongly suggests that asymmetry is a key driver of self-serving biases and overharvesting. Resource dilemmas represent a critical area where ambiguity enables individuals to justify what they *want* to do (take a larger share of a limited resource) instead of what they *should* do (practice self-restraint). One current example is the overfishing of bluefin tuna to near extinction. The most valuable fish in the ocean, the majestic bluefin tuna can grow to be ten feet long and 1,500 pounds; in Japan, just one of these fish can fetch up to $150,000 (Bazerman & Tenbrunsel, 2011). Back in 1969, when bluefin tuna were plentiful in the North, Baltic, and Mediterranean seas, the Madrid-based International Commission for the Conservation of Atlantic Tunas (ICCAT) was established to ensure that the fish was not overharvested. Yet it seems ICCAT has failed miserably at its mission. Stocks of bluefin tuna have collapsed in the decades of the organization's existence, to the point that it may be too late for the species to rebound in the northeast Atlantic and Mediterranean. Despite setting strict fishing quotas, ICCAT does little to police the fishing behavior of its 46 member states, leaving their egocentrism unchecked (Economist, 2008). And in 2008, even after most countries agreed to an international resolution calling for a moratorium on bluefin tuna fishing, their governments backed away from the pledge. Because individual fishers—and the nations that support them—are subject to self-serving fairness interpretations, it would be unrealistic to expect them to police their own behavior. Rather, changes at the system level are needed in the form of better policing and tougher penalties for rule-breakers.

Moving beyond the fishing industry, current debates about how to cope with global climate change tend to be rooted in countries' different viewpoints about their right to develop and claim their "fair share" of natural resources. In particular, developing nations have been at loggerheads with more developed nations over the question of which side deserves more blame for climate change—and, consequently, which bears a greater responsibility for addressing it. China, India, and other rapidly developing nations have blamed the West for its ongoing industrialization and excessive consumption, while Western countries blame emerging nations for engaging in unregulated economic expansion. This difference in opinion leads to differing perspectives on how to remedy the looming problem.

Discussions between the United States and China, which together are estimated to be responsible for 42 percent of human-caused greenhouse gas emissions, have become particularly heated (Bazerman & Tenbrunsel, 2011). In December 2009, United Nations representatives tried and failed to negotiate a comprehensive global climate change agreement in Copenhagen, Denmark. China and the United States reached an impasse on a key issue. China had committed to reductions in its emissions growth, but refused to accept international monitoring of these efforts. U.S. officials objected to this stance and complained that China's emissions targets were too modest. Only after U.S. President Barack Obama insisted on meeting face to face with Chinese Premier Wen Jiabao did the two sides reach a compromise on the monitoring issue. Yet the Copenhagen talks as a whole remained deadlocked, and real remedies to climate change again were put off until another day. Egocentrism causes all nations to believe they deserve less responsibility for addressing climate change than an objective judge would deem fair.

When it comes to self-serving negotiation biases, the source of the problem is not our desire to be unfair, but rather the difficulty we have interpreting information in an unbiased manner (Messick & Sentis, 1983). Our egocentric perceptions of fairness prevent us from recognizing our personal responsibility to help forge a compromise. Communication-building strategies, including asking questions, seeking tradeoffs, and making concessions, can help to reduce self-serving biases and can facilitate negotiated solutions that benefit not only the interested parties, but society as a whole.

ANCHORING IN NEGOTIATION

From Chapter 3, we know that people tend to be overly affected by an initial anchor, without realizing this effect. Northcraft and Neale (1987) surveyed real-estate brokers who claimed they could assess the value of a property to within 5 percent of the true or appraised value. These brokers were unanimous in stating that, when looking at an actual house on the market, they did not factor the listing price of the property into their personal estimate of its "true" value. Northcraft and Neale then asked the brokers, and separately a group of undergraduate students, to estimate the value of an actual house. Both brokers and students were randomly assigned to one of four experimental groups. In each group, all participants were given a ten-page information packet about the house being sold, which included considerable information about the house, as well as data on prices and characteristics of recently sold homes in the area. The only difference in the information given to the four groups was the house's listing price, which was listed as +11 percent, +4 percent, −4 percent, or −11 percent of the actual appraised value of the property. After reading the material, all participants toured the house and the surrounding neighborhood. Participants were then asked to estimate the house's true value. The values estimated by both the brokers and the students suggest that both groups were significantly and strongly affected by the listing price (the anchor). While the students readily admitted the role that the listing price played in their decision-making process, the brokers flatly denied their use of the listing price as an anchor—despite the evidence to the contrary. This anchoring effect has been replicated in many other contexts, including auto mechanics' estimates of a car's value (Mussweiler, Strack, & Pfeiffer, 2000) and art experts' estimates of a painting's value (Beggs & Graddy, 2009).

Ritov (1996) finds that even very subtle shifts in how negotiations are anchored can create big differences in final outcomes. In her study, she varied whether buyers and sellers in a simulation are looking at possible agreements in an order that moves from best-for-the-buyer to best-for-the-seller, or in an order that moves from the best-for-the-seller to best-for-the-buyer. She finds surprisingly big effects, such that negotiators end up closer to the end of the bargaining zone that corresponds with the starting point (the price listed at the top of the page). As a simplified example, Ritov's research suggests that if possible prices are listed as $1,000, $800, $600, $400, $200, and $0, a higher price will result, on average, than if possible prices are listed as $0, $200, $400, $600, $800, and $1,000. In addition, Ritov found that the first offer is positively correlated with the final outcome, a phenomenon that we will explore below.

In negotiation, one party must make the first offer. Should it be the buyer or the seller? While first offers have the power to anchor the negotiation, unreasonable first offers can scare away the other side. Ideally, an effective first offer will seem reasonable to the other side, while also being close to your preferred end of the bargaining zone. Galinsky and Mussweiler (2001) show that first offers have a strong anchoring effect when great ambiguity exists. If your opponent has a good sense of the bargaining zone or knows what the item is worth to him or her, your first offer will have little value. However, when your opponent lacks information, he or she may actually make inferences about the value of the item based on your first offer.

Often, we may be inclined to make initial offers at a nice round number that easily pops to mind. Presumably, it should not matter how round our number appears if our goal is to get someone to anchor to our initial offer. Jansewski and

Uy (2008) show that we are likely to be better off coming up with an initial offer that appears precise and not rounded, even if it is slightly less than we otherwise would have used to anchor the negotiation. Through a series of lab experiments and the analysis of a dataset containing real-estate sale prices, Jansewski and Uy demonstrated that people tend to adjust less from precise anchors. For example, in examining the sale prices of real estate, Jansewski and Uy found that houses with list prices specified to the nearest hundred dollars sold for a final price closer to the list price than houses with list prices specified to the nearest thousand dollars, which sold for a final price closer to the list price than houses with a list price specified to the nearest ten thousand dollars. How can you protect yourself from first offers that benefit your opponent at your expense? Galinsky and Mussweiler (2001) show that your opponent's first offer will have little effect on you if you focus on your own alternatives and your own objectives. While we learn a great deal in the process of negotiation, we should avoid learning from the potential manipulative effect of the other side's first offer.

CONCLUSIONS

Chapters 10 and 11 have offered an overview of what is commonly known as the decision perspective to negotiation, which can be traced to Raiffa's "asymmetrically prescriptive/descriptive" approach to negotiation. In his groundbreaking 1982 book *The Art and Science of Negotiation,* Raiffa focused on providing the best advice to a focal negotiator (prescriptive) based on the best possible description of the likely behavior of the negotiator's opponent (descriptive). Raiffa's work represented a turning point in negotiation research for a number of reasons. First, by departing from game-theoretic perspectives that assumed full rationality by all parties, Raiffa explicitly acknowledged the importance of developing accurate descriptions of opponents. In addition, his realization that negotiators need advice implicitly acknowledged the fact that we do not intuitively follow purely rational strategies. Finally, Raiffa initiated the groundwork for a dialogue between prescriptive and descriptive researchers, which we have overviewed in these last two chapters.

Chapter 10 provided the basic analytic structure for Raiffa's prescriptive analysis, while Chapter 11 dealt with questions that Raiffa's work left unexamined. For example, if the negotiator and his or her opponent do not act rationally, what systematic departures from rationality result? A successful negotiator will use descriptive models to anticipate the likely behavior of the opponent and to identify errors to avoid in his or her own negotiating behavior.

CHAPTER TWELVE

Improving Decision Making

At this point in the book, you may be wondering why human judgment is so terrible. In fact, the situation is not as bad as it seems. Our brains generally serve us well. We are able to perform computational miracles with the three pounds of gray matter between our ears. To pick just two examples, our ability to understand verbal language and to recognize human faces is far beyond that of even the fastest and most powerful computers.

Researchers who study judgment and decision making focus our work on the frailties and shortcomings of human judgment because such examination provides us with the best opportunities to understand the human mind. We learn the most about how we accomplish our goals not by observing successes, but by taking account of failures. When do we confuse one face with another? When do we confuse one word with another? Answers to these questions have helped us understand how our minds process visual and auditory information (Holt & Lotto, 2008; Yovel & Kanwisher, 2005). Just so, the study of judgment biases has revealed a great deal about how people make decisions.

The study of biases is also of immense practical value. Abundant evidence shows that the decisions of smart managers are routinely impaired by biases. Studying how organizations fail can provide useful lessons about what helps them succeed (Bazerman & Watkins, 2004; Perrow, 1984; Ross & Staw, 1986; Sitkin, 1992; Weick, 1993). The good news is that many interventions to improve decision making have emerged in the behavioral decision research literature, and many of these interventions have been developed and have succeeded in the real world.

One story of an effective decision-changing process appears in Michael Lewis's 2003 book *Moneyball* and the 2011 film adaptation. Lewis tells the story of how Billy Beane, the general manager of the Oakland Athletics, transformed his baseball team by questioning the intuition of baseball professionals. From 1999, when Beane took over as general manager of the Oakland Athletics, through 2002, the team achieved a truly amazing record. The year Beane took over, the team ranked eleventh of fourteen in the American League in terms of payroll yet placed fifth out of fourteen in wins. In both the 2000 and 2001 seasons, the Athletics ranked twelfth in payroll and second in wins in the American League. In 2002, they were twelfth in payroll and first in wins in the league. Over this four-year period, the team had the second-best record in Major League Baseball with one of the two smallest payrolls in the entire league. The players earned less than a third of the amount earned by the New York Yankees yet won more games than the Yankees.

How did the Athletics achieve this success? The simple answer is that manager Billy Beane, with the help of Paul DePodesta, a recent Harvard economics graduate, realized that the intuition of baseball executives was limited and systematically biased, and that their perceived "wisdom" nonetheless had been incorporated into personnel management in ways that created enormous inefficiencies. Lewis (2003) argues that baseball executives were consistently guilty of three mistakes. First, they overgeneralized from their personal experiences. Second, they were overly influenced by players' recent performances. Third, they were overly influenced by what they saw with their own eyes, when players' multiyear records provided far better data.

More broadly, Beane and DePodesta found that expert intuition in baseball systematically overweighted some variables and underweighted other variables. The results made it clear that, in baseball, statistics have outperformed the experts. After allowing intuition to rule decision making in baseball for over one hundred years, teams are only now replacing their "experts" with nerds who know how to run regression equations. In Lewis's (2003) words, "the market for baseball players was so inefficient, and the general grasp of sound baseball strategy so weak, that superior management could run circles around taller piles of cash." Following Beane's success, many teams tried to hire DePodesta as their general manager, and most teams learned to rely more heavily on statistical analysis to predict players' future performance (Schwarz, 2005).

The story of the Athletics' success raises some interesting questions. Why did it take so long for rationality to enter into decision making in baseball? To what extent are managers in other industries still relying on false expertise when better strategies exist? As Thaler and Sunstein (2003) note in their insightful review of *Moneyball*, baseball professionals are not stupid, but they are human. Like all of us, they have tended to rely on simple heuristics, traditions, and habits, which in turn created the conventional wisdom that governed baseball for over a century. It takes time, effort, and courage for an organization to move from relying on faulty intuition to carefully assessing data and using appropriate statistical techniques.

Lewis (2003) argues that the mistakes documented in Major League Baseball are probably more severe in other industries. After all, the sport of baseball is full of excellent, reliable data. Thaler and Sunstein (2003) compare the tendency of baseball executives to overlook a wealth of statistics to the tendency of personnel managers to base hiring decisions on their "gut" reactions to job interviews rather than on the hard data available on applicants. Executives tend to trust their intuitive reactions to interviews, despite extensive research showing that interviews provide little predictability about future performance. Thaler and Sunstein (2003) argue for personnel selection based on real performance predictors (grades, test scores, past company performance, etc.) rather than on intuition gathered from interviews.

In this chapter, we argue that most organizations have the opportunity to significantly increase the effectiveness of their decision-making processes. We will not argue that executives are lacking in intelligence. Rather, like baseball executives, most professionals make decisions that fall short of objectively rational behavior and do so in specific and systematic ways. The critical question is: What can we do to correct these deficiencies? This concluding chapter examines seven concrete and complementary strategies for making better decisions: (1) use decision-analysis tools, (2) acquire expertise, (3) debias your judgment, (4) reason analogically, (5) take an outsider's view, (6) understand biases in others, and (7) nudge people toward wiser and more ethical decisions.

STRATEGY 1: USE DECISION-ANALYSIS TOOLS

Because we do not make optimal decisions intuitively or automatically, when decision quality really matters, it makes sense to rely on procedures that can help direct us toward more optimal decisions. The field of study that specializes in giving this sort of prescriptive decision advice is generally called *decision analysis*. A number of books have distilled the field's wisdom to provide useful guides for making decisions (for example, see Goodwin, 1999; Hammond, Keeney, & Raiffa, 1999). These approaches usually require you to quantify both your preferences and the value you place on each of the various decision options. Rational decision-making strategies also require you to be specific about the probabilities associated with uncertain future outcomes.

Decision analysis usually guides decision making using the logic of *expected value*. To compute an option's expected value, you multiply its value by its probability. So, for instance, to compute the dollar value of a lottery ticket, you would need to multiply the dollar value of its payout by the probability of receiving that payout. Because the expected value of lottery tickets is almost always less than it costs to buy them, purchasing lottery tickets is usually not a good use of your money. When a decision has multiple dimensions, such as a choice between two houses, one that is expensive and newly renovated and another whose price is more reasonable but that requires more work, the decision usually requires some sort of multi-attribute utility computation. This computation forces the decision maker to weigh her willingness to spend money against her willingness to perform home improvement work.

Often, however, businesses need to make a series of similar decisions over and over. For instance, corporations need to decide which applicants to hire. Executives need to decide which employees to promote and how big each employee's bonus should be. Bank loan officers need to decide whether to extend credit to loan applicants. Venture capitalists need to decide whether to fund an entrepreneur's new venture. These complex decisions can be guided by the use of a linear model.

What is a Linear Model?

A linear model is a formula that weights and adds up the relevant predictor variables in order to make a quantitative prediction. As an example, when his older son was five, Don asked the boy's pediatrician to predict how tall Josh would grow to be. The pediatrician offered a simple linear model in response. She said that a child's adult height is best predicted with the following computation. First, average the parents' heights. Second, if the child is a boy, add two inches to the parents' average. If the child is a girl, subtract two inches from the parents' average. Innumerable linear models such as this exist to help us make informed predictions. A linear model called PECOTA, for instance, helps baseball teams predict players' future performances using data such as their prior performances, ages, heights, and weights (Schwarz, 2005). There is even a company that uses a secretive linear model to help movie studios predict how much money their movies will earn (Gladwell, 2006).

Why Linear Models Can Lead to Superior Decisions

Researchers have found that linear models produce superior predictions than experts across an impressive array of domains. In addition, research has found that more complex models produce only marginal improvements above a simple linear framework. Dawes (1979) argues that linear models are superior because people are much better at selecting and coding information (such as what variables to put in the model) than they are at integrating the information (using the data to make a prediction). Einhorn (1972) illustrates this point in a study of physicians who coded biopsies of patients with Hodgkin's disease and then made an overall rating of disease severity. The individual ratings were not able to predict the survival time of the patients, all of whom died of the disease. However, the variables that the physicians selected to code did predict survival time when optimal weights were determined with a multiple regression model. The doctors knew what information to consider, but they did not know how to integrate this information consistently into valid predictions.

In addition to having difficulty integrating information, we are also inconsistent. Given the same data, we will not always make the same decision. Our judgment is affected by mood, subjective interpretations, environment, deadlines, random fluctuations, and many others nonstable characteristics. In contrast, a linear model will always make the same decisions with the same inputs. Thus, such models capture the underlying policy that an expert uses while avoiding the expert's random error. Furthermore, experts are likely to be affected by certain biases triggered by specific cases. In contrast, linear models include only the actual data that are empirically known to have predictive power, not the salience or representativeness of that or any other available data. In short, linear models can be programmed to sidestep biases that are known to impair human judgment.

Such bias is common in financial decisions, corporate personnel decisions, bank loan decisions, and routine purchasing decisions. In each of these domains, the decision maker must make multiple routine decisions based on the same set of variables—a task well suited to a linear model. Such models allow the organization to identify the factors that are important in the decisions of its experts. Thus, independent of their superior predictive powers, the feedback and training opportunities provided by linear models make them a valuable managerial tool.

Why We Resist Linear Models

While evidence amply supports the power of linear models, such models have not been widely used. Why not? Resistance to them is strong. Some have raised ethical concerns, such as this one described by Dawes:

> I overheard a young woman complain that it was "horribly unfair" that she had been rejected by the Psychology Department at the University of California, Santa Barbara, on the basis of mere numbers, without even an interview. "How could they possibly tell what I'm like?" The answer is they can't. Nor could they with an interview.

Dawes argues that decision makers demonstrate irresponsible conceit in believing that a half-hour interview leads to better predictions than the information contained in a transcript covering three-and-a-half years of work and the carefully devised aptitude assessment of graduate board exams.

Now consider the response that Max received when he asked a well-known arbitrator to make a number of decisions as part of a study of arbitrator decision-making processes:

> You are on an illusory quest! Other arbitrators may respond to your question-naire; but in the end you will have nothing but trumpery and a collation of responses which will leave you still asking how arbitrators decide cases. Telling you how I would decide in the scenarios provided would really tell you nothing of any value in respect of what moves arbitrators to decide as they do. As well ask a youth why he is infatuated with that particular girl when her sterling virtues are not that apparent. As well ask my grandmother how and why she picked a particular "mushmelon" from a stall of "mushmelons." Judgment, taste, experience, and a lot of other things too numerous to mention are factors in the decisions (Bazerman, 1985).

In contrast with this arbitrator's denial of the possibility of systematically studying decision processes, research in this area does show that linear models are capable of capturing his decision-making model (or his grandmother's choice of mushmelon).

Another argument commonly made against decision-analysis tools such as linear models is that they rule out the inclusion of intuitions or gut feelings. In an apocryphal story, Howard Raiffa was on the faculty at Columbia and received an offer from Harvard. According to the story, he visited his dean at Columbia, who was also his friend, and asked for help with his decision. Sarcastically, the dean, borrowing from Raiffa's writings on decision analysis, told Raiffa to identify the relevant criteria, weight each criterion, rate each school on each criterion, do the arithmetic, see which school had the best overall score, and go there. Supposedly,

Raiffa protested, "No, this is a serious decision!" While he enjoys this story, Raiffa says it simply isn't true. The more important the decision is, he continues to believe, the more important it is to think systematically about it.

Finally, people sometimes argue that the use of linear models will require difficult changes within organizations. What will bank loan officers or college admissions officers do when computers make the decisions? Such concerns express the fear that people are not necessary for linear models to make decisions. In fact, people play a crucial role in models. People decide which variables to put into the model and how to weight them. People also monitor the model's performance and determine when it needs to be updated. Nevertheless, resistance to change is natural, and resistance to the use of linear models is clearly no exception. Overcoming a bias against expert-based, computer-formulated judgments is yet another step you can take toward improving your decision-making abilities. We will now look more closely at two domains in which evidence shows that linear models can lead to better organizational outcomes: graduate-school admissions decisions and hiring decisions.

Improving Admissions Decisions

The value of using linear models in hiring, admissions, and selection decisions is highlighted by research on the interpretation of grades (Moore, Swift, Sharek, & Gino, 2010). There are substantial differences in the grading practices of colleges, even between institutions of similar quality and selectivity. It turns out that students from colleges with more lenient grading are more likely to get in to graduate school, even after controlling for the quality of the institution and the quality of its students. In one study, due to a variant of the representativeness heuristic called the *correspondence bias* (Gilbert & Malone, 1995), graduate schools mistook the high GPAs of alumni from lenient-grading institutions as evidence of high performance. The correspondence bias describes the tendency to take others at face value by assuming that their behavior (or their GPAs) corresponds to their innate traits. The researchers found that this bias persisted even when those making the admissions decisions had full information about different institutions' grading practices. It seems that people have trouble sufficiently discounting high grades that are due to lenient grading.

By contrast, it would be easy to set up a linear program to avoid this error. Indeed, Dawes (1971) did just that in his work on graduate-school admissions decisions. Dawes used a common method for developing his linear model: he first modeled the admission decisions of a four-person committee. In other words, he systematically analyzed how the committee made its admissions decisions, relying on three factors: (1) Graduate Record Examination scores, (2) undergraduate GPA, and (3) the quality of the undergraduate school. Dawes then used the variable weightings he obtained from modeling the experts in a linear model to predict the average rating of 384 other applicants. He found that the model could be used to rule out 55 percent of the applicant pool without ever rejecting an applicant that the selection committee had in fact accepted. In addition, the linear model was better than the committee itself in predicting future ratings of the accepted and matriculated applicants by faculty! In 1971, Dawes estimated that the use of a linear model as a screening device by the nation's graduate schools could result in an annual savings of about $18 million in professional time. Adjusted for today's dollars and the current number of graduate-school applications, that number would easily exceed $500 million. And this figure neglects many larger domains, including undergraduate admissions and corporate recruiting.

Improving Hiring Decisions

Hiring decisions are among the most important decisions an organization can make. Virtually every corporation in the world relies on unstructured, face-to-face employment interviews as the most important tool for selecting employees who have passed through an initial screening process. The effectiveness of employment interviews for predicting future job performance has been the subject of extensive study by industrial psychologists. This research shows that job interviews do not work well. Specifically, employment interviews predict only about 14 percent of the variability in employee performance (Schmidt & Hunter, 1998). In part, this figure is so low because predicting job performance is difficult and few tools do it well. Yet some assessment tools do predict performance substantially better than the unstructured interview, and at a substantially lower cost.

So why do people continue to believe so strongly in employment interviews? Managers' robust faith in the value of interviews is the result of a "perfect storm" of cognitive biases:

- *Availability*: Interviewers may think they know what constitutes superior employee performance, but their information is highly imperfect. Few companies bother to collect useful data on the attributes that employees need to succeed within specific positions or within the broader organization. As a result, managers must rely on their intuitions to determine whether or not a job candidate has the qualities needed for success.

- *Affect heuristic*: People make very quick evaluations of whether they like others or not based on superficial features, such as physical attractiveness, mannerisms, or similarity to oneself (Ambady, Krabbenoft, & Hogan, 2006; Ambady & Rosenthal, 1993). Managers rarely revise these first impressions in the course of an employment interview (Dougherty, Turban, & Callender, 1994). Managers sometimes claim that interviews allow them to assess a potential candidate's "fit" with the firm, but this assessment is usually not based on systematic measurement of a candidate's qualities and is little more than the interviewer's intuitive, affective response.

- *Representativeness*: Intuition also leads managers to believe that if a person can speak coherently about her goals, the organization, or the job, then she will perform well at the job. For most jobs, however, interview performance is weakly related to actual job performance. Extroverted, sociable, tall, attractive, and ingratiating people often make more positive interview impressions than others. However, these traits are often less critical to job performance than other, less immediately observable traits, such as conscientiousness and intelligence.

- *Confirmation heuristic*: After interviewing a number of people for a position and hiring one of them, managers only learn about the performance of the person selected. Without knowing whether that person is performing better than the rejected applicants would have, managers lack the data they would need to assess whether their selection mechanisms are effective (Einhorn & Hogarth, 1978).

What is a better alternative to face-to-face, unstructured employment interviews? A number of other selection tools are available, most of which are less expensive to implement than interviews, including simple intelligence tests. But if organizations insist on conducting interviews, they ought to use structured ones in which all job candidates are reviewed by the same set of interviewers and in which each interviewer asks the same questions of each candidate (Schmidt & Hunter, 1998). In addition, interviewers' quantitative assessments ought to be just one component fed into a linear model, along with intelligence measures, years of relevant work experience, and so on.

STRATEGY 2: ACQUIRE EXPERTISE

Many of the biases we have examined in this book were identified in experiments with student participants who were not rewarded for accurate performance and who were making decisions in task domains unfamiliar to them. Thus, one optimistic possibility is that experts or experienced decision makers facing important real-world decisions might be far less affected by biases than most research participants. Does this book unfairly exaggerate the prevalence of judgment biases? This is certainly an important question, since experience and expertise might be useful tools for improving decision making.

Some researchers believe that the process of improving judgment will occur naturally as individuals receive feedback about their past decisions. This view is represented by Kagel and Levin (1986, p. 917) in their analysis of the winner's curse in competitive bidding discussed in Chapter 4:

> Given sufficient experience and feedback regarding the outcomes of their decisions, we have no doubt that our experimental participants, as well as most bidders in "real world" settings, would eventually learn to avoid the winner's curse in any particular set of circumstances. The winner's curse is a disequilibrium phenomenon that will correct itself given sufficient time and the right kind of information feedback.

In fact, Kagel and Levin (1986) do show a reduction in the winner's curse in the auction context as the market (but not necessarily specific players) "learns" over time. However, much of this learning can be attributed to the phenomenon in which the most aggressive bidders go broke and drop out of the market. Additional learning occurs by observing the consistent losses being suffered by "winners" in the auction.

Clearly, life experiences help us to improve numerous skills and abandon many bad habits. Unfortunately, our judgmental distortions might not be among them. Tversky and Kahneman (1986) have argued that basic judgmental biases are unlikely to correct themselves over time. Responsive learning requires accurate and immediate feedback, which is rarely available in the real world because:

> (i) outcomes are commonly delayed and not easily attributable to a particular action; (ii) variability in the environment degrades the reliability of feedback. . . ; (iii) there is often no information about what the outcome would have been if another decision had been taken; and (iv) most important decisions are unique and therefore provide little opportunity for learning (see Einhorn and Hogarth, 1978) . . . any claim that a particular error will be eliminated by experience must be supported by demonstrating that the conditions for effective learning are satisfied (pp. s274–s275).

Even if accurate and immediate feedback is available in a given situation, we face another crucial challenge: we are likely to misremember our own forecasts (Meyvis, Ratner, & Levav, 2010). We often anchor to current states and fail to accurately recall our prior predictions. Thus, it is common for us to underestimate the extent to which our prior predictions deviated from actual outcomes, and this underestimation leads to us inadequately learn from prior experience (Morris & Moore, 2000).

Using the "Acquiring a Company" problem described in Chapter 4, Ball, Bazerman, and Carroll (1991) tested the ability of individuals to learn to avoid the winner's curse by incorporating the decisions of others into their decision making. Participants in this experiment played for real money, played in 20 trials, and were given full feedback immediately after each trial based on a random determination of the value of the firm up for sale; in addition, they could observe changes in their asset balance (which virtually always went down). Thus, when compared to the limitations cited by Tversky and Kahneman, ideal conditions existed for learning from past mistakes. The only limitation that was not eliminated—namely, the variability of the environment (ii above)—is a natural part of the winner's curse phenomenon. Thus, we were able to look at whether or not the ability to consider the cognitions of the other party in a bilateral negotiation problem can be learned in a highly favorable environment.

Remembering that $0 is the correct answer and that $50 to $75 is the answer typically obtained when decision makers ignore the cognitions of others, examine the mean bids across the 20 trials in Figure 12.1. Across the 20 trials, there is no obvious trend indicating that participants learned the correct response. In fact, only five of 72 participants from a leading MBA program learned over the course of the trials. Our general conclusion? Individuals are unlikely to overcome the winner's curse simply through experience or feedback.

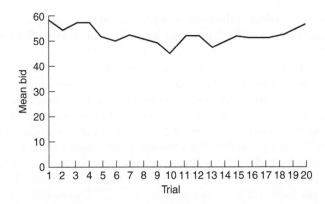

Figure 12.1 Mean Offers Across 20 Trials of the "Acquiring a Company" Problem.

This evidence paints a pessimistic picture of the idea that experience will cure the decision biases identified in this book. In fact, Bereby-Meyer and Grosskopf (2008) documented that even hundreds of trials do not lead most study participants to solve the Acquiring a Company problem. This evidence is consistent with the documentation of extensive bias in decision making by actual investors, real-estate agents, medical doctors, and numerous other "expert" groups. Neale and Northcraft (1989) proposed that biased decision-making outcomes could be eliminated or ameliorated through the development of expertise. While we often think of experience and expertise as closely related, Neale and Northcraft defined experience simply as repeated feedback. By contrast, they assert that expertise results when individuals develop a "strategic conceptualization" of what constitutes a rational decision-making process and learn to recognize the biases that limit rationality.

Neale and Northcraft's experience/expertise distinction is highly relevant to the question of whether or not experienced decision makers can benefit from the study of decision making. Northcraft and Neale's (1987) study of anchoring and adjustment among real-estate agents suggests that experienced decision makers can be very biased. In addition, while most "effective decision makers" are successful in a specific domain, experience without expertise can be quite dangerous when it is transferred to a different context or when the environment changes. Evidence from Chapter 2 suggests that as the amount of ignorance increases, individuals become more overconfident regarding their fallible judgment.

If you think that experience should help negotiators do a better job of understanding the other side's reservation price, think again. Larrick and Wu (2007) find that, when it comes to estimating the size of the bargaining zone, experience will only help us correct one type of error: overestimation of the bargaining zone's size. When you think the bargaining zone is much bigger than it is, your negotiating counterpart will help you identify and correct your error by refusing to agree to deal at the price you propose. When, on the other hand, you underestimate the size of the bargaining zone, you will end up offering the other side more than was necessary. Though she probably will be anxious to accept your offer, she may try to get you to concede a bit more first, so that you will think that your offer is close to her reservation price. This type of experience will generally lead negotiators to believe that bargaining zones are smaller than they actually are and that they need to make more generous offers to their negotiating opponents.

Stressing the drawbacks of relying on experience for knowledge, Dawes (1988) notes that Benjamin Franklin's famous quote "experience is a dear teacher" is often misinterpreted to mean "experience is the best teacher," when in fact Franklin was using "dear" as a synonym for expensive. After all, the quote continues, "yet fools will learn in no other [school]." Dawes writes,

> Learning from an experience of failure . . . is indeed "dear," and it can even be fatal. . . . moreover, experiences of success may have negative as well as positive results when people mindlessly learn from them. . . . People who are extraordinarily successful—or lucky—in general may conclude from their "experience" that they are invulnerable and consequently court disaster by failing to monitor their behavior and its implications.

Or in the words of Confucius: "By three methods we may learn wisdom: First, by reflection, which is noblest; Second, by imitation, which is easiest; and third, by experience, which is the bitterest."

This view of experience reiterates the comparative value of gaining a conceptual understanding of how to make a rational decision rather than simply depending upon the relatively mindless, passive learning obtained via experience. Expertise requires much more than the unclear feedback of uncertain, uncontrollable, and often delayed results. Rather, it necessitates constant monitoring and awareness of our decision-making processes. The final benefit of developing a strategic conceptualization of decision making concerns transferability. If you ask experienced decision makers for the secrets of their success, they routinely insist that their skills have developed over years of observation and experience that cannot be taught. This obviously reduces their ability to pass on their knowledge to others. Thus, experience without expertise limits the ability to transfer knowledge to future generations.

A key element of developing a strategic conceptualization of decision making is to become aware of the many biases in individual and group contexts that we have discussed in Chapters 1 through 11. However, awareness is just one step in the process. Another strategy, debiasing, is the topic of the next section.

STRATEGY 3: DEBIAS YOUR JUDGMENT

Debiasing refers to a procedure for reducing or eliminating biases from the cognitive strategies of the decision maker. Fischhoff (1982) proposed four steps that decision-making teachers or trainers can follow to encourage their students to make wiser judgments: (1) offer warnings about the possibility of bias, (2) describe the direction of the bias, (3) provide a dose of feedback, and (4) offer an extended program of training with feedback, coaching, and whatever else it takes to improve judgment. Fischhoff also argues that debiasing is an extremely difficult process that must be closely monitored and guided by a psychological framework for change. For example, research on the hindsight bias (Fischhoff, 1977), described in Chapter 3, has shown that even when the bias is explicitly described to participants and they are instructed to avoid it, the bias remains.

In contrast, a review by Larrick (2004) paints a rosier picture of our ability to overcome bias through training. Yet Larrick (2004) also notes that most successful debiasing strategies tend to be context- and bias-specific; training and testing must be closely linked and must occur in close time proximity. For example, research on the overconfidence bias has found that intensive, personalized feedback is moderately effective in improving judgment (Lichtenstein & Fischhoff, 1980), but only in the short term. Occasionally, a broader effect of training has been documented. For example, simply encouraging people to "consider the opposite" of whatever they are deciding reduces overconfidence, hindsight, and anchoring effects (Larrick, 2004; Mussweiler, Strack, & Pfeiffer, 2000). Larrick (2004) also highlights the partial debiasing success of using groups instead of individuals, training in statistical reasoning, and making people accountable for their decisions (Lerner & Tetlock, 1999).

Based on Lewin's framework outlined in Chapter 1, Fischhoff's debiasing research, Larrick's review, and our own judgment-training programs with MBA and executive students, this section makes specific suggestions for debiasing judgment.

Unfreezing

Chapter 1 noted that many behaviors at the individual, group, and organizational levels are ingrained, or part of a standard repertoire, and are therefore quite difficult to change. Factors that inhibit individuals from changing their behavior include satisfaction with the status quo, risk aversion, and a preference for the certain outcomes of known behavior to the uncertain outcomes of innovative behavior. For improved decision making to occur and continue over time, an explicit "unfreezing" process of ingrained thinking and behaviors must take place. For at least three key reasons, unfreezing old strategies is crucial to changing the decision-making processes of individuals.

First, individuals will have typically relied on their current intuitive strategy for many years. To want to change would be to admit that past strategies were flawed, and this realization is likely to be disturbing. Thus, individuals may be motivated to avoid the disconcerting truth about their judgmental deficiencies.

Second, individuals who have achieved a certain level of professional success (such as students in MBA and executive education programs) are likely to have received positive reinforcement for many of their past decisions. According to the basics of reinforcement theory, individuals tend to continue behaviors that are positively rewarded. For example, because many successful executives rise to the top using intuitive strategies, they tend to resist information indicating that their judgment is systematically deficient in some demonstrable manner.

A third, related point has to do with balance theory (Heider, 1958), which suggests that individuals try to manage their cognitions into a consistent order. For successful managers, the notion that "there is something fundamentally wrong with my decision-making processes" clashes with their awareness of their success. The belief "I am currently an excellent decision maker" is much more harmonious with the notion of success; therefore, according to balance theory, that cognition is more likely to dominate.

Overall, a pattern emerges of an intelligent manager who has multiple reasons for believing in the high quality of his or her decision-making processes and resisting any change to his or her intuitive strategies. Most successful people will be motivated to view their intuition as a talent rather than a handicap. In fact, this book has provided substantial evidence that there is significant room for improvement in the intuitive strategies of even the brightest, most successful managers. Thus, we conclude that improving on intuition is an important activity for successful managers to attempt, but that cognitive resistance to change is a predictable pattern.

This book has sought to create changes in your judgment by exposing you to concrete evidence that leads you to question your current strategies. The quiz-and-feedback format was designed specifically to unfreeze your decision-making processes. Most readers make a substantial number of mistakes on these items and are then ready to learn where they went wrong and how they could have performed better. This format unfreezes the notion that your decision-making processes do not require improvement. As you begin to question your current strategies, you become receptive to alternatives. In other cases (such as the dollar auction), vivid examples were intended to unfreeze your thinking by leading you to identify with individuals who fell victim to judgmental deficiencies.

Change

Once you has unfrozen past behaviors, you will become willing to consider alternatives. The next stage consists of making the change itself. However, change is far from guaranteed; internal resistance is likely, causing you to continually reassess the desirability of change. There are three critical steps to changing your decision-making process: (1) clarification of the existence of specific judgmental deficiencies, (2) explanation of the roots of these deficiencies, and (3) reassurance that these deficiencies should not be taken as a threat to your self-esteem.

The first step consists of abstracting from the concrete example that was used for unfreezing to identify the more general bias that exists. In addition, for the bias to have face validity to you, an explanation of why the bias exists is necessary; this often consists of clarifying the heuristic or phenomenon that underlies the bias. Finally, this information may be threatening enough to increase the resistance that you partially overcame in the unfreezing stage. Thus, it is critical that you understand that virtually everyone is subject to judgment biases and that having them does not imply that you are a poor decision maker, but simply human.

Perhaps the most general-purpose debiasing strategy is what Lord, Lepper, and Preston (1984) call "consider the opposite." They advise us to play devil's advocate with ourselves and to think about reasons our tentative conclusions could be wrong. This strategy is obviously most useful for counteracting the confirmation trap—the tendency to seek out information that supports our chosen point of view while overlooking disconfirming evidence. Baron (1994) has given more specific advice. He suggests that, when assessing any piece of data, you should do two things. First, ask yourself: "How likely is a yes answer, if I assume that my hypothesis is false?" For instance, imagine you are considering investing money in a friend's new business idea. You take it as a good sign that his business plan projects he will turn a profit in one year. The hypothesis you've been entertaining is that this is a good investment for your money. But what if you assume the hypothesis is false: that this investment is a terrible idea because it puts both your money and your friendship in peril? Is it possible that your friend came up with a plausible business plan but that his chances of success are not particularly great?

Second, try to think of alternative hypotheses, then choose a test most likely to distinguish them. Could you devise a test that could tell whether your friend's plan was actually a viable one? Maybe the fact that he has had trouble getting start-up funding from banks or venture capitalists is a sign that his business plan doesn't stack up that well against those of other aspiring entrepreneurs. This process is useful not only for counteracting the confirmation bias but also for reducing overconfidence. Admittedly, it's not always fun to consider ways in which we might be wrong, but this is a crucial step when sound decisions and accurate judgments are more important than ego gratification.

Refreezing

After we make a positive change, it is tempting to revert to past practices and bad habits. The old biases still exist and can be easily and even accidentally used. Meanwhile, the new procedures are foreign and must develop into intuitive strategies, a process that takes place with practice over time. As you consciously use new strategies in multiple applications, these strategies slowly become second nature, taking the place of old patterns. However, frequent application and overviews of past training are necessary if change is to last.

For refreezing to occur, you must continue to examine your decisions for bias long after you have finished this book. You should schedule routine "checkups" to evaluate your recent important decisions—those you made on your own, as a negotiator, and as a member of a group—while remaining aware of the limits of your judgment.

STRATEGY 4: REASON ANALOGICALLY

Analogical reasoning, or the process of abstracting common lessons from two or more situations, turns out to be a remarkably simple debiasing approach (D. Gentner, G. Loewenstein, & L. Thompson, 2003a; Loewenstein, Thompson,

& Gentner, 1999; L. Thompson, D. Gentner, & J. Loewenstein, 2000). Research shows that people learn far more from cases, simulations, and real-world experiences when they are able to take away an abstract form of the learning message. In the context of learning to negotiate through simulations, Gentner, Loewenstein, & Thompson (2003b) found that greater debiasing occurred among participants when they took part in two exercises that had the same lesson and were asked how the two simulations were related than when they assessed the same two exercises and were asked to explain the lesson of each one. When people learn from one episode at a time, they too often focus on superficial characteristics of the situation and assume that the message applies only to the specific context of the decision (such as learning how to buy a house). By contrast, the process of abstracting similar lessons from two episodes (such as learning to overcome the mythical fixed pie of negotiation following a house purchase and a workplace negotiation) creates more generalizable insight.

By assessing participants' performance on a third task, Gentner, Loewenstein, and Thompson (2003a) have demonstrated evidence of debiasing decision-making and negotiation behavior through this type of analogical reasoning. They have replicated their research conclusions across a number of studies, many involving executives and consultants. Thompson, Gentner, & Loewenstein (2000) claim that when people make a comparison, they focus on the similarities between examples, whose common structure becomes more transparent. Identifying the common structure—the principle shared by both examples—helps the learner form a schema that is less sensitive to the irrelevant surface or context features of the particular examples. Such an abstract principle is more likely to be transferred to new situations with different contexts than a principle that is not abstracted from its original context. These impressive findings on the effectiveness of analogical reasoning open up important new directions for debiasing research and offer guidance on how to use cases and simulations to maximize generalizable learning.

Building on Thompson et al.'s analogical reasoning work, Idson, Chugh, Bereby-Meyer, Moran, Grosskopf, and Bazerman (2004) suggest that understanding differences, as well as similarities, across problems may also be a very useful means of transferring knowledge. Idson et al. (2004) show that training based on differences can reduce bias in the Acquiring a Company problem, which, as discussed earlier, had proven resistant to many other debiasing techniques. Using the five problems from Tor and Bazerman (2003), Idson et al. (2004) had study participants either (1) examine the two versions of the Monty Hall problem and the two versions of the Dividing a Pie problem as four separate problems, or (2) presented the problems in pairs. All participants were then given multiple trials to solve the Acquiring a Company problem, with pay based on performance. They also gave the same Acquiring a Company problem to other study participants who were not trained on the Monty Hall problem and the Dividing a Pie problem. Idson et al. (2004) found that allowing study participants to view the Monty Hall and Dividing a Pie problems as pairs helped them understand the differences between the two versions of each problem and generalize the importance of focusing on the decisions of other parties and the rules of the game. These lessons, which were also the keys to solving the Acquiring a Company problem, indeed enabled participants to perform substantially better on this problem. This research offers evidence that examining differences between seemingly related problems may be a successful direction for improving decision making.

What is the optimal level of abstraction that should occur to help people form analogies across problems? Moran, Bereby-Meyer, and Bazerman (2008) argue that teaching people more *general* negotiation principles (such as "Value can be created" or "It is important to understand how parties' interests interrelate") enables successful transfer to a broader range of new negotiation tasks than the focused analogies of Loewenstein et al. (2003). Moran et al. (2008) argue that learning general principles will improve not only the ability to positively transfer specifically learned principles but also the ability to discriminate their appropriateness—i.e., to determine when a principle should and should not be applied.

Moran et al. (2008) found that learners who previously received training in analogical reasoning for one specific negotiation strategy (namely, logrolling issues to create value) did not perform well when confronted with a diverse, face-to-face negotiation with a very different structure. Thus, logrolling may have limited generalizability to other value-creating processes. To test this idea, Moran et al. adapted Thompson et al.'s analogical reasoning training to teach negotiators broad thought processes for creating value in negotiations. Moran et al. (2008) compared *specific training*, wherein learners compare two cases that illustrate the same specific strategy instances (e.g., logrolling), with *diverse training*, wherein learners compare two cases that illustrate different value-creating strategies (e.g., one illustrates logrolling and the other compatibility). Training effectiveness was assessed by looking at performance and outcomes in a negotiation simulation with potential for various value-creating strategies, some of which learners previously had learned and others which they had not.

Moran et al. (2008) found that more diverse analogical training, wherein negotiators learn and compare several different value-creating strategies, fostered greater learning of underlying value-creating negotiation principles than did more specific analogical training. This method facilitated transfer to a very distinctive task and improved performance on a variety of value-creating strategies, including some that participants had never previously encountered. Improved performance was accompanied by a deeper understanding of the potential to create value. Thus, more diverse analogical training can be effective for attaining greater expertise, which fosters understanding of which particular strategies might be effective in different situations and why. At the same time, when training becomes too diverse, the applicability of the message may be lost. The optimal level of abstraction remains an interesting question for future research, as does the question of how analogical reasoning can be applied to improve individual decision making.

STRATEGY 5: TAKE AN OUTSIDER'S VIEW

In Chapter 2, we asked you to estimate ten obscure quantities and to place 98 percent confidence intervals around your estimates. As we noted, most people answer only three to seven of the ten items correctly, despite being 98 percent confident of their intervals. This study bolsters the widespread finding that people are overconfident in their decisions. Interestingly, after people make these ten assessments and are asked to estimate the total number of questions for which the correct answer will be within their confidence interval, these more global estimates are fairly accurate (Gigerenzer, Hoffrage, & Kleinbölting, 1991; Kahneman & Lovallo, 1993). That is, participants generally understand that only three to seven of their 98 percent confidence intervals will actually contain the true estimate!

Kahneman and Lovallo (1993) explain this apparent contradiction by theorizing that we all have two perspectives on decision making: an *insider* view and an *outsider* view. The insider is the biased decision maker who looks at each situation as unique. The outsider, on the other hand, is more capable of generalizing across situations and identifying similarities. Because these two viewpoints exist simultaneously, a member of a consulting team might be well aware that most projects take longer to complete than initial estimates suggest (outsider view) while also believing that her own optimistic estimate of an upcoming project's duration is somehow accurate and unbiased (insider view). Similarly, people who undertake a new home construction or major home renovation know from their friends that such projects typically end up being overdue and 20–50 percent over budget (outsider view). Nevertheless, most people who initiate such a building project believe that theirs will be different—that their home will be completed on time and near the projected costs (insider view).

Kahneman identified a classic situation of insider optimism within a group of colleagues he was working with to define a new curriculum (Kahneman & Lovallo, 1993). The group estimated that the project would take 18–30 months to complete. Kahneman asked a member of the team, who was a distinguished expert in curriculum design, "We are surely not the only team to have tried to develop a curriculum where none existed before. Please try to recall as many cases as you can. Think of them as they were in a stage comparable to ours at present. How long did it take them, from that point, to complete their project?" The team member answered that 40 percent of the projects were never completed, and none were completed in less than seven years. As it turned out, the team took *eight years* to finish its project.

This pattern resonates well with writers. Most of us understand that books take a long time to write; nonetheless, we are optimistic about meeting our own unrealistic deadlines when we sit down to write the first chapter. We may never complete the book, but we will probably believe that the next project will be different. Similarly, Cooper, Woo, and Dunkelberg (1988) found that over 80 percent of entrepreneurs perceived their chances of success to be 70 percent or better, and one-third of them described their success as certain. In contrast, they estimated the mean success rates of businesses similar to their business to be 59 percent. Meanwhile, the five-year survival rate for new businesses is only about 33 percent (Kahneman & Lovallo, 1993).

Kahneman and Lovallo provide convincing evidence that the outsider makes better estimates and decisions than the insider. The outsider view incorporates more relevant data from previous decisions—yet we tend to believe and act on the insider view. Why? Certainly, optimism and overconfidence are factors. In addition, Kahneman and Lovallo document the human tendency to consider all of a decision's various details into our judgment process and, as a consequence, to view each decision as unique. This focus on the here and now leads us to overlook historic data and to let our biases run wild. As a result, we follow the insider view despite the readily available insights of the outsider view.

The insider-outsider distinction suggests another strategy to reduce bias: When making an important decision, invite an outsider to share his or her insight. This may mean conferring with a trusted friend or colleague who has experience with similar decisions. Interestingly, when a friend is building a house, we often predict that construction will cost more and take longer than expected. Our friend is the only one who doesn't know this! So, for decisions that really matter, ask friends you trust for their estimate of what will happen and understand that their outsider perspective may be more accurate than your biased insider view. Alternatively, ask yourself what your outsider self thinks of the situation. To assess this, imagine that the decision was a friend's, and ask yourself what advice you would give him or her. The key is to figure out how to give the outsider a stronger voice in the decision-making process.

STRATEGY 6: UNDERSTAND BIASES IN OTHERS

The nature of managerial life requires you to work closely with the decisions of others, reviewing recommendations, transforming recommendations into decisions, and adjusting decisions made by others in the past. The task of evaluating the decisions of others is fundamentally different from the task of auditing your own decisions. Nonetheless, from reading this book, you have learned that everyone's decisions are influenced to some degree by a shared set of biases. How can you systematically detect bias in the decisions of those around you? Consider the following managerial situation:

> You are the director of marketing for a retail chain that has 40 stores in 14 cities. Annual sales in these stores average between $2 million and $4 million with mean sales of $3 million. Twenty-five of the stores have opened in the last three years, and the company plans to open 30 new stores in the next four years. Because of this growth, you have hired a site location analyst to predict the sales in each potential site. Unfortunately, predicting sales in new markets is difficult, and even the best analyst faces a great deal of uncertainty. As the marketing director, you are evaluated in part by the accuracy of the forecasts coming out of your department. The site location analyst has just given you her latest forecast, $3.8 million in annual sales for a potential site. Demographic data backs up

the analyst's claim that this area should make the store one of the top producers in the chain. What is your reaction to the forecast?

At a naive level, there is reason to have confidence in the analyst's forecast. After all, she knows more than you about the details of the data that underlie the prediction. In addition, your overview of the area also predicts that the store will do well in comparison to existing stores; this evaluation is based on matching the representativeness of this site to other existing sites. The prediction begins to lose force, however, when we consider the prediction in light of a basic but counter-intuitive statistical concept: regression to the mean. In Chapter 3, we saw that the extremeness of our predictions should be moderated toward the mean by the degree of uncertainty in the prediction (Kahneman & Tversky, 1982).

With this rule in mind, let's imagine that the site location analyst is known for her extreme accuracy. In fact, her predictions are almost perfectly accurate and have a correlation of actual sales equal to 1.0. If this is true, it would be appropriate to rely on the $3.8 million prediction. Now let's consider the case in which there is a correlation of zero between the analyst's predictions (based on demographic data) and actual sales. If this is true, her forecast is meaningless, and the only pertinent information is that the average store has sales of $3 million. Therefore, this figure becomes your best estimate. It is most likely, in fact, that the analyst has achieved neither total success nor total failure, but an intermediate level of predictability over the course of her career. The forecast should then fall between sales of the mean store and the analyst's estimate, becoming progressively closer to the analyst's estimate as her ability to predict sales increases (Kahneman & Tversky, 1982). This analysis suggests that, as the director, you will want to reduce the forecast to somewhere between $3 million and $3.8 million, depending on your assessment of the correlation between the analyst's forecasts and actual sales. In essence, the understanding of human judgment taught by this book should help you to systematically adjust the analyst's initial decision.

The preceding analysis offers a rough guide to adjusting the decisions of others. Kahneman and Tversky (1982) have formalized this process into a five-step procedure whose steps are outlined here, using the site location problem as an example. In reviewing each step, you should think about how you might convert this systematic training into an intuitive, natural response. This will allow you, as a manager, to recognize the existence and direction of a wide range of biases across a wide range of decisions and make adjustments accordingly.

1. **Select a comparison group.** This first step consists of selecting the set of past observations to which the current decision or forecast is to be compared. In the site location problem, comparing the new store to the population of all company stores is an obvious group. Other comparison groups often exist. For example, you might decide that only stores that have opened in the last three years are appropriate for comparison, particularly if recent stores are closer in description to the future store than established stores. A more inclusive group allows for a larger basis of

comparison, but its heterogeneity may reduce its comparability to the targeted forecast.

2. **Assess the distribution of the comparison group.** The next step involves assessing the characteristics of the past observations to which the current decision is being compared. If the comparison group consists of all stores, we know the range and mean from the data presented. If we limit the group to recent stores, these data would need to be recalculated. In addition, we might want to get additional data about the shape of the distribution around the mean.

3. **Incorporate intuitive estimation.** This step calls for identification of the decision or forecast of the expert. In this case, the site location analyst's assessment, $3.8 million, is the intuitive estimate that needs to be adjusted. The next two steps attempt to improve this forecast.

4. **Assess the predicted results of the decision.** This is the most difficult step in the corrective procedure, as it requires us to determine the correlation between the decision or forecast and the comparison group data. It may be possible to assess this correlation by comparing past estimates to actual sales. In the absence of these data, you must determine some subjective procedure for this assessment. Kahneman and Tversky (1982) discuss this process in more detail. For our purposes, the key point is that the analyst's estimate assumes a correlation of 1.0 between her prediction and actual sales. In virtually all cases, we must adjust away from this biased estimate.

5. **Adjust the intuitive estimate.** In this step we must calculate the adjustment that reduces the bias error of the initial decision or forecast. For example, this procedure should produce an estimate of $3.8 million when the correlation in Step 4 is 1.0, an estimate of $3 million when the correlation is zero, and estimates proportionally in between when the correlation falls between zero and one. This adjustment can be formalized as follows:

adjusted estimate = group mean + correlation (initial estimate − group mean)

In our example, it is easy to see that this leads to a prediction of $3.4 million when the correlation is 0.5, $3.6 million when the correlation is 0.75, and so on. The person making the adjustment should fully understand the logic of the procedure and evaluate its relevance to the decision at hand. When arguing for this adjustment, you must recognize that you are likely to face resistance to change.

These five steps provide a clearly delineated process for debiasing an individual's intuition by adjusting for the regression-to-the-mean bias. The formal procedure will typically improve the forecast. More important, a manager who understands the process will become capable of intuitively assessing the degree to which an initial estimate should be regressed to the mean.

This section shows that we can use an understanding of biases to identify systematic error in the decisions of others. Adjusting for regression to the mean is simply one example of how such a technique can be systematized. When we consult with organizations, our knowledge of the various biases documented in this book allows us to identify biases across a variety of problem types.

We now have a model for adjusting a wide range of biased decisions in both individual and multiparty contexts. Broadly, it involves three phases. First, we need to accurately perceive and analyze the context within which the decision is being made. Next, we need to distinguish the potential bias(es) surrounding the decision and the decision makers. Finally, we need to identify and make the appropriate logical adjustments for that decision. This judgment-improvement technique can be used to evaluate and adjust our own, as well as others', intuitive judgments in a variety of situations.

You can also use your new knowledge of the biases of others to identify optimal moves in a competitive environment. Richard Thaler, whose ideas we have cited often in this book, teamed up with Russell Fuller to create the Fuller-Thaler mutual funds (www.fullerthaler.com). These funds buy securities by taking advantage of the predictable biases of key market participants. Fuller and Thaler argue that these biases result in mispricing of securities. For example, they argue that most analysts underreact to new, positive information about firms. By identifying how decision biases create under- and overvalued firms, Fuller and Thaler have created funds that outperform the market.

STRATEGY 7: NUDGE WISER AND MORE ETHICAL DECISIONS

Which option do you prefer (from Bazerman, Baron, and Shonk, 2001):

(a) If you die in an accident, your heart will be used to save another person's life. In addition, if you ever need a heart transplant, there will be a 90 percent chance that you will get a heart.

(b) If you die in an accident, you will be buried with your heart in your body. In addition, if you ever need a heart transplant, there will be a 45 percent chance that you will get a heart.

In this problem, most people chose (a). So why does the United States maintain an organ donation policy that resembles (b)? The answer lies in the psychology of the evaluation of losses and gains. As we discussed in Chapter 5, Tversky and Kahneman (1991) have documented that losses loom larger in our minds than gains. Moving to an opt-out program would save lives (an important gain) but would also have costs salient to some individuals, such as the prospect of being buried without all of their organs.

As a result, in the United States alone, about 50,000 people are on waiting lists for organs at any given time. More than a third of them will die before an organ is found. The number of organ donors has declined in recent decades, due to increased use of seatbelts and motorcycle helmets, and only 4,500 of the 11,000 eligible donors actually donate their organs. If we could double this figure, we could save an additional one-quarter of the approximately 15,000 people who die each year in the United States because of the lack of organs.

This situation exists despite the fact that we know how to increase the number of organs available for donation. Bazerman et al. (2001) argued that like many other countries (including Austria, Belgium, France, and Sweden), we could presume consent to organ donation (an opt-out program) rather than presuming non-consent (an opt-in program). That is, we could change the default in the United States to assume that eligible people are organ donors upon death unless they specifically opt out of the organ-donation system. Thanks to the clever empirical work of Johnson and Goldstein (2003), we already know what the result would be. European countries with an opt-in program similar to that of the United States have organ donations rates between 4 and 28 percent. In contrast, European countries with opt-out programs have rates ranging from 86 to 100 percent.

Enormously costly inefficiencies such as the U.S. organ donation system are surprisingly common in society. In their fascinating book *Nudge*, Thaler and Sunstein (2008), outline a structure for thinking about devising more efficient and beneficial organizational and societal systems. They argue that we can anticipate the mistakes humans make on a regular basis and then create systems that correct for these mistakes in a way that will nudge them toward better and more ethical decisions. Thaler and Sunstein's "libertarian paternalism" is libertarian in the sense that people have control over maintaining or expanding the options available to them and paternalistic in the sense that the system's architects attempt to guide people toward wiser decisions.

One of the most famous examples of Thaler's prior work in the area of nudges comes from a study by Thaler and Benartzi (2004) focusing on how to increase employees' enrollment in retirement plans that will benefit them over the long term. Using the psychological principles described in our book, they motivate people to increase their contributions to their 401(k) plans through a program called "Save More Tomorrow." Under this program, workers have the option of committing in advance to increase their retirement savings rates when they get a raise. The creation of the program was based on an understanding of the concepts of discounting, procrastination, and loss aversion. The design encourages commitment because people are more likely to choose what they know they *should* do when considering future rather than present events. The program remains effective over time thanks to inertia: people rarely take the initiative to opt out of the program once they have committed to it. Finally, the contribution increases are not difficult for the saver to stomach because the savings rate increases with the size of one's paycheck and never leads to a decrease in disposable income. The additional savings come from foregone consumption of anticipated gains rather than from a decrease in current disposable income.

In just over two years, the Save More Tomorrow pilot plan more than tripled the savings rates of those who joined. Since then, numerous retirement-plan administrators have implemented the Save More Tomorrow concept, including Vanguard, T. Rowe Price, TIAA-CREF, Fidelity, and Hewitt Associates. According to the Profit Sharing Council of America, as of 2007, 39 percent of large U.S. employers have adopted an automatic retirement contribution escalation plan (Thaler & Sunstein, 2008). Automatic enrollment dramatically increases participation in such programs. The Safelite Group, the first to adopt an "opt out" enrollment (in which employees must actively decline participation), automatically enrolled 93 percent of program participants in 2003. Only 6 percent chose to opt out over the next year, leaving the bulk of participants to save much more than they would have if they had been required to actively "opt in" to the program. Thaler and Sunstein (2008) provide numerous examples of common-sense nudges that suggest how, by thinking about human barriers to wise decisions, we can design systems that will lead to more positive results.

Nudges can be quite simple. Bohnet, van Geen, and Bazerman (2012) focus on how to nudge employers to make personnel decisions based on individual capabilities rather than stereotypes. They start by showing that when evaluating employees one at a time, many people rely on gender stereotypes: they select men for mathematical tasks and women for verbal tasks. When the hiring system is adjusted so that two or more potential employees are considered jointly, the focus of decision makers shifts to the ability of the potential employees, and they make decisions that are more ethical to the job candidates and that lead to better organizational performance. By making such small changes in how we make common decisions in organizations, we can inspire wiser and more ethical decisions.

CONCLUSION

In this final chapter, we have introduced seven strategies for correcting the deficiencies in our decision making. The first three strategies seek to create broad change in our intuitive responses to decision-making situations. In general, they strive to heighten our awareness of our cognitive limitations and our susceptibility to bias. The last four strategies provide techniques for improving specific decisions in specific contexts. They offer concrete methods for testing and adjusting actual decisions. Together, these seven strategies provide tools for changing and "refreezing" your intuitive decision-making processes in the future.

An optimistic but naive view of this book is that you are now immediately capable of improving your decision making. Why naive? Because it would be premature to expect you to have fully integrated the process of changing your judgment for the better. If unfreezing did not take place, then the book failed. If you were not provided with sufficient information for change, the book again failed. However, the responsibility for refreezing new processes and using the decision-improvement strategies suggested in this last chapter lies with you.

Refreezing requires a period in which you constantly review your decision-making processes for the errors identified in this book. Refreezing also requires that you be vigilant in your search for biases in the more complex world of decisions that you face. Creating lasting internal improvement in decision making is a complex task that occurs gradually over time through persistent monitoring. It is far easier to identify a bias while you are reading a book about decision making than when you are in the midst of an organizational crisis. Raiffa (1984) has found that his students were likely to use appropriate decision-making strategies on one of his exams but failed to generalize the relevance of these strategies to similar problems in courses taught by other instructors. Thus, making adjustments to your decision-making processes requires constant attention.

In addition to improving your own decisions, the ideas in this book should be very useful for informing you about the decisions of others. We are often faced with situations in which we are suspicious of another party's decision making, but we lack the vocabulary to articulate the flaws in their logic. This book offers systematic clues for understanding and explaining the biases of others. You can practice spotting others' biases while reading the newspaper or watching a sporting event on television. Reporters, sportscasters, politicians, and other information providers and public servants constantly make statements that exemplify the biased decision-making processes outlined in this book.

We hope that this book has dispelled some of your assumptions about decision making. We also hope to have raised your awareness of the importance of the decision-making process itself, rather than just the results of this process. We are disturbed by the fact that most managers reward results rather than good decisions. As we have seen, managers make many decisions for the wrong reasons. Nevertheless, because so many important decisions involve uncertainty, plenty of good decisions turn out badly, and some bad decisions turn out well. To the extent that a manager rewards results and not sound decision making, the manager is likely to be rewarding behaviors that may not work in the future.

Davis (1971) argues that "interesting" writing leads readers to question issues that they never thought about before. Thus, identifying new issues may be more important than providing new answers to old questions. In this sense, we hope this book has succeeded at being interesting by making you aware of aspects of your decision-making process that inspire new questions and solutions.

References

Abeler, J., Falk, A., Goette, L., & Huffman, D. (2011). Reference points and effort provision. *The American Economic Review, 101*(2), 470–492.

Adaval, R., & WyerJr, R. S. (2011). Conscious and Nonconscious Comparisons with Price Anchors: Effects on Willingness to Pay for Related and Unrelated Products. *Journal of Marketing Research, 48*(2), 355–365.

Ager, J. W., & Dawes, R. M. (1965). Effect of judges' attitudes on judgment. *Journal of Personality and Social Psychology, 1*(5), 533–538.

Ainslie, G. (1975). Specious reward: A behavioral theory of impulsiveness and impulse control. *Psychological Bulletin, 82*, 463–509.

Akerlof, G. (1970). The market for lemons: Qualitative uncertainty and the market mechanism. *Quarterly Journal of Economics, 89*, 488–500.

Akerlof, G. A., & Yellen, J. L. (1990). The fair wage-effort hypothesis and unemployment. *Quarterly Journal of Economics, 105*, 255–283.

Alicke, M. D. (1985). Global self-evaluation as determined by the desirability and controllability of trait adjectives. *Journal of Personality and Social Psychology, 49*(6), 1621–1630.

Allison, S. T., Messick, D. M., & Goethals, G. R. (1989). On being better but not smarter than others: The Muhammad Ali effect. *Social Cognition, 7*(3), 275–295.

Alpert, M., & Raiffa, H. (1969/1982). A progress report on the training of probability assessors. In D. Kahneman, P. Slovic & A. Tversky (Eds.), Judgment under uncertainty: Heuristics and biases. Cambridge, UK: Cambridge University Press.

Ambady, N., & Rosenthal, R. (1993). Half a minute: Predicting teacher evaluations from thin slices of nonverbal behavior and physical attractiveness. *Journal of Personality and Social Psychology, 64*, 431–441.

Ambady, N., Krabbenoft, M. A., & Hogan, D. (2006). The 30-sec sale: Using thin-slice judgments to evaluate sales effectiveness. *Journal of Consumer Psychology, 16*(1), 4–13.

Anderson, C., Srivastava, S., Beer, J. S., Spataro, S. E., & Chatman, J. A. (2006). Knowing your place: Self-perceptions of status in face-to-face groups. *Journal of Personality and Social Psychology, 91*(6), 1094–1110.

Angelone, B. L., Levin, D., & Simons, D. J. (2003). The relationship between change, detection, and recognition of centrally attended objects in motion pictures. *Perception, 32*(8), 947–962.

Asendorpf, J. B., Banse, R., & Muecke, D. (2002). Double dissociation between implicit and explicit personality self-concept: the case of shy behavior. *Journal of Personality & Social Psychology, 83*(2), 380–393.

Åstebro, T., Jeffrey, S. A., & Adomdza, G. K. (2007). Inventor perseverance after being told to quit: The role of cognitive biases. *Journal of Behavioral Decision Making, 20*(3), 253–272.

Babcock, L., & Loewenstein, G. (1997). Explaining bargaining impasse: The role of self-serving biases. *Journal of Economic Perspectives, 11*(1), 109–126.

Babcock, L., Loewenstein, G., Issacharoff, S., & Camerer, C. F. (1995). Biased judgments of fairness in bargaining. *American Economic Review, 85*(5), 1337–1343.

Badaracco, J. L., Jr., & Webb, A. P. (1995). Business Ethics: The View from the Trenches. *California Management Review* (winter).

Bajaj, V. (2005, December 28). FDA puts restrictions on Guidant. *New York Times*, p. C1.

Balcetis, E., & Dunning, D. (2006). See what you want to see: Motivational influences on visual perception. *Journal of Personality and Social Psychology, 91*(4), 612–625.

Ball, S. B., Bazerman, M. H., & Carroll, J. S. (1991). An evaluation of learning in the bilateral winner's curse. *Organizational Behavior and Human Decision Processes, 48*, 1–22.

Banaji, M. R. (2001). Ordinary prejudice. *Psychological Science Agenda, 14* (Jan–Feb), 8–11.

Banaji, M. R. (2004). The opposite of a great truth is also true: Homage of Koan #7. In J. T. Jost & M. R. Banaji (Eds.), *Perspectivism in social psychology: The yin and yang of scientific progress*. Washington, DC, US: American Psychological Association.

Banaji, M. R., & Bhaskar, R. (2000). Implicit stereotypes and memory: The bounded rationality of social beliefs. In D. L. Schacter & E. Scarry (Eds.), Memory, brain, and belief. Cambridge, Mass.: Harvard University Press.

Banaji, M. R., Bazerman, M. H., & Chugh, D. (2003). How (un)ethical are you? *Harvard Business Review, December*.

Barber, B. M., & Odean, T. (2000). Trading is hazardous to your wealth: The common stock investment performance of individual investors. *Journal of Finance, 55*(2), 773–806.

Barber, B. M., & Odean, T. (2002). Online investors: Do the slow die first? *Review of Financial Studies, 15*(2), 455–487.

Barber, B. M., Odean, T., & Zheng, L. (2005). Out of sight, out of mind: The effects of expenses on mutual fund flows. *Journal of Business, 78*, 2095–2120.

Barber, B., & Odean, T. (2000b). Too many cooks spoil the profits: The performance of investment clubs. *Financial Analyst Journal* (Jan-Feb), 17–25.

Barber, B., & Odean, T. (2001). Boys will be boys: Gender, overconfidence, and common stock investment. *Quarterly Journal of Economics, 116*(1), 261–293.

Barberis, N., & Xiong, W. (forthcoming). Realization utility. *Journal of Financial Economics*.

BarclayHedge. (2012). *Hedge Fund Industry Assets Under Management*. Retrieved February 14, 2012, from http://www.barclayhedge.com/research/indices/ghs/mum/HF_Money_Under_Management.html

Bargh, J. A., Chen, M., & Burrows, L. (1996). Automaticity of social behavior: Direct effects of trait construct and stereotype activation on action. *Journal of Personality and Social Psychology, 71*(3), 230–244.

Bar-Hillel, M. (1973). On the subjective probability of compound events. *Organizational Behavior and Human Performance, 9*, 396–406.

Baron, J. (1994). Thinking and deciding (2nd ed.). Cambridge [England]: Cambridge University Press.

Baumeister, R. F., Campbell, J. D., Krueger, J. I., & Vohs, K. D. (2003). Does high self-esteem cause better performance, interpersonal success, happiness, or healthier lifestyles? *Psychological Science in the Public Interest, 4*, 1–44.

Bazerman, M. H. (1985). Norms of distributive justice in interest arbitration. *Industrial and Labor Relations Review, 38,* 558–570.

Bazerman, M. H., & Chugh, D. (2005). Focusing in negotiation. In L. Thompson (Ed.), *Frontiers of Social Psychology: Negotiations*: Psychological Press.

Bazerman, M. H., & Gillespie, J. J. (1999). Betting on the future: The virtues of contingent contracts. *Harvard Business Review, Sept–Oct,*155–160.

Bazerman, M. H., & Neale, M. A. (1982). Improving negotiation effectiveness under final offer arbitration: The role of selection and training. *Journal of Applied Psychology, 67,* 543–548.

Bazerman, M. H., & Neale, M. A. (1992). Negotiating rationally. New York: Free Press.

Bazerman, M. H., & Samuelson, W. F. (1983). I won the auction but don't want the prize. *Journal of Conflict Resolution, 27*(4), 618–634.

Bazerman, M. H., & Tenbrunsel, A. E. (2011). Blind spots: Why we fail to do what's right and what to do about it. Princeton: Princeton University Press.

Bazerman, M. H., & Watkins, M. D. (2004). *Predictable surprises.* Boston: Harvard Business School Press.

Bazerman, M. H., Baron, J., & Shonk, K. (2001). *You can't enlarge the pie: The psychology of ineffective government.* New York: Basic Books.

Bazerman, M. H., Curhan, J. R., & Moore, D. A. (2000). The death and rebirth of the social psychology of negotiation. In G. J. O. Fletcher & M. S. Clark (Eds.), *Blackwell handbook of social psychology: Interpersonal processes* (pp. 196–228). Oxford, England: Blackwell.

Bazerman, M. H., Curhan, J. R., Moore, D. A., & Valley, K. L. (2000). Negotiation. *Annual Review of Psychology, 51,* 279–314.

Bazerman, M. H., Giuliano, T., & Appelman, A. (1984). Escalation of commitment in individual and group decision making. *Organizational Behavior and Human Decision Processes, 33*(2), 141–152.

Bazerman, M. H., Loewenstein, G., & Moore, D. A. (2002). Why good accountants do bad audits. *Harvard Business Review, 80*(1), 87–102.

Bazerman, M. H., Loewenstein, G., & White, S. B. (1992). Psychological determinants of utility in competitive contexts: The impact of elicitation procedure. *Administrative Science Quarterly, 37,* 220–240.

Bazerman, M. H., Moore, D. A., Tenbrunsel, A. E., Wade-Benzoni, K. A., & Blount, S. (1999). Explaining how preferences change across joint versus separate evaluation. *Journal of Economic Behavior and Organization, 39,* 41–58.

Bazerman, M. H., Morgan, K. P., & Loewenstein, G. (1997). The impossibility of auditor independence. *Sloan Management Review, 38*(4), 89–94.

Bazerman, M. H., Russ, L. E., & Yakura, E. (1987). Post-settlement settlements in two-party negotiations. *Negotiation Journal, July,* 283–291.

Bazerman, M. H., Tenbrunsel, A. E., & Wade-Benzoni, K. A. (1998). Negotiating with yourself and losing: Understanding and managing competing internal preferences. *Academy of Management Review, 23*(2), 225–241.

Bazerman, M. H., Wade-Benzoni, K. A., & Benzoni, F. J. (1996). A behavioral decision theory perspective to environmental decision making. In D. M. Messick & A. E. Tenbrunsel (Eds.), *Ethical Issues in Managerial Decision Making.* New York: Russell Sage.

Bechara, A., Damasio, H., Damasio, A. R., & Lee, G. P. (1999). Different contributions of the human amygdala and ventromedial prefrontal cortex to decision-making. *Journal of Neuroscience, 19,* 5473–5481.

Bechara, A., Damasio, H., Tranel, D., & Damasio, A. R. (1997). Deciding advantageously before knowing the advantageous strategy. *Science, 275,* 1293–1294.

Beggs, A., & Graddy, K. (2009). Anchoring Effects: Evidence from Art Auctions. *American Economic Review, 99*(3), 1027–1039.

Belsky, G., & Gilovich, T. (1999). *Why smart people make big money mistakes.* New York: Simon and Schuster.

Benartzi, S., & Thaler, R. H. (2001). Naive diversification strategies in defined contribution saving plans. *American Economic Review, 91*(1), 79–98.

Ben-David, I., Graham, J. R., & Harvey, C. R. (2010). Managerial miscalibration. *Unpublished manuscript.*

Benton, M. J. (2005). *When life nearly died: The greatest mass extinction event of all time.* London: Thames & Hudson.

Bereby-Meyer, Y., & Grosskopf, B. (2008). Overcoming the winner's curse: an adaptive learning perspective. *Journal of Behavioral Decision Making, 21*(1), 15–27.

Bernhard, H., Fischbacher, U., & Fehr, E. (2006). Parochial altruism in humans. *Nature, 442,* 912–915.

Bernheim, B. D., & Rangel, A. (2009). Beyond Revealed Preference: Choice-Theoretic Foundations for Behavioral Welfare Economics. *The Quarterly Journal of Economics, 124*(1), 51–104.

Bernoulli, D. (1738/1954). Exposition of a new theory on the measurement of risk. *Econometrica, 22,* 22–36.

Bertrand, M., & Mullainathan, S. (2001). Are CEOs rewarded for luck? The ones without principals are. *Quarterly Journal of Economics, 116*(3), 901–932.

Bertrand, M., Karlan, D., Mullainathan, S., Shafir, E., & Zinman, J. (2010). What's advertising content worth? Evidence from a consumer credit marketing field experiment. *The Quarterly Journal of Economics, 125*(1), 263.

Blanton, H., & Jaccard, J. (2006). Arbitrary metrics in psychology. *American Psychologist, 61,* 27–41.

Blount, S., & Bazerman, M. H. (1996). The inconsistent evaluation of comparative payoffs in labor supply and bargaining. *Journal of Economic Behavior and Organization, 891,* 1–14.

Bodenhausen, G. V., Gabriel, S., & Lineberger, M. (2000). Sadness and susceptibility to judgmental bias: The case of anchoring. *Psychological Science, 11*(4), 320–323.

Bodenhausen, G. V., Kramer, G. P., & Suesser, K. (1994). Happiness and stereotypic thinking in social judgment. *Journal of Personality and Social Psychology, 66*(4), 621–632.

Bogle, J. C. (1994). *Bogle on mutual funds.* New York: Irwin.

Bohnet, I., van Geen, & Bazerman, M. H. (2012). When performance trumps gender bias. *Unpublished manuscript.*

Boltz, M. G., Kupperman, C., & Dunne, J. (1998). The role of learning in remembered duration. *Memory & Cognition, 26*(5), 903–921.

Bowles, H. R., Babcock, L., & McGinn, K. L. (2005). Constraints and triggers: Situational mechanics of gender in negotiation. *Journal of Personality and Social Psychology, 89,* 951–965.

Bradsher, K. (2009, July 15). U.S. officials press China on climate. *New York Times.*

Brawley, L. R. (1984). Unintentional egocentric biases in attributions. *Journal of Sport Psychology, 6,* 264–278.

Brickman, P., & Campbell, D. T. (1971). Hedonic relativism and planning the good society. In M. H. Appley (Ed.), *Adaptation level theory: A symposium*. New York: McGraw-Hill.

Brickman, P., Coates, D., & Janoff-Bulman, R. (1978). Lottery winners and accident victims: Is happiness relative? *Journal of Personality and Social Psychology*, *36*(8), 917–927.

Brief, A. P., Dietz, J., Cohen, R. R., Pugh, S., & Vaslow, J. B. (2000). Just doing business: Modern racism and obedience to authority as explanations for employment discrimination. *Organizational Behavior & Human Decision Processes*, *81*(1), 72–97.

Brodt, S. E. (1990). Cognitive illusions and personnel management decisions. In C. Cooper & I. T. Robertson (Eds.), *International Review of Industrial and Organizational Psychology* (Vol. 5, pp. 229–279). New York: Wiley.

Brosnan, S. F., & de Waal, F. B. M. (2003). Monkeys reject unequal pay. *Nature*, *425*, 297–299.

Budiansky, S., Gest, T., & Fischer, D. (1995, January 30). How lawyers abuse the law. *U.S. News and World Report*, *118*, 50.

Buehler, R., Griffin, D., & Ross, M. (1994). Exploring the "planning fallacy": Why people underestimate their task completion times. *Journal of Personality and Social Psychology*, *67*(3), 366–381.

Burt, C. D. B., & Kemp, S. (1994). Construction of activity duration and time management potential. *Applied Cognitive Psychology*, *8*(2), 155–168.

Cain, D. M., Loewenstein, G., & Moore, D. A. (2005). The dirt on coming clean: Perverse effects of disclosing conflicts of interest. *Journal of Legal Studies*, *34*, 1–25.

Caldwell, D. F., & O'Reilly, C. A. (1982). Responses to failures: The effects of choices and responsibility on impression management. *Academy of Management Journal*, *25*, 121–136.

Calvet, L. E., Campbell, J. Y., & Sodini, P. (2009). Fight or Flight? Portfolio Rebalancing by Individual Investors. *Quarterly Journal of Economics*, *124*, 301–348.

Camerer, C. F. (2000). Prospect theory in the wild: Evidence from the field. In D. Kahneman & A. Tversky (Eds.), *Choices, values, and frames* (pp. 288–300). New York: Russell Sage Foundation.

Camerer, C. F., & Lovallo, D. (1999). Overconfidence and excess entry: An experimental approach. *American Economic Review*, *89*(1), 306–318.

Camerer, C. F., Babcock, L., Loewenstein, G., & Thaler, R. (1997). Labor supply of New York City cabdrivers: One day at a time. *Quarterly Journal of Economics*, *112*(2), 407–441.

Camerer, C. F., Loewenstein, G., & Weber, M. (1989). The curse of knowledge in economic settings: An experimental analysis. *Journal of Political Economy*, *97*(5), 1232–1254.

Cameron, L. (1999). Raising the stakes in the ultimatum game: Experimental evidence from Indonesia. *Economic Inquiry*, *37*(1), 47–59.

Cannell, J. J. (1989). How public educators cheat on standardized achievement tests: The "Lake Wobegon" report.

Carhart, M. M. (1997). On persistence in mutual fund performance. *Journal of Finance*, *52* (1), 57–82.

Carroll, J. S., Bazerman, M. H., & Maury, R. (1988). Negotiator cognitions: A descriptive approach to negotiators' understanding of their opponents. *Organizational Behavior and Human Decision Processes*, *41*(3), 352–370.

Caruso, E. M., Epley, N., & Bazerman, M. H. (2005). The good, the bad, and the ugly of perspective taking in groups. In E. A. Mannix, M. A. Neale & A. E. Tenbrunsel (Eds.), *Research on Managing Groups and Teams: Ethics and Groups* (Vol. 8) JAI Press.

Caruso, E. M., Epley, N., & Bazerman, M. H. (2006). The costs and benefits of undoing egocentric responsibility assessments in groups. *Journal of Personality and Social Psychology, 91,* 857–871.

Caruso, E. M., Epley, N., & Bazerman, M. H. (2007). *Leader of the packed: Unpacking, egocentrism, and the costs and benefits of perspective taking in groups.* Unpublished manuscript.

Cassidy, J. (2007, July 2). Hedge clipping: Is there any way to get above-average returns on the cheap? *The New Yorker,* 28–33.

Cassidy, J. (2011, July 25). Mastering the machine: How Ray Dalio built the world's richest and strangest hedge fund. *The New Yorker.*

CBS News. (2004, September 29). *Kerry's top ten flip-flops.* Retrieved July 11, 2007, from http://www.cbsnews.com/stories/2004/09/29/politics/main646435.shtml

Chabris, C. F., & Simons, D. J. (2010). *The invisible gorilla.* New York: Crown.

Chambers, J. R., Windschitl, P. D., & Suls, J. (2003). Egocentrism, event frequency, and comparative optimism: When what happens frequently is "more likely to happen to me." *Personality and Social Psychology Bulletin, 29*(11), 1343–1356.

Chen, M. K., Lakshminarayanan, V., & Santos, L. R. (2006). How basic are behavioral biases? Evidence from capuchin monkey trading behavior. *Journal of Political Economy, 114*(3), 517–537.

Chicago Tribune. (2011, June 30, 2011). NBA lockout begins as sides fail to reach deal. *Chicago Tribune.*

Choi, J., Laibson, D., Madrian, B. C., & Metrick, A. (2003). Active Decisions: A Natural Experiment in Savings.

Chugh, D. (2004). Societal and Managerial Implications of Implicit Social Cognition: Why Milliseconds Matter. *Social Justice Research, 17*(2).

Chugh, D., Bazerman, M. H., & Banaji, M. R. (2005). Bounded ethicality as a psychological barrier to recognizing conflicts of interest. In D. A. Moore, D. M. Cain, G. Loewenstein & M. H. Bazerman (Eds.), *Conflicts of Interest* (pp. 74–95). Cambridge, UK: Cambridge University Press.

College Board. (1976–1977). *Student descriptive questionnaire.* Princeton, NJ: Educational Testing Service.

Cooper, A. C., Woo, C. Y., & Dunkelberg, W. C. (1988). Entrepreneurs' perceived chances for success. *Journal of Business Venturing, 3*(2), 97–109.

Correll, J., Park, B., Judd, C. M., Wittenbrink, B., Sadler, M. S., & Keesee, T. (2007). Across the thin blue line: Police officers and racial bias in the decision to shoot. *Journal of Personality and Social Psychology, 92*(6), 1006.

Cowherd, D. M., & Levine, D. I. (1992). Product Quality and Pay Equity Between lower-Level Employees and Top Management: An Investigation of Distributive Justice Theory. *Administrative Science Quarterly, 37*(2 Special Issue: Process and outcome: Perspectives on the Distribution of Rewards in Organizations), 302–320.

Coy, P. (2008, February 27th). Bill Clinton's drive to increase homeownership went way too far. *Business Week.*

Crupi, V., Tentori, K., & Lombardi, L. (2009). Pseudodiagnosticity revisited. *Psychological Review, 116*(4), 971.

Cryder, C. E., Lerner, J. S., Gross, J. J., & Dahl, R. E. (2007). *The material self: Sadness, self-focus, and spending.* Unpublished manuscript.

Curhan, J. R., Neale, M. A., & Ross, L. (2004). Dynamic valuation: Preference change in the context of active face-to-face negotiations. *Journal of Experimental Social Psychology, 40,* 142–151.

Dalai Lama XIV. (1999). *Ethics for the new millennium.* New York: Riverhead Books.

Dana, J., Cain, D., & Dawes, R. M. (2006). What you don't know won't hurt me: Costly (but quiet) exit in a dictator game. *Organizational Behavior & Human Decision Processes, 100,* 193–201.

Dana, J., Weber, R. A., & Kuang, J. X. (2007). Exploiting moral wiggle room: Behavior inconsistent with a preference for fair outcomes. *Economic Theory, 33*(1), 67–80.

Danziger, S., Levav, J., & Avnaim-Pesso, L. (2011). Extraneous factors in judicial decisions. *Proceedings of the National Academy of Sciences, 108*(17), 6889.

Darley, J. M., & Gross, P. H. (1983). A hypothesis-confirming bias in labeling effects. *Journal of Personality and Social Psychology, 44*(1), 20–33.

Dasgupta, N. (2004). Implicit ingroup favoritism, outgroup favoritism, and their behavioral manifestations. *Social Justice Research, 17*(2), 143–170.

Davis, M. S. (1971). That's interesting! *Philosophy of Social Science,* 309–344.

Dawes, R. M. (1971). A case study of graduate admissions: Application of three principles of human decision making. *American Psychologist, 26*(2), 180–188.

Dawes, R. M. (1979). The robust beauty of improper linear models in decision making. *American Psychologist, 34*(7), 571–582.

Dawes, R. M. (1988). Rational choice in an uncertain world. Fort Worth, TX: Harcourt Brace.

Dawson, E., Gilovich, T., & Regan, D. (2002). Motivated reasoning and performance on the Wason Selection Task. *Personality and Social Psychology Bulletin, 28*(10), 1379–1387.

de Quervain, D. J. F., Fischbacher, U., Treyer, V., Schellhammer, M., Schnyder, U., Buck, A., et al. (2004). The neural basis of altruistic punishment. *Science, 305,* 1254–1258.

DeBondt, W. F. M., & Thaler, R. H. (1985). Does the stock market overreact? *Journal of Finance, 53,* 1839–1885.

DeBondt, W. F. M., & Thaler, R. H. (1995). Financial decision-making in markets and firms: A behavioral perspective. In R. A. Jarrow, V. Maksimovic & W. T. Ziemba (Eds.), *Finance, Handbooks in Operations Research and management Science* (Vol. 9, pp. 385–410). North Holland, Amsterdam: Elsevier.

den Ouden, E. (2006). *Developments of a design analysis model for consumer complaints: Revealing a new class of quality failures.* Unpublished doctoral dissertation. Technical University of Eindhoven, Eindhoven.

Depken, C. A. (2000). Wage disparity and team productivity: Evidence from Major League Baseball. *Economic Letters, 67,* 87–92.

Diekmann, K. A., Samuels, S. M., Ross, L., & Bazerman, M. H. (1997). Self-interest and fairness in problems of resource allocation: Allocators versus recipients. *Journal of Personality and Social Psychology, 72*(5), 1061–1074.

Diekmann, K. A., Tenbrunsel, A. E., Shah, P. P., Schroth, H., & Bazerman, M. H. (1996). The descriptive and prescriptive use of previous purchase price in negotiations. *Organizational Behavior and Human Decision Processes, 66*(2), 179–191.

Ditto, P. H., & Lopez, D. F. (1992). Motivated skepticism: Use of differential decision criteria for preferred and nonpreferred conclusions. *Journal of Personality and Social Psychology, 63*(4), 568–584.

Dougherty, T. W., Turban, D. B., & Callender, J. C. (1994). Confirming first impressions in the employment interview: A field study of interviewer behavior. *Journal of Applied Psychology*, 79(5), 656–665.

Duncan, B. L. (1976). Differential social perception and attribution of intergroup violence: Testing the lower limits of stereotyping of Blacks. *Journal of Personality and Social Psychology*, 34, 590–598.

Dunning, D. (2005). *Self-insight: Roadblocks and detours on the path to knowing thyself.* New York: Psychology Press.

Dunning, D., Heath, C., & Suls, J. M. (2004). Flawed self-assessment: Implications for health, education, and the workplace. *Psychological Science in the Public Interest*, 5 (3), 69–106.

Economist, T. (2008, October 30). Editorial: Managed to death. *The Economist*.

Einhorn, H. J. (1972). Expert measurement and mechanical combination. *Organizational Behavior and Human Performance*, 7, 86–106.

Einhorn, H. J., & Hogarth, R. M. (1978). Confidence in judgment: Persistence of the illusion of validity. *Psychological Review*, 85(5), 395–416.

Ekman, P. (1992). Are there basic emotions? *Psychological Review*, 99(3), 550–553.

Englich, B., & Mussweiler, T. (2001). Sentencing under uncertainty: Anchoring effects in the courtroom. *Journal of Applied Social Psychology*, 31(7), 1535–1551.

Englich, B., Mussweiler, T., & Strack, F. (2006). Playing dice with criminal sentences: The influence of irrelevant anchors on experts' judicial decision making. *Personality and Social Psychology Bulletin*, 32(2), 188–200.

Epley, N. (2004). A tale of Tuned Decks? Anchoring as accessibility and anchoring as adjustment. In D. J. Koehler & N. Harvey (Eds.), *Blackwell Handbook of Judgment and Decision Making* (pp. 240–256). Oxford: Blackwell.

Epley, N., & Gilovich, T. (2001). Putting adjustment back in the anchoring and adjustment heuristic: Differential processing of self-generated and experimenter-provided anchors. *Psychological Science*, 12(5), 391–396.

Epley, N., Caruso, E., & Bazerman, M. H. (2006). When perspective taking increases taking: Reactive egoism in social interaction. *Journal of Personality and Social Psychology*, 91, 872–889.

Epley, N., Keysar, B., VanBoven, L., & Gilovich, T. (2004). Perspective taking as egocentric anchoring and adjustment. *Journal of Personality and Social Psychology*, 87(3), 327–339.

Epley, N., Mak, D., & Idson, L. C. (2006). Rebate or bonus? The impact of income framing on spending and saving. *Journal of Behavioral Decision Making*, 19(4), 213–227.

Epstude, K., & Roese, N. J. (2008). The functional theory of counterfactual thinking. *Personality and Social Psychology Review*, 12(2), 168–192.

Evans, J. S. B. T. (2008). Dual-processing accounts of reasoning, judgment, and social cognition. *Annu. Rev. Psychol.*, 59, 255–278.

Feder, B. (2006, January 26). Quiet end to battle of the bids. *New York Times*, p. C1.

Feder, B., & Sorkin, A. R. (2005, November 3). Troubled maker of heart devices may lose suitor. *New York Times*, p. A1.

Fehr, E., & Fischbacher, U. (2003). The nature of human altruism. *Nature*, 425, 785–791.

Fehr, E., & Fischbacher, U. (2004). Third-party punishment and social norms. *Evolution and Human Behavior*, 25, 63–87.

Fehr, E., & Gächter, S. (2000). Cooperation and punishment in public goods experiments. *American Economic Review*, 90(4), 980–994.

Fehr, E., Kirchsteiger, G., & Reidl, A. (1993). Does fairness prevent market clearing? An experimental investigation. *Quarterly Journal of Economics, 108,* 437–459.

Fernbach, P. M., Darlow, A., & Sloman, S. A. (2011). Asymmetries in predictive and diagnostic reasoning. *Journal of Experimental Psychology: General, 140*(2), 168.

Fiedler, K. (2000). Beware of samples! A cognitive-ecological sampling approach to judgment biases. *Psychological Review, 107*(4), 659–676.

Fischer, P., Greitemeyer, T., & Frey, D. (2008). Self-regulation and selective exposure: The impact of depleted self-regulation resources on confirmatory information processing. *Journal of Personality and Social Psychology, 94*(3), 382.

Fischhoff, B. (1975). Hindsight is not equal to foresight: The effect of outcome knowledge on judgment under uncertainty. *Journal of Experimental Psychology: Human Perception and Performance, 1*(3), 288–299.

Fischhoff, B. (1977). Cognitive liabilities and product liability. *Journal of Products Liability, 1,* 207–220.

Fischhoff, B. (1982). Debiasing. In D. Kahneman, P. Slovic & A. Tversky (Eds.), *Judgment under uncertainty: Heuristics and biases.* Cambridge, Mass.: Cambridge University Press.

Fisher, R., Ury, W., & Patton, B. (1981). *Getting to yes.* Boston: Houghton Mifflin.

Flyvbjerg, B., Bruzelius, N., & Rothengatter, W. (2003). *Megaprojects and risk: An anatomy of ambition.* Cambridge, UK: Cambridge University Press.

Foot, P. (1978). *Virtues and vices and other essays in moral philosophy*: Oxford University Press, USA.

Forgas, J. P. (1995). Mood and judgment: The affect infusion model (AIM). *Psychological Bulletin, 117*(1), 39–66.

Forsyth, D. R., & Schlenker, B. R. (1977). Attributional egocentrism following a performance of a competitive task. *Journal of Social Psychology, 102,* 215–222.

Fox, C. R., & Tversky, A. (1998). A belief-based account of decision under uncertainty. *Management Science, 44*(7), 879–895.

Fredrickson, J. W., Davis-Blake, A., & Sanders, W. M. (2010). Sharing the wealth: social comparisons and pay dispersion in the CEO's top team. *Strategic Management Journal, 31*(10), 1031–1053.

Friedman, A. (1996). *High-altitude decision making.* Paper presented at the Jeffrey Z. Rubin Memorial Conference, Cambridge, Mass.

Friedman, D. (1998). Monty Hall's three doors: Construction and deconstruction of a choice anomaly. *American Economic Review, 88*(4), 933–946.

Fujita, K., & Roberts, J. C. (2010). Promoting prospective self-control through abstraction. *Journal of Experimental Social Psychology, 46*(6), 1049–1054.

Galinsky, A. D., & Mussweiler, T. (2001). First offers as anchors: The role of perspective-taking and negotiator focus. *Journal of Personality and Social Psychology, 81*(4), 657–669.

Gentner, D., Loewenstein, G., & Thompson, L. (2003a). Learning and transfer: a general role for analogical encoding. *Journal of Educational Psychology, 95*(2), 393–408.

Gentner, D., Loewenstein, J., & Thompson, L. (2003b). Learning and transfer: A general role for analogical encoding. *Journal of Educational Psychology, 95,* 393–405.

Gigerenzer, G., Hoffrage, U., & Kleinbölting, H. (1991). Probabilistic mental models: A Brunswikian theory of confidence. *Psychological Review, 98*(4), 506–528.

Gilbert, D. T. (1991). How mental systems believe. *American Psychologist, 46*(2), 107–119.

Gilbert, D. T. (2002). Inferential correction. In T. Gilovich, D. Griffin, & D. Kahneman (Eds.), *Heuristics and Biases: The psychology of intuitive judgment* (pp. 167–184). Cambridge, U.K.: Cambridge University Press.

Gilbert, D. T. (2006). *Stumbling on happiness*. New York: Random House.

Gilbert, D. T., & Malone, P. S. (1995). The correspondence bias. *Psychological Bulletin, 117*(1), 21–38.

Gilbert, D. T., & Wilson, T. D. (2000). Miswanting: Some problems in the forecasting of future affective states. In J. P. Forgas (Ed.), *Feeling and thinking: The role of affect in social cognition, Studies in emotion and social interaction* (xvi ed., Vol. 2, pp. 178–197).

Gilbert, D. T., Pinel, E. C., Wilson, T. D., Blumberg, S. J., & Wheatley, T. P. (1998). Immune neglect: A source of durability bias in affective forecasting. *Journal of Personality and Social Psychology, 75*(3), 617–638.

Gilovich, T. (1991). *How we know what isn't so: The fallibility of human reason in everyday life*. New York: Free Press.

Gilovich, T., Kerr, M., & Medvec, V. H. (1993). Effect of temporal perspective on subjective confidence. *Journal of Personality and Social Psychology, 64*(4), 552–560.

Gilovich, T., Medvec, V. H., & Chen, S. (1995). Commission, omission, and dissonance reduction: Coping with regret in the "Monty Hall" problem. *Personality and Social Psychology Bulletin, 21*(2), 182–190.

Gilovich, T., Vallone, R. P., & Tversky, A. (1985). The hot hand in basketball: On the misperception of random sequences. *Cognitive Psychology, 17*, 295–314.

Gino, F., & Bazerman, M. H. (2009). When misconduct goes unnoticed: The acceptability of gradual erosion in others' unethical behavior. *Journal of Experimental Social Psychology, 45*, 708–719.

Gino, F., Moore, D. A., & Bazerman, M. H. (2009). See no evil: When we overlook other people's unethical behavior. In M. H. Bazerman (Ed.), *Essays in honor of David M. Messick* (pp. 241–263).

Gladwell, M. (2006, October 16). The formula: What if you built a machine to predict hit movies? *The New Yorker*.

Gladwell, M. (2009, July 27). Cocksure: Banks, battles, and the psychology of overconfidence. *The New Yorker*.

Glassman, J. K., & Hassett, K. A. (1999). *Dow 36,000: The new strategy for profiting from the coming rise in the stock market*. New York: Times Business.

Gneezy, A., Gneezy, U., Nelson, L. D., & Brown, A. (2010). Shared social responsibility: A field experiment in pay-what-you-want pricing and charitable giving. *Science, 329*(5989), 325.

Goetzmann, W. N., & Peles, N. (1997). Cognitive dissonance and mutual fund investors. *Journal of Financial Research, 20*(2), 145–158.

Goodwin, P. (1999). *Decision analysis for management judgment* (2nd ed.). New York: Wiley.

Gore, A. (1992). *Earth in the Balance*. New York: Penguin Books USA.

Grabiner, D. (1996). Frequently asked questions about the baseball strike. *Web site: ftp:// baseball.berkelely.edu/pub/baseball/faq/strike.FAQ*.

Gramzow, R. H., & Gaertner, L. (2005). Self-esteem and favoritism toward novel in-groups: The Self as an evaluative base. *Journal of Personality and Social Psychology, 88*, 801–815.

Greene, J. D. (forthcoming). *The moral brain and how to use it*. New York: Penguin.

Greenwald, A. G. (1980). The totalitarian ego: Fabrication and revision of personal history. *American Psychologist, 35*(7), 603–618.

Greenwald, A. G., McGhee, D. E., & Schwartz, J. L. K. (1998). Measuring individual differences in implicit cognition: The implicit association test. *Journal of Personality and Social Psychology, 74*(6), 1464–1480.

Griffin, D. W., & Varey, C. A. (1996). Towards a consensus on overconfidence. *Organizational Behavior and Human Decision Processes, 65*(3), 227–231.

Grosskopf, B., Bereby-Meyer, Y., & Bazerman, M. H. (2007). On the robustness of the winner's curse phenomenon. *Theory and Decision, 63*(4), 389–418.

Grossman, S. J., & Stiglitz, J. E. (1980). On the impossibility of informationally efficient markets. *American Economic Review, 70*(3), 393–408.

Gruenfeld, D. H., Mannix, E. A., Williams, K. Y., & Neale, M. A. (1996). Group composition and decision making: How member familiarity and information distribution affect process and performance. *Organizational Behavior and Human Decision Processes, 67*(1), 1–15.

Güth, W., Schmittberger, R., & Schwarze, B. (1982). An experimental analysis of ultimatum bargaining. *Journal of Economic Behavior and Organization, 3*, 367–388.

Haidt, J. (2001). The emotional dog and its rational tail: A social intuitionist approach to moral judgment. *Psychological Review, 108*(4), 814–834.

Haidt, J. (2007). The new synthesis in moral psychology. *Science, 316*, 998–1002.

Haidt, J., Björklund, F., & Murphy, S. (2007). *Moral dumbfounding*. Unpublished manuscript, Charlotte, VA.

Hammond, J. S., Keeney, R. L., & Raiffa, H. (1999). *Smart choices: A practical guide to making better life decisions*. New York: Broadway.

Haran, U., Moore, D. A., & Morewedge, C. K. (2010). A simple remedy for overprecision in judgment. *Judgment and Decision Making, 5*(7), 467–476.

Hardin, G. (1968). The tragedy of the commons. *Science, 162*(3859), 1243–1248.

Harris, G., & Feder, B. (2006, January 27). FDA warns device maker over safety. *New York Times*, p. C1.

Hastorf, A. H., & Cantril, H. (1954). They saw a game: A case study. *Journal of Abnormal and Social Psychology, 49*, 129–134.

Hawken, P. (1993). *The ecology of commerce: A declaration of sustainability* (1st ed.) New York, NY: HarperBusiness.

Heider, F. (1958). *The psychology of interpersonal relations*. New York: Wiley.

Henrich, J., Boyd, R., Bowles, S., Camerer, C. F., Fehr, E., Gintis, H., et al. (2001). In search of Homo Economicus: Behavioral experiments in 15 small-scale societies. *AEA Papers and Proceedings*, 73–78.

Henrion, M., & Fischhoff, B. (1986). Assessing uncertainty in physical constants. *American Journal of Physics, 54*(9), 791–798.

Hershey, J. C., & Schoemaker, P. J. H. (1980). Prospect theory's reflection hypothesis: a critical examination. *Organizational Behavior and Human Performance, 3*, 395–418.

Herzog, S. M., & Hertwig, R. (2009). The wisdom of many in one mind. *Psychological Science, 108*, 9020–9025.

Highhouse, S. (2008). Stubborn reliance on intuition and subjectivity in employee selection. *Industrial and Organizational Psychology, 1*(3), 333–342.

Ho, T. H., Camerer, C. F., & Weigelt, K. (1998). Iterated dominance and iterated best response in experimental "p-beauty contests." *American Economic Review*, 88(4), 947–969.

Hoch, S. J. (1988). Who do we know: Predicting the interests and opinions of the American consumer. *Journal of Consumer Research*, 15(3), 315–324.

Hoffman, E., McCabe, K., & Smith, V. (1996). On expectations and the monetary stakes in ultimatum games. *International Journal of Game Theory*, 25, 289–302.

Holt, J. (2006, December 3). The new, soft paternalism. *New York Times*, p. 15.

Holt, L. L., & Lotto, A. J. (2008). Speech perception within an auditory cognitive science framework. *Current Directions in Psychological Science*, 17(1), 42–46.

Horberg, E. J., Oveis, C., Keltner, D., & Cohen, A. B. (2009). Disgust and the moralization of purity. *Journal of Personality and Social Psychology*, 97(6), 963–976.

Hsee, C. K. (1996). The evaluability hypothesis: An explanation for preference reversals between joint and separate evaluations of alternatives. *Organizational Behavior and Human Decision Processes*, 67(3), 247–257.

Hsee, C. K. (1998). Less is better: When low-value options are valued more highly than high-value options. *Journal of Behavioral Decision Making*, 11, 107–121.

Hsee, C. K., Loewenstein, G., Blount, S., & Bazerman, M. H. (1999). Preference reversals between joint and separate evaluations of options: A review and theoretical analysis. *Psychological Bulletin*, 125(5), 576–590.

Idson, L. C., Chugh, D., Bereby-Meyer, Y., Moran, S., Grosskopf, B., & Bazerman, M. H. (2004). Overcoming focusing failures in competitive environments. *Journal of Behavioral Decision Making*, 17(3), 159–172.

Iyengar, S. S. (2010). *The art of choosing*: Hachette.

Iyengar, S. S., & Lepper, M. R. (2000). When choice is demotivating: Can one desire too much of a good thing? *Journal of Personality and Social Psychology*, 79(6), 995–1006.

Iyengar, S. S., Jiang, W., & Huberman, G. (2004). How much choice is too much: Determinants of individual contributions in 401K retirement plans. In O. S. Mitchell & S. Utkus (Eds.), *Pension Design and Structure: New Lessons from Behavioral Finance* (pp. 83–95). Oxford: Oxford University Press.

James, W. (1890). *The principles of psychology*. New York: H. Holt.

Janiszewski, C., & Uy, D. (2008). Precision of the anchor influences the amount of adjustment. *Psychological Science*, 19(2), 121.

Janiszewski, C., Lichtenstein, D. R., & Belyavsky, J. (2008). Judgments about judgments: The dissociation of consideration price and transaction commitment judgments. *Journal of Experimental Psychology: Applied*, 14(2), 151.

Janofsky, M. (2004, March 19). Scalia refusing to take himself off Cheney case. *New York Times*, p. A1.

Jefferis, V. E., & Fazio, R. H. (2008). Accessibility as input: The use of construct accessibility as information to guide behavior. *Journal of Experimental Social Psychology*, 44(4), 1144–1150.

Jegadeesh, N., & Titman, S. (1993). Returns to Buying Winners and Selling Losers: Implications for Stock Market Efficiency. *Journal of Finance*, 48(1), 65–91.

Johnson, D. D. P. (2004). Overconfidence and war: The havoc and glory of positive illusions. Cambridge, MA: Harvard University Press.

Johnson, E. J., & Goldstein, D. G. (2003). Do defaults save lives? *Science*, 302, 1338–1339.

Johnson, E. J., & Tversky, A. (1983). Affect, generalization, and the perception of risk. *Journal of Personality and Social Psychology*, 45, 20–31.

Jordan, D. J., & Diltz, J. D. (2003). The profitability of day traders. *Financial Analysts Journal, 59*(6), 85–94.

Joyce, E. J., & Biddle, G. C. (1981). Anchoring and adjustment in probabilistic inference in auditing. *Journal of Accounting Research, 19,* 120–145.

Kagel, J. H., & Levin, D. (1986). The winner's curse and public information in common value auditing. *American Economic Review, 76,* 894–920.

Kahneman, D. (2003). A perspective on judgment and choice: Mapping bounded rationality. *American Psychologist, 58*(9), 697–720.

Kahneman, D., & Klein, G. (2009). Conditions for intuitive expertise: A failure to disagree. *American Psychologist, 64*(6), 515–526.

Kahneman, D., & Lovallo, D. (1993). Timid choices and bold forecasts: A cognitive perspective on risk and risk taking. *Management Science, 39,* 17–31.

Kahneman, D., & Miller, D. T. (1986). Norm theory: Comparing reality to its alternatives. *Psychological Review, 93*(2), 136–153.

Kahneman, D., & Ritov, I. (1994). Determinants of stated willingness to pay for public goods: A study in the headline method. *Journal of Risk and Uncertainty, 9,* 5–38.

Kahneman, D., & Tversky, A. (1972). Subjective probability: A judgment of representativeness. *Cognitive Psychology, 3*(3), 430–454.

Kahneman, D., & Tversky, A. (1973). On the psychology of prediction. *Psychological Review, 80,* 237–251.

Kahneman, D., & Tversky, A. (1979). Prospect theory: An analysis of decision under risk. *Econometrica, 47*(2), 263–291.

Kahneman, D., & Tversky, A. (1981). The framing of decisions and the psychology of choice. *Science, 211*(4481), 453–458.

Kahneman, D., & Tversky, A. (1982). The psychology of preferences. *Scientific American, 246*(1), 160–173.

Kahneman, D., & Tversky, A. (1982). The simulation heuristic. In D. Kahneman, P. Slovic & A. Tversky (Eds.), *Judgment under uncertainty: Heuristics and biases* (pp. 201–208). New York: Cambridge University Press.

Kahneman, D., Knetsch, J. L., & Thaler, R. H. (1986). Fairness as a constraint on profit seeking: Entitlements and the market. *American Economic Review, 76*(4), 728–741.

Kahneman, D., Knetsch, J. L., & Thaler, R. H. (1990). Experimental tests of the endowment effect and the Coase Theorem. *Journal of Political Economy, 98*(6), 1325–1348.

Kahneman, D., Krueger, A. B., Schkade, D., Schwarz, N., & Stone, A. A. (2006). Would you be happier if you were richer? A focusing illusion. *Science, 312,* 1908–1910.

Kahneman, D., Schkade, D. A., & Sunstein, C. R. (1998). Shared outrage and erratic awards: The psychology of punitive damages. *Journal of Risk and Uncertainty, 16,* 49–86.

Kant, I. (1964). *Groundwork of the metaphysics of morals.* New York: Harper & Row.

Kat, H. M., & Palaro, H. P. (2006). *Superstars or Average Joes? A Replication-Based Performance Evaluation of 1917 Individual Hedge Funds,* from http://ssrn.com/abstract=881105.

Kennedy, J. F. (1956). *Profiles in courage.* New York: Harper.

Keynes, J. M. (1936). *The general theory of interest, employment, and money.* London: Macmillan.

Keysar, B. (1994). The illusory transparency of intention: Linguistic perspective taking in text. *Cognitive Psychology, 26*(2), 165–208.

Khan, U., & Dhar, R. (2006). Licensing Effect in Consumer Choice. *Journal of Marketing Research*, *43*, 259–266.

Khan, U., & Dhar, R. (2007). Where there is a way, is there a will? The effect of future choices on self-control. *Journal of Experimental Psychology: General*, *136*, 277–288.

Klar, Y., & Giladi, E. E. (1999). Are most people happier than their peers, or are they just happy? *Personality and Social Psychology Bulletin*, *25*(5), 585–594.

Klar, Y., Karelitz, T. M., Roziner, I., & Levi, U. (2012). LOGE vs. Logic: Can every group member be taller than the others in the group? *Unpublished manuscript*.

Klar, Y., Ravid, D., & Hallak, Y. (2012). Nonselective optimism and pessimism among market experts and non-experts: Merely belonging to a potentially winning market can make each option more promising than the other options in the same market. *Unpublished manuscript*.

Klayman, J., & Ha, Y.-w. (1987). Confirmation, disconfirmation, and information in hypothesis testing. *Psychological Review*, *94*(2), 211–228.

Klayman, J., & Ha, Y.-won. (1987). Confirmation, disconfirmation, and information in hypothesis testing. *Psychological Review*, *94*(2), 211–228.

Koellinger, P., Minniti, M., & Schade, C. (2007). "I think I can, I think I can": Over-confidence and entrepreneurial behavior. *Journal of Economic Psychology*, *28*, 502–527.

Koole, S. L., Dijksterhuis, A., & vanKnippenberg, A. (2001). What's in a name: Implicit self-esteem and the automatic self. *Journal of Personality and Social Psychology*, *80*(4), 669–685.

Koriat, A., Fiedler, K., & Bjork, R. A. (2006). Inflation of conditional predictions. *Journal of Experimental Psychology: General*, *135*, 429–447.

Koriat, A., Lichtenstein, S., & Fischhoff, B. (1980). Reasons for confidence. *Journal of Experimental Psychology: Human Learning and Memory*, *6*(2), 107–118.

Kramer, R. M. (1994). Self-enhancing cognitions and organizational conflict, Working paper.

Kruger, J. (1999). Lake Wobegon be gone! The "below-average effect" and the egocentric nature of comparative ability judgments. *Journal of Personality and Social Psychology*, *77*(2), 221–232.

Kruger, J., & Burrus, J. (2004). Egocentrism and focalism in unrealistic optimism (and pessimism). *Journal of Experimental Social Psychology*, *40*(3), 332–340.

Kruger, J., Epley, N., Parker, J., & Ng, Z.-W. (2005). Egocentrism over e-mail: Can we communicate as well as we think? *Journal of Personality and Social Psychology*, *89*(6), 925–936.

Ku, G. (2008). Learning to de-escalate: The effects of regret in escalation of commitment. *Organizational Behavior and Human Decision Processes*, *105*(2), 221–232.

Ku, G., Galinsky, A. D., & Murnighan, J. K. (2006). Starting low but ending high: A reversal of the anchoring effect in auctions. *Journal of Personality and Social Psychology*, *90*(6), 975–986.

Ku, G., Malhotra, D., & Murnighan, J. K. (2005). Towards a competitive arousal model of decision making: A study of auction fever in live and Internet auctions. *Organizational Behavior and Human Decision Processes*, *96*(2), 89–103.

Kunda, Z. (1990). The case for motivated reasoning. *Psychological Bulletin*, *108*(3), 480–498.

Laibson, D. (1994). *Essays in Hyperbolic Discounting. Unpublished doctoral dissertation*. MIT, Cambridge, Mass.

Laibson, D., Repetto, A., & Tobacman, J. (1998). Self-control and saving for retirement. *Brookings paper on economic activity, 1,* 91–196.

Langer, E. J. (1975). The illusion of control. *Journal of Personality and Social Psychology, 32*(2), 311–328.

Larrick, R. P. (1993). Motivational factors in decision theories: The role of self-protection. *Psychological Bulletin, 113,* 440–450.

Larrick, R. P. (2004). Debiasing. In D. J. Koehler & N. Harvey (Eds.), *Blackwell Handbook of Judgment and Decision Making.* Oxford, England: Blackwell Publishers.

Larrick, R. P., & Wu, G. (2007). Claiming a large slice of a small pie: Asymmetric disconfirmation in negotiation. *Journal of Personality and Social Psychology, 93*(2), 212–233.

Larrick, R. P., Burson, K. A., & Soll, J. B. (2007). Social comparison and confidence: When thinking you're better than average predicts overconfidence (and when it does not). *Organizational Behavior & Human Decision Processes, 102*(1), 76–94.

Latane, B., & Darley, J. M. (1969). Bystander "apathy." *American Scientist, 57,* 244–268.

Lax, D. A., & Sebenenius, J. K. (1987). *Measuring the degree of joint gains achieved by negotiators.*

Lax, D. A., & Sebenius, J. K. (1986). Three ethical issues in negotiation. *Negotiation Journal, October,* 363–370.

Lax, D. A., & Sebenius, J. K. (2002). Dealcrafting: The substance of three dimensional negotiation. *Negotiation Journal, 18,* 5–28.

Leeson, N. (1997). *Rogue trader.* New York: Time Warner.

Leith, K. P., & Baumeister, R. F. (1996). Why do bad moods increase self-defeating behavior? Emotion, risk taking, and self-regulation. *Journal of Personality and Social Psychology, 71*(6), 1250–1267.

Lerner, J. S., & Keltner, D. (2000). Beyond valence: Toward a model of emotion-specific influences on judgement and choice. *Cognition and Emotion, 14*(4), 473–493.

Lerner, J. S., & Keltner, D. (2001). Fear, anger, and risk. *Journal of Personality and Social Psychology, 81*(1), 146–159.

Lerner, J. S., & Tetlock, P. E. (1999). Accounting for the effects of accountability. *Psychological Bulletin, 125*(2), 255–275.

Lerner, J. S., & Tiedens, L. Z. (2006). Portrait of the angry decision maker: How appraisal tendencies shape anger's influence on cognition. *Journal of Behavioral Decision Making, 19,* 115–137.

Lerner, J. S., Goldberg, J. H., & Tetlock, P. E. (1998). Sober second thought: The effects of accountability, anger, and authoritarianism on attributions of responsibility. *Personality and Social Psychology Bulletin, 24*(6), 563–574.

Lerner, J. S., Small, D. A., & Loewenstein, G. (2004). Heart strings and purse strings: Carryover effects of emotions on economic transactions. *Psychological Science, 15*(5), 337–341.

Levy, J., Pashler, H., & Boer, E. (2006). Central interference in driving: Is there any stopping the psychological refractory period? *Psychological Science, 17,* 228–235.

Lewin, K. (1947). Group decision and social change. In T. M. Newcomb & E. L. Hartley (Eds.), *Readings in social psychology.* New York: Holt, Rinehart and Winston.

Lewis, M. (2003). *Moneyball: The art of winning an unfair game:* W.W. Norton & Company.

Lichtenstein, S., & Fischhoff, B. (1980). Training for calibration. *Organizational Behavior and Human Decision Processes, 26*(2), 149–171.

Lieberman, M. D., Eisenberger, N. I., Crockett, M. J., Tom, S. M., Pfeifer, J. H., & Way, B. M. (2007). Putting feelings into words: Affect labeling disrupts amygdala activity to affective stimuli. *Psychological Science, 18*, 421–428.

Lind, E. A., & Tyler, T. R. (1988). *The social psychology of procedural justice.* New York: Plenum.

Lindell, M. K., & Perry, R. W. (2000). Household adjustment to earthquake hazard: A review of research. *Environment and Behavior, 32*, 461–501.

Loewenstein, G. (1996). Out of control: Visceral influences on behavior. *Organizational Behavior and Human Decision Processes, 65*(3), 272–292.

Loewenstein, G. F., & Prelec, D. (1993). Preferences for sequences of outcomes. *Psychological Review, 100*, 91–91.

Loewenstein, G., & Moore, D. A. (2004). When ignorance is bliss: Information exchange and inefficiency in bargaining. *Journal of Legal Studies, 33*(1), 37–58.

Loewenstein, G., & Thaler, R. H. (1989). Anomalies: Intertemporal choice. *Journal of Economic Perspectives, 3*(4), 181–193.

Loewenstein, G., Rick, S., & Cohen, J. D. (2008). Neuroeconomics. *Annu. Rev. Psychol., 59*, 647–672.

Loewenstein, G., Thompson, L., & Bazerman, M. H. (1989). Social utility and decision making in interpersonal contexts. *Journal of Personality and Social Psychology, 57*, 426–441.

Loewenstein, G., Weber, E. U., Hsee, C. K., & Welch, N. (2001). Risk as feelings. *Psychological Bulletin, 127*, 267–286.

Loewenstein, J., Thompson, L., & Gentner, D. (1999). Analogical encoding facilitates knowledge transfer in negotiation. *Psychonomic Bulletin and Review, 6*(4), 586–597.

Loewenstein, J., Thompson, L., & Gentner, D. (2003). Analogical learning in negotiation teams: Comparing cases promotes learning and transfer. *Academy of Management Learning and Education, 2*(2), 119–127.

Loftus, E. F. (1975). Leading questions and the eyewitness report. *Cognitive Psychology, 7*, 560–572.

Lord, C. G., Lepper, M. R., & Preston, E. (1984). Considering the opposite: A corrective strategy for social judgment. *Journal of Personality and Social Psychology, 47*(6), 1231–1243.

Lord, C. G., Ross, L., & Lepper, M. R. (1979). Biased assimilation and attitude polarization. *Journal of Personality and Social Psychology, 37*(11), 2098–2109.

Lowenthal, D. J. (1996). *What voters care about: How electoral context influences issue salience in campaigns.* Unpublished manuscript, Carnegie Mellon University.

Mack, A. (2003). Inattentional Blindness: Looking Without Seeing. *Current Directions in Psychological Science, 12*(5), 180–184.

Mack, A., & Rock, I. (1998). *Inattentional blindness.* Cambridge, MA: Bradford Books.

Macrae, C. N., & Bodenhausen, G. V. (2001). Social cognition: Categorical person perception. *British Journal of Psychology, 92*(1), 239–255.

Madrian, B. C., & Shea, D. F. (2001). The power of suggestion: Inertia in 401(k) participation and savings behavior. *Quarterly Journal of Economics, 116*(4), 1149–1187.

Malhotra, D., & Bazerman, M. H. (2007). *Negotiating genius.* New York: Bantam.

Malkiel, B. G. (2003). *A random walk down Wall Street* (8th ed.). New York: Norton.

Malkiel, B. G., & Saha, A. (2005). Hedge funds: Risk and return. *Financial Analyst Journal, 61*(6), 80–88.

Malmendier, U., & Tate, G. (2005). CEO overconfidence and corporate investment. *Journal of Finance, 60*(6), 2661–2700.

Malmendier, U., & Tate, G. (2008). Who makes acquisitions? CEO overconfidence and the market's reaction. *Journal of Financial Economics, 89*(1), 20–43.

Mannes, A., & Moore, D. A. (2012). *A behavioral demonstration of overconfidence in judgment. Unpublished manuscript.*

Mannix, E., & Neale, M. A. (2005). What differences make a difference? The promise and reality of diverse teams in organizations. *Psychological Science in the Public Interest, 6*, 31–55.

March, J. G., & Simon, H. A. (1958). *Organizations.* New York: Wiley.

Markopolos, H., & Casey, F. (2010). *No one would listen: A true financial thriller.* New York: Wiley.

Massey, C., Simmons, J. P., & Armor, D. A. (2011). Hope over experience: Desirability and the persistence of optimism. *Psychological Science, 22.*

McClure, S. M., Laibson, D., Loewenstein, G., & Cohen, J. D. (2004). Separate neural systems value immediate and delayed monetary rewards. *Science, 306*(5695), 503–507.

McConnell, A. R., & Leibold, J. M. (2001). Relations among the Implicit Association Test, discriminatory behavior, and explicit measures of racial attitudes. *Journal of Experimental Social Psychology, 37*(5), 435–442.

McGraw, A. P., Mellers, B. A., & Ritov, I. (2004). The affective costs of overconfidence. *Journal of Behavioral Decision Making, 17*(4), 281–295.

McKenzie, C. R. M., Liersch, M. J., & Yaniv, I. (2008). Overconfidence in interval estimates: What does expertise buy you? *Organizational Behavior & Human Decision Processes, 107*, 179–191.

Medvec, V. H., Madey, S. F., & Gilovich, T. (1995). When less is more: Counterfactual thinking and satisfaction among Olympic medalists. *Journal of Personality and Social Psychology, 69*(4), 603–610.

Meier, B. (2005, November 10). Guidant issues data on faulty heart devices. *New York Times,* p. C5.

Messick, D. M. (1991). Equality as a decision heuristic. In B. A. Mellers (Ed.), *Psychological issues in distributive justice.* New York: Cambridge University Press.

Messick, D. M., & Bazerman, M. H. (1996). Ethical leadership and the psychology of decision making. *Sloan Management Review, 37*(2), 9–22.

Messick, D. M., & Sentis, K. P. (1983). Fairness, preference, and fairness biases. In D. M. Messick & K. S. Cook (Eds.), *Equity theory: Psychological and sociological perspectives* (pp. 61–94). New York: Praeger.

Messick, D. M., Moore, D. A., & Bazerman, M. H. (1997). Ultimatum bargaining with a group: Underestimating the importance of the decision rule. *Organizational Behavior and Human Decision Processes, 69*(2), 87–101.

Meyvis, T., Ratner, R. K., & Levav, J. (2010). Why don'ft we learn to accurately forecast feelings? How misremembering our predictions blinds us to past forecasting errors. *Journal of Experimental Psychology: General2, 139*(4), 579–589.

Milgram, S. (1963). Behavioral study of obedience. *Journal of Abnormal & Social Psychology, 67*, 371–378.

Milkman, K. L., Beshears, J., Rogers, T., & Bazerman, M. H. (2008). *Mental accounting and small windfalls: Evidence from an online grocer.* Unpublished manuscript, Boston.

Milkman, K., Rogers, T., & Bazerman, M. H. (2007). *Film rentals and procrastination: A study of intertemporal reversals in preferences and intrapersonal conflict.* Unpublished manuscript, Boston, MA.

Minson, J. A., Liberman, V., & Ross, L. (2009). Two to tango: The effect of collaborative experience and disagreement on dyadic judgment. *Personality and Social Psychology Bulletin, 37,* 1325–1338.

Mitroff, S. R., Simons, D. J., & Franconeri, S. L. (2002). The Siren Song of implicit change detection. *Journal of Experimental Psychology: Human Perception & Performance, 28,* 798–815.

Moore, C. M., & Egeth, H. (1997). Perception without attention: Evidence of grouping under conditions of inattention. *Journal of Experimental Psychology: Human Perception & Performance, 23*(2), 339–352.

Moore, D. A. (2007). Not so above average after all: When people believe they are worse than average and its implications for theories of bias in social comparison. *Organizational Behavior and Human Decision Processes, 102*(1), 42–58.

Moore, D. A., & Cain, D. M. (2007). Overconfidence and underconfidence: When and why people underestimate (and overestimate) the competition. *Organizational Behavior & Human Decision Processes, 103,* 197–213.

Moore, D. A., & Kim, T. G. (2003). Myopic social prediction and the solo comparison effect. *Journal of Personality and Social Psychology, 85*(6), 1121–1135.

Moore, D. A., Cain, D. M., Loewenstein, G., & Bazerman, M. H. (Eds.). (2005). *Conflicts of interest: Challenges and solutions in law, medicine, and organizational settings.* New York: Cambridge University Press.

Moore, D. A., Kurtzberg, T. R., Fox, C. R., & Bazerman, M. H. (1999). Positive illusions and forecasting errors in mutual fund investment decisions. *Organizational Behavior and Human Decision Processes, 79*(2), 95–114.

Moore, D. A., Oesch, J. M., & Zietsma, C. (2007). What competition? Myopic self-focus in market entry decisions. *Organization Science, 18*(3), 440–454.

Moore, D. A., Swift, S. A., Sharek, Z., & Gino, F. (2010). Correspondence bias in performance evaluation: Why grade inflation works. *Personality and Social Psychology Bulletin, 36*(6), 843–852.

Moore, D. A., Tetlock, P. E., Tanlu, L., & Bazerman, M. H. (2006). Conflict of interest and the case of auditor independence: Moral seduction and strategic issue cycling. *Academy of Management Review, 31*(1), 10–29.

Moran, S., Bereby-Meyer, Y., & Bazerman, M. H. (2008). Getting more out of analogical training in negotiations: Learning core principles for creating value. *Negotiation and Conflict Management Research, 1*(2), 99–134.

Morewedge, C. K., & Kahneman, D. (2010). Associative processes in intuitive judgment. *Trends in Cognitive Sciences, 14*(10), 435–440.

Morewedge, C. K., Shu, L. L., Gilbert, D. T., & Wilson, T. D. (2009). Bad riddance or good rubbish? Ownership and not loss aversion causes the endowment effect. *Journal of Experimental Social Psychology, 45*(4), 947–951.

Morris, M. W., & Moore, P. C. (2000). The lessons we (don't) learn: Counterfactual thinking and organizational accountability after a close call. *Administrative Science Quarterly, 45*(4), 737–765.

Murnighan, J. K., Cantelon, D. A., & Elyashiv, T. (2004). Bounded personal ethics and the tap dance of real estate agency. In J. A. Wagner, J. M. Bartunek & K. D. Elsbach (Eds.), *Advances in qualitative organizational research* (Vol. 3) New York: Elsevier/JAI.

Murray, S. L., & Holmes, J. G. (1994). Storytelling in Close Relationships: The Construction of Confidence. *Personality and Social Psychology Bulletin, 20*(6), 650–663.

Mussweiler, T., & Englich, B. (2005). Subliminal anchoring: Judgmental consequences and underlying mechanisms. *Organizational Behavior and Human Decision Processes*, 98(2), 133–143.

Mussweiler, T., & Strack, F. (1999). Hypothesis-consistent testing and semantic priming in the anchoring paradigm: A selective accessibility model. *Journal of Experimental Social Psychology*, 35(2), 136–164.

Mussweiler, T., & Strack, F. (2000). The use of category and exemplar knowledge in the solution of anchoring tasks. *Journal of Personality and Social Psychology*, 78(6), 1038–1052.

Mussweiler, T., & Strack, F. (2001). The semantics of anchoring. *Organizational Behavior and Human Decision Processes*, 86(2), 234–255.

Myers, D. G. (1998). *Social psychology* (5th ed.). New York: McGraw-Hill.

Nalebuff, B. J. (1987). Puzzles: Choose a curtain, duel-ity, two point conversions, and more. *Economic Perspectives*, 1(1), 157–163.

Nalebuff, B. J., & Ayres, I. (2003). *Why Not? How to Use Everyday Ingenuity to Solve Problems Big and Small.* Boston: Harvard Business School Press.

Neale, M. A., & Bazerman, M. H. (1985). Perspectives for understanding negotiation: Viewing negotiation as a judgmental process. *Journal of Conflict Resolution*, 29, 33–55.

Neale, M. A., & Bazerman, M. H. (1985). The effects of framing and negotiator over-confidence on bargaining behaviors and outcomes. *Academy of Management Journal*, 28(1), 34–49.

Neale, M. A., & Northcraft, G. B. (1989). Experience, expertise, and decision bias in negotiation: The role of strategic conceptualization. In B. Sheppard, M. H. Bazerman & P. Lewicki (Eds.), *Research on negotiations in organizations* (Vol. 2) Greenwich, Conn.: JAI Press.

Neisser, U. (1979). The concept of intelligence. *Intelligence*, 3(3), 217–227.

Nelson, J. D., McKenzie, C. R. M., Cottrell, G. W., & Sejnowski, T. J. (2010). Experience Matters. *Psychological Science*, 21(7), 960–969.

Nelson, L. D., Meyvis, T., & Galak, J. (2009). Enhancing the Television-Viewing Experience through Commercial Interruptions. *Journal of Consumer Research*, 36(2), 160–172.

Nickerson, R. S. (1998). Confirmation bias: A ubiquitous phenomenon in many guises. *Review of General Psychology*, 2, 175–220.

Nisbett, R. E., & Ross, L. (1980). *Human inference: Strategies and shortcomings of social judgment.* Englewood Cliffs, NJ: Prentice-Hall.

Norem, J. K. (2002). *The positive power of negative thinking.* New York: Basic.

Norem, J. K., & Cantor, N. (1986). Defensive pessimism: Harnessing anxiety as motivation. *Journal of Personality and Social Psychology*, 51(6), 1208–1217.

Northcraft, G. B., & Neale, M. A. (1987). Expert, amateurs, and real estate: An anchoring-and-adjustment perspective on property pricing decisions. *Organizational Behavior and Human Decision Processes*, 39, 228–241.

Northcraft, G. B., & Neale, M. A. (1993). Negotiating successful research collaboration. In J. K. Murnighan (Ed.), *Social Psychology in organizations: Advances in theory and research.* Englewood Cliffs, N.J.: Prentice Hall.

Nosek, B. A., Banaji, M. R., & Greenwald, A. G. (2002). Harvesting implicit group attitudes and beliefs from a demonstration web site. *Group Dynamics: Theory, Research, and Practice*, 6(1), 101–115.

Null, C. 2007, (May 31, 2007). *Why your eBay auction didn't sell.* Retrieved August 22, 2007, from http://tech.yahoo.com/blog/null/28466

Nuttin, J. M. (1985). Narcissism beyond Gestalt and awareness: The name letter effect. *European Journal of Social Psychology*, 15, 353–361.

Nuttin, J. M. (1987). Affective consequences of mere ownership: The name letter effect in twelve European languages. *European Journal of Social Psychology*, 17, 381–402.

Ochs, J., & Roth, A. E. (1989). An experimental study of sequential bargaining. *American Economic Review*, 79(3), 355–384.

O'Connor, K. M., De Dreu, C. K. W., Schroth, H., Barry, B., Lituchy, T. R., & Bazerman, M. H. (2002). What we want to do versus what we think we should do: An empirical investigation of intrapersonal conflict. *Journal of Behavioral Decision Making*, 15(5), 403–418.

Odean, T. (1998). Are investors reluctant to realize their losses? *Journal of Finance*, 53(5), 1775–1798.

Odean, T. (1998). Volume, volatility, price, and profit when all traders are above average. *Journal of Finance*, 53(6), 1887–1934.

Odean, T. (1999). Do investors trade too much? *American Economic Review*, 89(5), 1279–1298.

O'Donoghue, T., & Rabin, M. (1999). Doing it now or later. *American Economic Review*, 89(1), 103–124.

Oppenheimer, D. M., LeBoeuf, R. A., & Brewer, N. T. (2008). Anchors aweigh: A demonstration of cross-modality anchoring and magnitude priming. *Cognition*, 106(1), 13–26.

Oskarsson, A. T., Van Boven, L., McClelland, G. H., & Hastie, R. (2009). What's next? Judging sequences of binary events. *Psychological Bulletin*, 135–2, 262–285.

Oveis, C., Horberg, E. J., & Keltner, D. (2010). Compassion, pride, and social intuitions of self-other similarity. *Journal of Personality and Social Psychology*, 98(4), 618–630.

Pager, D., & Shepherd, H. (2008). The sociology of discrimination: Racial discrimination in employment, housing, credit, and consumer markets. *Annual Review of Sociology*, 34, 181.

Paharia, N., Kassam, K., Greene, J. D., & Bazerman, M. H. (2007). *Washing your hands clean: Moral implications of indirection actions in business decisions*. Unpublished manuscript.

Palm, R. (1995). Catastrophic earthquake insurance: Patterns of adoption. *Economic Geography*, 71(2), 119–131.

Pedersen, W. C., Bushman, B. J., Vasquez, E. A., & Miller, N. (2008). Kicking the (barking) dog effect: The moderating role of target attributes on triggered displaced aggression. *Personality and Social Psychology Bulletin*, 34(10), 1382–1395.

Perrow, C. (1984). *Normal accidents: Living with high-risk technologies*. New York: Basic Books.

Petersen, T., Saporta, I., & Seidel, M. D. L. (2000). Offering a job: Meritocracy and social networks. *American Journal of Sociology*, 106(3), 763–816.

Plant, E. A., Devine, P. G., Cox, W. T. L., Columb, C., Miller, S. L., Goplen, J., et al. (2009). The Obama effect: Decreasing implicit prejudice and stereotyping. *Journal of Experimental Social Psychology*, 45(4), 961–964.

Plous, S. (1993). *The psychology of judgment and decision making*. New York: McGraw-Hill.

Pollan, S. M., & Levine, M. (1997). *Die Broke*. New York: Harper Business.

Pope, D. G., & Schweitzer, M. E. (2011). Is Tiger Woods loss averse? Persistent bias in the face of experience, competition, and high stakes. *The American Economic Review*, 101(1), 129–157.

Pronin, E., Gilovich, T., & Ross, L. (2004). Objectivity in the eye of the beholder: Divergent perceptions of bias in self versus others. *Psychological Review, 111*(3), 781–799.

Pronin, E., Lin, D. Y., & Ross, L. (2002). The bias blind spot: Perceptions of bias in self versus others. *Personality and Social Psychology Bulletin, 28*(3), 369–381.

Pruitt, D. G., & Rubin, J. Z. (1985). *Social conflict: Escalation, impasse, and resolution.* Reading, MA: Addison-Wesley.

Rabin, M., & Thaler, R. H. (2001). Anomalities: Risk aversion. *Journal of Economic Perspectives, 15*(1), 219–232.

Radzevick, J. R., & Moore, D. A. (2007). *Myopic biases in competitions.* Unpublished manuscript, Pittsburgh.

Radzevick, J. R., & Moore, D. A. (2011). Competing to be certain (but wrong): Social pressure and overprecision in judgment. *Management Science, 57*(1), 93–106.

Raiffa, H. (1968). *Decision analysis: Introductory lectures on choices under uncertainty.* Reading, MA: Addison-Wesley; reissued in 1997, New York. McGraw-Hill.

Raiffa, H. (1982). *The art and science of negotiation.* Cambridge, MA: Belknap.

Raiffa, H. (1984). *Invited address to the Judgment and Decision Making Society* (November), San Antonio, TX.

Raiffa, H. (1985). Post-settlement settlements. *Negotiation Journal, 1,* 9–12.

Raiffa, H. (2001). *Collaborative decision making.* Cambridge, Mass.: Belknap.

Ravenscraft, D. J., & Scherer, F. M. (1989). The profitability of mergers. *International Journal of Industrial Organization, 7*(1), 101–116.

Rayo, L., & Becker, G. S. (2007). Evolutionary efficiency and happiness. *Journal of Political Economy, 115*(2), 302–337.

Reifman, A. (2011). *Hot hand: The statistics behind sports' greatest streaks.* Washington, DC: Potomac.

Richeson, J. A., & Shelton, J. N. (2003). When prejudice does not pay: Effects of interracial contact on executive function. *Psychological Science, 14,* 287–290.

Richeson, J. A., & Shelton, J. N. (2005). Brief report: Thin slices of racial bias. *Journal of Nonverbal Behavior, 29,* 75–86.

Richeson, J. A., & Trawalter, S. (2005). Why do interracial interactions impair executive function? A resource depletion account. *Journal of Personality and Social Psychology, 88,* 934–947.

Risen, J. L., & Gilovich, T. (2008). Why people are reluctant to tempt fate. *Journal of Personality and Social Psychology, 95*(2), 293.

Ritov, I. (1996). Anchoring in simulated competitive market negotiation. *Organizational Behavior and Human Decision Processes, 67*(1), 16–25.

Roberts, R. R., & Kraynak, J. (2006). Flipping houses for dummies. New York: Wiley.

Robins, R. W., & Beer, J. S. (2001). Positive illusions about the self: Short-term benefits and long-term costs. *Journal of Personality and Social Psychology, 80*(2), 340–352.

Rogers, T., & Bazerman, M. H. (2008). Future lock-in: Future implementation increases selection of 'should' choices. *Organizational Behavior & Human Decision Processes, 105*(1), 1–20.

Rogers, T., Milkman, K. L., & Bazerman, M. H. (2007). *I'll Have the Ice Cream Soon and the Vegetables Later: Decreasing Impatience over Time in Online Grocery Stores.* Unpublished manuscript, Boston.

Rosenthal, R. (1974). *On the social psychology of the self-fulfilling prophecy: Further evidence for Pygmalion effects and their mediating mechanisms.* New York: M. S. S. Inf. Corp. Modular Publications.

Rosenthal, R., & Jacobson, L. (1968). *Pygmalion in the classroom; teacher expectation and pupils' intellectual development.* New York: Holt Rinehart and Winston.

Ross, J. M., & Staw, B. M. (1986). Expo 86: An escalator prototype. *Administrative Science Quarterly, 31*(2), 274–297.

Ross, L., & Stillinger, C. (1991). Barriers to conflict resolution. *Negotiation Journal, 7*(4), 389–404.

Ross, L., & Ward, A. (1996). Naive realism in everyday life: Implications for social conflict and misunderstanding. In E. Reed, E. Turiel & T. Brown (Eds.), Values and knowledge (pp. 103–135).

Ross, M., & Sicoly, F. (1979). Egocentric biases in availability and attribution. *Journal of Personality and Social Psychology, 37*, 322–336.

Rozin, P., Haidt, J., & McCauley, C. R. (1999). Disgust: The body and soul emotion. In *Handbook of cognition and emotion* (pp. 429–445). Chichester, England: John Wiley & Sons org.

Rozin, P., Markwith, M., & Ross, B. (1990). The sympathetic magical law of similarity, nominal realism and neglect of negatives in response to negative labels. *Psychological Science, 1*, 383–384.

Rudman, L. A., & Borgida, E. (1995). The afterglow of construct accessibility: The behavioral consequences of priming men to view women as sexual objects. *Journal of Experimental Social Psychology, 31*(6), 493–517.

Rudman, L. A., & Glick, P. (2001). Prescriptive gender stereotypes and backlash toward agentic women. *Journal of Social Issues, 57*(4), 743–762.

Samuelson, P. A. (1963). Risk and Uncertainty: A fallacy of large numbers. *Scientia, 98*, 108–113.

Samuelson, W. F., & Bazerman, M. H. (1985). Negotiation under the winner's curse. In V. Smith (Ed.), *Research in experimental economics* (Vol. 3, pp. 105–138). Greenwich, CT: JAI.

Samuelson, W. F., & Zeckhauser, R. J. (1988). Status quo bias in decision making. *Journal of Risk and Uncertainty, 1*, 7–59.

Sanfey, A. G., Rilling, J. K., Aronson, J. A., Nystrom, L. E., & Cohen, J. D. (2003). The neural basis of economic decision-making in the Ultimatum Game. *Science, 300* (5626), 1755–1758.

Saul, S. (2006, January 25). J&J passes on raising Guidant bid. *New York Times*, p. C1.

Saunders, E. M. (1993). Stock prices and Wall Street weather. *American Economic Review, 83*(5), 1337–1345.

Schelling, T. C. (1984). *Choice and consequence: Perspectives of an errant economist.* Cambridge, MA: Harvard University Press.

Schkade, D. A., & Kahneman, D. (1998). Does living in California make people happy? A focusing illusion in judgments of life satisfaction. *Psychological Science, 9*(5), 340–346.

Schmidt, F. L., & Hunter, J. E. (1998). The validity and utility of selection methods in personnel psychology: Practical and theoretical implications of 85 years of research findings. *Psychological Bulletin, 124*(2), 262–274.

Schmidt, P. (2007, April 6). Children of alumni are uniquely harmed by admissions preferences, study finds. *Chronicle of Higher Education.*

Schoemaker, P. J. H., & Kunreuther, H. (1979). An experimental study of insurance decisions. *Journal of risk and Insurance, 46*, 603–618.

Schoorman, F. D. (1988). Escalation bias in performance appraisals: An unintended consequence of supervisor participation in hiring decisions. *Journal of Applied Psychology*, 73(1), 58–62.

Schulz, K. (2010). *Being wrong*. New York: Ecco.

Schwartz, B. (2005). *The paradox of choice: Why more is less*: Harper.

Schwarz, A. (2005, Nov 13). Predicting futures in baseball, and the downside of Damon. *New York Times*.

Schwarz, N. (2001). Feelings as information: Implications for affective influences on information processing. In *Theories of mood and cognition: A user's guidebook* (pp. 159–176). Mahwah, NJ: Erlbaum.

Schwarz, N., & Strack, F. (1999). Reports of subjective well-being: Judgmental processes and their methodological implications. In D. Kahneman & E. Diener (Eds.), *Well-being: The foundations of hedonic psychology* (pp. 61–84). New York, NY, USA: Russell Sage Foundation.

Schwarz, N., Bless, H., Strack, F., Klumpp, G., Rittenauer-Schatka, H., & Simons, A. (1991). Ease of retrieval as information: Another look at the availability heuristic. *Journal of Personality and Social Psychology*, 61(2), 195–202.

Sebenius, J. K., & Wheeler, M. (1994, October 30, 1994). Let the game continue. *The New York Times*, pp. October 30, Sect. 33, p. 39.

Sedikides, C., & Gregg, A. P. (2008). Self-enhancement: Food for thought. *Perspectives on Psychological Science*, 3(2), 102–116.

Seligman, M. E. P. (1991). *Learned optimism*. New York: A. A. Knopf.

Selvin, S. (1975). [Letter to the editor]. *American Statistician*, 29, 67.

Shafir, E., & Thaler, R. H. (2006). Invest now, drink later, spend never: On the mental accounting of delayed consumption. *Journal of Economic Psychology*, 27(5), 694–712.

Shah, A. K., & Oppenheimer, D. M. (2008). Heuristics made easy: An effort-reduction framework. *Psychological Bulletin; Psychological Bulletin*, 134(2), 207–222. doi: 10.1037/0033–2909.134.2.207

Sharot, T., Riccardi, A. M., Raio, C. M., & Phelps, E. A. (2007). Neural mechanisms mediating optimism bias. *Nature*, 450(1), 102–106.

Sharpe, W. F. (1991). The arithmetic of active management. *Financial Analysts Journal*, 47, 7–9.

Shefrin, H. M. (2000). *Beyond greed and fear*. Boston: Harvard Business School Press.

Shelton, J. N., Richeson, J. A., & Vorauer, J. D. (2006). Threatened identities and interethnic interactions. *European Review of Social Psychology*, 17, 321–358.

Shepard, R. N. (1990). *Mind sight: Original visual illusions, ambiguities, and other anomalies*. New York: W.H. Freeman and Co.

Shiv, B., & Fedorikhin, A. (1999). Heart and mind in conflict: The interplay of affect and cognition in consumer decision making. *Journal of Consumer Research*, 26(3), 278–292.

Shiv, B., Loewenstein, G., Bechara, A., Damasio, H., & Damasio, A. R. (2005). Investment behavior and the negative side of emotion. *Psychological Science*, 16, 435–439.

Shleifer, A. (2000). *Inefficient markets*. New York: Oxford University Press.

Shubik, M. (1971). The dollar auction game: A paradox in noncooperative behavior and escalation. *Journal of Conflict Resolution*, 15, 109–111.

Simmons, J. P., Nelson, L. D., Galak, J., & Frederick, S. (2011). Intuitive biases in choice versus estimation: Implications for the wisdom of crowds. *Journal of Consumer Research*, 38(1), 1–15.

Simon, H. A. (1957). *Models of man*. New York: Wiley.

Simons, D. J. (2000). Current approaches to change blindness. *Visual Cognition, 7*(1–3), 1–15.

Simons, D. J., & Chabris, C. F. (1999). Gorillas in our midst: Sustained inattentional blindness for dynamic events. *Perception, 28*(9), 1059–1074.

Simons, D. J., & Levin, D. (2003). What makes change blindness interesting? In D. E. Irwin & B. Ross (Eds.), *The psychology of learning and motivation*. San Diego, CA: Academic Press.

Simons, D. J., & Rensink, R. A. (2005). Change blindness: Past, present, and future. *Trends in Cognitive Sciences, 9*, 16–20.

Simons, D. J., Chabris, C. F., Schnur, T., & Levin, D. (2002). Evidence for preserved representation in change blindness. *Consciousness & Cognition: An International Journal, 11*(1), 78–97.

Sitkin, S. B. (1992). Learning through failure: The strategy of small losses. *Research in Organizational Behavior, 14*, 231–266.

Slovic, P., & Fischhoff, B. (1977). On the psychology of experimental surprises. *Journal of Experimental Psychology: Human Perception & Performance, 3*(4), 544–551.

Slovic, P., & Peters, E. (2006). Risk perception and affect. *Current Directions in Psychological Science, 15*(6), 323–325.

Slovic, P., Finucane, M., Peters, E., & MacGregor, D. G. (2002). The affect heuristic. In T. Gilovich, D. Griffin & D. Kahneman (Eds.), *Heuristics and Biases: The psychology of intuitive judgment* (pp. 397–420): Cambridge University Press.

Slovic, P., Fischhoff, B., & Lichtenstein, S. (1982). Response mode framing and information processing effects in risk assessment. In R. M. Hogarth (Ed.), *New Directions for Methodology and Social and Behavioral Science: Question Framing and Response Consistency*. San Francisco: Jossey-Bass.

Slovic, P., Lichtenstein, S., & Fischhoff, B. (1982). Characterizing perceived risk. In R. W. Kataes & C. Hohenemser (Eds.), *Technological hazard management*. Cambridge, MA: Oelgesschlager, Gunn and Hain.

Sniezek, J. A., & VanSwol, L. M. (2001). Trust, confidence, and expertise in a judge-advisor system. *Organizational Behavior and Human Decision Processes, 84*(2), 288–307.

Solomon, S., Qin, D., Manning, M., Chen, Z., Marquis, M., Averyt, K. B., et al. (Eds.). (2007). *Climate change 2007: The physical science basis: Contribution of Working Group I to the Fourth Assessment Report of the Intergovernmental Panel on Climate Change*. Cambridge, UK: Cambridge University Press.

Stanovich, K. E., & West, R. F. (2000). Individual differences in reasoning: Implications for the rationality debate. *Behavioral & Brain Sciences, 23*, 645–665.

Stanovich, K. E., & West, R. F. (2008). On the relative independence of thinking biases and cognitive ability. *Journal of Personality and Social Psychology, 94*(4), 672.

Stasser, G. (1988). Computer simulation as a research tool: The DISCUSS model of group decision making. *Journal of Experimental Social Psychology, 24*(5), 393–422.

Stasser, G., & Stewart, D. (1992). Discovery of hidden profiles by decision-making groups: Solving a problem versus making a judgment. *Journal of Personality and Social Psychology, 63*(3), 426–434.

Stasser, G., & Titus, W. (1985). Pooling of unshared information in group decision making: Biased information sampling during discussion. *Journal of Personality and Social Psychology, 48*(6), 1467–1478.

Stasser, G., Vaughn, S. I., & Stewart, D. D. (2000). Pooling unshared information: the benefits of knowing how access to information is distributed among group members. *Organizational Behavior & Human Decision Processes*, 82(1), 102–116.

Staw, B. M. (1976). Knee-deep in the Big Muddy: A study of escalating commitment to a chosen course of action. *Organizational Behavior and Human Decision Processes*, 16(1), 27–44.

Staw, B. M. (1980). Rationality and justification in organizational life. In B. M. Staw & L. L. Cummings (Eds.), *Research in organizational behavior* (Vol. 2) Greenwich, CT: JAI Press.

Staw, B. M. (1981). The escalation of commitment to a course of action. *Academy of Management Review*, 6(4), 577–587.

Staw, B. M., & Hoang, H. (1995). Sunk costs in the NBA: why draft order affects playing time and survival in professional basketball. *Administrative Science Quarterly*, 40, 474–494.

Staw, B. M., & Ross, J. M. (1978). Commitment to a policy decision: A multi-theoretical perspective. *Administrative Science Quarterly*, 23, 40–64.

Staw, B. M., & Ross, J. M. (1980). Commitment in an experimenting society, An experiment on the attribution of leadership from administrative scenarios. *Journal of Applied Psychology*, 65, 249–260.

Staw, B. M., & Ross, J. M. (1987). Behavior in escalation situations: Antecedents, proto-types, and solutions. *Research in Organizational Behavior*, 9.

Stillinger, C., Epelbaum, M., Keltner, D., & Ross, L. (1990). The reactive devaluation barrier to conflict resolution. Unpublished manuscript, Stanford University.

Straub, P. G., & Murnighan, J. K. (1995). An experimental investigation of ultimatum games: Information, fairness, expectations, and lowest acceptable offers. *Journal of Economic Behavior and Organization*, 27, 345–364.

Sunstein, C. R. (2002). Toward behavioral law and economics. In Judgments, decisions, and public policy (pp. 218–240). New York, NY, US: Cambridge University Press.

Svenson, O. (1981). Are we less risky and more skillful than our fellow drivers? *Acta Psychologica*, 47, 143–151.

Swanson, J. (2008). *Ratings Agencies Hit for Role in Financial Crisis*. Retrieved February 28, 2012, from http://www.mortgagenewsdaily.com/10232008_Ratings_Agencies_.asp

Swift, S. A., Moore, D. A., Sharek, Z., & Gino, F. (2009). Inflated applicants: Attribution errors in performance evaluation by professionals. *Unpublished manuscript*.

Taleb, N. N. (2001). *Fooled by randomness*. New York: Texere.

Taylor, K. M., & Shepperd, J. A. (1998). Bracing for the worst: Severity, testing, and feedback timing as moderators of the optimistic bias. *Personality and Social Psychology Bulletin*, 24(9), 915–926.

Taylor, S. E. (1989). *Positive illusions: Creative self-deception and the healthy mind*. New York, NY, US: Basic Books, Inc.

Taylor, S. E., & Brown, J. D. (1988). Illusion and well-being: a social psychological perspective on mental health. *Psychological Bulletin*, 103(2), 193–210.

Taylor, S. E., Lerner, J. S., Sage, R. M., Lehman, B. J., & Seeman, T. E. (2004). Early environment, emotions, responses to stress, and health. *Journal of Personality*, 72, 1365–1393.

Teger, A. (1980). *Too much invested to quit*. New York: Pergamon.

Tenbrunsel, A. E., & Bazerman, M. H. (1995). *Moms.com simulation*: Dispute Resolution Research Center, Northwestern University.

Tenbrunsel, A. E., & Messick, D. M. (2004). Ethical fading: The role of self-deception in unethical behavior. *Social Justice Research*, *17*(2), 223–236.

Tenney, E. R., MacCoun, R. J., Spellman, B. A., & Hastie, R. (2007). Calibration trumps confidence as a basis for witness credibility. *Psychological Science*, *18*(1), 46–50.

Tesser, A. (1988). Toward a self evaluation maintenance model of social behavior. In L. Berkowitz (Ed.), *Advances in experimental social psychology* (Vol. *21*, pp. 181–227). New York: Guilford.

Tetlock, P. E. (1986). A value pluralism model of ideological reasoning. *Journal of Personality and Social Psychology*, *50*(4), 819–827.

Tetlock, P. E., Kristel, O. V., Elson, S. B., Green, M. C., & Lerner, J. S. (2000). The psychology of the unthinkable: Taboo trade-offs, forbidden base rates, and heretical counterfactuals. *Journal of Personality and Social Psychology*, *78*(5), 853–870.

Tetlock, P. E., Peterson, R. S., & Lerner, J. S. (1996). Revising the value pluralism model: Incorporating social content and context postulates. In C. Seligman, J. Olson & M. Zanna (Eds.), *Values: Eighth Annual Ontario Symposium on Personality and Social Psychology* (pp. 25–51). Hillsdale, NJ: Erlbaum.

Thaler, R. H. (1980). Toward a positive theory of consumer choice. *Journal of Economic Behavior and Organization*, *1*, 39–80.

Thaler, R. H. (1985). Using mental accounting in a theory of purchasing behavior. *Marketing Science*, *4*, 12–13.

Thaler, R. H. (1991). *Quasi rational economics*. New York, NY, USA: Russell Sage Foundation.

Thaler, R. H. (1999). Mental accounting matters. *Journal of Behavioral Decision Making*, *12*(3), 183–206.

Thaler, R. H. (2000). From homo economicus to homo sapiens. *Journal of Economic Perspectives*, *14*, 133–141.

Thaler, R. H. (2004). Unrestricted teaching files, faculty website at University of Chicago School of Business: http://gsb.uchicago.edu/fac/richard.thaler/.

Thaler, R. H., & Benartzi, S. (2004). Save more tomorrow: Using behavioral economics to increase employee saving. *Journal of Political Economy*, *112*(1), S164–S187.

Thaler, R. H., & DeBondt, W. F. M. (1992). A mean reverting walk down Wall Street. In R. H. Thaler (Ed.), *The winner's curse: Paradoxes and anomalies of economic life*. New York: Free Press.

Thaler, R. H., & Shefrin, H. M. (1981). An economic theory of self control. *Journal of Political Economy*, *89*, 392–406.

Thaler, R. H., & Sunstein, C. R. (2003, September 9). Who's on first? *The New Republic*, Sept. 9 p. 27.

Thaler, R. H., & Sunstein, C. R. (2008). Nudge: Improving decisions about health, wealth, and happiness. New Haven, CT: Yale University Press.

Thaler, R. H., & Ziemba, W. T. (1988). Anomalies: Parimutual Betting Makes Markets: Racetracks and Lotteries. *Journal of Economic Perspectives*, *2*(2), 161–174.

The Economist. (2004, January 8). The curse of nepotism. *The Economist*.

Thompson, L. (2001). *The mind and the heart of the negotiator*. Upper Saddle River, N.J.: Prentice Hall.

Thompson, L., & Loewenstein, G. (1992). Egocentric interpretations of fairness and interpersonal conflict. *Organizational Behavior and Human Decision Processes*, & *51*(2), 176–197.

Thompson, L., Gentner, D., & Loewenstein, J. (2000). Avoiding missed opportunities in managerial life: Analogical training more powerful than case-based training. *Organizational Behavior and Human Decision Processes*, 82(1), 60–75.

Thompson, L., Gentner, D., & Loewenstein, J. (2000). Avoiding missed opportunities in managerial life: Analogical training more powerful than individual case training. *Organizational Behavior and Human Decision Processes*, 82(1), 60–75.

Thompson, S. C. (1999). Illusions of control: How we overestimate our personal influence. *Current Directions in Psychological Science*, 8(6), 187–190.

Tiedens, L. Z., & Linton, S. (2001). Judgment under emotional certainty and uncertainty: The effects of specific emotions on information processing. *Journal of Personality and Social Psychology*, 81(6), 973–988.

Todd, A. R., Hanko, K., Galinsky, A. D., & Mussweiler, T. (2011). When focusing on differences leads to similar perspectives. *Psychological Science*, 22(1), 134.

Tor, A., & Bazerman, M. H. (2003). Focusing failures in competitive environments: Explaining decision errors in the Monty Hall game, the acquiring a company problem, and multiparty ultimatums. *Journal of Behavioral Decision Making*, 16(5), 353–374.

Trabasso, T., Rollins, H., & Shaughnessy, E. (1971). Storage and verification stages in processing concepts. *Cognitive Psychology*, 2, 239–289.

Tversky, A., & Kahneman, D. (1971). Belief in the law of small numbers. *Psychological Bulletin*, 76(2), 105–110.

Tversky, A., & Kahneman, D. (1973). Availability: A heuristic for judging frequency and probability. *Cognitive Psychology*, 5(2), 207–232.

Tversky, A., & Kahneman, D. (1974). Judgment under uncertainty: Heuristics and biases. *Science*, 185, 1124–1131.

Tversky, A., & Kahneman, D. (1981). The framing of decisions and the psychology of choice. *Science*, 211(4481), 453–458.

Tversky, A., & Kahneman, D. (1983). Extensional versus intuitive reasoning: The conjunction fallacy in probability judgment. *Psychological Review*, 90(4), 293–315.

Tversky, A., & Kahneman, D. (1986). Judgment under uncertainty: Heuristics and biases. In H. R. Arkes & K. R. Hammond (Eds.), *Judgment and decision making: An interdisciplinary reader* (pp. 38–55). Cambridge, UK: Cambridge University Press.

Tversky, A., & Kahneman, D. (1991). Loss aversion in riskless choice: A reference-dependent model. *Quarterly Journal of Economics*, 106(4), 1039–1061.

Tversky, A., & Koehler, D. J. (1994). Support theory: A nonextensional representation of subjective probability. *Psychological Review*, 101(4), 547–567.

Tyler, T. R., & Hastie, R. (1991). The social consequences of cognitive illusions. In R. J. Bies, R. J. Lewicki & B. H. Sheppard (Eds.), *Research on negotiation in organizations* (Vol. 3, pp. 69–98). Greenwich, CT: JAI.

Ubel, P. A., Loewenstein, G., Hershey, J., Baron, J., Mohr, T., Asch, D. A., et al. (2001). Do nonpatients underestimate the quality of life associated with chronic health conditions because of a focusing illusion? *Medical Decision Making*, 21(3), 190–199.

Valley, K. L., Moag, J., & Bazerman, M. H. (1998). A matter of trust: Effects of communication on the efficiency and distribution of outcomes. *Journal of Economic Behavior and Organization*, 34, 211–238.

Van Boven, L., Dunning, D., & Loewenstein, G. (2000). Egocentric empathy gaps between owners and buyers: Misperceptions of the endowment effect. *Journal of Personality and Social Psychology*, 79(1), 66–76.

Vancouver, J. B., & Kendall, L. N. (2006). When self-efficacy negatively relates to motivation and performance in a learning context. *Journal of Applied Psychology*, *91*(5), 1146.

Vaughn, D. (1996). *The Challenger launch Decision: Ricky Technology, Culture, and Deviance at NASA*. Chicago, IL: University of Chicago.

Vohs, K. D., Baumeister, R. F., Schmeichel, B. J., Twenge, J. M., Nelson, N. M., & Tice, D. M. (2008). Making choices impairs subsequent self-control: A limited-resource account of decision making, self-regulation, and active initiative. *Journal of Personality and Social Psychology*, *94*(5), 883.

von Hippel, W., & Trivers, R. L. (2011). The evolution and psychology of self-deception. *Behavioral and Brain Sciences*, *34*, 1–56.

von Hippel, W., Lakin, J. L., & Shakarchi, R. J. (2005). Individual Differences in Motivated Social Cognition: The Case of Self-Serving Information Processing. *Personality and Social Psychology Bulletin*, *31*, 1347–1357.

vos Savant, M. (1990a). Ask Marilyn. *Parade Magazine*, New York, NY.

vos Savant, M. (1990b). Ask Marilyn. *Parade Magazine*, New York, NY.

vos Savant, M. (1991). Ask Marilyn. *Parade Magazine*, New York, NY.

Wade-Benzoni, K. A., Li, M., Thompson, L., & Bazerman, M. H. (2007). The malleability of environmentalism. *Analyses of Social Issues and Public Policy*, *7*(1), 163–189.

Wade-Benzoni, K. A., Tenbrunsel, A. E., & Bazerman, M. H. (1996). Egocentric interpretations of fairness in asymmetric, environmental social dilemmas: Explaining harvesting behavior and the role of communication. *Organizational Behavior and Human Decision Processes*, *67*(2), 111–126.

Wason, P. C. (1960). On the failure to eliminate hypotheses in a conceptual task. *Quarterly Journal of Experimental Psychology*, *12*, 129–140.

Webb, J. 2004, (September 3). *Bush's bid to connect with voters*. Retrieved July 11, 2007, from http://news.bbc.co.uk/2/hi/americas/3623560.stm

Wegner, D. M. (2002). *The illusion of conscious will*. Cambridge, Mass.: MIT Press.

Weick, K. E. (1993). The collapse of sensemaking in organizations: The Mann Gulch disaster. *Administrative Science Quarterly*, *38*(4), 628–653.

Whitman, W. (1855/2001). *Song of myself*. Mineola, New York: Dover.

Williams, J. E., Patson, C. C., Siegler, I. C., Eigenbrodt, M. L., Neieto, F. J., & Tyroler, H. (2000). Anger proneness predicts coronary heart disease risk. *Circulation*, *101*, 2034–2039.

Wilson, T. D., Wheatley, T., Meyers, J. M., Gilbert, D. T., & Axsom, D. (2000). Focalism: A source of durability bias in affective forecasting. *Journal of Personality and Social Psychology*, *78*(5), 821–836.

Windschitl, P. D., Kruger, J., & Simms, E. (2003). The influence of egocentrism and focalism on people's optimism in competitions: When what affects us equally affects me more. *Journal of Personality and Social Psychology*, *85*(3), 389–408.

Windschitl, P. D., Rose, J. P., Stalkfleet, M. T., & Smith, A. R. (2008). Are people excessive or judicious in their egocentrism? A modeling approach to understanding bias and accuracy in people's optimism within competitive contexts. *Journal of Personality and Social Psychology*, *95*(2), 253–273.

Yaniv, I., & Kleinberger, E. (2000). Advice taking in decision making: Egocentric discounting and reputation formation. *Organizational Behavior and Human Decision Processes*, *84*(2), 260–281.

Yates, J. F., & Carlson, B. W. (1986). Conjunction errors: Evidence for multiple judgment procedures, including 'signed summation.' *Organizational Behavior & Human & Decision Processes*, 37, 230–253.

Yovel, G., & Kanwisher, N. (2005). The neural basis of the behavioral face-inversion effect. *Current Biology*, 15, 2256–2262.

Zander, A. (1971). *Motives and goals in groups*. New York: Academic Press.

Zauberman, G., Kim, B. K., Malkoc, S. A., & Bettman, J. R. (2009). Discounting time and time discounting: Subjective time perception and intertemporal preferences. *Journal of Marketing Research*, 46(4), 543–556.

Zell, E., & Alicke, M. D. (2009). Contextual Neglect, Self-Evaluation, and the Frog-Pond Effect. *Journal of Personality and Social Psychology*, 97(3), 467–482.

Zickfeld, K., Morgan, M. G., Frame, D. J., & Keith, D. W. (2010). Expert judgments about transient climate response to alternative future trajectories of radiative forcing. *Proceedings of the National Academy of Sciences*, 107(28), 12451.

Ziemba, S. (1995, November 10). American to United: Avoid bidding war carrier won't draw first in USAir fight. *Chicago Tribune*, p. B1.

Zuckerman, G. (2010). *The greatest trade ever: The behind-the-scenes story of how John Paulson defied Wall Street and made financial history*. New York: Crown Business.

Zweig, J. (2000, August). Mutual competition: Are the new rivals to traditional funds a better bet? *Money Magazine*.

Index

A

Abeler, J., 101

Acquiring a Company problem, 71, 73, 75–76, 214–215, 215*f*, 220–221

Acquisition utility, 92

Active trading, 170–171

Adaval, R., 51

Admissions, decisions about, 211–212

Adomdza, G. K., 26

Advisers, ethics of, 154–155

Affect heuristic, 10, 212

African Americans, implicit attitudes toward, 147–148, 151

Ager, J. W., 109

Ainslie, G., 106

Akerlof, G. A., 74, 139

Alicke, M. D., 23, 27

Allison, S. T., 29

Alpert, M., 16

Altruistic punishment, 142

Ambady, N., 212

Analogical reasoning, in decision-making improvement, 219–221
  diverse training, 221
  specific training, 221

Anchoring, 10, 49–53, 167–169
  in accounting firms, 52
  affecting decisions, 50
  in everyday life, 51–52
  hindsight bias and, 55–56
  in negotiation, 203–205
  processes leading to anchoring bias, 53

Anderson, C., 29, 155

Andrus, Elvis, 43

Angelone, B. L., 66

Appelman, A., 122

Armor, D. A., 80

Art and Science of Negotiation, The, 205

Asendorpf, J. B., 149

Åstebro, T., 26

Asymmetry in self-serving biases, 202

Attitudes, implicit, 147–151

Auctions, 77–79

Availability heuristic, 7–8
  biases emanating from, 34–38
    during performance appraisals, 36
    ease of recall (based on vividness and recency), 34–37
    internal feelings about tempting fate, 36
    retrievability (based on memory structures), 37–38

Avnaim-Pesso, L., 107

Awareness. *See* Bounded awareness

Axsom, D., 67

Ayres, I., 64–65

B

Babcock, L., 51, 101, 112, 200

Badaracco, J. L., Jr., 158

Bajaj, V., 125

Balance theory, 218

Balcetis, E., 112–113

Ball, S. B., 76, 214

Banaji, M. R., 143–144, 148–149, 158

Banse, R., 149

Barber, B. M., 21, 161, 163, 169, 170–171, 174

Bargaining zone concept, 179
  negative bargaining zone, 180
  positive bargaining zone, 180

Bargh, J. A., 147
Bar-Hillel, M., 53
Baron, J., 80, 219, 226
Barry, B., 99
Base rates, insensitivity to, 38–39, 58*t*
Basketball, commitment to draft
    choices in, 122
  focusing illusion in, 67–69
BATNA. *See* Best Alternative To a
    Negotiated Agreement
    (BATNA)
Baumeister, R. F., 29, 115
Bazerman, M. H., 26, 29, 39, 63, 67,
    71–72, 75–76, 77–78, 80–81, 95,
    98–99, 105–106, 109, 112, 114,
    122, 140, 143, 145, 147, 149,
    151, 154, 156–157, 159, 165,
    177, 184–186, 189, 190, 195,
    197, 199, 201–203, 206, 210,
    214, 220–221, 227–228
Bechara, A., 106
Becker, G. S., 101
Beer, J. S., 29
Beggs, A., 204
Behavioral finance, 161–162
Belsky, G., 167
Belyavsky, J., 51
Benartzi, S., 167–168, 172, 227
Ben-David, I., 18
Benton, M. J., 153
Benzoni, F. J., 109
Bereby-Meyer, Y., 76, 215, 220–221
Bernhard, H., 146
Bernheim, B. D., 80
Bernoulli, D., 83
Bertrand, M., 80, 140
Beshears, J., 95
Best Alternative To a Negotiated
    Agreement (BATNA), 177, 179,
    180, 191
Bets, value creation through, 184–185
"Better-than-average" effect, 26
Bettman, J. R., 109
Bhaskar, R., 144
Biases, 31–59

availability heuristic, 7–8, 34–37
bounded ethicality, 6, 143–145,
    158–159
common, 31–32
confirmation bias, 9–10, 20, 46–57,
    67, 69, 162, 213, 219
conjunctive event bias, 53–54
curse of knowledge, 54–57
debiasing judgment and, 216–219
disjunctive event bias, 53–54
hindsight bias, 10, 54–56
in employment interviews,
    212–213
inappropriate application of
    heuristics, 31
increased through disclosure,
    154–155
investments and, 162–170
judgmental, 128–129
overconfidence, 14–30
perceptual, 127–129
rationality and, 5
from representativeness heuristic,
    38–46, 58t
retrievability, 37–38, 48
self-serving, 112–114, 200–203
serial decision making and, 128
status quo, 167–169
understanding in others, 223–226
vulnerability to, 22, 113–114
Bidding. *See* Auctions
Biddle, G. C., 52
Bjork, R. A., 55
Björklund, F., 153
Blanton, H., 149
Blount, S., 99, 140
Blumberg, S. J., 102
Bodenhausen, G. V., 114, 147
Boer, E., 66
Bogle, J. C., 166
Bohnet, I., van Geen, 228
Boltz, M. G., 24
Bonus framing, 96–97
Borgida, E., 149
Bounded awareness, 6, 60–81

bounds of others, understanding, 80
change blindness, 66–67
focalism, 67–69
focusing illusion, 67–69
in groups, 69–71
inattentional blindness, 65–66
'slippery slope' of unethical
behaviour, 67
in strategic settings, 71–80. *See also*
Strategic settings, bounded
awareness in
Bounded ethicality, 6, 143–145
Bounded rationality, 5–6
Bowles, H. R., 51
Bradsher, K., 112
Brawley, L. R., 145
Brewer, N. T., 51
Brickman, P., 102
Brief, A. P., 150
Brodt, S. E., 28
Brosnan, S. F., 138
Brown, A., 138
Brown, J. D., 28
Budiansky, S., 112
Burrows, L., 147
Burrus, J., 25, 27
Burson, K. A., 26
Burt, C. D. B., 24
Bushman, B. J., 52
Buyers, endowment effect and,
93–94

C
Cain, D. M., 27, 79, 152, 154–155
Caldwell, D. F., 127
Callender, J. C., 51, 212
Calvet, L. E., 169
Camerer, C. F., 15, 56, 79, 101, 112,
200
Cameron, L., 138
Campbell, D. T., 102
Campbell, J. D., 29
Campbell, J. Y., 169
Camp David Accords (1978), value
creation in, 181–182

Cannell, J. J., 26
Cantelon, D. A., 144
Cantor, N., 25
Cantril, H., 112
Carhart, M. M., 163, 166
Carlson, B. W., 46
Carroll, J. S., 76, 214
Caruso, E. M., 145
Casey, F, 60
Casino betting, 79
Cassidy, J., 18, 161
Certainty, 87–90
perception of, 88
pseudocertainty,
87–90
Chabris, C. F., 65–66
Challenger space shuttle disaster,
69
Chambers, J. R., 25, 27
Change blindness, 66–67
Chatman, J. A., 29
Chen, M. K., 101, 147
Chen, S., 117
Choi, J., 169
Chugh, D., 4, 63, 81, 143–144, 149,
150, 220
Claiming value in negotiation,
179–180
Coates, D., 102
Cognition in decision making,
105–111
emotion and, 105–111
internal conflicts, 110–111
multiple selves theory,
106–107
Cohen, A. B., 114
Cohen, J. D., 106
Cohen, R. R., 150
Cold War, self-serving reasoning
about, 194
Colleges, admission decisions in,
211–212
Commitment, escalation of, 119–131.
See also Escalation of
commitment

Common investment mistakes,
160–174. *See also* Poor
investment decisions
action steps, 171–174
investment goals, determining,
172–173
in stock market prediction,
173–174
Competitive escalation paradigm,
123–127
dollar bill auction, 124
in reverse-bid auctions, 126
Competitive irrationality, 130–131
Confidence, 15–20. *See also*
Overconfidence
Confirmation heuristic, 9–10, 213
biases emanating from, 46–57
confirmation trap, 46–49
reasons we fall prey to, 47
Conflicts of interest, 154–158
disclosure as a solution to, 154
motivated blindness, 155–158
psychology of, 154–158
Conjunction fallacy, 45–46
Conjunctive events bias, 53–54
"Consider the opposite," as debiasing
strategy, 217, 219
Contingent contracts, 184
Cooper, A. C., 184, 222
Corporate scandals, ethics and, 143
Corporate takeovers, 78
Correll, J., 150
Cottrell, G. W., 57
Cowherd, D. M., 139
Coy, P., 109
Creativity problems, 64
Credit, overclaiming of, 145–146
Cross-species generality, in fairness
judgments, 138
Crupi, V., 57
Cryder, C. E., 114
Curhan, J. R., 177, 194
Culture, ultimatum game and,
138–139
Curse of knowledge, 56–57

D

Dahl, R. E., 114
Damasio, A. R., 106
Damasio, H., 106
Dana, J., 152
Danziger, S., 107
Darley, J. M., 51, 158
Darlow, A., 9
Dasgupta, N., 146
Davis, M. S., 229
Davis-Blake, A., 139
Dawes, R. M., 109, 152, 209–211,
216
Dawson, E., 112
Daytrading, 170
Dealcrafting, 183
Death penalty, evidence for and
against, 48
Debiasing, 216–219
changing decision-making process,
218–219
refreezing, 219
unfreezing, 217–218
DeBondt, W. F. M., 15, 166–167
Decision-analytic approach to
negotiations, 176–179
Decision making, 103–118
Decision making, improving, 206–229
by acquiring expertise, 213–216
analogical reasoning, 219–221
admissions decisions, 211–212
hiring decisions, 212–213
by using decision-analysis tools,
208–213
linear models, 208–209
debiasing, 216–219
refreezing, 219
by taking an outsider's view, 222–223
by understanding biases in others,
223–226
comparison group, 224–225
intuitive estimation, 225
Decisions, anatomy of, 1–3
De Dreu, C. K. W., 99
Den Ouden, E., 56

Deontological approach in ethical decision making, 103
Depken, C. A., 139
de Quervain, D. J. F., 142
de Waal, F. B. M., 138
Dhar, R., 107
Dictator game, 137–138
  cross-cultural consistency in, 138
Diekmann, K. A., 112, 197
Dietz, J., 150
Dijksterhuis, A., 23
Diltz, J. D., 171
Discounting concept, 107
  exponential discounting, 107
  hyperbolic discounting, 108
Disjunctive-events bias, 53–54
Ditto, P. H., 112
Diverse training, 221
Dividing a Pie problem, 220
Dollar bill auction, 124
Dougherty, T. W., 51, 212
Duncan, B. L., 52
Dunkelberg, W. C., 184, 222
Dunne, J., 24
Dunning, D., 23, 28, 112–113
Dynamic game-theoretic equilibrium, 73n2

E
Economist, T., 202
Egeth, H., 66
Einhorn, H. J., 209, 213–214
Ekman, P., 114
Elson, S. B., 153
Elyashiv, T., 144
Emotional influences on decision making, 114–117. *See also under* Cognition in decision making
  emotion and cognition, 105–111
  financial decisions, 115
  influencing judgment, 115
  mood-congruent recall, 115–116
  regret avoidance, 116–117
  self-serving reasoning, 112–114
specific emotions, 114–115
  anger, 114
  disgust, 114
  happiness, 114
  sadness, 114
  effect of weather, 116
Employment interviews, 212–213
Endowment effect, 94–95
Englich, B., 50, 53
Epelbaum, M., 194
Epley, N., 21, 50, 53, 57, 97, 145
Epstude, K., 80
Equality norms, perverse consequences of, 141–142
Escalation of commitment, 119–131
  competitive escalation paradigm, 123–127
  reasons for occurrence, 127–131
  tendency to escalate, 121
  unilateral escalation paradigm, 121–123
Escalation of conflict, 196–198
Ethical decision making, 103
  deontological approach, 103
  utilitarian approach, 103
Ethics in decision making, 132–159.
  See also Fairness
  conflicts of interest, 154–158
  indirectly unethical behavior, 151–152
  sacred values, 152–154
  value pluralism, 152–154
Evaluability hypothesis, 99
Evans, J. S. B. T., 106
Executive ethics, 159
Expectations, self-serving bias and, 112
Expected value, 208
Experience, in negotiations, 115, 210–216
Expertise, for decision making, 213–216
Exploitation, camouflaging intentionality behind, 152
Exponential discounting, 107

F

Fairness, 132–159
  concerns about outcomes of others,
    139–142
  in decision making, 132–159
  fairness judgments, importance of,
    142–143
  perceptions of, 133–135
  persistent desire for, 138–139
  "unfair" ultimatums, resistance to,
    135–139
Falk, A., 101
Fallacies, conjunction, 45–46
Favoritism, in-group, 146–147
Favors, bounded ethicality and, 143
Fazio, R. H., 148
Feder, B., 125–126
Fedorikhin, A., 107
Feedback, 213
Fehr, E., 139, 142, 146
Fernbach, P. M., 9
Fiedler, K., 55
Finance, behavioral, 161–162
Finucane, M., 10, 98, 105
Fischbacher, U., 142, 146
Fischer, D., 23, 112
Fischer, P., 49
Fischhoff, B., 18, 20, 55–56, 88,
    216–217
Fisher, R., 177
Fixed-pie assumption, of negotiation,
    193–194
Flyvbjerg, B., 23
Focalism, 67–69
Focusing illusion, 67–69
Fooled by Randomness, 166
Foot, P., 103
Forgas, J. P., 114
Forsyth, D. R., 145
Fox, C. R., 68, 165
Framing of preferences, 82–102
  insurance, framing and overselling
    of, 90–91
  and irrationality of sum of our
    choices, 85–87
  rebate/bonus framing, 96–97
  value placement, 93–94
Franconeri, S. L., 66
Frederick, S., 101
Fredrickson, J. W., 139
Frey, D., 49
Friedman, A., 122
Friedman, D., 75
Fujita, K., 106
Fuller-Thaler mutual funds, 226
Future, discounting of, 109

G

Gabriel, S., 114
Gächter, S, 142
Gaertner, L., 23
Galak, J., 68, 101
Galinsky, A. D., 57, 131, 204–205,
    219–220
Gest, T., 23, 112
Gigerenzer, G., 222
Giladi, E. E., 28
Gilbert, D. T., 10, 23, 47, 67–68, 102,
    112
Gillespie, J. J., 184–185
Gilovich, T., 15, 21, 25, 36, 42, 47, 50,
    53, 112, 116–117, 167
Gino, F., 39, 67, 211
Giuliano, T., 122
Gladwell, M., 15, 209
Glassman, J. K., 162
Glick, P., 149
Gneezy, A., 138
Gneezy, U., 138
Goethals, G. R., 29
Goette, L., 101
Goetzmann, W. N., 165
Goldberg, J. H., 117
Goldstein, D. G., 125
Goodwin, P., 208
Gore, A., 112
Grabiner, D., 196
Graddy, K, 204
Graham, J. R., 18
Gramzow, R. H., 23

Green, M. C., 153
Greene, J. D., 104, 151
Greenwald, A. G., 28, 148
Gregg, A. P., 23
Greitemeyer, T., 49
Griffin, D. W., 14
Gross, J. J., 114
Gross, P. H., 51
Grosskopf, B., 76, 215, 220
Grossman, S. J., 162
Groups, bounded awareness in, 69–71
    overcoming, 70–71
Gruenfeld, D. H., 70
Güth, W., 137, 198

H
Ha, Y. W., 9, 20
Haidt, J., 114, 117, 153
Hallak, Y., 27
Hammond, J. S., 3, 208
Hanko, K., 57
Haran, U., 20
Hardin, G., 201
Harris, G., 125
Harvey, C. R., 18
Hassett, K. A., 162
Hastie, R., 20, 28, 41
Hastorf, A. H., 112
Hawken, P., 109
Heath, C., 28
Hedge funds, 18, 161–162
Heider, F., 218
Henrich, J., 138
Henrion, M., 18
Hershey, J. C., 90
Hertwig, R., 19
Herzog, S. M., 19
Heuristics, 6, 57–59. *See also* Affect
        heuristic; Availability heuristic;
        Confirmation heuristic;
        Judgmental heuristics;
        Representativeness heuristic
Highhouse, S., 22
Hindsight bias, 10, 54–56
Hiring decisions, improving, 212–213

affect heuristic, 212
availability, 212
confirmation heuristic, 213
representativeness, 212–213
Ho, T. H., 79
Hoang, H., 122
Hoch, S. J., 56
Hoffman, E., 138
Hoffrage, U., 222
Hogan, D., 212
Hogarth, R. M., 213–214
Holmes, J. G., 144
Holt, J., 110
Holt, L. L., 206
Horberg, E. J., 114–115
Hsee, C. K., 98–99, 107, 115
Huberman, G., 80
Huffman, D., 101
Hunter, J. E., 22, 212–213
Hyperbolic discounting, 108–109
Hypothesis testing, positive, 10

I
Idson, L. C., 97, 220
Illusion of control, 23
Implicit attitudes, 147–151
    behavior prediction by, 149
    control of, 149
    Implicit Associations Test (IAT), 148
Impression management, 129–130
Inattentional blindness, 65–66
Incentives, for retirement investment,
        167–168
Incompatibility bias, 194
Index funds, 160–161, 165–167
Indirectly unethical behavior, 151–152
Inferences, availability heuristic and,
        35
Information overload, 61
In-group favoritism, 146–147
In-group members, favors for, 147
Insider view in decision making,
        222–223
Integration, escalation of commitment
        and, 131

Internal conflicts, reconciling, 110–111
Internal dissonance, 19
Investment decisions, 160–174.
  overconfidence resulting in excessive
    trading, 163–164
    gender difference and, 164
    stock-market investing strategies,
    163
    psychology of, 162–170, *See also*
      Common investment mistakes;
      Optimism about investment
      decisions; Poor investment
      decisions
Irrationality, competitive, 130–131
Issacharoff, S., 112, 200
Iyengar, S. S., 80

J
Jaccard, J., 149
Jacobson, L., 51
James, W., 61, 149
Janiszewski, C., 51, 205
Janoff-Bulman, R., 102
Janofsky, M., 144
Jefferis, V. E., 148
Jeffrey, S. A., 26
Jegadeesh, N., 166–167
Jiang, W., 80
Job interviews, 22
Johnson, D. D. P., 21
Johnson, E. J., 117, 125, 227
Joint-versus-separate preference
  reversals, 98–100
Jordan, D. J., 171
Joyce, E. J., 52
Judgmental biases in escalation,
  occurrence, 128–129
Judgmental heuristics, 7–10
  affect heuristic, 10
  anchoring, 10
  availability heuristic, 7–8
  confirmation bias, 10
  confirmation heuristic, 9–10
  hindsight bias, 10
  representativeness heuristic, 8–9

K
Kagel, J. H., 213
Kahneman, D., 3, 6–7, 10, 31–32, 35,
  37, 39, 41–42, 44–46, 50, 53–54,
  68, 81–82, 84–86, 88–90, 92, 98,
  100, 102, 116, 133–135, 140,
  195, 214, 222–226
Kant, I., 103
Kanwisher, N., 206
Karelitz, T. M., 27
Karlan, D., 80
Kassam, K., 151
Kat, H. M., 161
Keeney, R. L., 3, 208
Keltner, D., 114–115, 194
Kemp, S., 24
Kendall, L. N., 29
Kennedy, J. F., 129
Kerr, M., 25
Keynes, J. M., 173
Keysar, B., 21, 56
Khan, U., 107
Kim, B. K., 109
Kim, T. G., 28
Kirchsteiger, G., 139
Klar, Y., 27–28
Klayman, J., 9, 20
Klein, G., 31
Kleinberger, E., 21
Kleinbölting, H., 222
Knetsch, J. L., 93, 115, 133
Knowledge, from experience, 216
Koehler, D. J., 69
Koellinger, P., 26
Koole, S. L., 23
Koriat, A., 20, 55
Krabbenoft, M. A., 212
Kramer, G. P., 114
Kramer, R. M., 28
Kristel, O. V., 153
Krueger, A. B., 102
Krueger, J. I., 29
Kruger, J., 25–27, 57
Ku, G., 128, 131
Kuang, J. X., 152

Kunda, Z., 29, 48
Kunreuther, H., 90
Kupperman, C., 24
Kurtzberg, T. R., 165

L
Laibson, D., 106, 169, 172
Lakin, J. L., 29
Lakshminarayanan, V., 101
"Lake Wobegon effect", 26
Langer, E. J., 23
Larrick, R. P., 117, 215, 217
Latane, B., 158
Law of small numbers, misconceptions
　of chance and, 42
Lax, D. A., 177, 179, 183
Learning, 18
　debiasing and, 216, 219–220
　from mistakes, 214
LeBoeuf, R. A., 51
Lee, G. P., 106
Leeson, N., 128–129
Lehman, B. J., 115
Leibold, J. M., 149
Leith, K. P., 115
Lepper, M. R., 48, 80, 219
Lerner, J. S., 114–115, 117, 153
Let's Make a Deal game show, 72
Levav, J., 107
Levi, U., 27
Levin, D., 65–66, 213
Levine, D. I., 139
Levine, M., 172
Levy, J., 66
Lewin, K., 11
Lewis, M., 207
Li, M., 29
Liberman, V., 21
Lichtenstein, D. R., 51
Lichtenstein, S., 20, 88, 217
Lieberman, M. D., 117
Liersch, M. J., 16
Life decisions, information available
　for, 35
Lin, D. Y., 22

Lind, E. A., 133
Lindell, M. K., 37
Linear models in decision analysis,
　208–211
Lineberger, M., 114
Linton, S., 115
Lituchy, T. R., 99
Loewenstein, G. F., 23, 25–26, 56,
　98–99, 101, 106, 109, 111–112,
　115, 140, 154–156, 189, 200,
　201, 219–220
Loewenstein, J., 220–221
Loftus, E. F., 47
Logic
　base-rate sensitivity and, 38–39
　of heuristics, 41
Lombardi, L., 57
Lopez, D. F., 112
Lord, C. G., 48, 219
Lotto, A. J., 206
Lovallo, D., 15, 79, 87, 222–223
Lowenthal, D. J., 99

M
MacCoun, R. J., 20
MacGregor, D. G., 10, 98, 105
Mack, A., 65–66
Macrae, C. N., 147
Madey, S. F., 116
Madrian, B. C., 168–169
Magellan Fund, 8
Mak, D., 97
Malhotra, D., 131, 186, 190
Malkiel, B. G., 161, 174
Malkoc, S. A., 109
Malmendier, U., 15, 26
Malone, P. S., 211
Managerial decision making, 1–13
　anatomy of decisions, 1–3
　bounded rationality and, 5–6
　rational decision-making, steps in, 2
Mannix, E. A., 70
March, J. G., 5
Marginal utility of gains, declining, 83
Markopolos, H., 60

Markwith, M., 4
Massey, C., 80
Maury, R., 76
McCabe, K., 138
McCauley, C. R., 114
McClelland, G. H., 41
McClure, S. M., 106
McConnell, A. R., 149
McGhee, D. E., 148
McGinn, K. L., 51
McGraw, A. P., 25, 29
McKenzie, C. R. M., 16, 57
Mean, regression to, 42–45
Medvec, V. H., 25, 116–117
Meier, B., 126
Mellers, B. A., 25
Mental accounting, 94–96
Mergers, classroom auction strategy
    and, 123–124
Messick, D. M., 29, 67, 71–72, 75, 112,
    133, 141 147, 158–159, 203
Metrick, A., 169
Meyers, J. M., 67
Meyvis, T., 68
Milgram, S., 158
Milkman, K. L., 95, 106
Miller, D. T., 116
Miller, N., 52
Minniti, M., 26
Minorities, exclusion of, 146
Minson, J. A., 21
Misconceptions of chance, 40–42
Mistakes, learning from, 174
Mitroff, S. R., 66
Moag, J., 76
"Moment of truth" effect, 25
Moneyball, 206–207
Money managers, 160, 166
Monty Hall game, 72–73
Mood-congruent recall, 115–116
Moore, C. M., 66
Moore, D. A., 20, 26–28, 39, 71–72, 79,
    99, 114, 154–156, 165, 177, 201,
    209, 211
Moore, P. C., 28, 214

Moral judgments, emotions and, 153
Moran, S., 220–221
Morewedge, C. K., 20, 23, 31
Morgan, K. P., 156
Morris, M. W., 28, 214
Motivated blindness, 155–158
Motivational influence on decision
    making, 103–118
Muecke, D., 149
Mullainathan, S., 80, 140
Multiparty ultimatum games,
    71–72
Multiple selves theory, 106–107
Murnighan, J. K., 131, 138, 144
Murphy, S., 153
Murray, S. L., 144, 153
Mussweiler, T., 50, 53, 55, 57, 204–205,
    217
Myers, D. G., 26
Mythical fixed pie of negotiation,
    193–194

N
Nalebuff, B. J., 64–65, 73
NASA, *Challenger* disaster and, 69
Natural resources, tragedy of the
    commons and, 203
Neale, M. A., 26, 70, 177, 183, 194–195,
    199, 203–204, 215
Negative bargaining zone, 180
Negotiations, 175–192. *See also*
    Anchoring; Rational decisions
    in negotiations; Self-serving
    biases in negotiation
    Best Alternative To a Negotiated
        Agreement (BATNA), 177
    claiming value in, 179–180
    decision-analytic approach to,
        176–179
    value creation in, 180–185. *See also*
        Value creation in negotiation
Negotiator cognition, 193–205
    escalation of conflict, 196–198
    mythical fixed pie of negotiation,
        193–194

negotiator judgment, framing of,
191–196
overestimation in negotiation,
198–199
Neisser, U., 65
Nelson, J. D., 57
Nelson, L. D., 68, 101, 138
Neuroscience, multiple-selves theory
and, 106
Ng, Z. W., 57
Nickerson, R. S., 10
Nisbett, R. E., 8, 11, 53
Nonrational escalation, elimination of,
119
Norem, J. K., 25
Northcraft, G. B., 183, 203, 215
Nosek, B. A., 148
Null, C., 93
Number sequences, confirmation trap
and, 46–47
Nuttin, J. M., 23

O

Oakland Athletics, transformation of,
206–207
Objectivity, conflicts of interest and,
154
O'Connor, K. M., 99
O'Donoghue, T., 106
O'Reilly, C. A., 127
Ochs, J., 137
Odean, T., 15, 21–22, 101, 161–163,
166, 169–171
Oesch, J. M., 28, 39, 79
Omission bias, 28
Online trading, 170
Oppenheimer, D. M., 31, 51
Optimism about investment decisions,
164–170
anchoring, 167–169
denying random events as random,
166–167
keeping losers, 169–170
procrastination, 167–169
prospect theory, 169–170

selling winners, 169–170
status quo, 167–169
Optimistic biases, 24–26
Oskarsson, A. T., 41
Outrage heuristic, 10
Outsider's view, in decision-making,
222–223
Oveis, C., 114–115
Overclaiming credit, 145–146
Overconfidence, 14–30
as mother of all biases, 14–15
resulting in excessive trading,
163–164
ways to study, 15. *See also*
Overestimation;
Overplacement; Overprecision
Overestimation, 15, 22–26
illusion of control, 23
"moment of truth" effect, 25
in negotiation, 198–199
optimistic biases, 24–26
planning fallacy, 23–24
self-enhancement, 23
Overplacement, 15, 26–28
"better-than-average" effect, 26
errors of, 27
"Lake Wobegon effect," 26
Overprecision, 15, 16–22
causes of, 19–20
consequences of, 20–21
Overvaluation, 94

P

Pager, D., 38
Paharia, N., 151
Palaro, H. P., 161
Palm, R., 37
Pareto-superior agreement,
189
Parker, J., 57
Pashler, H., 66
Patton, B., 177
Pay-what-you-want pricing, 137
Pedersen, W. C., 52
Peles, N., 165

Perceptions, self-serving, 112
  biased perception, automatic nature
    of, 113
Perceptual biases in escalation,
    occurrence, 127–128
Performance, overestimation of, 23
Performance appraisals, availability
    heuristic in, 36
Perrow, C., 206
Perry, R. W., 37
Persistent desire for fairness, 138–139
Peters, E., 10, 98, 105, 115
Petersen, T., 38
Peterson, R. S., 153
Pfeiffer, T., 204, 217
Phelps, E. A., 24
Pinel, E. C., 102
Planning fallacy, 23–24
Plant, E. A., 150
Plous, S., 15
Pollan, S. M., 172
Pope, D. G., 101
Positive bargaining zone, 180
Positive frame, of negotiator, 195–196
Positive hypothesis testing, 10
Positive illusions, 28
  advantages, 28–29
  disadvantages, 29
Post-settlement settlement (PSS), 189–
    190
Preferences
  framing and reversal of, 82–102
    endowment effect, 94
  joint-versus-separate preference
    reversals, 98–100
Prejudice, testing of, 148
Prelec, D., 25
Prescriptive decision making models, 5
Preston, E., 219
Price increases, fairness and, 134
Price offers, distribution of, 75f
Probability
  conjunction fallacy and, 45–46
  representativeness heuristic and,
    38–46

of risk, 90–91
  weighting of events and, 53
Procrastination, 167–169
Professional associations, codes of
    ethics of, 155
Profiles in Courage, 129
Pronin, E., 15, 22, 112, 114
Prospect theory, 84, 169–170
Pruitt, D. G., 181
Pseudocertainty, 87–90
Pugh, S., 150
Punishment
  misconceptions about regression
    and, 44
  of unfair treatment, 142

Q
Questioning, in value creation,
    186–187

R
Rabin, M., 87, 106
Radzevick, J. R., 20, 79
Raiffa, H., 3, 16, 176–177, 180, 189,
    190, 205, 208, 210, 229
Raio, C. M., 24
Random events, denying random
    nature of, 166–167
Random Walk Down Wall Street, A,
    174
Rangel, A., 80
Rational decision making, steps in, 2
Rational decisions in negotiations,
    175–192. *See also* Negotiations;
    Value creation in negotiation
Rational model, 5–6
Ravenscraft, D. J., 26
Ravid, D., 27
Rayo, L., 101
Real estate, estimating value in,
    203–204
Reasoning
  analogical, 219–221
  self-serving, 112–114
Rebate/bonus framing, 96–97

Recall, ease of, based on availability
 heuristic, 34–37, 58*t*
Recency, 34–37
Reference group neglect, 79
Reference points
 in salary fairness, 135
 shifting of, 85
Refreezing, 219
Regan, D., 112
Regression-to-the-mean concept,
 42–45
Regret avoidance, 116–117
Reidl, A., 139
Reifman, A., 42
Reinforcement theory, 217
Rensink, R. A., 66
Repetto, A., 172
Representativeness heuristic, 8–9,
 38–46
 biases emanating from, 38–46
 conjunction fallacy, 45–46
 insensitivity to base rates, 38–39
 insensitivity to sample size, 39–40
 misconceptions of chance, 40–42
 regression-to-the-mean concept,
  42–45
Representativeness, 212
Retirement
 allocation of money in plans for,
  172–173
 investing for, 172–173
Retrievability bias, 37–38
Reversal of preferences, 82–102
Rewards
 misconceptions about regression
  and, 46
 short-term, 107
Reverse-bid auctions, escalation in, 126
Riccardi, A. M., 24
Richeson, J. A., 148
Rick, S., 106
Risen, J. L., 36
Risk
 emotions and, 98
 gains from, 84

probability of, 88
 reference point and, 84
Risk-averse choice, 83, 91
Risk neutrality, 87
Risk preferences, expected value and,
 83
Ritov, I., 25, 98, 204
Roberts, J. C., 106
Robins, R. W., 29
Rock, I., 65
Roese, N. J., 80
Rogers, T., 95, 106
Rogue Trader, 128
Rollins, H., 10
Rose, J. P., 27
Rosenthal, R., 51, 212
Ross, B., 4
Ross, J. M., 122, 129–130, 206
Ross, L., 8, 11, 15, 21–22, 48, 53, 112,
 194
Ross, M., 145
Roth, A. E., 137
Rozin, P., 4, 114
Roziner, I., 27
Rubin, J. Z., 122, 181
Rudman, L. A., 149
Rules of thumb. *See* Heuristics
Russ, L. E., 189

S
Sadness, 114–115
Sage, R.M., 115
Saha, A., 161
Salaries, fairness of, 139
SALT treaty, fixed-pie assumption and,
 194
Sample size, insensitivity to, 39–40
Samuels, S. M., 112
Samuelson, P. A., 87
Samuelson, W. F., 76–78, 168
Sanders, W. M., 139
Sanfey, A. G., 138
Santos, L. R., 101
Saporta, I., 38
Satisficing, 5–6

Saul, S., 125
"Save More Tomorrow" program, 227–228
Savings, for retirement, 227–228
Schade, C., 26
Schelling, T. C., 106, 110
Scherer, F. M., 26
Schkade, D. A., 10, 68, 102
Schlenker, B. R., 145
Schmidt, F. L., 22, 212–213
Schmidt, P., 147
Schmittberger, R., 137, 198
Schnur, T., 66
Schoemaker, P. J. H., 90
Schoorman, F. D., 122
Schroth, H., 99, 197
Schulz, K., 15, 20
Schwartz, B., 80, 207, 209
Schwartz, J. L. K., 148
Schwarz, N., 36, 102, 116–117
Schwarze, B., 137, 198
Schweitzer, M. E., 101
Search strategies, availability heuristic and, 37–38
Sebenenius, J. K., 177, 179, 183
Sebenius, J. K., 197
Securities and Exchange Commission (SEC), ethical issues and, 156
Sedikides, C., 23
Seeman, T. E., 115
Seidel, M. D. L., 38
Sejnowski, T. J., 57
Self-enhancement, 23
Self-interest, in ultimatum game, 138–139, 152
Self-serving biases in negotiation, 200–203
    asymmetry in, 202
Self-serving reasoning, 112–114
    expectations, 112
    perceptions, 112
Seligman, M. E. P., 28
Sellers, endowment effect and, 93
Selvin, S., 73
Sentis, K. P., 112, 203

Separate preference reversal, 98–100
Serial decision making, 128
Shafir, E., 80, 95
Shah, A. K., 31
Shah, P. P., 197
Shakarchi, R. J., 29
Sharek, Z., 39, 211
Sharot, T., 24
Sharpe, W. F., 161
Shaughnessy, E., 10
Shea, D. F., 168
Shefrin, H. M., 110, 162, 167, 228
Shelton, J. N., 148
Shepard, R. N., 4
Shepherd, H., 38
Shepperd, J. A., 25
Shiv, B., 106–107
Shleifer, A., 162
Shonk, K., 80, 226
Short-term reward, 107
Shu, L. L., 23
Shubik, M., 124
Sicoly, F., 145
Simmons, J. P., 80, 101
Simms, E., 27
Simon, H. A., 5
Simons, D. J., 65–66
Sitkin, S. B., 206
Slippery slope, of unethical behavior, 67
Sloman, S. A., 9
Slovic, P., 56, 88, 90, 115
Small, D. A., 115
Smith, A. R., 27
Smith, V., 138
Sniezek, J. A., 20
Social dilemmas, 201–202
Social issues, joint-vs.-separate preference reversals and, 98
Sodini, P., 169
Soll, J. B., 26
Solomon, S., 17
Sorkin, A. R., 125–126
Spataro, S. E., 29
Spellman, B. A., 20

Srivastava, S., 29
Stalkfleet, M. T., 27
Stanovich, K. E., 1, 3, 31, 70
Stasser, G., 70
Statistics
    regression to the mean and, 42–45
    sample-size insensitivity and, 39–40
Status quo bias, 167–169
Staw, B. M., 121–122, 127, 130, 198, 206
Stereotypes, 147–150
Stewart, D. D., 70
Stiglitz, J. E., 162
Stillinger, C., 194
Stock market
    investment strategies, 162–164
    prediction, difficulty of, 173–174
Stone, A. A., 102
Strack, F., 50, 53, 55, 117
Strategic settings, bounded awareness in, 71–80
    acquiring a company, 73–75
    auctions, 77–79
    Monty Hall game, 72–73
    multiparty ultimatum games, 71–72
    reference group neglect, 79
    special-interest groups, 80
Straub, P. G., 138
Subjectivity utility scale, 101
Subsets, conjunction fallacy and, 46
Suesser, K., 114
Suls, J. M., 25, 28
Sunk costs, 120–122
Sunstein, C. R., 10, 118, 207
Supply and demand, fairness and, 133–135
Supreme Court, bounded ethicality and, 144
Surplus, rebate/bonus framing and, 97
Svenson, O., 26
Swanson, J., 157
Swift, S. A., 39, 211
System 1 (automatic) thought, 3–4, 106
System 2 (deliberative) thought, 3–4, 106

T
Takeovers, corporate, 78
Tanlu, L., 114
Tate, G., 15, 26
Taxation, investments and, 168
Taxpayers, rebate/bonus framing and, 96–97
Taylor, K. M., 25
Taylor, S. E., 28, 43
Teger, A., 124
Temporal differences impact, 107–110
    discounting concept, 107–109
Tenbrunsel, A. E., 67, 99, 109, 149, 156–158, 184, 197, 201–203
Tenney, E. R., 20
Tentori, K., 57
Tesser, A., 27
Tetlock, P. E., 114, 117, 152–153, 217
Thaler, R. H., 6, 15, 87, 91, 93–96, 101, 109–110, 115, 133, 135, 139, 166–168, 172, 207, 226–228
Thompson, L., 26, 29, 177, 189, 194, 200, 219–220
Thompson, S. C., 23, 1999
Tiedens, L. Z., 114–115
Time preferences, in trade, 183
Titman, S., 166–167
Titus, W., 70
Tobacman, J., 172
Todd, A. R., 57
Tor, A., 75–76, 220
Trabasso, T., 10
Tracking, mental accounting for, 94–96
Trading
    active, 170–171
    in financial markets, 162
Tragedy of the commons, 201
Training, overcoming bias through, 217
Tranel, D., 106
Transactional utility, 92
Trawalter, S., 148
Trivers, R. L., 114
Trust, in value creation, 186
Turban, D. B., 51, 212

Tversky, A., 6–7, 32, 35, 37, 39, 41–42, 45–46, 50, 53–54, 68–69, 81–86, 88–89, 90, 92, 110, 116–117, 140, 195, 214, 224–226
Two-party negotiations, 78, 176
Tyler, T. R., 28, 133

U
Ubel, P. A., 68
Ultimatums, fairness of, 135–139
Underplacement, 26–27
Unethical behavior, detecting change and, 143–144
"Unfair" ultimatums, resistance to, 135–139
Unfreezing, 217–218
Unilateral escalation paradigm, 121–123
Ury, W., 177
Utilitarian approach in ethical decision making, 103
Uy, D., 205

V
Valley, K. L., 76, 177
Vallone, R. P., 42
Value creation in negotiation, 180–185
1978 Camp David Accords, 181–182
through bets, 184–185
tools of, 185–191
trading on issues to create value, 182–184
Value pluralism, 152–154
Van Boven, L., 21, 23, 41
Vancouver, J. B., 29
Van Knippenberg, A., 23
Van Swol, L. M., 20
Varey, C. A., 14
Vaslow, J. B., 150
Vasquez, E. A., 52
Vaughn, D., 69
Vaughn, S. I., 70
Vividness, 34–37
Vohs, K. D., 29, 80
von Hippel, W., 29, 114

Vorauer, J. D., 148
vos Savant, M., 73

W
Wade-Benzoni, K. A., 29, 99, 109
Wages, fairness of, 133–143
Want/should conflict, 99, 106, 108, 110–111
Ward, A., 21
Warranties, framing of, 90–91
Wason, P. C., 46–47
Wason's rule, 47
Watkins, M. D., 206
Weather, moods and, 116
Webb, A. P., 158
Webb, J., 129
Weber, E. U., 115
Weber, M., 56
Weber, R. A., 152
Wegner, D. M., 144
Weick, K. E., 206
Weigelt, K., 79
Welch, N., 115
Well-calibrated decision making, 28–30
West, R. F., 1, 3, 31
Wheatley, T. P., 102
Wheatley, T., 67
Wheeler, M., 197
White, S. B., 98, 140
Whitman, W., 110
Williams, J. E., 115
Williams, K. Y., 70
Willpower, bounded nature of, 6
Wilson, T. D., 23, 67–68, 102
Windschitl, P. D., 25, 27
Winner's curse, 74
Women, and investment overconfidence, 163–164
Woo, C. Y., 184, 222
Wu, G., 214
Wyer Jr, R. S., 51

Y
Yakura, E., 189
Yaniv, I., 16, 21

Yates, J. F., 46
Yellen, J. L., 139
Yovel, G., 206

Z
Zander, A., 145
Zauberman, G., 109
Zeckhauser, R. J., 168
Zell, E., 27

Zheng, L., 169
Zickfeld, K., 17
Ziemba, S., 125
Ziemba, W. T., 101
Zietsma, C., 28, 39, 79
Zinman, J., 80
Zuckerman, G., 25
Zweig, J., 162–163